Abuse of Rights in International Arbitration

Abuse of Rights in International Arbitration

AHMED EL FAR

OXFORD
UNIVERSITY PRESS

OXFORD
UNIVERSITY PRESS

Great Clarendon Street, Oxford, OX2 6DP,
United Kingdom

Oxford University Press is a department of the University of Oxford.
It furthers the University's objective of excellence in research, scholarship,
and education by publishing worldwide. Oxford is a registered trade mark of
Oxford University Press in the UK and in certain other countries

First Edition published in 2020

Impression: 1

Published in the United States of America by Oxford University Press
198 Madison Avenue, New York, NY 10016, United States of America

British Library Cataloguing in Publication Data
Data available

Library of Congress Control Number: 2019948468

ISBN 978–0–19–885038–0

Printed and bound by
CPI Group (UK) Ltd, Croydon, CR0 4YY

Acknowledgements

As the progenitor of this book is a doctoral thesis submitted to Queen Mary University of London, I would first like to express my sincere gratitude to Professor Stavros Brekoulakis. His academic expertise, coupled with his practical experience in international arbitration, made a substantial contribution to the former guise of this book. His prefatory comments at the early stages of my research helped me refine the topic, and his guidance throughout influenced the development of this book. My gratitude also extends to Professor Julian Lew, an eminent arbitration scholar and practitioner who I was fortunate to work with. His guidance and valuable insight helped develop my ideas in its primitive stages.

I am also in the debt of my examiners for the degree of PhD, Professor Jan Paulsson and Ms Norah Gallagher, for having shared their invaluable knowledge and their practical experience. This revised work has indeed benefitted from their perceptive commentary.

I would also like to acknowledge a longstanding debt to Dr Mohamed Abdel Wahab who encouraged me to embark on my doctoral studies, and offered me continuous support throughout. He is a mentor and a friend, from whom I have learnt, and continue to learn, the theoretical aspects of the law as well as the art of advocacy in international arbitration.

Above all, I would like to thank my family for all the moral and intellectual support they have always given me. My mother, who has faithfully devoted her life to bringing up three children; her presence in mine is the one precious gift that cannot be replaced. My father, the man who taught me the importance and value of education, demonstrating the true meaning of a role model; a man of principle and professional integrity like no other. I wholeheartedly dedicate this book to them in deep gratitude and appreciation for what they both relinquished for my sisters and me.

Finally, my love extends to my beautiful wife, who has endured my incessant stress and bore my irregular work patterns, to my precious two sisters for always being supportive, and to my friends with whom I have shared my life, despite our physical presence in different parts of the world.

Contents

Table of Cases and Arbitral Awards

NATIONAL COURT DECISIONS

Argentina

Australia

Belgium

Canada

Egypt

England

France

Germany

Japan

Kuwait

Netherlands

Paris

Qatar

South Africa

United States of America

Switzerland

DECISIONS OF INTERNATIONAL COURTS AND TRIBUNALS

Court of Justice of the European Union

International Court of Justice

Permanent Court of International Justice

ARBITRAL AWARDS

CRCICA

Geneva Chamber of Commerce and Industry

ICC

ICSID

WTO

Table of Legislation

EUROPEAN LEGISLATION

INTERNATIONAL INSTRUMENTS

Introduction and Delimitation of the Subject

I. Setting out the Framework of Discussion

Referring existing or future disputes to international arbitration primarily rests on the will of the parties. In that sense, international arbitration has a clear contractual and consensual nature.[1] This implies that international arbitration is regarded as an exceptional mechanism for the settlement of disputes.[2] While this was the prevalent perception of international arbitration, it has drastically changed.[3] It is now generally recognized that international arbitration is the preferred method for resolving disputes in international trade,[4] and the normal means for resolving commercial and investment disputes.[5] **0.01**

As the size and complexity of international commercial and investment transactions continue to grow, so will transnational business disputes. Thus, the dire need for appropriate and efficient dispute resolution schemes remains a global reality. **0.02**

[1] Gary B Born, *International Arbitration and Forum Selection Agreements: Drafting and Enforcing* (3rd edn, Kluwer Law International 2010) 2.

[2] Egyptian Court of Cassation, Challenge No 86, Judicial Year 70, Session held on 26 November 2002, 1095.

[3] Simon Greenberg, Christopher Kee, and J Romesh Weeramantry, *International Commercial Arbitration: An Asia Pacific Perspective* (Cambridge University Press 2011) 3.

[4] Richard Garnett, 'National Court Intervention in Arbitration as an Investment Treaty Claim' (2011) 60 International and Comparative Law Quarterly 485, 485; Ucheora Onwuamaegbu, 'International Dispute Settlement Mechanisms—Choosing Between Institutionally Supported and Ad Hoc; and Between Institutions' in Katia Yannaca-Small (ed), *Arbitration Under International Investment Agreements: A Guide to the Key Issues* (Oxford University Press 2010) 64; L Yves Fortier, 'Arbitrating in the Age of Investment Treaty Disputes' (2008) 31 The University of Southern Wales Law Journal 1, 2; MIM Aboul-Enein, 'Arbitration of Foreign Investment Disputes: Responses to the New Challenges and Changing Circumstances' in Albert Jan Van Den Berg (ed), *New Horizons in International Commercial Arbitration and Beyond* (Kluwer Law International 2010) 181.

[5] Jean-François Poudret and Sébastien Besson, *Comparative Law of International Arbitration* (2nd edn, Sweet & Maxwell 2007) 24; Joseph T McLaughlin, 'Arbitration and Developing Countries' (1979) 13 The International Lawyer 211, 211.

0.03 Any major concern that is left unremedied may grow to become an arbitral nightmare that can adversely impact the arbitral process and induce distrust and disbelief in the system.

0.04 In recent years, international arbitration has been plagued by different forms of procedural abuse. Abusive practices developed by parties may not only cause paramount prejudice to their opposing parties, but can also undermine the fair resolution of disputes and frustrate the administration of arbitral justice.

0.05 Thus, we have witnessed cases where parties restructure their investments in an abusive manner by altering one of its features, not for commercial purposes but to gain access to ICSID arbitration.[6] Similarly, the rise of abusive parallel arbitral proceedings and the undesirable risk of inconsistent decisions may pose an impediment to standards of fairness, requirements of due process, and the broader notion of administration of justice.[7]

0.06 There are pre-existing classic tools and legal rules at the disposal of arbitrators that can be utilized to prevent abuse and administer arbitral justice. However, these tools have a defined and narrow scope, are inherently rigid in their application, and fail to remedy different forms of abuse.

0.07 A general principle of abuse of rights is vital in international arbitration. The virtue of a single theory with a wide scope and an overarching premise is that it is a principle which involves equity considerations, enjoys the flexibility of general principles of law, and can be used to address different abusive behaviours.

0.08 The importance of endorsing a general principle of abuse of rights in order to ensure the good administration of justice is not only appealing because of its comprehensiveness and its ability to remedy forms of abuse that other rules fail to remedy. As shall be discussed, its potency stems equally from the fact that it is a general principle that can also remedy any form of abuse that is not currently regulated by a specific rule.

II. Scope of the Book

0.09 The book discusses the principle of abuse of rights in international arbitration. Specifically, it explores the possibility of developing and applying the principle of abuse of rights as a general principle of law in international commercial and investment arbitration to tackle different forms of substantive and procedural abuse.

0.10 The principal issues/questions addressed in this book are:

- The meaning of abuse of rights;

[6] *CME Czech Republic BV v The Czech Republic*, UNCITRAL Arbitration Proceedings, Final Award of 14 March 2003.

[7] *ST-AD GmbH v Republic of Bulgaria*, UNCITRAL, PCA Case No 2011-06, Award on Jurisdiction of 18 July 2013, para 423.

- The recognition, or lack thereof, of a principle of abuse of rights in different legal systems;
- The essential elements of abuse of rights and the conditions *sine qua non* for its application;
- Limitations/concerns of the principle of abuse of rights;
- The legal basis of abuse of rights in international commercial and investment arbitration and whether it is applied as a general principle of substantive and procedural law;
- Whether it is considered an overriding principle of substantive and procedural law in international arbitration;
- Justification for the principle's application in international arbitration and its importance in ensuring the administration of arbitral justice;
- An examination of how it ensures the administration of arbitral justice.

III. Theoretical Background on Abuse of Rights in International Arbitration

The study of abuse of rights has not been subject to much legal analysis in English legal literature. This is frustrating, given that a principle so pivotal in the civil legal systems, and equally an intrinsic part of international law, has not stimulated the interest of jurists in that part of the world. **0.11**

Moreover, the study of the principle of abuse of rights and its application in international arbitration is far from being a recognized topic of discussion in the law and practice of international arbitration. While recent trends in arbitral practice may reveal a frequent, albeit scattered, use of the principle as shall be discussed in this book, its application has been left to the judicial whim of arbitral tribunals, especially in the absence of any sufficiently detailed analysis where the principle's core elements have been addressed or its application in international arbitration scrupulously discussed. **0.12**

In this section one endeavours to provide an abridged overview of the existing theoretical background on the principle of abuse of rights in general, and a succinct overview on its application in international arbitration in particular. **0.13**

Whilst the relevant literature is analysed in each section of the book, this prefatory section is important in order to grasp the current discussion of the issues addressed, to highlight the originality of the study, and to pinpoint its theoretical and practical significance. **0.14**

A. Abuse of Rights: Demystifying the Principle

0.15 Individuals possess substantive and procedural rights in every legal system. The law protects and enforces any normal exercise of a right.[8] However, the question arises whether an exercise of a right in an abusive manner may trigger the right holder's liability. This posits the question: when does an exercise of a right become an abuse of a right?

0.16 In broad terms, abuse of rights denotes the malicious or unreasonable exercise of an otherwise lawful right, or an exercise of a right for a purpose other than that for which it was granted.[9] According to Hersch Lauterpacht, an abuse of right occurs when a right is exercised in an unreasonable or arbitrary manner in a way that inflicts upon another harm that cannot be legitimately justified.[10]

0.17 Many legal systems have sought to design rules to prohibit the abusive exercise of rights.[11] Such sanctions are not necessarily imposed for the mere wrongdoing of the individual, but rather to preserve another more important right.[12] Thus, it seems that the gist of abuse of rights comprises the constructive analysis and evaluation of various competing legal rights, where the legislator and/or court, upon prudent consideration, decides to sacrifice one right to preserve another.[13]

0.18 Although abuse of rights is not generally acknowledged in the common law, it is widely recognized in civil law jurisdictions.[14] As shall be discussed below, while some States adopt a strict approach to the principle and limit its application to certain areas of law, others tend to encompass a broader scope, and further extend its application to different legal areas.[15]

[8] Viktor Knapp, *International Encyclopedia of Comparative Law* (Springer 1983) Part I, Chapter 2, 105.

[9] Anna Di Robilant, 'Abuse of Rights: The Continental Drug and the Common Law' (2010) 61 Hastings Law Journal 687, 688; David Angus, 'Abuse of Rights in Contractual Matters in the Province of Quebec' (1962) 8 McGill Law Journal 150, 151; Glenda Redmann, 'Abuse of Rights: An Overview of the Historical Evolution and the Current Application in Louisiana Contracts' (1987) 32 Loyola Law Review 946, 946–47; Tobi Goldoftas, 'Abuse of Process' (1964) 13 Cleveland-Marshall Law Review 163, 163; Robert Kolb, 'General Principles of Procedural Law' in Andreas Zimmermann and others (eds), *The Statute of the International Court of Justice: A Commentary* (Oxford University Press 2006) 831.

[10] Hersch Lauterpacht, *The Function of Law in the International Community* (Oxford University Press 2011) 294. For a similar definition, see Michael Byers, 'Abuse of Rights: An Old Principle, A New Age' (2002) 47 McGill Law Journal 389, 406. FA Mann equally recognized the importance of abuse of right: Francis A Mann, *The Legal Aspects of Money* (5th edn, Oxford University Press 1992) 476.

[11] Byers (n 10) 406.

[12] In some cases, damages are granted even though the right holder is found to have not committed any fault, given the harm caused to another individual as a result of the exercise of the right. Albert Mayrand, 'Abuse of Rights in France and Quebec' (1974) 34 Louisiana Law Review 993, 1000–02; John H Crabb, 'The French Concept of Abuse of Rights' (1964) 6 Inter-American Law Review 1, 19–20; Lauterpacht (n 10) 303–04.

[13] Ernest J Weinrib, *Corrective Justice* (Oxford University Press 2012) 112–15.

[14] For example, Article 2 of the Swiss Civil Code; Articles 226 and 242 of the German Civil Code; Article 281 of the Greek Civil Code; Article 6.1 of the Luxembourgish Civil Code; Article 3:13 of the Dutch Civil Code; Article 833 of the Italian Civil Code; Article 1295.2 of the Austrian Civil Code; Article 334 of the Portuguese Civil Code; Article, 7.2 of the Spanish Civil Code; Article 334 of the Portuguese Civil Code; Article 7 of the Quebec Civil Code; Article 10 of the Russian Civil Code; Article 107 of the Bolivian Civil Code; Article 840 of the Mexican Civil Code; Article 372 of the Paraguayan Civil Code; Article 5 of the Egyptian Civil Code; Article 106 of the UAE Federal Civil Code; Article 30 of the Kuwaiti Civil Code; and Article 63 of the Qatari Civil Code.

[15] Byers (n 10) 392.

Scholars have different views regarding abuse of rights. Those who deny the validity of the principle argue that it is a vague concept that lacks defined content capable of application.[16] Moreover, as its application traditionally rests on the determination of the motive of the right holder (the subjective element), many have opposed the principle and argued that one's motive is immaterial.[17] Some also oppose its adoption owing to the fact that it grants extensive discretionary power to decision makers. In this regard, Gutteridge opined that a principle, which leaves it to the discretion of the decision maker to determine the purpose of a right, is subject to 'grave objection'.[18] **0.19**

Those who support the need for the prohibition of abuse of rights argue that it: grants courts/arbiters the flexibility needed to deal with the uncertainties and undeterminable variable parameters of which any right bears, aids decision makers in reaching a fair and equitable outcome,[19] and is employed to defeat any attempt to utilize a rule of law for an improper purpose.[20] Herch Lauterpacht noted that the prohibition of abuse of rights 'must exist in the background in any system of administration of justice in which courts are not purely mechanical agencies'.[21] To its proponents, it is a potent legal tool which precludes '*summum ius*' (supreme justice) becoming '*summa iniuria*' (supreme injustice),[22] given that it ameliorates the rigidity of legal rules and advocates reasonableness.[23] **0.20**

A prudent review of scholarly writings and decisions/awards dealing with abuse of rights reveal that it functions either as a curative mechanism or, more prominently, as a corrective mechanism, and aims to ensure the administration of justice.[24] **0.21**

Firstly, whilst all legal systems have articulated legal rules to ensure fairness and the good administration of justice, no legal system exists that has exhaustive legal rules to govern an infinite number of cases and all diversified issues that may arise. In this regard, while rights may be effectively defined in scope and qualified in their reach, it is tenuous to presume that legislators are omniscient, that is, can predict all exceptions and qualifications covered by a given right.[25] In these particular cases, abuse of rights may act as a curative mechanism, as it may be employed to grant courts/arbiters the **0.22**

[16] GDS Taylor, 'The Content of the Rule Against Abuse of Rights in International Law' (1973) 46 Ybk of International Law 323, 324; Shael Herman, 'Classical Social Theories and the Doctrine of "Abuse of Right"' (1977) 37 Louisiana Law Review 747, 747.

[17] *The Mayor, Aldermen and Burgesses of the Borough of Bradford v Edward Pickles* [1895] AC 587, 594.

[18] Harold C Gutteridge, 'Abuse of Rights' (1935) 5 Cambridge Law Journal 22, 42.

[19] Angus (n 9) 157.

[20] Redmann (n 9), 947; Gutteridge (n 18) 42.

[21] Herch Lauterpacht, *The Development of International Law by the International Court* (Cambridge University Press 1982) 165.

[22] A legal maxim which denotes cases where justice may turn into injustice if one strictly follows the legal rule. María José and Falcón Tella, *Equity and Law* (Martinus Nijhoff 2008) 192; Alexandre Kiss, 'Abuse of Rights' in Rudolf Bernhardt (ed), *Encyclopedia of Public International Law* (North-Holland 1992) vol 1, para 1.

[23] Wim Decock, *Theologians and Contract Law: The Moral Transformation of the Ius Commune* (Martinus Nijhoff 1983) 292.

[24] Chester Brown, 'The Inherent Powers of International Courts and Tribunals' (2005) 76 British Ybk of International Law 195, 231.

[25] Frederick Schauer, 'Can Rights be Abused?' (1981) 31 Philosophical Quarterly 225, 229; Pannal A Sanders, '"At Will" Franchise Terminations and the Abuse of Rights Doctrine' (1981) 42 Louisiana Law Review 210, 223.

flexibility needed to deal with the uncertainties and undeterminable variable parameters of which any right bears. As stipulated by Joseph Voyame, Bertil Cottier, and Bolivar Rocha:

> [T]he great majority of commentators agree on the usefulness of the remedial function of the rules forbidding abuse of rights. Indeed, the legislator is no more infallible today than he was in the past. While the rules he promulgates are becoming increasingly precise and detailed, he cannot foresee every eventuality. Only the proscription of abuse of rights makes it possible to establish the connection between the justice ostensibly guaranteed by positive law and genuine justice.[26]

0.23 Accordingly, it serves to fill the lacuna that may exist in all legal systems.[27] Thus, as shall be discussed below, abuse of rights has been utilized in certain cases to create new contractual obligations to avoid an unjust or inequitable outcome.[28]

0.24 Secondly, abuse of rights functions as a corrective mechanism, as it softens and ameliorates the rigidity of strict legal rules.[29]

0.25 The principle has arguably presented elements that were peculiar to the positivistic legal school: courts are bestowed with a parochial right to apply an existing legal provision on a given set of facts.[30] With the introduction of abuse of rights, courts are conferred with a rather broad role, that is, to ameliorate the harshness of positive law or contractual provisions.[31]

0.26 The corrective function of abuse of rights is further fortified by the words of the Swiss Federal Supreme Court where it provided that:

> The fundamental theory of this article is the recognition that positive legislation is unable to affect in detail all the controversies which may arise in the society of men, and it is equally impossible for it to regulate these controversies in advance. However much the legislator may try to build up a legal structure that shows no gaps in the laws, there will always be special cases in which *a rigid application of the statutory principles would lead to injustice, and this the judge is not permitted to tolerate.* This happens in particular if individual rights are exercised contrary to good faith. Section 2 of article

[26] Joseph Voyame, Bertil Cottier, and Bolivar Rocha, 'Abuse of Right in Comparative Law' in 'Abuse of Rights and Equivalent Concepts: The Principle and Its Present Day Application' (Proceedings of the 19th Colloquy on European Law, Luxembourg, 6–9 November 1989) (Council of Europe 1990) 48.

[27] Lauterpacht (n 10) 308.

[28] Quebec Superior Court in *Posluns v Enterprises Lormil Inc* [1990] Quebec 200-05-001584-858, JE 90-1131 (CS), cited in Rosalie Jukier, 'Banque Nationale du Canada v. Houle (S.C.C.): Implications of an Expanded Doctrine of Abuse of Rights in Civilian Contract Law' (1992) 37 McGill Law Journal 221, 235 (where the Court applied abuse of rights to create a contractual provision of a guarantee of exclusivity which was not part of the contract).

[29] AN Yiannopoulos, 'Civil Liability for Abuse of Right: Something Old, Something New . . . ', (1994) 54 Louisiana Law Review 1173, 1195.

[30] Julio Cueto-Rua, 'Abuse of Rights' (1975) 35 Louisiana Law Review 965, 972.

[31] Yiannopoulos (n 29), 1195; James Gordley, 'The Abuse of Rights in the Civil Law Tradition' in Rita de la Feria and Stefan Vogenauer (eds), *Prohibition of Abuse of Law: A New General Principle of EU Law?* (Hart Publishing 2011) 35.

> 2, which denies legal protection to the manifest abuse of a right, forms the necessary amendment to the duty which is set down in section 1 of article 2, namely, to act always in good faith. *The purpose of this provision is to either limit or to annul the formal validity of positive laws whenever the judge deems this to be in the interests of substantive justice.*[32] (Emphasis added)

On a different note, characterizing and labelling abuse of rights as a term of art is not an easy task. Scholars have engaged in a futile logomachy in this regard. **0.27**

Some, influenced by the views of Marcel Planiol, have rejected the use of the words 'abuse' and 'right', holding that it is a 'contradiction in terms' as a right ceases to be given such status when tainted with abuse and consequently, it is futile to speak of it as the abuse of a right:[33] **0.28**

> This new doctrine is based entirely on language insufficiently studied; its formula 'abusive use of rights' is a logomachy, for if I use my right, my act is licit; and when it is illicit it is because I exceed my right and act without right.[34]

This emanates from the perception that one who abuses his rights is no longer within the formal limits of the right, but has necessarily exceeded the limits of that right. Others prefer to use terms such as 'distortion of rights', 'competitive rights', or 'conflict of rights'.[35] **0.29**

Regardless of such terminological juxtaposition, it is submitted that, for reasons of convenience and given the scope of the book, the best term to be used is 'abuse of rights'. **0.30**

As a term of art, one may argue that there is no contradiction in terms given the distinction between one's subjective right (*droits subjectifs*) and the objective law (*droit objectif*); the abuse 'is in accord with such a right, but is against the law in its entirety'.[36] **0.31**

Finally, choosing to employ such terminology equally emanates from reasons of convenience, as it is the term used in the existing literature and it easily depicts the principle's legal concept and purpose. From a purely logical stance, the main purpose of words is to indicate a specific meaning to those in receipt. If such purpose is effectively **0.32**

[32] Judgment of the Swiss Federal Supreme Court, BGE 72.2.39 (1946), cited and translated in Vera Bolgar, 'Abuse of Rights in France, Germany, and Switzerland: A Survey of a Recent Chapter in Legal Doctrine' (1975) 35 Louisiana Law Review 1015, 1034.

[33] Robilant (n 9) 83, citing Marcel Planiol, *Traité Élémentaire De Droit Civil* (Paris 1907) vol 2, No 870: 'The formula abuse of rights is a logomachy, since if I use my own right, my act is licit and when it is illicit it is because I have exceeded my right and *acted sine jus, iniuria* as the *Lex Aquilia* says. To reject the category abuse of rights is not to try to hold licit the various damaging activities repressed by our courts. It is only to note that an abusive act to the extent that it is illicit is not the exercise of a right and that abuse of rights is not a category distinct from "illicit act". In other words, the right ends where the abuse begins'; Gutteridge (n 18) 24; Herman (n 16) 747; Cueto-Rua (n 30) 974–75; Mayrand (n 12) 993.

[34] Marcel Planiol, *Treatise on the Civil Law* (Louisiana State Law Institution tr, 1959) 477; Redmann (n 9) 949.

[35] Cueto-Rua (n 30) 976; Gutteridge (n 18) 24–25.

[36] Annekatrien Lenaerts, 'The General Principle of the Prohibition of Abuse of Rights: A Critical Position on Its Role in a Codified European Contract Law' (2010) 18 European Review of Private Law 1121, 1122; José and Tella (n 22) 191–92; Josserand, 'De l'esprit des droits et de leur relativitd', cited in Gutteridge (n 18) 24.

satisfied, any debate regarding the use of the words seems of a purely linguistic nature and is futile from a strict legal point of view.

0.33 Despite its historical imbroglio, 'abuse of right', as a term of art, largely satisfies its main purpose by alluding its characteristic elements, as a legal construct, to readers.

B. Scope of Application

0.34 An examination of the principle of abuse of rights in different legal systems reveals that the principle's conditions of application comprise the existence of a right, and that such right ceases legal protection given that it has been abused.[37]

0.35 In relation to what conduct constitutes an abuse, courts and tribunals rely on different criteria. It is generally recognized[38] that abuse is established if any of the following criteria is fulfilled.

0.36 Firstly, abuse is established if a right is exercised with an intent to cause harm. Most scholars and legal systems that recognize abuse of rights endorse this criterion.[39] Scholtens held that abuse is established whereby the right holder exercises his/her right with an intention to cause harm to another, and this may be presumed where the exercise brings no advantage to the right holder, or where the benefit derived is minimal and the detriment caused thereby is great.[40] Other scholars opposed endorsing the subjective element of malice because of the difficulty in proving it.[41]

0.37 Secondly, abuse is established if a right is exercised for a purpose other than that for which it was granted. The supporters of this criterion of abuse note that it presupposes that rights do not exist in a vacuum; they are conferred upon the right holder for a specific social purpose. If the holder of the right derogates from its purpose, it may be tantamount to an abuse of right.[42]

0.38 Thirdly, abuse may be established if one exercises his/her right unreasonably. It is often held that unreasonableness is determined where the right holder exercises the right

[37] Yiannopoulos (n 29) 1195; Kiss (n 22) para 2; Gianluigi Palombella, 'The Abuse of Rights and the Rule of Law' in András Sajó (ed), *Abuse: The Dark Side of Fundamental Rights* (Eleven International 2006) 9–10; Babatunde O Iluyomade, 'The Scope and Content of a Complaint of Abuse of Right in International Law' (1975) 16 Harvard International Law Journal 47, 48; Qatari Court of Cassation, Session held on 7 January 2014, Challenge No 176, Judicial Year 2013.

[38] Cueto-Rua (n 30) 985–1003; Yiannopoulos (n 29) 1180; Joseph M Perillo, 'Abuse of Rights: A Pervasive Legal Concept' (1996) 27 Pacific Law Journal 37, 47; James C Exnicios, 'Abuse of Rights: An Overview of the Historical Evolution and the Current Application in Louisiana Contracts' (1987) 32 Law Review 946, 946–49.

[39] Cueto-Rua (n 30) 991; Crabb (n 12) 13; Mayrand (n 12) 994; Article 226 of the German Civil Code.

[40] JE Scholtens, 'Abuse of Rights' (1958) 75 South African Law Journal 39, 43.

[41] B Edmeades, 'Abuse of Rights' (1978) 24 McGill Law Journal 136, 137; Pierre Catala and John A Weir, 'Delict and Torts: A Study in Parallel, Part II' (1964) 38 Tulane Law Review 221, 224; Gutteridge (n 18) 26.

[42] FP Walton, 'Motive as an Element in Torts in the Common and in the Civil Law' (1909) 22 Harvard Law Review 501, 501; Louis Josserand, *De I 'esprit des droits et de leur Relativité: Théorie dite dès l'Abus des Droits* (2nd edn, 1925), cited in Cueto-Rua (n 30) 1001; *Prest v Petrodel Resources Ltd* [2013] 2 AC 415, 17; *Barcelona Traction (Belgium v Spain)* [1970] ICJ 39, 56, judgment of 5 February 1970.

with minimal serious or legitimate interest,[43] or where there is disparity between the interests which are served by its effectuation and the interests which are, or could be, damaged as a result thereof.[44]

Finally, some also note that abuse may be established if a right is exercised in violation of good faith.[45] **0.39**

On a different note, the application of abuse of rights has clearly developed throughout the years. While its scope of application was limited to the area of property law, it subsequently extended to other areas and is now said to have a general application.[46] **0.40**

As noted by John Crabb, abuse of rights has been applied in cases pertaining to contract law, law of procedures, including the legal process, the process of appeal, and the execution of judicial decisions, and to family law.[47] Other scholars equally note that abuse of rights applies in every department of the law.[48] **0.41**

C. Abuse of Rights in the Context of International Arbitration

Whilst the application of abuse of rights in international arbitration has not been addressed in detail, the growing phenomenon of abuse and procedural misconduct in the context of arbitration is acknowledged by many. **0.42**

Parties principally refer their disputes to international arbitration owing to the presumed advantages and benefits that the arbitration system aspires to offer, including procedural efficiency and obtaining a fair resolution of the dispute.[49] However, the arbitral system is currently subject to challenges and criticism,[50] owing to the perception that it is failing to accommodate the needs of its users.[51] In recent surveys and empirical **0.43**

[43] *Karaha Bodas Co v Perusahaan Pertambangan Minyak Das Gas Bumi Negara*, 364 F 3d 274 (5th Cir 2004), ('An action violates abuse of rights doctrine if [. . .] the action is totally unreasonable given the lack of any legitimate interest in the exercise of the right and its exercise harms another'); Gutteridge (n 18) 32.

[44] Edmeades (n 41) 138; Perillo (n 38) 47; Lauterpacht (n 10), 303–04; Kiss (n 22) para 4; Case C-373/97 *Diamantis* [2000] ECR I-1705, para 43; Weinrib (n 13) 112–15, discussing that courts may award damages in lieu of an injunction on the basis of abuse of right. If monetary compensation is adequate for the plaintiff, while issuing an injunction would be oppressive to the defendant and the plaintiff would derive no substantial benefit therefrom, courts may use abuse of right to *balance the competing interests* and reach equipoise (remedial fairness).

[45] Cueto-Rua (n 30) 996; Michael Joachim Bonell, *An International Restatement of Contract Law: The UNIDROIT Principles of International Commercial Contracts* (3rd edn, Transnational Publishers 2005) 133; Egyptian Court of Cassation, Session held on 27 April 2006, Challenge No 3473, Judicial Year 75.

[46] Walton (n 42) 505; Byers (n 10) 392, it is widely applied in 'property law, labour law, contractual obligations, and legal proceedings'; Cueto-Rua (n 30) 967; FP Walton, 'Delictual Responsibility in the Modern Civil Law (More Particularly in the French Law) as Compared with the English Law of Torts' (1933) 49 Law Quarterly Review 70, 87; MS Amos, 'Abusive Exercise of Rights According to French Law' (1900) 2 Journal of the Society of Comparative Legislation 453, 453–54.

[47] Crabb (n 12) 3–4; Walton (n 42) 508; Catala and Weir (n 41) 225–26; Walton (n 46) 87.

[48] Walton (n 42) 505.

[49] William W Park, 'Arbitrators and Accuracy' (2010) 1 Journal of International Dispute Settlement 25, 27.

[50] Bernard Hanotiau, 'International Arbitration in a Global Economy: The Challenges of the Future' (2011) 28 Journal of International Arbitration 89, 99.

[51] Alan Redfern and others, *Law and Practice of International Commercial Arbitration* (4th edn, Sweet & Maxwell 2004) paras 1-46; Irene Welser and Susanna Wurzer, 'Formality in International Commercial Arbitration—For Better or for Worse?' in Gerold Zeiler and others (eds), *Austrian Arbitration Yearbook 2008*

studies, users have complained primarily because of costs, delays, and procedural misconduct during the arbitration process.[52]

0.44 Scholars have noted that different forms of abuse in arbitration may be detrimental to the arbitral system,[53] if an effective remedy is not established. To that effect, one scholar emphasized that the arbitral system will self-destruct unless there is recourse against procedural abuse.[54] Professor Emmanuel Gaillard also acknowledged the rising phenomenon of abuse in international arbitration. He emphasized that parties have developed an exceptional array of procedural abuse, and noted that specific tools need to be developed to prevent procedural misconduct.[55]

0.45 The problem of abuse in arbitration is significant owing to the fact that it is frequently resorted to[56] and can be employed during any phase in international arbitration.[57]

0.46 This was also confirmed by another scholar who acknowledged that abuse is becoming widespread, is negatively impacting the arbitration system, and may pertain to any right conferred upon the parties by the applicable arbitration rules or laws.[58]

0.47 There is general consensus in legal discourse that the frequent abuse of the arbitral system is detrimental to arbitration and that finding a principle to remedy such abuse would be serving the parties' interests, the integrity of the arbitral system, and the overall administration of justice.[59]

(Manz'sche Verlags- und Universitätsbuchhandlung 2008); Irene Welser and Christian Klausegger, 'Fast Track Arbitration: Just Fast or Something Different?' in Gerold Zeiler and others (eds), *Austrian Arbitration Yearbook 2009* (Manz'sche Verlags- und Universitätsbuchhandlung 2009) 260; Piero Bernardini, 'International Arbitration: How to Make it More Effective' in Laurent Levy and Yves Derains (eds), *Liber Amicorum En l'Honnour de Serge Lazareff* (ICC Publication 2011); Klaus Peter Berger, 'The Need for Speed in International Arbitration' (2008) 25 Journal of International Arbitration 595, 595; Jeffrey Waincymer, 'Promoting Fairness and Efficiency of Procedures in International Commercial Arbitration—Identifying Uniform Model Norms' (2010) 3 Contemporary Asia Arbitration Journal 25, 45; William K Slate II, 'Cost and Time Effectiveness of Arbitration' (2010) 3 Contemporary Asia Arbitration Journal 185, 186; Jorg Risse, 'Procedural Risk Analysis: An ADR-Tool in Arbitration Proceedings' (2009) Austrian Arbitration Ybk 461, 461.

[52] Queen Mary University of London and PricewaterhouseCoopers LLP, '2015 International Arbitration Survey: Improvements and Innovations in International Arbitration' (2015) 7.

[53] Jan Paulsson,'International Arbitration is Not Arbitration' (2008) 2 Stockholm International Arbitration Review 1, 3.

[54] Patrick M Lane, 'Dilatory Tactics: Arbitral Discretion' in Albert Jan van den Berg (ed), *Improving the Efficiency of Arbitration Agreements and Awards: 40 Years of Application of the New York Convention* (Kluwer Law International 1999) 425.

[55] Emmanuel Gaillard, 'Abuse of Process in International Arbitration' (2017) 32 ICSID Review 17, 17.

[56] Edward R Leahy and Kenneth J Pierce, 'Sanctions to Control Party Misbehavior in International Arbitration' (1986) 26 Virginia Journal of International Law 291, 299.

[57] Günther J Horvath and others, 'Categories of Guerrilla Tactics' in Stephan Wilske and Günther J Horvath (eds), *Guerrilla Tactics in International Arbitration* (Kluwer Law International 2013) 4–5.

[58] Klaus Sachs, 'Time and Money: Cost Control and Effective Case Management' in Julian Lew and Loukas Mistelis (eds), *Pervasive Problems in International Arbitration* (Kluwer Law International 2006) 113.

[59] Stephan Wilske, 'Crisis? What Crisis? The Development of International Arbitration in Tougher Times' (2009a) 2 Contemporary Asia Arbitration Journal 187, 208; Martin Raible and Stephan Wilske, 'The Arbitrator as Guardian of International Public Policy: Should Arbitrators go Beyond Solving Legal Issues' in Catherine A Rogers and Roger P Alford (eds), *The Future of Investment Arbitration* (Oxford University Press 2009b) 269; Leahy and Pierce (n 56) 293; Nadia Darwazeh and Baptiste Rigaudeau, 'Clues to Construing the New French Arbitration Law' (2011) 28 Journal of International Arbitration 381, 383.

Whilst scholars have carefully accentuated the problem, they have not enunciated the procedural principle that can operate effectively to tackle the different forms of abuse. **0.48**

Despite this, there have been clear attempts by commentators and arbitral tribunals to introduce, or revive, the principle of abuse of rights to tackle *specific* forms of abuse in arbitration, particularly in investment arbitration.[60] **0.49**

For example, it is generally acknowledged that the principle is vital to deal with abusive subsequent proceedings in arbitration. Eminent scholars confirm the need to apply abuse of rights to bar subsequent proceedings that fall outside the scope of *res judicata*.[61] Thus, Audley Sheppard stipulated that: **0.50**

> [W]here the conditions for *res judicata* are not met, I would suggest that a tribunal nevertheless should consider whether it should not allow the second claim from proceeding, on grounds of abuse of process or abuse of rights.[62]

Similarly, in the context of parallel arbitral proceedings, Gaillard recently noted that a principle of abuse of rights is the most promising tool to tackle the problem of abusive parallel proceedings in arbitration, and advocated for this in a number of ICSID arbitration proceedings.[63] **0.51**

Based on the above, it seems clear that abuse of rights has recently gained a pivotal role in the context of international arbitration and its application is slowly gaining momentum. Commentators have raised the application of the principle and arbitrators have been willing to apply it to preclude certain forms of abuse in international arbitration. **0.52**

IV. Originality and Structure of the Book

The above analysis reveals that there is an apparent lacuna in this context, where no substantial legal work has been undertaken to: carefully establish the core elements of **0.53**

[60] Hervé Ascensio, 'Abuse of Process in International Investment Arbitration' (2014) 13 Chinese Journal of International Law 763, 764–65; Eric De Brabandere, '"Good Faith", "Abuse of Process" and the Initiation of Investment Treaty Claims' (2012) 3 Journal of International Dispute Settlement 609; John P Gaffney, '"Abuse of Process" in Investment Treaty Arbitration' (2010) 11 Journal of World Investment and Trade 515; *Phoenix Action v The Czech Republic*, ICSID Case No ARB/06/5, Award of 15 April 2009; *Philip Morris Asia Limited v The Commonwealth of Australia*, PCA Case No 2012-12, Award on Jurisdiction and Admissibility of 17 December 2015, under UNCITRAL Rules.

[61] Yuval Shany, *The Competing Jurisdictions of International Courts and Tribunals* (Oxford University Press 2003) 259; Vaughan Lowe, 'Overlapping Jurisdiction in International Tribunals' (1999) 20 Australian Ybk of International Law 191, 269; Campbell Mclachlan, *Lis Pendens in International Litigation* (Martinus Nijhoff Publishers 2009) 420–32; Gary B Born, *International Commercial Arbitration* (2nd edn, Kluwer Law International 2014) 3736–37; International Law Association, Resolution No 1/2006, Recommendation 5.

[62] Audley Sheppard, 'Res Judicata and Estoppel' in Bernardo M Cremades and Julian DM Lew (eds), *Parallel State and Arbitral Procedures in International Arbitration* (ICC Institute of World Business Law 2005) 235.

[63] Gaillard (n 55) 32–34; *Ampal-American Israel Corp, et al v Arab Republic of Egypt*, ICSID Case No ARB/12/11, Decision on Jurisdiction of 1 February 2016; *Orascom TMT Investments Sàrl v Republic of Algeria*, ICSID Case No ARB/12/35, Award of 31 May 2017.

abuse of rights; determine if it elevates to a general or transnational principle of law; and shed light on its multifaceted functions when applied in international arbitration.

0.54 Moreover, its application as a general principle of law in international arbitration is to be examined. A careful analysis of the possibility of approaching abuse of rights as a general principle of law has serious legal manifestations. Particularly, it enables arbitrators to utilize it to address all procedural tactics, and different forms of abuse, designed to undermine the arbitral process. It also dispenses with the current compartmentalized approach to abusive conduct, where different abusive behaviours fit into different rules or doctrines that are generally rigid and fail to effectively tackle the panoply of abusive practices.

0.55 Additionally, this book addresses a novel aspect of abuse of rights in the context of arbitration. Whilst some may have advocated the applicability of the principle in arbitration, it appears that the legal basis, or the justification for its application in arbitration, have not been discussed before. The book argues that the principle is vital not merely because it is considered, as shall be discussed, a general principle of law, but more importantly, as it functions to ensure the administration of arbitral justice. Thus, the principle's interrelation with, and its effect on, the administration of arbitral justice shall be carefully addressed.

0.56 Moreover, the status of the principle in international arbitration is of particular importance. While abuse of rights may be applied as part of the applicable law, or as a general substantive and procedural principle of law, it is of theoretical and practical significance to examine if it constitutes a principle of transnational public policy that remains applicable irrespective of the *lex arbitri* and *lex causae*.

0.57 In light of the above, the significance of this book not only stems from the importance of the issues covered and their theoretical and practical significance and ramifications, or the relative scarcity of specialized resources. Equally important is the fact that it represents a comprehensive study on abuse of rights in international arbitration and amongst the few examples, if any, that address the principle's core elements, question its legitimacy in international arbitration, and discusses its nature and/or function when applied to different legal areas in arbitration law.

0.58 The book is divided into four chapters. Chapter 1 provides a comparative overview of the principle of abuse of rights and its application in national legal systems and in international law. In order to provide that abuse of rights is a general principle of law, this chapter examines its recognition and application in different legal systems. Thus, epitomes of its application in a number of civil and common law systems and international law are discussed to establish the generality/universality of the principle.

0.59 Chapter 2 addresses the particulars of abuse of rights and distils the concept to its essential elements. This chapter seeks to articulate the principle's conditions of application and to shed light on any concerns that may arise from its application.

Chapter 3 discerns the nature of abuse of rights in international arbitration. It determines the legal basis of abuse of rights, questions the transnational nature of the principle, and examines whether it comprises a principle of transnational public policy. **0.60**

Chapter 4 examines the importance of applying abuse of rights in international arbitration. It analyses how the principle's application in arbitration ensures the administration of arbitral justice. In particular, this chapter discusses how the application of the principle may achieve fairness during arbitral proceedings, fetter the effective resolution of disputes, enable arbitrators to reach equitable outcomes, and preserve the integrity of the arbitration system. **0.61**

Finally, the book includes a general conclusion that summarizes the legal questions discussed and the findings of each question examined. **0.62**

V. Research Methodology

Descriptive, comparative, and analytical approaches are employed in examining the issues raised in this book. **0.63**

The descriptive approach is utilized to elucidate the gist of the principle of abuse of rights, its scope of application, and to examine the *status quo* of the field and of the issues raised. **0.64**

A comparative approach is equally indispensable to the study of abuse of rights in international arbitration. The study examines the application of abuse of rights as a general principle of law in international arbitration. Generally, for a principle to be considered transnational or a general principle of law, one should: (1) examine its generality and universality; (2) distil the concept to its essential elements; and (3) ascertain whether the principle is suitable to be transposed into international arbitration.[64] **0.65**

Thus, in order to ascertain the universality of abuse of rights, an examination of the principle in different legal systems is crucial. In this regard, it is generally acknowledged that the principle's recognition in all systems of law is not required.[65] Thus, the study shall ascertain the prevailing trend within legal systems and establish wide recognition of the principle in question, rather than unanimous recognition.[66] **0.66**

[64] Charles T Kotuby and Luke A Sobota, *General Principles of Law and International Due Process* (Oxford University Press 2017) 17–27; Jaye Ellis, 'General Principles and Comparative Law' (2011) 22 European Journal of International Law 949, 955–59; *International Status of South West Africa* (Advisory Opinion) [1950] ICJ Rep 128, 148, Separate Opinion of Lord McNair, discussing general principles of law.

[65] Emmanuel Gaillard, *Legal Theory of International Arbitration* (Martinus Nijhoff 2010) 48–51.

[66] Harold C Gutteridge, *Comparative Law* (2nd edn, Cambridge University Press 1949) 65; Ellis (n 64) 949, 953–54 ('This methodology [. . .] is the object of a reasonably solid doctrinal and jurisprudential consensus'); LC Green, 'Comparative Law as a "Source" of International Law' (1968) 42 Tulane Law Review 52; Emmanuel Gaillard, 'General Principles of Law in International Commercial Arbitration—Challenging the Myths' (2011) 5 World Arbitration and Mediation Review 161, 162.

0.67 As the recognition of abuse of rights, its function, and its legal basis are questioned, the comparative analysis and the functional approach being utilized shall focus on the principle's mechanism of operation in a number of civil legal systems, including French law, German law, Swiss law, the law of Louisiana, and Egyptian law. This method will generally focus on: (1) outlining the statutory and/or judicial formation of the principle; (2) the policy adopted, that is, a restrictive policy or endorsement of a general principle of abuse of rights; (3) the application of the principle; and (4) the criteria adopted to determine if there is an abuse of right. The recognition and application of abuse of rights in international law shall also be examined. This comparative methodology will assess whether the mentioned legal systems apply abuse of rights in the same manner or, at least, if there exists sufficient elements of commonality in its application.

0.68 Whilst abuse of rights is not readily recognized in the common law legal systems, as shall be discussed, this derogation does not necessarily deprive it from its status as a transnational or general principle.[67] This study employs a functional approach to identify and discuss other existing rules and principles in order to establish elements of commonality, that is *tertium comparationis.*

0.69 In parts related to the application of abuse of rights in international arbitration, the book employs an international comparative perspective. Thus, national court decisions and arbitral case law of various jurisdictions are reviewed and analysed.

0.70 Furthermore, the analytical method is similarly employed throughout the book in order to examine the elements of abuse of rights; the limitation of its scope of application; its relation to the administration of justice; and its function, transnational nature, and application in the context of international arbitration.

0.71 In doing so, one shall analyse the operation of the principle of abuse of rights in international arbitration as acknowledged by prominent scholars; as reflected in international legal instruments such as uniform laws; and as applied by arbitral tribunals. This methodology is particularly used in the arena of international arbitration.[68]

0.72 The analysis of the mentioned legal issues shall be attained by examining the law and practice of commercial and investment arbitration. However, emphasis may be given to investment arbitration materials in relation to some issues and to commercial arbitration materials in others. In doing so, one is mandated and restricted by the existence and availability of materials for the relevant issue. That said, it is submitted that any conclusion reached in relation to the nature and application of the principle should extend to, and apply in, international commercial and investment arbitration.

[67] Thus, whilst the principle of good faith is not recognized as a general principle under English law, it constitutes a general principle of law: Michael Nolan, 'Issues of Proof of General Principles of Law in International Arbitration' (2009) 3 World Arbitration and Mediation Review 505, 510–12.

[68] Note, 'General Principles of Law in International Commercial Arbitration' (1988) 101 Harvard Law Review 1816, 1824–25.

1

Abuse of Rights in National Legal Systems and International Law

I. Introduction

To determine if abuse of rights constitutes a general principle of law, its recognition must first be examined in the different legal systems in order to establish its generality[1] and then subsequently one must distil the concept to its essential elements. This is necessary to determine if there is a need to modify its conditions of application in order to make it suitable for the particularities of international arbitration.[2] **1.01**

The application of the principle in civil legal systems (II) is briefly discussed: mainly in (A) French Law, (B) German Law, (C) Swiss Law, (D) Louisiana Law, and (E) Egyptian Law. **1.02**

Subsequently, an abridged discussion of the recognition, or lack thereof, of abuse of rights in the common law legal systems is undertaken (III). By doing so, one aims to highlight the general view shared in this context, and discuss the existence of functional equivalents that achieve the same purpose as that of abuse of rights. Finally, a succinct examination of the recognition and application of abuse of rights in international law is undertaken (IV). **1.03**

[1] Konrad Zweigert and Hein Kötz, *An Introduction to Comparative Law* (3rd edn, Oxford University Press 1998) 34–36; Ralf Michaels, '*The Functional Method of Comparative Law*' in Mathias Reimann and Reinhard Zimmermann (eds), *The Oxford Handbook of Comparative Law* (Oxford University Press 2008) 342 and 346.

[2] Jaye Ellis, 'General Principles and Comparative Law' (2011) 22 European Journal of International Law 949, 955–59; *International Status of South West Africa* (Advisory Opinion) [1950] ICJ Rep 128, 148, Separate Opinion of Lord McNair, discussing general principles of law.

1.04 For obvious spatial-temporal considerations, the author chose these particular legal systems given: the influence they had on other legal systems; the important role they played in establishing and developing the principle; the different policies they adopt; and because they represent epitomes of legal systems from different regions in the world.

II. Abuse of Rights in Civil Legal Systems

A. French Law

1.05 Abuse of rights was formulated in France by jurisprudence and legal literature, and was further developed by French courts. The principle emanated from the general rules on civil liability enshrined in Article 1382 of the French Civil Code.[3] The said Article is the normative foundation of delictual liability. It fixes the responsibility of any harm on the author, whether he/she deliberately inflicted such harm, or if it was because of his/her negligence or imprudence.

1.06 While, from a purely vernacular perspective, Article 1382 does not refer explicitly to abuse of rights, French courts have used the sufficiently broad terms of the Article to apply the principle and extend it to different areas of the law.[4] Moreover, Article 32.1 of the French Code of Civil Procedure acknowledges abuse of procedural rights.[5]

1.07 Although the acknowledgement of the principle in French law and its application by French courts is unequivocal, the conditions of application may seem ambiguous, as the French case law and jurisprudence have adopted different criteria of abuse.[6]

1.08 A review of the conditions under French law reveals that French courts establish an abuse of right if a right is exercised: (a) to cause harm to another; or (b) in bad faith; or (c) unreasonably; or (d) contrary to its social purpose. The satisfaction of one of the mentioned criteria warrants the application of the principle. However, French courts prefer certain criteria to others. This is discussed in more detail as follows.

1.09 One of the first cases where the French courts explicitly applied the principle was seen in 1855. The case involved the owner of some land and a house built thereon. The owner had built a chimney on top of the house, without any legitimate or serious interest, but

[3] Glenda Redmann, 'Abuse of Rights: An Overview of the Historical Evolution and the Current Application in Louisiana Contracts' (1987) 32 Loyola Law Review 946, 948; Article 1382 of the French Civil Code stipulates that 'Tout fait quelconque de l'homme, qui cause à autrui un dommage, oblige celui par la faute duquel il est arrivé à le réparer'. Article 1383 provides that 'Chacun est responsable du dommage qu'il a causé non seulement par son fait, mais encore par sa négligence ou par son imprudence'.

[4] Mateusz Krauze, 'English Law and the Doctrine of Abuse of Rights' (2012) 1 Oxford University Undergraduate Law Journal 2; Michael Byers, 'Abuse of Rights: An Old Principle, A New Age' (2002) 47 McGill Law Journal 389, 392; Vera Bolgar, 'Abuse of Rights in France, Germany, and Switzerland: A Survey of a Recent Chapter in Legal Doctrine' (1975) 35 Louisiana Law Review 1015, 1019–20.

[5] Article 32.1 of the French Code of Civil Procedures; and Articles 118, 123, 550, 559, and 560; Emmanuel Gaillard, 'Abuse of Process in International Arbitration' (2017) 32 ICSID Review 17, 33.

[6] Harold C Gutteridge, 'Abuse of Rights' (1935) 5 Cambridge Law Journal 22, 32.

for the *sole purpose* of harming his neighbour. The owner argued that property rights were absolute and were not subject to limitations, and that his motive was irrelevant and could not render a legal act into an illegal one. However, in endorsing the principle, the Court of Appeal of Colmar stipulated that:

> [I]t is a principle of law that the right of ownership is, in a fashion, an *absolute* right, entitling the owner abuse of his thing; *however*, the exercise of this right, as the exercise of any other right, ought to be *limited by the satisfaction of a serious and licit interest* [. . .] Principles of morals and equity prevent the court from protecting an action motivated by ill will, performed under the sway of a wicked passion, which while not providing any personal benefit to the performer, causes serious damages to another.[7] (Emphasis added)

Thus, while acknowledging that the right holder was merely exercising a right conferred by the law, such a right is not conferred without restrictions. The right holder must have a legitimate and serious interest to exercise his right, and cannot be acting solely to harm his neighbour. It is important to note that the Court's decision pertains to an ownership right, which was considered to be the epitome of unrestricted and absolute rights. The decision further fortifies the submission that the term 'absolute right' is an oxymoron: the language used, per se, negates the very characteristics of an absolute right, as the Court clearly limited the extent of the exercise of the right by the 'satisfaction' of a 'serious' and 'licit interest'. It was thus clear that French law would not extend its protection to an act which was performed in malevolence, and that a right holder may not attempt to inflict harm on another and evade legal liability by hiding behind the defence of exercising a 'legal right'. **1.10**

The above case demonstrates the classic form of conduct tainted with abuse. When the right holder exercises his/her right with a malicious intent for no other purpose but to inflict harm on another individual, he/she is held liable for abusing his/her right.[8] **1.11**

The case in question also demonstrates how courts deduce an intent to inflict harm. As is evident from the decision, the Court deduced malice, 'ill will', by the fact that the right holder did not have a serious interest to exercise the right. Thus, the lack of a legitimate or serious interest may be evidence of malice. **1.12**

The Court of Appeal of Lyon confirmed the above submission in a case regarding adjacent springs producing mineral water. The owner of the spring had installed a powerful pump which had the effect of decreasing the water yielded by the spring owned by his neighbour. The owner argued that he may not be found accountable for any damages caused as a result of his exercise of a right: *nemo injuria facit qui jure suo utitur*.[9] While **1.13**

[7] *Colmar*, 2 May 1855, DP 1856.2.9, 10, cited in Julio Cueto-Rua, 'Abuse of Rights' (1975) 35 Louisiana Law Review 965, 965 (1975); James Gordley, 'The Abuse of Rights in the Civil Law Tradition' in Rita de la Feria and Stefan Vogenauer (eds), *Prohibition of Abuse of Law: A New General Principle of EU Law?* (Hart Publishing 2011) 34.

[8] John H Crabb, 'The French Concept of Abuse of Rights' (1964) 6 Inter-American Law Review 1, 13.

[9] Cueto-Rua (n 7) 966.

the factual matrix of the case did not reveal or evince a palpable intention to harm another, the Court concluded that such intention was *presumed*, given that the owner *did not benefit* by the additional water yielded because of the installed pump, and that it was merely wasted. Thus, the Court decided that the lack of a legitimate or serious interest proved that the action was inspired by an intention to inflict harm on another.[10]

1.14 In the seminal case of *affaire Clément-Bayard*, which is generally considered to be the decisive authority on this matter, the French Court of Cassation was caught on the horns of a dilemma, in that there were complex/a mixture of motives involved and the Court had to decide whether abuse could be established notwithstanding the existence of a legitimate motive. The case involved an owner, Coquerel, of land adjoining land owned by Clément-Bayard, who had built hangars for storing dirigibles. Coquerel wanted to sell his land to Clément-Bayard, but the latter refused to buy at the proposed price. Accordingly, Coquerel had built wooden scaffolds and installed steel spikes, which negatively impacted upon Clément-Bayard's dirigibles. In fact, one of Clément-Bayard's aircraft had collided with the structures built by Coquerel, and was manifestly damaged.[11]

1.15 In a suit brought by Clément-Bayard, requesting the removal of the spikes and the payment of damages, Coquerel vehemently argued that he was exercising a legally acknowledged right. Precisely, he was simply seeking an economic advantage by attempting to exert pressure on Clément-Bayard to buy the land and to obtain the highest profit from the sale thereof.

1.16 In its decision, the French Court of Cassation held that Coquerel was liable, ordered the removal of the scaffolds and spikes, and granted the damages requested by Clément-Bayard. The Court held that Coquerel's actions were abusive. It acknowledged that his primary intention was to force Clément-Bayard to buy the land by obtaining an economic advantage. In doing so, Coquerel's conduct was abusive, as he necessarily expected the possible damages that might occur to the aircraft, and accepted such damages, with the purpose of reaching his ends on capitalizing his profits, to the detriment of Clément-Bayard. Thus, it was held that, despite the existence of more than one motive, the *dominant* motive was to inflict harm on another.[12]

1.17 This decision clearly supports the principle of abuse of rights from a practical perspective. Any other conclusion would lead to rendering its viability vacuous in content as any right holder may evade liability by having any secondary, albeit legitimate, purpose for exercising his right. To that end, Josserand stipulated that 'if we were to admit that a few good grains would purify the weeds, we would be opening the doors to human malice. In the great majority of cases, the holder of the right could invoke an acceptable

[10] Redmann (n 3) 948; Gutteridge (n 6) 33.

[11] The case of *affaire Clément-Bayard*, Req, 3 August 1915, DP III.1917.1.79, cited in Cueto-Rua (n 7) 981; and Gutteridge (n 6) 33.

[12] Gutteridge (n 6) 34.

motive, a legitimate interest [. . .]'.[13] It would thus encourage right holders to circumvent their legal obligations and escape liability by hiding behind a secondary motive. Granting courts the power to examine the motives of the right holder, as demonstrated by his conduct, and discerning the primary motive that shall be considered decisive in establishing any liability, greatly prevents the manipulation of the principle.

Based on the above, it seems evident that French courts apply abuse of rights where the right holder exercises the right with an intent to inflict harm on another. This intention is presumed if there is no legitimate or serious interest to exercise the right. Additionally, intention to cause harm is not negated where it is associated with another secondary legitimate intention. **1.18**

The cases referred to above are the leading authorities on abuse of rights. Recent cases confirm that French courts predominantly rely on the right holder's primary intention to cause harm, as deduced from the lack of a legitimate and serious interest, in relation to substantive as well as procedural rights.[14] **1.19**

The second alternative criterion that French courts apply is good/bad faith. Where the conduct of the right holder does not strictly demonstrate malice, French courts rely on the principle of bad faith to establish abuse.[15] In a case pertaining to one's right to appeal, the French Court provided that abuse is established where the conduct of the right holder constitutes: 'an act of malice or of bad faith or, at least, a gross error equivalent to wantonness.'[16] It should be mentioned here that good faith/bad faith as a criterion of abuse, as well as its relation to abuse of rights is discussed in another section of the book. **1.20**

Reasonableness is another criterion that French courts may use to establish an abuse of right. This is precisely the situation in the case of a service contract, such as a business agency, that has no stipulation as to the contract duration. From a strictly contractual perspective, either party has the right to terminate the contract without being liable. However, the principle operates to possibly indemnify the dismissed party if he/she proves that it was unreasonable.[17] **1.21**

[13] Louis Josserand, *De I 'esprit des droits et de leur Relativité: Théorie dite dès l'Abus des Droits* (2nd edn 1925), cited in Crabb (n 8) 13 and Cueto-Rua (n 7) 990.

[14] French *Cour de Cassation*, Civ 1re, 24 June 2015, no 14-17795; French *Cour de Cassation*, Civ 2e, 13 November 2015, no 13-28180; French *Cour de Cassation*, Civ 3re, 8 October 2015, no 14-16216; French *Cour de Cassation*, Civ 2re, 25 June 2015, no 14-19745; French *Cour de Cassation*, Civ 3e, 7 July 2015, no 14-17644; French *Cour de Cassation*, Civ 3e, 7 July 2015, no 14-15211; Montpellier *Cour d'Appel*, 1re Chambre, Section C2, 21 October 2015, no 14.06363 (regarding right of an action).

[15] French *Cour de Cassation*, Commercial Chamber, 3 November 2015, no 14-19191 (inconsistent behaviour may constitute an abuse of right and contrary to good faith); French *Cour de Cassation*, Civ 3e, 7 July 2015, no 14-17644; Montpellier *Cour d'Appel*, 1re Chambre, Section C2, 21 October 2015, no 14.06363 (right of an action may be abusive on grounds of malice or bad faith).

[16] The Case of *Berjont v Andre de Giraud d'Agay and Rousset, Req. 8 June 1931, Sirey 1931.1*.332, cited by Crabb (n 8) 12–13; French *Cour de Cassation*, Commercial Chamber, 3 November 2015, no 14-19191 (inconsistent behaviour may constitute an abuse of right and contrary to good faith); Montpellier *Cour d'Appel*, 1re Chambre, Section C2, 21 October 2015, no 14.06363 (regarding right of an action).

[17] MS Amos, 'Abusive Exercise of Rights According to French Law' (1900) 2 Journal of the Society of Comparative Legislation 453, 457–58.

1.22 *Ex analogia*, a promise of marriage is treated by French courts and jurisprudence as *un contrat à durée indéterminée*. While a promise of marriage does not constitute an enforceable contract, French courts engage in a balancing exercise and evaluate the competing interest of the parties to determine if the revocation of the promise was unreasonable.[18] Amos and Walton provide that:

> [T]he defendant has the *right* to revoke his promise, but he must not, on pain of damages, exercise this right *unreasonably*; if he does so, he commits an *abus de droit* and makes himself liable in delict.[19] (Emphasis added)

1.23 A case brought before the French courts against the Benetton Group[20] involved an advertising campaign which included pictures of human torsos apparently belonging to HIV-positive individuals. An AIDS charity and three HIV-positive individuals brought a suit against the Benetton Group, and requested damages on the grounds that the Benetton Group used sensational issues to promote its brand. Despite the fact, acknowledged by the Court, that there was no intention to inflict harm upon the plaintiffs or any other individual, the Court used the criterion of reasonableness and prudence to establish an abuse of right to freedom of expression. In this regard, it appears that the Court established fault from the fact that the Benetton Group expected that possible damages might have occurred, and accepted such damages, with the purpose of reaching its end.

1.24 On a related note, French courts have extended the application of abuse of rights and granted damages in cases that not only lacked any malice or bad faith, but that also involved *no fault* from the right holder.[21] An example of this is where abuse of rights applies, given the gravity of damages caused to an individual from the exercise of a right 'notwithstanding the absence of fault'.[22] In doing so, courts justify their decision on the criterion of reasonableness in the exercise of rights.

1.25 In a case that involved a company engaged in operating a refinery and refining oil, fumes were emitted which caused air pollution and nuisance to its neighbours. While the company did not commit any wrongdoing in the conduct of its business, the Court concluded that damages caused exceeded the limits that the neighbours were expected to endure.[23] This case demonstrates that abuse of rights may even extend to cases where no fault is strictly established and, a fortiori, no malice or bad faith is alleged.[24]

[18] Maurice Amos and Walton FP, *Introduction to French Law* (3rd edn, Oxford University Press 1967) 58; Amos (n 17) 458.

[19] Amos and Walton (n 18) 58.

[20] Case of *X . . . et autres v Sté Benetton Group SpA autres, Recueil Dalloz-Sirey* 1995 J 569; the case was subsequently upheld by the Court of Appeal, *Recueil Dalloz-Sirey* 1996 J 617. This case is referred to in Elspeth Reid, 'Abuse of Rights in Scots Law' (1998) 2 Edinburgh Law Review 129, 139.

[21] Albert Mayrand, 'Abuse of Rights in France and Quebec' (1974) 34 Louisiana Law Review 993, 1000–02; Crabb (n 8) 19–20.

[22] *Epoux Vullion v Société immobilière Vernet- Christophe Subsequent Developments*, JCP 1971. 2. 16781 (Tony Weir tr), available at: <https://law.utexas.edu/transnational/foreign-law-translations/french/case.php?id=1204> accessed 1 February 2018.

[23] Mayrand (n 21) 1000–01.

[24] Another French case is *Epoux Vullion v Société immobilière Vernet- Christophe Subsequent Developments*, JCP 1971. 2. 16781 (Tony Weir tr). Cases have been decided similarly in Quebec, Canada. The Supreme Court decided

Finally, another test that is invoked in the realm of abuse of rights under French law pertains to the deviation from the social-economic purpose of the right. This criterion of abuse presupposes that rights are conferred upon the right holder for a specific social-economic purpose, and the exercise of the right is merely a means to satisfy such purpose. Any deviation from the purpose amounts to an abuse of right.[25] The main protagonist of this criterion is Louis Josserand, who produced his seminal work on the theory of *relativity of rights*, which links the extent of the exercise of a right to its social purpose.[26] However, due to the difficulty in applying this criterion, as shall be discussed in a later section, French courts rarely rely on it to establish abuse.[27] **1.26**

While it may seem, prima facie, that abuse of rights is primarily applied in relation to property rights, the principle extended to other areas and is now said to have a general application.[28] It has been constantly applied by French courts in cases pertaining to, inter alia, contract law; law of procedures, including the legal process; the process of appeal and the execution of judicial decisions; and family law.[29] Moreover, one submits that the essence of abuse of rights also applies in administrative law, as manifested in the concept of *détournement de pouvoir*, which sanctions the use of discretion/power for a purpose other than that for which it was conferred.[30] **1.27**

In relation to abuse of procedural rights, French courts rely on the same criteria of abuse discussed above. Thus, courts have used the tests of malice and lack of legitimate interest as well as good faith and reasonableness in relation to different procedural rights, including: the right to bring an action, the right of defence, and the right to appeal.[31] **1.28**

As to the legal basis of the principle under French law, one who abuses his right commits a delict, which triggers the delictual liability for the wrongdoer.[32] Courts constantly base abuse of rights decisions on Article 1382 of the Civil Code,[33] which states **1.29**

that, while the defendant had exercised *utmost prudence* in the exercise of his rights, he was nevertheless responsible for the damages caused thereby. Mayrand (n 21) 1001.

25 FP Walton, 'Motive as an Element in Torts in the Common and in the Civil Law' (1909) 22 Harvard Law Review 501, 501; Louis Josserand, *De I 'esprit des droits et de leur Relativité: Théorie dite dès l'Abus des Droits* (2nd edn 1925), cited in Cueto-Rua (n 7) 1001.

26 Bolgar (n 4) 1018; Gutteridge (n 6) 27–28.

27 Viktor Knapp, *International Encyclopedia of Comparative Law* (Springer 1983) Part I, Chapter 2, 114; Pirovano, 'La fonction sociale des droits: Réflexions sur le destin des théories de Josserand', in Recueil Dalloz Sirey, sec. Chronique 67, 70 (1972), cited and translated in Cueto-Rua (n 7) 1001–02.

28 Walton (n 25) 505; Byers (n 4) 392, it is widely applied in 'property law, labour law, contractual obligations, and legal proceedings'; Cueto-Rua (n 7) 967; Walton (n 25) 87; Amos (n 17) 453–54.

29 Crabb (n 8) 3–4; Walton (n 25) 508; Pierre Catala and John A Weir, 'Delict and Torts: A Study in Parallel, Part II' (1964) 38 Tulane Law Review 221, 225–6; DJ Devine, 'Some Comparative Aspects of the Doctrine of Abuse of Rights' (1964) Acta Juridica 148, 154; Amos and Walton (n 18) 219; Articles 32.1, 559, and 581 of the French Code of Civil Procedures.

30 Babatunde O Iluyomade, 'The Scope and Content of a Complaint of Abuse of Right in International Law' (1975) 16 Harvard International Law Journal 47, 55; GDS Taylor, 'The Content of the Rule Against Abuse of Rights in International Law' (1973) 46 Ybk of International Law 323, 324–35.

31 Montpellier *Cour d'Appel*, 1re Chambre, Section C2, 21 October 2015, no 14-06363; French *Cour de Cassation*, Civ 1re, 24 June 2015, no 14-17795; French *Cour de Cassation*, Civ 2re, 25 June 2015, no 14-19745; French *Cour de Cassation*, Civ 3e, 7 July 2015, no 14-17644; French *Cour de Cassation*, Civ. 2e, 13 November 2015, no 13-28180 (seizure procedures).

32 Crabb (n 8) 7; Mayrand (n 21) 1011; Cueto-Rua (n 7) 966.

33 French *Cour de Cassation*, Civ 2e, 13 November 2015, no 13-28180.

that: 'anyone who, through his act, causes damage to another by his fault shall be obliged to compensate the damage.' Moreover, while the principle equally applies to contracts, that is abuse of contractual rights, any abuse of a contractual right is 'generally considered as a delictual or a quasi-delictual fault'.[34]

1.30 On a related note, one submits that abuse of contractual rights may constitute a contractual breach and trigger one's contractual liability.[35] To that end, based on Article 1134.3 of the French Civil Code, which mandates performance of agreements in good faith, one holds that any abusive exercise of a contractual right is a contractual breach. Thus, if a 'party acts maliciously in the performance of a contract, he violates a rule of law and he therefore commits a fault'.[36] The scope of abuse of rights extends to sanction the abusive exercise of rights associated with contracts, but not stemming from a contract, such as the right to refuse to conclude an agreement.[37] In this case, the right holder's liability is based on delictual fault (Articles 1382 and 1383 of the French Civil Code).[38] Thus, it appears that the principle of good faith can be utilized with the principle of abuse of rights to address different forms of abuse.

B. German Law

1.31 The adoption of abuse of rights (*Rechtmissbrauch*) in German law differs from the French approach. German law explicitly acknowledges and regulates the principle of abuse of rights. Its legal basis is multifaceted: while it is found under section 226, other scattered sections of the Civil Code also relate to the principle, which broadens its scope of application, and extends its reach to different legal areas.

1.32 Section 226 of the German Civil Code (*Schikaneverbot*) stipulates that 'the exercise of a right is forbidden if it can have no other purpose than to harm some other person'.[39] This testifies to the effect that German law opted for a restrictive approach to abuse of rights.[40]

1.33 Only where it is established that a right holder has exercised his right for the sole purpose of inflicting harm will the principle's application be triggered. Thus, it seems sensible and logical to assume that cases where acts are driven by a complexity of motives,

[34] Mayrand (n 21) 1011. The position in Quebec in Canada is divided. However, the prevailing view is that an abuse of a contractual right constitutes a contractual breach. *Marcotte v Assomption Cie mutuelle d'assurancevie*, [1981] CS 1102; *Macaulay v Imperial Life Assurance Co of Canada*, Sup Ct Montréal, No 50005015231804, 19 April 1984; *Drouin v Électrolux Canada Ltée Division de les Produits CFC Ltée*, [1988] RJQ 950, 95–53, all summarized and translated in *Banque Nationale du Canada v Houle*, [1990] 3 SCR 122, 50–57.

[35] Reinhard Zimmermann and Simon Whittaker, *Good Faith in European Contract Law* (Cambridge University Press 2000) 35; Mayrand (n 21) 1010–11.

[36] Mayrand (n 21) 1010.

[37] Reid (n 20) 139–40.

[38] Zimmermann and Whittaker (n 35) 35.

[39] Article 226 of the German Civil Code, translated in Gutteridge (n 6) 36.

[40] Some held that the narrowness of Section 226 renders it practically inoperative. H Foster, 'Abuse of Rights—Civil Law—Legal Reasoning: Bradford v Pickles Revisited' (1973) 8 University of British Columbia Law Review 343, 346.

some serious and other(s) illegitimate, such as in the French case of *affaire Clément-Bayard*, no abuse can be established. Even in cases where the right holder's dominant motive was to inflict harm on another, he may easily escape liability by asserting the existence of another legitimate motive, notwithstanding how ancillary it is.[41] This is vindicated by the choice of words 'have *no other purpose* than to harm some other person'. (Emphasis added)

Opting for such a narrow scope was primarily driven by the fear of adopting a general application of the principle, given its serious limitation on the exercise of individual rights.[42] While it is held that the aforementioned section was adopted to cover cases of abuse related to proprietary rights, it was later expanded on, and extended, to have a general application, and to effectively address all forms of abuse.[43] However, unlike French law, some hold that abuse of rights as embodied in section 226 of the Civil Code, does not apply to procedural rights.[44] **1.34**

Notwithstanding the above-mentioned, it is important to consider the provisions of section 226 in conjunction with section 242 of the German Civil Code, *Treu und Glauben* (Faith and Credit) provision, which encompasses the general obligation of good faith.[45] Given the narrow scope of section 226, the prohibition against abuse of rights is held to fall within the scope of the good faith obligation.[46] In this regard, Wolfgang Siebert supports the view that the abusive exercise of rights that do not fall within the narrow terms of section 226, can still be seen to be contrary to the duty to act in good faith. He submitted that those who fail to expediently exercise their rights in a timely manner may lose such rights on the basis of abuse of right: 'a person can lose rights by sleeping on them or by leading others to believe he will not exercise them.'[47] Thus, abuse may be established if one fails to exercise/use the right in a timely manner. **1.35**

It is worth mentioning that abuse of rights as a constituent element of section 242 governs the exercise of any right and thus extends to all areas of the law, including the law of procedures.[48] **1.36**

[41] Knapp (n 27) 109; VE Greaves, 'The Social-Economic Purpose of Private Rights: Section 1 of the Soviet Civil Code. A Comparative Study of Soviet and Non-communist Law' (1935) 12 New York University Law Quarterly Review 439, 446.

[42] Bolgar (n 4) 1024.

[43] Gutteridge (n 6) 36.

[44] German Supreme Court, Judgment of 10 February 1940, 162 RGZ 65, (1940), cited in Bolgar (n 4) 1028.

[45] The *Treu und Glauben* concept is said to be tested by objective standards. Greaves (n 41) 445.

[46] Willi E Joachim, 'The "Reasonable Man" in United States and German Commercial Law' (1992) 15 Comparative Law Ybk of International Business 341, 353; Zimmermann and Whittaker (n 35) 694; BGH, 29 April 1959, BGHZ 30, 140; Bernardo M Cremades, 'Good Faith in International Arbitration' (2012) 27 American University International Law Review 761, 773; Shael Herman, 'Classical Social Theories and the Doctrine of "Abuse of Right"' (1977) 37 Louisiana Law Review 747, 747–48; Krauze (n 4) 3; Bolgar (n 4) 1024; Knapp (n 27) 109; Gutteridge (n 6) 38. According to *Gutteridge*, Article 157 and Article 242 of the German Civil Code oblige parties to a business contract to perform their contractual undertaking in accordance with good faith as understood by men of affairs.

[47] Gordley (n 7) 41.

[48] Zimmermann and Whittaker (n 35) 694–95; Krauze (n 4) 3, referring to Z Prebble and J Prebble, 'Comparing the General Anti-Avoidance Rule of Income Tax Law with the Civil Law Doctrine of Abuse of Law' (2008) 62 Bulletin for International Taxation 151, 158.

1.37 Accordingly, the various other applications of abuse of rights that do not fall within the ambit of the narrow provisions of section 226 remain legally proscribed by the overarching principle of good faith.[49] This stems from the fact that abuse of rights is intertwined with the concept of good faith, where acts of the former are necessarily contrary to the latter.[50] *Exempli gratia*, an exercise of a right with a mixture of motives is not deemed abusive as per section 226 given that it is not exercised for the sole purpose of harming another individual. However, it has been held that such an exercise remains abusive as it is contrary to the good faith obligation enshrined in section 242.[51] This demonstrates the different policy adopted in Germany: the divergent abusive conduct will be tackled, not merely by the explicit abuse of rights provision, but may also be barred by relying on similar provisions such as that of good faith.

1.38 On a related note, some scholars hold the view that abuse of rights may also fall under the ambit of sections 138 and 826 of the German Civil Code, which pertain to acts that are *contra bonos mores*.[52] In particular, the said Articles address respectively: legal transactions that contravene with public policy; and the liability of individuals who inflict harm on another in a manner *contra bonos mores*.[53]

1.39 The test utilized to determine if there is an abuse of right based on section 242 or if the act is *contra bonos mores*, is that of the 'reasonable man'; that the act will be abusive if found *contra bonos mores* to the general popular conscience.[54]

1.40 According to Gutteridge: 'it is difficult to conceive of any case in which the malevolent exercise of a right could not be checked by the application of the principle of boni mores.'[55]

1.41 Filtering the exercise of rights by applying the said provisions overcomes a number of limitations, namely: (a) the narrow scope of section 226; (b) dispenses with the enigmas associated with a subjective criterion; and (c) adopts an objective test to establish abuse: acts that the average German citizen regarded as *contra bonos mores* are abusive.[56]

1.42 Thus, Julio Cueto-Rua noted that: 'typical cases of abuse of rights have been decided, instead, by application of article (826) of the same Code, where proof of the intent to harm is not required.'[57]

[49] Reid (n 20) 135.

[50] Saul Litvinoff, 'Good Faith' (1997) 71 Tulane Law Review 1645, 1660–61; Yasuhei Taniguchi, 'Good Faith and Abuse of Procedural Rights in Japanese Civil Procedure' (2000) 8 Tulane Journal of International and Comparative Law 167, 173–75.

[51] Cases that included acts of an economic nature done to harm a competitor and buy his shares were found contrary to good faith and thus abusive. Cases cited in Cueto-Rua (n 7) 991–92, footnote 88.

[52] Joachim (n 46) 353.

[53] Herman (n 46) 748.

[54] Joachim (n 46) 353; Ludwig Enneccerus, Martin Wolff, and Theodor Kipp, '*Tratado De Derecho Civil: Derecho De Obligaciones*, (1950), 2666, cited in Cueto-Rua (n 7) 998.

[55] Gutteridge (n 6) 38.

[56] ibid 37–38.

[57] Cueto-Rua (n 7) 995, footnote 92.

While the sufficiently broad terms of the general good faith provision grant decision makers the power to prohibit any abusive act, certain acts have been consistently rendered abusive. German courts established abuse where: (a) a right is exercised to inflict harm; (b) rights are exercised in a manner contrary to equity; (c) rights are exercised without any regard to the interests of third parties; (d) an exercise of right is contrary to former conduct; (e) a right is established or acquired as a result of a wrongdoing or in bad faith.[58] **1.43**

Thus, German courts generally rely on good faith in finding an abuse of right, unless malice is palpable. The leading case on abuse of rights based on the criterion of malice involved a father who prohibited his son from visiting the grave of his mother which was situated on the father's property. The German Supreme Court found that this was a manifest abuse of ownership rights.[59] **1.44**

Where malice is not evident, courts generally rely on the general principle of good faith. In one case involving the liability of a member of a limited liability company, the German Court held that it would be contrary to the principle of good faith, and thus an abuse of right, if it upheld the separation of the assets of the company from its members, given the circumstances of the case.[60] In another case, the Court noted that while a services contract provided for rescission at will, the circumstances of the case may render such rescission contrary to the principle of good faith and thus abusive.[61] Similarly, the Court found that the delaying of proceedings by presenting meritless defences was deemed abusive and contrary to good faith.[62] **1.45**

Based on the above, abuse of rights forms a fundamental legal principle under German law.[63] While its scope may appear limited given the narrowness of section 226, other provisions similarly encompass the principle, broaden its scope, and extend its application to, inter alia, contractual obligations, corporate law, public law, and law of procedures.[64] Thus, in any abuse of rights allegation, German courts may either grant relief based on section 226 of the Civil Code, if malice is palpable, or establish an abuse of right and grant relief based on the more general provisions of sections 242 and 826.[65] **1.46**

58 For a list of cases providing the said legal rules based on abuse of rights, see Bolgar (n 3) 1027–28.
59 Bolgar (n 4) 1028.
60 Judgment of 29 November 1956, 22 BGHZ 226, 230 (1957) translated and cited in Bolgar (n 4) 1029–30; Zimmermann and Whittaker (n 35) 515–16.
61 Bolgar (n 4) 1027.
62 Cueto-Rua (n 7) 991–92, footnote 88.
63 Bolgar (n 4) 1026–27.
64 Krauze (n 4) 3; Judgment of 30 January 1956, 20 BGHZ 4 (1956); Judgment of 9 October 1956, 21 BGHZ 378, (1956); Judgment of 29 November 1956, 22 BGHZ 226, (1957); Judgment of 20 May 1968, 50 BGHZ 191 (1969), cited in Bolgar (n 4) 1029–30.
65 Bolgar (n 4) 1026–27.

C. Swiss Law

1.47 Abuse of rights is an integral part of Swiss law. It is mentioned in the introductory section of the Civil Code. This testifies to the effect that there is a general prohibition against the abuse of rights under Swiss law and it is not limited to a specific area of the law.[66] Thus, Swiss law acknowledges that any right, whether substantive or procedural, is susceptible to abuse.[67]

1.48 Unlike most national laws, the Swiss perception is to minimize, to a large extent, the extensive regulation of the abuse of rights principle.[68] By merely incorporating under Article 2.2 that 'the manifest abuse of a right is not protected by law',[69] it is evident that the Swiss legislator intends to ensure the proper exercise of all rights, without attempting to specify certain elements that constitute abuse. Thus, Swiss law seems to grant courts and tribunals a wide discretionary power to decide on the scope, criteria, and application of abuse of rights.[70]

1.49 The Swiss legislator went further than its German counterpart and directly linked abuse of rights to the principle of good faith.[71] Article 2.1 reads: 'every person must act in good faith *in the exercise of his or her rights* and in the performance of his or her obligations' (emphasis added). From a mere vernacular perspective, it is argued that Article 2.1 also pertains to the principle of abuse of rights, given the terms: 'in the exercise of his or her rights'.

1.50 The relationship between the good faith principle and the prohibition against abuse of rights, as encompassed in Article 2, has been subject to heated debates. Specifically, there are different views as to whether they are different principles or if abuse of rights is merely an emanation of the good faith principle.[72] The predominant view holds that a contextual analysis of Article 2 in its entirety reveals that abuse of rights is merely an illustration and an application of the principle of good faith.[73]

1.51 It is submitted that this representation of abuse of rights is similar to the juridical basis of the principle under German law. As previously mentioned, section 242 of the German Civil Code governs the exercise of any right and extends to all areas of the law. It has been stipulated that a German observer 'cannot fail to be struck by the fact that Art. 2 ZGB appears to perform a very similar function, and to be applied in a very similar way, to § 242 BGB'.[74]

66 Zimmermann and Whittaker (n 35) 51.
67 Gutteridge (n 6) 40; Bolgar (n 4) 1032–33.
68 John P Gaffney, '"Abuse of Process" in Investment Treaty Arbitration' (2010) 11 Journal of World Investment and Trade 517.
69 Article 2.2 of the Swiss Civil Code.
70 WT Tête, 'Tort Roots and Ramifications of the Obligations Revision' (1987) 32 Loyola Law Review 47, 67; Bolgar (n 4) 1032; Gaffney (n 68) 517.
71 Also see Article 2 of the Turkish Civil Code.
72 Zimmermann and Whittaker (n 35) 51.
73 ibid 51; Gutteridge (n 6) 40.
74 Zimmermann and Whittaker (n 35) 51–52.

A prudent review of the Swiss legal practice reveals that courts often rely on the criterion of 'good faith' to establish abuse of substantive[75] or procedural rights.[76] **1.52**

The Swiss Federal Supreme Court stipulated that an abuse of right is committed if: **1.53**

> [I]ndividual rights are exercised *contrary to good faith*. Section 2 of article 2, which denies legal protection to the manifest abuse of a right, forms the necessary amendment to the duty which is set down in section 1 of article 2, namely, to act always in good faith. The purpose of this provision is to either limit or to annul the formal validity of positive laws whenever the judge deems this to be in the interests of substantive justice.[77] (Emphasis added)

This further confirms that Swiss courts adopt the criterion of good faith to determine whether abuse has taken place. To the same effect, in discussing abuse of rights under Swiss law, A Von Tuhr writes: **1.54**

> The exercise of rights, as the law indicates, is subject to the *postulates of good faith*, that is to say, those exigencies should be respected which are proper of the circumstances, and that the holder of the right, correctly behaving, owes to the interests of the other party. Otherwise, he will be responsible for an abuse of right.[78] (Emphasis added)

Despite the sufficiently broad terms of good faith, which grants decision makers the power to prohibit any abusive act, certain acts have been consistently rendered abusive as contrary to good faith. These include: (a) the exercise of a right without a serious or legitimate interest; (b) the unreasonable exercise of rights; (c) the exercise of rights without any regard to the interests of third parties; (d) any exercise of right that is contrary to former conduct in application of the well-established principle of *allegans contraria non est audiendus*; and (e) if the right is exercised for a purpose other than that for which the right was granted.[79] **1.55**

In a case involving the dismissal of a member of an association, the Swiss Court applied the criterion of good faith and held that it would be an abuse of right if the exclusion of such a member was not motivated by the interests of the association.[80] In a similar case, the Court held that a decision of the general assembly of a company was abusive and contrary to good faith where it did not serve a principal interest to the majority and damaged the interests of the minority.[81] **1.56.**

[75] BGE 95.2.157 (1970), Journal des Tribunaux 344 (1970), (finding the decision of the general assembly of a corporation abusive) cited in Bolgar (n 4) 1036.

[76] BGE 94.1.659, Journal des Tribunaux 216 (1970); BGE 86.2.417 (1961), Journal des Tribunaux 325 (1961), (regarding the abuse of legal institutions if used for a purpose contrary to that prescribed by the law) cited in Bolgar (n 4) 1036.

[77] Judgment of the Swiss Federal Supreme Court, BGE 72.2.39 (1946), translated in Bolgar (n 4) 1034.

[78] A Von Tuhr, 'Tratado De Las Obligaciones' (1934) 270, translated in Cueto-Rua (n 7) 998.

[79] Bolgar (n 4) 1033 and 1036.

[80] BGE 85.2.525 (1965), Journal des Tribunaux 538 (1960); BGE 90.2.346, Journal des Tribunaux 258 (1965), cited in Bolgar (n 4) 1036.

[81] BGE 95.2.157 (1970), Journal des Tribunaux 344 (1970), in Bolgar (n 4) 1036.

1.57 It is of particular interest to note the manifestation of abuse of rights in the realm of Swiss arbitration law and practice. Swiss courts utilize the principle of abuse of rights to correct the rigidity of consent rules in arbitration, particularly in relation to the extension of arbitration agreements to non-signatories.[82] It is predominantly held that Swiss law accepts piercing the corporate veil of companies (*Durchgriff*) only if there is an abuse of right.[83] The Swiss Federal Supreme Court, as well as arbitral tribunals applying Swiss law, often decide to extend an arbitration clause to a non-signatory by applying abuse of rights and the principle of good faith as enshrined in Article 2 of the Swiss Civil Code.[84]

1.58 The existence, scope, and application of the abuse of rights in Switzerland is founded on, and greatly influenced by, the concept of justice and equity.[85] Article 4 provides that where the law confers discretion on the courts, the 'courts must reach its decision in accordance with the principles of justice and equity'. Given that the Swiss Code refrained from carefully defining the scope of abuse of rights or expressing a specific test to be used, leaving it to courts and tribunals, one submits that Article 2 must be read and construed in *pari materia* with Article 4.[86] Therefore, in exercising such discretionary power, the decision maker is to decide based on considerations of equity and justice.

1.59. The broad terms of Article 2 may be criticized given that there seems to be no guidance on what constitutes a manifest abuse and the fact that the provision grants wide discretionary power to decision makers.[87]

1.60 While Swiss law adopts a broad approach to abuse of rights and there is no statutory limitation on acts that may be abusive, from a practical stance, this corrective tool has not been abused by the courts. A contrario, courts have exercised prudence and caution when dealing with abuse of rights and only resorted to it in cases of manifest abuse.[88]

[82] Marc Bauen and Robert Bernet, *Swiss Company Limited by Shares*, (Bruylant and Schulthess 2007) 226; Andrea Meier, 'Multi-party Arbitrations' in Manuel Arroyo (ed), *Arbitration in Switzerland* (Kluwer Law International 2013) 1330; Bernhard Berger and Franz Kellerhals, *International and Domestic Arbitration in Switzerland* (3rd edn, Stämpfli Publishers 2015) 199.

[83] Ad-hoc Interim Award, in the case of *FR German Engineering Company v Polish buyer*, 9 September 1983, (1987) 12 Ybk Commercial Arbitration 63, 72; Swiss Federal Tribunal, 24 November 2006, 4C.327/2005; Ad-hoc Award of 1991, in the case of *SA v Alpha Beta & Co*, 10 ASA Bulletin 202, (1992); Swiss Federal Tribunal, 16 October 2003, 22 ASA Bulletin 364, (2004); Bernard Hanotiau, Complex Arbitrations, Multiparty, Multicontract, Multi-issue and Class Actions (Kluwer Law International 2005) 79–80; Werner Wenger, 'Art. 178 SPILA' in Stephen V Berti (ed), *International Arbitration in Switzerland: An Introduction to and a Commentary on Articles 176-194 of the Swiss Private International Law Statute* (Helbing & Lichtenhahn and Kluwer International 2000) 350–51, para 56.

[84] Swiss Federal Tribunal 4A_450/2013 of 7 April 2014, ground 3.5.5.1.1, available at: <http://www.swissarbitrationdecisions.com> accessed 15 February 2019; Swiss Federal Tribunal, First Civil Division, 29 January 1996, 14 ASA Bulletin 496, (Kluwer Law International 1996); Stephan Wilske, Laurence Shore and Jan-Michael Ahrens, 'The "Group of Companies Doctrine" —Where is it Heading?' (2006) 17 American Review of International Arbitration 1, 3; Ad-hoc Interim Award, in the case of *FR German Engineering Company v Polish buyer*, 9 September 1983, in Albert Jan van den Berg (ed), (1987) 12 Ybk Commercial Arbitration 63, 72; *Westland Helicopters Ltd v Arab Organization, et al*, Interim Award, ICC Case No 3879 of 1984, (1986) XI Ybk Commercial Arbitration 127, 132.

[85] Judgment of the Swiss Federal Supreme Court, BGE 72.2.39 (1946), cited and translated in Bolgar (n 4) 1034.

[86] Tête (n 70) 80–81.

[87] Bolgar (n 4) 1032.

[88] Gutteridge (n 6) 40.

Accordingly, where the law necessitates strict adherence to specific legal form for certain transactions, Swiss courts emphasize the importance of legal certainty and security. In such cases, courts tend to reject allegations of abuse, even when it is alleged that the exercise of the right is contrary to the purpose prescribed by the law.[89] **1.61**

Thus, where an employee of the plaintiff witnessed the conclusion of the contract, it was held that no abuse of rights is established if the plaintiff himself is responsible for the formal defect.[90] Moreover, in a case regarding a request for the rescission of a long-term contract because of an increase in the price, the Court found no abuse of rights if the party refused to amend the provisions of the contract given the change of circumstances.[91] **1.62**

Accordingly, it is submitted that Swiss law recognizes a general principle of abuse of rights. Its application is neither limited to certain rights nor confined to a specific legal area. Moreover, a prima facie examination of the judicial and legal opinion seems to hold that good faith comprises the criterion of abuse under Swiss law. However, as shall be discussed in Chapter 2, one shall challenge this approach given that good faith is broader than abuse of rights and cannot be an effective criterion of abuse. It will be submitted that the criterion of good faith, as applied by courts and tribunals, is not a stand-alone criterion, but emulates one of the other criteria of abuse (malice, reasonableness, or deviation of the purpose of the right in question). **1.63**

D. Law of Louisiana

The law of Louisiana is based on a variety of legal sources. It has been greatly influenced by the Justinian legislations, the French and Spanish laws.[92] While the Louisiana Civil Code does not explicitly refer to the principle of abuse of rights, it is unequivocally acknowledged, scrupulously regulated, and applied by the Louisiana courts. **1.64**

At the outset, the Louisiana Civil Code clearly establishes liability, on the basis of abuse of rights, in relation to ownership rights.[93] **1.65**

Aside from the statutory confirmation, Louisiana courts have often adopted an abuse of rights analysis on cases before it. This was evident from its seminal decision rendered in 1919 in a case pertaining to property rights. As this was one of the first decisions related to abuse of rights, the Court primarily relied on French authorities, albeit not overlooking the scattered provisions of the Louisiana Civil Code which also endorse the principle. In its decision, the Court provided: **1.66**

89 Bolgar (n 4) 1034–35.

90 BGE 72.2.39 (1946) cited in Bolgar (n 4) 1035.

91 BGE 47.2.440 (1921) cited in Bolgar (n 4) 1035–36.

92 AN Yiannopoulos, 'The Civil Codes of Louisiana', (2008) 1 Civil Law Commentaries 1, 8; AN Yiannopoulos, 'Civil Liability for Abuse of Right: Something Old, Something New . . .', (1994) 54 Louisiana Law Review 1173.

93 This is evident from Articles 667, 668, and 669 of the Louisiana Civil Code; Yiannopoulos (n 92) 1174.

> [C]ases like the present one are not to be decided by the application of any broad or inflexible rule, but by a careful weighing of all the circumstances attending them, by diagnosing them, to use the expression of Baudry- Lacantinerie and Chaveau, with the aid and guidance of two principles, that the owner must not injure seriously any right of his neighbour, and, even in the absence of any right on the part of the neighbour, must not in an unneighbourly spirit do that which, while of no benefit to himself causes damage to the neighbour.[94]

1.67 While the application of abuse of rights was first limited to ownership rights[95] and property disputes, the Louisiana courts later extended its application to all legal matters. To that effect, in 1975[96] the Louisiana Supreme Court explicitly adopted the principle, endorsed the terminology and, while acknowledging that the principle was primarily premised on Article 667, which pertains to ownership rights, the Court extended its scope and reach, *ex analogia*, to all legal matters:[97] 'Louisiana adopts a general theory or principle of law that in *all areas of legal relationships* a legal right can be exercised in such a manner as to constitute a legal abuse' (emphasis added).[98]

1.68 In relation to the scope of the principle and the criteria of abuse, it is well established that abuse of rights is not limited to cases of *mala fide*. It applies whenever the right holder fails to show a serious and/or a legitimate interest in exercising his/her right. To that effect, the Louisiana Supreme Court stated that 'the exercise of a right [. . .] without legitimate and serious interest, even where there is neither alleged nor proved an intent to harm, constitutes an abuse of right which courts should not countenance'.[99]

1.69 However, in the case of *Illinois Cent Gulf v International Harvester* of 1979, the Louisiana Supreme Court went further and engaged in a scrupulous analysis of the principle, examined its scope in other jurisdictions, and set out what constitutes an abuse of right. The Court stipulated that an abuse of right is not limited to acts which done to inflict harm on another, but is also established if the right holder's predominant motive was to cause harm; or if there was no serious and/or legitimate interest worthy of judicial protection, regardless of the motive associated with the conduct.[100] Additionally, the Court went further to include cases where one exercises a right in a way which is considered

[94] *Higgins Oil & Fuel Co v Guaranty Oil Co*, 145 La 233, 82 So 206 (1919), 211; Yiannopoulos (n 92) 1177; Pannal A Sanders, '"At Will" Franchise Terminations and the Abuse of Rights Doctrine' (1981) 42 Louisiana Law Review 210, 223–33.

[95] Redmann (n 3) 950.

[96] It must be noted that earlier decisions pertaining to contractual disputes were rendered on the basis of an abuse of rights analysis and equitable considerations, but without an explicit reference thereto. *Onorato v Maestri*, 173 La 375, 137 So 67 (1931); and *Lawton v Smith*, 146 So 2d 461 (La App Cir 1933); Yiannopoulos (n 92) 1178.

[97] *Morse v J Ray McDermott & Co*, 344 So 2d 1353 (La 1977); *Illinois Central Gulf RR v International Harvester Co*, 368 So 2d 1009 (La 1979); *Travelers Indemnity Co v Hunt*, 371 So 2d 342 (La App 4th Cir), writ denied, 374 So 2d 657 (1979); *Cox v Kirkpatrick*, 404 So 2d 999 (La App 1st Cir 1981); *Sanborn v Oceanic Contractors, Inc*, 448 So 2d 91 (La 1984); *Breland v Louisiana Hospital Services, Inc*, 488 So 2d 1215 (La App 1st Cir 1984), vacated on rehearing, 468 So 2d 1223 (La App 1st Cir 1985); Redmann (n 3) 958–68.

[98] *Hero Lands Co v Texaco, Inc*, 310 So 2d 93, 99 (La 1975).

[99] *Morse v J Ray McDermott & Co*, 344 So 2d 1353 (La 1977), 1369; Byers (n 4) 394; Redmann (n 3) 960.

[100] *Illinois Central Gulf RR v International Harvester Co*, 368 So 2d 1009 (La 1979).

contrary to moral rules, good faith, or elementary fairness, or if the right is exercised for a purpose other than that for which the right was granted.[101]

Following the above decision, Louisiana courts have continually examined the conduct of the parties to establish an abuse based on any of the following criteria: **1.70**

> [I]f the predominant motive for it was to cause harm; (2) if there was no serious or legitimate motive for refusing; (3) if the exercise of the right to refuse is against moral rules, good faith, or elementary fairness; (4) if the right to refuse is exercised for a purpose other than that for which it is granted.[102]

Based on the above, it seems that Louisiana courts have adopted broad criteria of what constitutes an abuse of right. While the Swiss approach is highlighted by the minimal regulation of the principle's scope of application, Louisiana stands as a relative antinomy in terms of its regulation and its expressed criteria of what constitutes an abuse. **1.71**

Driven by the desire to avoid applying a stringent positivistic rule, the courts tend to carefully examine the factual matrix of the case and weigh any conflicting interests to determine whether the act or conduct in question is abusive.[103] **1.72**

In essence, while it may appear that the courts apply an objective standard of what constitutes abuse, that is, standard of reasonableness, it remains evident that emphasis is given to the state of mind of the right holder. This is particularly true in cases where courts have refused to grant remedies on the ground of a negligent, or non-negligent, albeit non intentional abuse of right.[104] This defies the corrective nature of abuse of rights which should entail emphasis on the repercussions of one's action/conduct, rather than fishing in one's state of mind in order to discern motive: 'there are some circumstances where a person who, in the course of exercising a right, has *inadvertently* caused damage to another would be in *bad faith*, in effect at fault, in failing to repair the damage even though not caused by negligence' (emphasis added).[105] It is submitted that in such cases, bad faith in the exercise of rights, or abuse of rights, is merely presumed, however such presumption becomes irrebuttable if the right holder fails to repair, or refrain from causing, the damage. **1.73**

On a related note, one submits that the criteria adopted by the courts may seem of tenuous character and nebulous in scope. The mentioned criteria greatly overlap, where some clearly fall under the ambit of others, which arguably render some of these criteria superfluous. For example, if one examines the criterion that prohibits the exercise **1.74**

[101] ibid.

[102] *Trushinger v Pak*, 513 So 2d 1151, 1154 (La 1987); *Ballaron v Equitable Shipyards, Inc* 521 So 2d 481 (La 1988); *Ouachita National Bank in Monroe v Palowsky*, 554 So 2d 108 (La 1989); *Addison v Williams*, 546 So 2d 220 (La 1989); *Fidelity Bank and Trust Co v Hammons*, 540 So 2d 461 (La 1989); *210 Baronne St Ltd Partnership v First Nat'l Bank of Commerce*, 543 So 2d 502, 507 (La App 4th Cir), *writ denied*, 546 So 2d 1219 (1989).

[103] *Higgins Oil & Fuel Co v Guaranty Oil Co*, 145 La 233, 82 So 206 (1919), 211; *Langlois v Allied Chemical Corporation*, 249 So 2d 133, 258 La 1067 (1971).

[104] *McCoy v Arkansas Natural Gas Co*, 175 La 487, 143 So 383 (1932); Yiannopoulos (n 92) 1196–97.

[105] Tête (n 70) 72.

of a right that violates moral rules, good faith, and/or elementary fairness, it is self-evident that it is broad enough to encompass, a fortiori, the one which forbids an exercise merely to cause harm to another, or that which precludes the exercise of a right with no serious or legitimate motive.

1.75 Thus, the Louisiana courts are vested with a potentially praetorian authority; unprecedented discretionary power to determine what constitutes an abuse of right, which emanates from the multiplicity and scope of the mentioned criteria. However, from a practical stance, this corrective tool has not been abused by the courts. A contrario, courts have exercised prudence and caution when dealing with the abuse of rights principle and only resorted to it in cases of manifest abuse.[106] This is particularly evident in contractual disputes that have been dominated by claims of abuse of rights.[107] In this regard, courts often examine the four criteria of the principle's application, and reach the decision that no abuse is established.[108]

1.76 This is clearly demonstrated in a case heard before the Louisiana Supreme Court, where it carefully weighed the interests at stake, examined the four criteria of abuse, and decided that, given the factual matrix of the case, there was no abuse of rights.[109] The case pertained to an insurance dispute which involved an employee who suffered severe damage and was quadriplegic due to an accident which was unrelated to work. Subsequently, the employer terminated the employment contract and thus the employee was not covered by the insurance group policy. Although consistent with the contractual provisions, the employee argued that it would be an abuse of a contractual right to terminate the insurance coverage. The trial judge and the Court of Appeal confirmed that termination of the insurance policy was consistent with the contractual provision and held that abuse of rights was not applicable.

1.77 The Louisiana Supreme Court recognized the principle of abuse of rights, but expressed that it should only apply in limited circumstances given the possible encroachment to individual rights and interests. Upon a prudent examination of all criteria of abuse, the Court held that it was inapplicable.

1.78 The case is significant as it clearly reflects that the principle is narrowly construed and applied in cases of blatant abuse, despite the adopted criteria which may seem, prima facie, extensively broad. Precisely, it is to be highlighted that the Court did not find the termination of the policy contrary to considerations of moral rules, good faith, or elementary fairness. The latter criterion obviously could have entertained the action given

[106] *Mcinnis v Mcinnis*, 618 So 2d 672 (La App Cir 1993), 676 ('Because the "abuse of rights" approach would render unenforceable a party's otherwise judicially protected rights, the doctrine is sparingly invoked in Louisiana'); *Fidelity Bank and Trust Co v Hammons*, 540 So 2d 461 (La 1989); *Massachusetts Mutual Life Insurance Company v Steven F Nails*, 549 So 2d 826 (La 1989); *Illinois Cent. Gulf RR v International Harvester Co*, 368 So 2d 1009 (La 1979) ('the doctrine of abuse of rights has been invoked sparingly in Louisiana').

[107] Redmann (n 3) 947.

[108] For a detailed examination of how Louisiana courts have acknowledged the application of the principle, yet did not find any abuse, in relation to lease disputes, employment disputes, insurance disputes, lender liability, and other contractual and non-contractual disputes, see Yiannopoulos (n 92).

[109] *Massachusetts Mutual Life Insurance Company v Steven F Nails*, 549 So 2d 826 (1989).

its broad and undetermined scope.[110] The Court, upon weighing the interests at stake, decided that the words of the contract were clear and explicit, and thus the paramount principle of sanctity of contracts prevailed over a potential abuse of right.

Even in cases where abuse might be flagrant, courts tend to rely on other legal principles to grant relief. For example, in a lease dispute, the parties agreed that no sublease can take place unless the lessor agreed in writing, which would not be unreasonably withheld. The trial judge decided that the lessor had abused his right by unreasonably refusing to permit the sublease. Precisely, the trial judge held that the lessor's refusal to permit the sublease was contrary to moral rules, good faith, and/or elementary fairness. On appeal, the Court of Appeal affirmed the decision but refrained from basing it on abuse of rights. The Court relied on the contractual provisions, the parties' common intention, and the reasonableness provision to uphold the appealed decision.[111] **1.79**

It is especially interesting to note that the Court was sceptical about applying abuse of rights. In the words of the Court: 'while we express no opinion as to the trial court's use of the equitable abuse of rights doctrine, we decline to follow his reasoning because we find no need to resort to equity here.' Thus, refraining from applying the principle stemmed from the rather moot view of the Court that abuse of rights is an equitable principle and thus courts need not resort to equity unless the application of existing law fails to remedy the victim and serve the ends of justice.[112] **1.80**

The view that the principle of abuse of rights is an equitable principle under Louisiana law is shared by scholars and hailed by some courts.[113] Given that it is perceived as an equitable principle, some courts provide that remedies based on abuse of rights would only be granted where the aggrieved party has acted reasonably and was blameless. In other words, some courts submit that the adage *he who comes to equity must come with clean hands* constitutes a condition *sine qua non* under the law of Louisiana.[114] Similarly, some authors stipulate that the principle applies in contractual disputes only where there is an unequal bargaining power between the parties.[115] **1.81**

However, one disagrees with such a proposition. While abuse of rights could be considered equitable in the sense that it corrects the law and clearly reflects equitable considerations, it is not based on equity, which is often resorted to in the absence of law.[116] **1.82**

[110] Yiannopoulos (n 92) 1187.
[111] *Maurin-Ogden-1978 Pinhook Plaza v The Wiener Corporation*, 430 So 2d 747, (La App 5th Cir 1983).
[112] Article 21 of the Louisiana Civil Code stipulates: 'in all civil matters, where there is no express law, the judge is bound to proceed and decide according to equity. To decide equitably, an appeal is to be made to natural law and reason, or received usages, where positive law is silent'.
[113] *Maurin-Ogden-1978 Pinhook Plaza v The Wiener Corporation*, 430 So 2d 747, (La App 5th Cir 1983); *Cataldie v Louisiana Health Services & Indemnity Co*, 456 So 2d 1373 (La 1984); Redmann (n 3) 968.
[114] *Fox v City of Monroe*, 15 La App 192, 131 So 483 (La App 2d Cir 1930); *City of New Orleans v Levy*, 233 La 844, 98 So 2d 210 (1957); *Dipuma v Dipuma*, 136 So 2d 505 (La App 1st Cir 1961); *Sanborn v Oceanic Contractors, Inc*, 448 So 2d 91 (La 1984); *Lambert v Maryland Casualty Co*, 418 So 2d 553 (La 1982); *Cox v Kirkpatrick*, 404 So 2d 999 (La App 1st Cir 1981); *Illinois Central Gulf RR v International Harvester Co*, 368 So 2d 1009 (La 1979); Sanders (n 94) 237; Redmann (n 3) 972.
[115] Redmann (n 3) 977.
[116] Yiannopoulos (n 92) 1192–95.

This is confirmed by the fact that its legal basis stems from various provisions that are of an equitable character in the Louisiana Civil Code and its scope has been delineated by the courts.[117]

1.83 However, this does not negate the fact that courts should take into consideration the bargaining power between the parties, the blameworthy conduct of the parties, as well as all other factual particulars of the case to assist courts in finding if there is an abuse of right.[118]

1.84 Courts often resort to, and find it more appropriate to grant remedies based on, the notion of good faith which is stipulated under the Louisiana Civil Code.[119] In doing so, courts reach the same outcomes that would otherwise be reached on the basis of abuse of rights.[120] That said, not only does the good faith provision under the Louisiana Civil Code embrace the prohibition against abuse of right,[121] but it is submitted that any provision pertaining to good faith includes a prohibition against the abuse of rights: good faith in the exercise of rights.[122]

1.85 It remains questionable as to why courts opt to rely on good faith rather than on abuse of rights, particularly given that the former notion is broader and far vaguer than the latter. The only plausible and sensible explanation seems to stem from the courts' belief that, unlike the notion of good faith, abuse of rights is an equitable principle rather than a legal one, and precedence is thus given to applying good faith rather than resorting to the concept of equity, as abovementioned.

1.86 By and large, it appears that abuse of rights triggers one's delictual liability under Louisiana law. However, it is submitted that in relation to contractual disputes, the principle of good faith may also operate as abuse of rights and be used to dismantle forms of abuse of contractual rights.[123]

E. Egyptian Law

1.87 Many of the legal systems in the Middle East and North Africa have adopted the principle of abuse of rights. In this regard, prior to the enactment of the Egyptian Civil Code of 1948, there was no explicit reference to abuse of rights, however there were

[117] ibid.

[118] ibid 1194; Hervé Ascensio, 'Abuse of Process in International Investment Arbitration' (2014) 13 Chinese Journal of International Law 763, 781–82;

[119] Article 1759 of the Louisiana Civil Code; Irina Petrova, '"Stepping on the Shoulders of a Drowning Man" The Doctrine of Abuse of Right as a Tool for Reducing Damages for Lost Profits: Troubling Lessons from the Patuha and Himpurna Arbitrations' (2004) 35 Georgetown Journal of International Law 455, 466.

[120] Yiannopoulos (n 92) 1185 and 1190.

[121] Tête (n 70) 65; Yiannopoulos (n 92) 1185.

[122] Bin Cheng, *General Principles of Law as Applied by International Courts and Tribunals* (Cambridge University Press 2006) 121.

[123] Tête (n 70) 89.

scattered provisions that embraced the principle.[124] Given its potency, the Egyptian legislator opted to include a specified article in the new Civil Code to that effect. It is worth pinpointing that many of the Arab legal systems have been greatly influenced by the Egyptian approach in this regard and adopted similar provisions.[125]

Article 5 of the Egyptian Civil Code reads: **1.88**

> Usage of right shall be illicit in the following cases: (a) if it was only intended to harm a third party; (b) if the interests pursued are of minor importance, so that they are manifestly disproportionate to the harm caused to others; (c) if the interests pursued are illicit.[126]

The principle forms a fundamental part of Egyptian law, and is mentioned in the introductory section of the Civil Code under the general provisions.[127] This vindicates the fact that: (a) it comprises a sacrosanct tenet under Egyptian law; (b) it dominates all legal relationships, tortious and contractual; (c) it is not limited to a specific area of the law, but applies to public law and private law; and (d) it acts as a limitation to the exercise of rights *in rem* as well as rights *in personam*.[128] Thus, Egyptian law recognizes that any right is susceptible to abuse.[129] This includes, inter alia, substantive rights such as those pertaining to a contract between the parties,[130] and procedural rights,[131] such as the right of access to the courts. **1.89**

[124] Soliman Morcos, *Al Wafi Fi Sharh Al Qanun Al Madani (A Treatise on the Explanation of the Civil Code)* (Cairo 1988 edn) vol 3, 363.

[125] Article 106 of the Civil Code of the United Arab Emirates; Article 30 of the Kuwaiti Civil Code; Article 66 of the Jordanian Civil Code; Article 19 of the Civil Code of Yemen; Article 6 of the Syrian Civil Code; Article 5 of the Libyan Civil Code; Articles 6 and 7 of the Iraqi Civil Code; Article 63 of the Qatari Civil Code; Article 124 of the Algerian Civil Code; Article 28 of the Bahraini Civil Code; Anis Al-Qasem, 'The unlawful exercise of rights in the Civil Code of the Arab Countries of the Middle East', (1990) International and Comparative Law Quarterly 396, 401–02; Mohamed S Abdelwahab, 'The Nuts and Bolts of Construction Arbitration in the MENA: Principles and Practice' in Stavros Brekoulakis and David Thomas (eds), *The Guide to Construction Arbitration* (Global Arbitration Review 2017).

[126] Article 5 of the Egyptian Civil Code (translated by the author).

[127] Abd El-Razzak El Sanhouri, *Al Wasit Fi Sharh Al Qanun Al Madani (A Treatise on the Explanation of the Civil Code)* (Dar Al Shorouk 2010 edn) vol 1, 753.

[128] The Explanatory Memorandum of the Egyptian Law No 131 of 1948 Promulgating the Civil Code, 31–35; Egyptian Court of Cassation, Session held on 10 March 2003, Challenge No 2803, Judicial Year 71; Sanhouri (n 127) 753; Morcos (n 124) 368; Egyptian Court of Cassation, Session held on 24 March 1991, Challenge No 1238, Judicial Year 56; Egyptian Court of Cassation, Session held on 25 April 1981, Challenge No 2, Judicial Year 46.

[129] Egyptian Court of Cassation, Session held on 10 March 2003, Challenge No 2803, Judicial Year 71.

[130] Egyptian Court of Cassation, Session held on 27 February 2005, Challenge No 871, Judicial Year 74; Egyptian Court of Cassation, Session held on 8 May 2000, Challenge No 8388, Judicial Year 64; Egyptian Court of Cassation, Session held on 2 January 1997, Challenge No 1481, Judicial Year 62; Egyptian Court of Cassation, Session held on 7 November 1993, Challenge No 1468, Judicial Year 57; Egyptian Court of Cassation, Session held on 28 June 1989, Challenge No 143, Judicial Year 52; Egyptian Court of Cassation, Session held on 28 April 1983, Challenge No 1710, Judicial Year 52; Egyptian Court of Cassation, Session held on 17 May 1980, Challenge No 633, Judicial Year 46.

[131] Egyptian Court of Cassation, Session held on 27 February 2012, Challenge No 266, Judicial Year 71; Egyptian Court of Cassation, Session held on 13 February 2010, Challenge No 3317, Judicial Year 67; Egyptian Court of Cassation, Session held on 26 October 2008, Challenge No 15487, Judicial Year 77; Egyptian Court of Cassation, Session held on 26 May 2004, Challenge No 5036, Judicial Year 72; Egyptian Court of Cassation, Session held on 4 May 1999, Challenge No 4464, Judicial Year 68; Egyptian Court of Cassation, Session held on 13 July 1999, Challenge No 2886, Judicial Year 68; Egyptian Court of Cassation, Session held on 9 June 1997, Challenge No 11865, Judicial Year 65; Egyptian Court of Cassation, Session held on 29 April 1993, Challenge No 306, Judicial Year 59; Egyptian Court of Cassation, Session held on 15 January 1989, Challenge No 132, Judicial Year 56;

1.90 While it is acknowledged that the Egyptian legal system is principally influenced by French law, a review of court decisions and scholarly contributions reveal that the generality of the principle under Egyptian law is largely inspired by Shari'a law[132] and Islamic jurisprudence.[133] Precisely, the Egyptian Court of Cassation has confirmed that the principle is primarily premised on the following sacrosanct adages of Shari'a law: (a) the prohibition of infliction of harm; (b) prevention of harm/damage takes precedence over reaping benefits; and (c) in case of inevitable damages to all parties, one shall prevent the more serious damage.[134]

1.91 The Egyptian legislator has identified three criteria of what constitutes an abuse of right.

1.92 Firstly, abuse is established if the right holder exercises his/her right to inflict harm on another.[135] While it may appear that courts apply a subjective standard of an abuse, they tend to apply the reasonable person construct to establish if there is an abuse, that is, examining the conduct of the right holder as opposed to that of a reasonable individual.[136] Moreover, the intention to inflict harm is often presumed if the right holder fails to show a serious and/or a legitimate interest in exercising his/her right.[137] Finally, in cases of a right holder who is driven by plurality of motives, Egyptian courts follow the French approach in determining abuse on the basis of the predominant and primary motive in the exercise of the right.[138]

1.93 The second criterion denotes disproportionality between the benefit(s) and prejudice(s) resulting from the exercise of the right. The reasonable person construct is the applicable standard in relation to this criterion as well.[139] It assumes and presupposes that

Egyptian Court of Cassation, Session held on 30 December 1982, Challenge No 1834, Judicial Year 51; Egyptian Court of Cassation, Session held on 1 April 1982, Challenge No 1739, Judicial Year 51.

132 According to Shari'a law, rights were first perceived as absolute: it was held that rights conferred upon individuals by God are meant to be unqualified, and that one shall not bear the consequences of the exercise of an acknowledged right. However, this liberalistic individualism philosophy was later set aside by the Hanafi school of thought, and the essence of abuse of rights was acknowledged in Islamic jurisprudence in the year of 6 AH (*Anno Hegirae*) which equates to 628 AD; Morcos (n 124) 357–58.

133 The Explanatory Memorandum of the Egyptian Law No 131 of 1948 Promulgating the Civil Code, 31–35; Sanhouri (n 127) 750; Abdul Hamid El-Ahdab, *Arbitration with the Arab Countries* (2nd edn, Kluwer Law International 1999) 573; Mohamed K Abdelaziz, *The Civil Code in Light of the Jurisprudence and Doctrine* (Cairo 1985) vol 1, 83.

134 Egyptian Court of Cassation, Session held on 14 April 2008, Challenge No 18318, Judicial Year 76; Egyptian Court of Cassation, Session held on 10 March 2003, Challenge No 2803, Judicial Year 71.

135 ibid.

136 Egyptian Court of Cassation, Session held on 12 July 1997, Challenge No 4338, Judicial Year 61; Sanhouri (n 127) 757.

137 The Explanatory Memorandum of the Egyptian Law No 131 of 1948 Promulgating the Civil Code, 32–33; Sanhouri (n 127) 759–60; Morcos (n 124) 371; Egyptian Court of Cassation, Session held on 9 February 2012, Challenge No 15906, Judicial Year 80; Egyptian Court of Cassation, Session held on 26 May 2004, Challenge No 5036, Judicial Year 72; Egyptian Court of Cassation, Session held on 22 April 2003, Challenge No 2633, Judicial Year 72; Egyptian Court of Cassation, Session held on 4 May 1999, Challenge No 4464, Judicial Year 68; Egyptian Court of Cassation, Session held on 13 July 1999, Challenge No 2886, Judicial Year 68

138 Sanhouri (127) 757–59.

139 Egyptian Court of Cassation, Session held on 24 March 1991, Challenge No 1238, Judicial Year 56, confirming that even in cases where the right holder shows a legitimate and serious interest in exercising his/her right, courts are obliged to weigh the competing interests and consider the potential harm caused thereby to establish whether there is an abuse; Egyptian Court of Cassation, Session held on 4 April 1985, Challenge No 1244, Judicial Year 54; Egyptian Court of Cassation, Session held on 25 April 1985, Challenge No 2, Judicial Year 46; Sanhouri (n 127) 760–61; Morcos (n 124) 372–73.

reasonableness and unrestricted egoism are antinomies. If a reasonable person, acting in the same circumstances, envisages/expects that his/her exercise of a right may cause serious damage, equity, justice, reason, and sensibility mandate the right holder to refrain from exercising the right in such manner to prevent harm caused thereby. However, he who envisages the possible damage that may occur and accepts it in order to materialize his minimal interests, defies reasonableness and commits an abuse of right.

The potency of this criterion emanates from its nature: a thermometer that effectively measures the potential prejudice that may be caused as a result of the exercise of right. This 'balancing factor' criterion grants wide discretionary power to courts/tribunals.[140] It entails that courts shall engage in an interest and justice-oriented analysis of the competing concerns to discern which right ought to prevail given the factual matrix of the dispute. In engaging in such analysis, Egyptian courts disregard the individualistic circumstances of the parties and engage in a rather abstract justice-oriented analysis. Courts weigh the competing interests and risks objectively regardless of the subjective circumstances of the parties. It is often held that this approach emanates from the perception that abuse of rights is premised on considerations of equity and justice and not a reflection of pity for the aggrieved party.[141] **1.94**

Thirdly, the principle applies whenever the right holder fails to show a legitimate interest in exercising his/her right.[142] Again, abuse on the basis of this criterion is ascertained objectively and primarily entails investigating the conduct of the right holder as opposed to that of the reasonable person.[143] **1.95**

An element of commonality between the above three criteria is the examination of the right holder's external behaviour rather than the quest of examining his/her internal belief to deduce an intent. While deducing the right holder's intention remains a potent element in abuse of rights, a constructive analysis of the criteria as applied by the courts demonstrates that abuse is often presumed by objectively evaluating the conduct of the right holder as opposed to that of a reasonable person.[144] **1.96**

[140] Egyptian Court of Cassation, Session held on 27 February 2005, Challenge No 871, Judicial Year 74; Egyptian Court of Cassation, Session held on 10 March 2003, Challenge No 2803, Judicial Year 71; Egyptian Court of Cassation, Session held on 8 May 2000, Challenge No 8388, Judicial Year 64.

[141] Egyptian Court of Cassation, Session held on 9 February 2012, Challenge No 15906, Judicial Year 80; Egyptian Court of Cassation, Session held on 14 December 2004, Challenge No 1302, Judicial Year 73; Egyptian Court of Cassation, Session held on 30 April 2001, Challenge No 1193, Judicial Year 69; Egyptian Court of Cassation, Session held on 23 November 1995, Challenge No 2845, Judicial Year 59; Egyptian Court of Cassation, Session held on 28 June 1989, Challenge No 143, Judicial Year 52; Egyptian Court of Cassation, Session held on 26 January 1980, Challenge No 108, Judicial Year 45.

[142] Abdelaziz (n 133) 79–80.

[143] This is further confirmed by the fact that the Egyptian legislator opted for the term 'illegitimate interest' rather than 'illegitimate purpose', as the latter was seen to shift the test of abuse to a subjective standard which was not preferable. Sanhouri (n 127) 726; Egyptian Court of Cassation, Session held on 27 December 1993, Challenge No 2451, Judicial Year 57; Egyptian Court of Cassation, Session held on 4 April 1985, Challenge No 1244, Judicial Year 54.

[144] A review of court decisions testifies to the fact that bad faith is often *presumed* and *objectively* ascertained. Egyptian Court of Cassation, Session held on 14 December 2004, Challenge No 1302, Judicial Year 73; Egyptian Court of Cassation, Session held on 12 July 1997, Challenge No 4338, Judicial Year 61.

1.97 In relation to the legal basis of the principle, it is the predominant view that one who abuses his right commits a delict, which triggers the delictual liability for the wrongdoer.[145] Moreover, eminent scholars and courts regularly hold that any abuse of a contractual right is equally tantamount to an abuse of right[146] and triggers the tortfeasor's delictual liability.[147]

1.98 In conclusion, Egyptian law embraces the abuse of rights principle and extends its application to all areas of law. The Egyptian approach is featured by its relative adoption of an objective standard of abuse.

III. Abuse of Rights in the Common Law

1.99 This section discusses the recognition, or lack thereof, of the principle of abuse of rights in the common law.

1.100 It is widely recognized that the principle of abuse of rights is alien to the common law systems.[148] However, as shall be discussed hereunder, it is submitted that the essence of the principle has crystallized its potent manifestations in various rules and principles endorsed in the common law systems. Thus, it is argued that while the principle does not exist, there are various principles and rules that have common elements and may achieve the same purpose.

1.101 For obvious spatial-temporal reasons, it is not the purpose of this section to engage in a detailed comparative analysis of equivalent rules and principles. In order to reach the conclusion that the essence of abuse of rights is not entirely foreign to the common law systems, one seeks to merely highlight particular fields of law where the essence of the principle has crystallized and gained acceptance.

1.102 Prior to embarking on an analysis of some of the those rules/principles, in an attempt to highlight the elements of commonality between them and abuse of rights, it is in order to first shed light on the generally acknowledged rejection of abuse of rights in the common law. In doing so, one shall focus on English law and US law.

[145] Morcos (n 124) 353; Sanhouri (n 127) 755–56.

[146] Egyptian Court of Cassation, Session held on 2 January 1997, Challenge No 1481, Judicial Year 62.

[147] Morcos (n 124) 45; Sanhouri (n 127) 756.

[148] Byers (n 4) 395. However, some authors advocate that abuse of rights exist in the United States. Joseph M Perillo, 'Abuse of Rights: A Pervasive Legal Concept' (1996) 27 Pacific Law Journal 37, 40.

A. Rejection of Abuse of Rights

It is the predominant view that the principle of abuse of rights forms no part of English law.[149] The case of *Mayor of Bradford v Pickles*,[150] a case decided in 1895, is often cited to support the view that the principle has been decisively rejected. **1.103**

In this case, *Pickles*, the Respondent, was the owner of land containing underground water which percolated through channels to the land of a neighbour, the Appellant. That the Appellant had no legal right to the water was undisputed. *Pickles* used his right to divert the water on his own land in an alleged attempt to improve the value of his land and minerals. In doing so, *Pickles*' apparent motive was to deprive his neighbours of the water in order to induce them to purchase his land or give him some other compensation. **1.104**

In rejecting the appeal, the Court provided that the state of mind of the person exercising the right is irrelevant and does not affect the status of the right. The Court stipulated that: **1.105**

> If it was a lawful act, however ill the motive might be, he had a right to do it. If it was an unlawful act, however good his motive might be, he would have no right to do it. Motives and intentions in such a question [. . .] seem to me absolutely irrelevant.[151]

The endorsement of an absolutist view of rights was further manifested by the Court as it stated that, while *Pickles* had deliberately deprived his neighbour of the water, conduct which 'may be churlish, selfish, and grasping', it did not violate English law. However, it may only be frowned upon from a moral perspective: 'His conduct may seem shocking to a moral philosopher.'[152] **1.106**

Moreover, it was stated in *Pickles* that Scottish law is consistent with English law in that it does not endorse abuse of rights and that the motive is irrelevant.[153] This conclusion is flawed as it failed to examine the well-established Scottish law principle of *aemulatio vicini*.[154] **1.107**

According to the latter principle, a landowner has the right to use his land in the way he desires except if his use is solely motivated by an intention to cause harm to another. The *aemulatio vicini* principle is a limitation on the exercise of rights founded on equity **1.108**

[149] Gutteridge (n 6) 22; *Chapman v Honig* [1963] 2 QB 502, 520, where the majority noted that contractual rights can be exercised for good reason or bad reason or no reason at all. However, Lord Denning dissented and recognized that it is an abusive exercise of right and held that the tenant should be remedied.

[150] *The Mayor, Aldermen And Burgesses of the Borough of Bradford v Edward Pickles* [1895] AC 587.

[151] ibid 594.

[152] ibid 601.

[153] ibid 598.

[154] Michael Taggart, *Private Property and Abuse of Rights in Victorian England: The Story of Edward Pickles and The Bradford Water Supply* (Oxford University Press 2002) 149–50; Elspeth Reid, 'The Doctrine of Abuse of Rights: Perspective from a Mixed Jurisdiction' (2004) 8 Electronic Journal of Comparative Law 1, 9; Reid (n 20) 153.

and elementary fairness.[155] While it is not frequently used, it is the predominant view that it forms part of Scottish law.[156] However, it should be noted that the *aemulatio vicini* principle differs from abuse of rights in that the former is limited to cases of property law and applies only in cases of malice.[157]

1.109 While some scholars have received such decision with equanimity,[158] others have criticized the decision.[159] Gutteridge rightly provided that the decision is a palpable manifestation of the adage '*dura lex sed lex*' (the law is harsh but it is the law).[160] He further stipulated:

> The possibility that a legal right may be exercised with impunity in a spirit of malevolence or selfishness is one of the unsatisfactory features of our law, and there would appear to be a prima facie case to reform in this direction, a belief which is strengthened by the fact that ours is the only modern system which has not endeavoured to evolve some means by which it may be ensured that a rule of law shall not be transformed into an instrument for the gratification of private spite or the promotion of chicanery.[161]

1.110 Subsequently, in the English case of *Allen v Flood*, a trade union delegate persuaded the employer to stop employing the Plaintiff's shipwrights. While there was no breach of contract as the Plaintiffs were employed 'for the job' and were liable to be discharged at any time, the Plaintiffs alleged that this conduct gave rise to tortious liability given that the Defendant interfered with their contracts of employment and maliciously induced the employer to discharge them. The fact that the Defendant (trade union delegate) acted maliciously was immaterial to the outcome of the case. The Court provided that the 'existence of a bad motive, in the case of an act which is not in itself illegal, will not convert that act into a civil wrong for which reparation is due'.[162]

1.111 The position adopted in this case is not prevailing in other common law systems. Thus, some American cases illustrate that at-will employees may be granted a cause of action if they were discharged maliciously.[163]

1.112 It is worth mentioning that the early cases in America were similar to the English position mentioned above.[164] However, while not endorsing a general principle of abuse

[155] Henry Home, *Principles of Equity* (Bell & Bradfute, Manners & Miller, A. Constable & Co, and John Fairbairn 1825) 36.
[156] David Johnston, 'Owners and Neighbours: From Rome to Scotland' in R Evans-Jones (ed), *The Civil Law Tradition in Scotland* (Stair Society 1995) 176; Reid (n 20); Taggart (n 154) 149–50.
[157] Reid (n 20) 155.
[158] John W Salmond, *The Law of Torts* (Sweet & Maxwell 1936) 8.
[159] Alfred Denning, *Freedom Under the Law* (Stevens & Sons 1949) 68–69; Crabb (n 8) 2; Wolfgang Friedmann, *Legal Theory* (2nd edn, Stevens & Sons 1949) 355–56; James Reid, 'The Law and the Reasonable Man' (1968) 54 Proceedings of the British Academy 189, 198; Foster (n 40) 351; Glanville L Williams, 'The Foundation of Tortious Liability' (1939) 7 Cambridge Law Journal 111, 127.
[160] Gutteridge (n 6) 22.
[161] ibid 22–23.
[162] *Allen v Flood* [1898] AC 1, 92.
[163] For a case that was decided in America at the same time as *Allen v Flood*, see *Lucke v Clothing Cutters & Trimmers*, 77 Md 396, 26 A. 505, 509 (1893).
[164] *Jenkins v Flower*, 24 Pa 308 (1855), 310.

of rights, some American courts subsequently denied the recognition of property rights which were exercised maliciously, under the notion of nuisance.[165] As stated by one court:

> A landowner has a right to build a fence along the boundary or division line of his property [. . .] But the right *is not absolute*; this is to say that *it is not unfettered or exercisable without reference to its impact upon others.* On the contrary, a right to fence, like so many other species of property rights, is not exercised in a vacuum and the law is not indifferent to the impact which that exercise may have on others.[166] (Emphasis added)

In this regard, some note that the common law's avoidance of endorsing a general principle of abuse of rights is primarily premised on the perception that the principle's determination involves an examination of one's state of mind, which renders the principle difficult to apply.[167] Moreover, some submit that the common law's rejection of the principle stems from the fact that it bears undeterminable variable parameters as it relies on an individual assessment of each decision maker, which would necessarily defy legal certainty.[168] **1.113**

While these may seem to be logical arguments, one submits that they are questionable given that: (a) abuse of rights does not merely rely on the right holder's intent; (b) the principle's scope of application is broader than the element of malice; and (c) the element of intent is not only a constituent of abuse of rights, but is also an element in other rules that are endorsed by the common law legal systems,[169] including, inter alia, the obligation to perform in good faith under US law,[170] nuisance,[171] and the tort of malicious prosecution.[172] **1.114**

Moreover, such concerns seem misplaced if the principle of abuse of rights is defined objectively, that is, by examining one's external behaviour and the particulars of the dispute to decide if the exercise of a right is reasonable.[173] **1.115**

[165] *Burke v Smith*, 37 NW 838 (Mich 1888); *Greenleaf v Francis*, 35 Mass 117 (1836); Perillo (n 148) 44; James B Ames, 'How Far An Act May be a Tort Because of the Wrongful Motive of the Actor' (1905) 18 Harvard Law Review 411, 414; Reid (n 20) 144.

[166] *Brittingham v Robertson*, 280 A 2d 741 (Del 1971).

[167] Taggart (n 154) 156; Mayrand (n 21) 996.

[168] *Allen v Flood* [1898] AC 1, 118; Arthur L Goodhart, *English Law and the Moral Law* (Stevens & Sons Ltd 1955) 145.

[169] Walton (n 25) 518–19; Ames (n 163) 412 and 416; *Secretary of State for Employment v Associated Society of Locomotive Engineers and Fireman (No 2)*, [1972] 2 QB 455, 492 (Lord Denning): 'There are many branches of our law when an act which would otherwise be lawful is rendered unlawful by the motive or object with which it is done'.

[170] Robert S Summers, '"Good Faith" in General Contract Law and the Sales Provisions of the Uniform Commercial Code' (1968) 54 Virginia Law Review 195.

[171] Anna Di Robilant, 'Abuse of Rights: The Continental Drug and the Common Law' (2010) 61 Hastings Law Journal 687, 704; GHL Fridman, 'Motive in the English Law of Nuisance' (1954) 40 Virginia Law Review 583, 586–87; *Hollywood Silver Fox Farm Ltd v Emmett* [1936] 2 KB 468; *Christie v Davey* [1893] 1 Ch 316; Reid (n 20) 145; Williams (n 159) 128.

[172] FP Walton, 'Delictual Responsibility in the Modern Civil Law (More Particularly in the French Law) as Compared with the English Law of Torts' (1933) 49 Law Quarterly Review 70, 88.

[173] ibid 87–89.

B. Functional Equivalents in the Common Law

1.116 As previously stated, it is evident that a general principle of abuse of rights has no place in the common law. However, it would be disingenuous to claim that the essence of the principle is peculiar to the common law.[174]

1.117 Thus, it is submitted that the common law systems have effectively implemented other rules/principles in different legal areas to limit cases of manifest substantive and procedural abuse. This is conspicuous, for example, when one recognizes the interrelation between abuse of rights and the broader notion of equity,[175] the prohibition against abuse of process and malicious prosecution to limit abuse of procedural rights.[176] Moreover, the role of reasonableness in limiting landlords' right to refuse renewing lease agreements,[177] retaliatory eviction in tenancy disputes,[178] and in the common law rules relating to nuisances further strengthen this submission.[179]

1. Substantive abuse: the notion of reasonableness and good faith

1.118 The notion of reasonableness, or the reasonable man construct, is a flexible standard for guiding conduct.[180] It is a legal fiction that allows the evaluation of conduct, and enables an objective and balanced approach to legal issues in order to reach an acceptable outcome.[181] As noted by one scholar, the conduct in question can be labelled reasonable 'if the activities can be valued as fair, just, or equitable'.[182]

[174] Gutteridge (n 6) 30.

[175] Taggart (n 154) 152–55; Tony Weir, 'The Common Law System' in R. David and others (eds), *International Encyclopedia of Comparative Law* , *The Legal Systems of the World: Their Comparison and Unification* (Martinus Nijhoff 1975) vol II; David Anderson, 'Abuse of Rights', (2006) 11 Judicial Review 348, 350. The interrelation is also manifested by the critiques of equity. Equity is often criticized for its vagueness, flexibility, broadness, and for the discretionary power it grants to the decision maker. John Selden, *Table-Talk: Being the Discourses of John Selden, Esq* (2nd edn, JM Dent & Co 1819) 45–46; Henry E Smith, 'Property, Equity and the Rule of Law' in Lisa M Austin and Dennis Kilmchuk (eds), *Private Law and the Rule of Law* (Oxford University Press 2014) 13; David Lieberman, *The Province of Legislation Determined: Legal Theory in Eighteenth-Century Britain* (Cambridge University Press 1989) 80 and 167; Michael Levenstein, *Maxims of Equity: A Juridical Critique of the Ethics of Chancery Law* (Algora 2014) 44–45; Roscoe Pound, *Jurisprudence* (West Publishing Co 1959) vol 1, 407; Alfred William Brian Simpson, *A History of the Common Law of Contract: The Rise of the Action of Assumpsit* (Clarendon Press 1975) 396–402; María José and Falcón Tella, *Equity and Law* (Martinus Nijhoff 2008) 64–65; Roscoe Pound, 'The End of Law as Developed in Legal Rules and Doctrines' (1914) 27 Harvard Law Review 195, 226–27; Roscoe Pound, *The Spirit of the Common Law* (Marshall Jones Company 1921) 185–86.

[176] Charles T Kotuby and Luke A Sobota, *General Principles of Law and International Due Process* (Oxford University Press 2017) 110.

[177] Iluyomade (n 30) 58–9 ('There are many instances where common law legislatures have written into laws restrictions on possible abuses of rights. An example is the English Landlord and Tenant Act, which limits a landlord's right of refusing the renewal of a lease').

[178] George M Armstrong and John C LaMaster, 'Retaliatory Eviction as Abuse of Rights: A Civilian Approach to Landlord-Tenant Disputes' (1986) 47 Louisiana Law Review 1, 18; Perillo (n 148) 58.

[179] Gutteridge (n 6) 30; Crabb (n 8) 1; Byers (n 4) 396–97; William Prosser, *Law of Torts* (3rd edn, West Publishing Co 1964) 618–19, discussing that US law recognizes that acting maliciously may trigger one's liability for nuisance; Krauze (n 4) 2.

[180] *Rath Packing Company v Joseph W Jones*, 530 F 2d 1295 (9th Cir 1975).

[181] Joachim (n 46) 341.

[182] ibid 342.

The common law's predilection for, and its pervasive reference to, reasonableness arguably permeates various areas of the law (contractual and tortious).[183] It is submitted that the standard of reasonableness often operates to limit different forms of abuse, as it arguably defies fairness, justice, and equity to allow rights to be exercised maliciously or in a disproportionate/unreasonable manner.[184] **1.119**

Thus, while no unitary concept of abuse of rights exists in the common law, courts have employed functional equivalents of abuse of rights, such as the standard of reasonableness, in their quest for tackling different forms of abuse.[185] It is said that the term 'reasonable' encompasses criteria 'that are the same as or similar to those invoked in assessing "abuse of rights" '.[186] In further demystifying the analogy, one scholar noted that while the principle of abuse of rights imposes a limitation to the exercise of private property rights, common law advocates that 'everyone has the right to the reasonable use of his or her property'.[187] **1.120**

In practice, this may be conspicuous, *ex analogia*, in the law of torts such as water disputes as well as the tort of nuisance under English and US law.[188] In this regard, scholars generally acknowledge that although the principle of abuse of rights 'is not readily apparent in the common law, the principle operates there as well in the form of torts such as nuisance, duress, and abuse of process'.[189] Similarly, Lauterpacht advocated that 'there is in this respect no difference of substance between English law and other legal systems. The major part of the law of torts is nothing else than the affirmation of the prohibition of abuse of rights'.[190] **1.121**

Whilst disputes arising out of the unreasonable erection of fences were manifestations of abuse of rights in civil law, they were deemed as a nuisance that may trigger one's tortious liability in the common law: **1.122**

> In systems of law derived from the Digest a great deal is said about abuse of rights; and the law is certainly made simpler and more patently straightforward by provisions in codes and case law developments therefrom, dealing with *jus abutendi*, *abus des droits*, or *schikanerverbot*. Such ideas are not to be found as part of the common law. But it

[183] George P Fletcher, 'The Right and the Reasonable' (1985) 98 Harvard Law Review 949, 949–50. For an overview of the principle's application in different legal areas, see Joachim (n 46).

[184] Ugo Mattei, *Basic Principles of Property Law: A Comparative Legal and Economic Introduction* (Greenwood Press 2000) 149, ('the doctrine of abuse of right as such is absent in the common law, where it is perfectly well substituted for by the reasonableness limit'); Joachim (n 46) 353.

[185] Robilant (n 171) 698; Zimmermann and Whittaker (n 35) 696.

[186] Fletcher (n 183) 953.

[187] ibid.

[188] Amos and Walton (n 18) 219; Reid (n 20) 145; David Campbell, 'Gathering the Water: Abuse of Rights After the Recognition of Government Failure', (2010) 7 Journal Jurisprudence 487, 523; Fridman (n 171) 586–87; William Prosser and others, *Prosser and Keeton on the Law of Torts* (5th edn, West Publishing Co 1984) 626–27, noting that unreasonable interference is the basis for the law of nuisance.

[189] Kotuby and Sobota (n 176) 110–11; Andreas Zeigler and Jorun Baumgartner, '*Good faith as a General Principle of (International) Law*' in Andrew Mitchell and others (eds), *Good Faith and International Economic Law* (Oxford University Press 2015) 30–31.

[190] Hersch Lauterpacht, *The Function of Law in the International Community* (Oxford University Press 2011) 303.

> should not be thought that the common law provides no remedy for such wrongs. There is an ample provision in the present law relating to the tort nuisance for control of activities envisaged by the continental codes.[191]

1.123 In the case of *Horan v Byrnes*, a dispute arose where the defendant maintained a fence on his land allegedly to harm the occupant of the adjoining premises. An applicable statute precluded a landowner from erecting a fence exceeding five feet in height, if the purpose of such erection is the annoyance of the adjoining occupant. The Claimant asserted that the statute is unconstitutional as it interfered with one's inherent right of protecting his property and deprived him from its enjoyment. In upholding the statute, the Supreme Court of New Hampshire noted:

> While one may in general put his property to any use he pleases not in itself unlawful, his neighbour has the same right to the undisturbed enjoyment of his adjoining property. What standard does the law provide? Whatever may be the law in other jurisdictions, it must be regarded as settled in this state that *the test is the reasonableness or unreasonableness of the business in question under all the circumstances*. The common law right of the ownership of land [. . .] does not sanction or authorize practical injustice to one landowner by the arbitrary and *unreasonable exercise of the right* of dominion by another (Franklin v. Durgee), but makes the test of the right the reasonableness of the use under all circumstances. In such case *the purpose of the use*, whether understood by the landowner to be necessary or useful to himself, or *merely intended to harm another*, may be *decisive* upon the question of right. *It cannot be justly contended that a purely malicious use is a reasonable use.*[192] (Emphasis added)

1.124 From the above decision, it may be inferred that the standard of reasonableness is broad and includes certain elements that parallel the criteria of abuse found in the civil legal systems, that is, malice, reasonableness and the purpose of the exercise of the right. Moreover, the standard of reasonableness is as flexible as the principle of abuse of rights. There is no set of rigid rules of what is considered reasonable, as this will largely depend on the particulars of each case.[193]

1.125 The role of the reasonableness test to preclude different forms of abuse is also apparent in contractual disputes. Whilst the prevailing view is that there is no general duty to perform the contract in good faith under English law, the abuse of contractual rights may be typically avoided whereby the 'content of right is cut down from within by the implication of "reasonableness," with reference to the intention of the parties, in much the same way as is done with statutory rights'.[194]

1.126 This may be demonstrated in cases where one refuses to consent to the assignment of a contract. Courts apply the test of reasonableness to determine if refusal to consent is

[191] Fridman (n 171) 586.
[192] *Horan v Byrnes*, 72 NH 93, 100 (NH 1903); Robilant (n 171) 705–06.
[193] Fletcher (n 183) 980.
[194] Catala and Weir (n 29) 258.

arbitrary or abusive.[195] This was the case in *Cohen v Ratinoff*, whereby the California Court of Appeal addressed whether the lessor can abusively withhold consent to an assignment, and held that:

> [W]here [. . .] the lease provides for an assignment or subletting only with the prior consent of the lessor, a lessor may refuse consent *only* where he has a good faith *reasonable* objection to the assignment or sublease, *even in the absence of a provision prohibiting the unreasonable or arbitrary withholding of consent to an assignment.*[196] (Emphasis added)

Similarly, in the case of *Larese v Creamland*, a dispute arose out of a franchise agreement that provided that the agreement should not be assigned without the prior consent of the franchisor. In refusing to consent, the franchisor asserted that this contractual right was absolute and unqualified, which is an assertion often raised in cases of abuse of rights as previously mentioned. The US Courts of Appeal did not agree with the franchisor, imposed a duty of reasonableness, and held that the franchisor's conduct was abusive/unreasonable.[197] **1.127**

Finally, in the case of *Eastleigh BC v Town Quay Developments Ltd*, a piece of land was transferred from the Claimant's predecessor to the Defendant subject to a reservation of a right for itself and/or its successors to enter the transfer land to do works subject to the consent of the defendant. There was *no* express qualification that such right (consent) should not be unreasonably withheld. Given that the Claimant, the owner of an adjacent land, wished to develop his land, he required access onto the land; however the Defendant withheld its consent. The issue before the English Court of Appeal was whether there was an implied term that the defendant should not unreasonably refuse consent. The court confirmed that implying the qualification of reasonableness was necessary as a matter of business efficacy.[198] **1.128**

In this regard, it is submitted that the element of reasonableness acts in a manner similar to abuse of rights.[199] This becomes evident if one considers that the same type of disputes are dealt with under the principle of abuse of rights in civil law. Thus, in France[200] as well as in Louisiana, courts have regularly assessed whether such refusal constituted an abuse of right.[201] **1.129**

[195] Byron R Lane, 'Kendall v Ernest Pestana, Inc: Landlords May Not Unreasonably Withhold Consent to Commercial Lease Assignments', (1986) 14 Pepperdine Law Review 81; *Lovelock v Margo* [1963] 2 All ER 13 (CA); *Schweiso v Williams*, 150 Cal App 3d 883, 886, (Cal Ct App 1984); *Prestin v Mobil Oil Corp*, 741 F 2d 268, 271 (9th Cir 1984); *Basnett v Vista Village Mobile Home Park*, 699 P 2d 1343, 1346–47 (Colo Ct App 1984); *Fernandez v Vazquez*, 397 So 2d 1171, 1173–74 (Fla Ct App 1981).

[196] *Cohen v Ratinoff*, 147 Cal App 3d 321, 330, 195 Cal Rptr 84 (1983).

[197] *Larese v Creamland Dairies, Inc*, 767 F 2d 716, 718 (10 Cir 1985).

[198] *Eastleigh BC v Town Quay Developments Ltd* [2009] EWCA Civ 1391.

[199] Fridman (n 171) 594–95, stating that the element of reasonableness may determine whether one's conduct amounts to a nuisance.

[200] Perillo (n 148) 78.

[201] *Illinois Central Gulf RR v International Harvester Co*, 368 So 2d 1009 (La 1979).

1.130 Another concept that may similarly limit the abusive exercise of rights is the principle of good faith under US law. The interrelation between abuse of rights and the broader principle of good faith shall be discussed in another section. However, suffice it to mention that such interrelation has serious practical implications. The perception that a general principle of good faith embodies the prohibition against abuse of rights, indicates that jurisdictions that do not explicitly endorse the principle of abuse of rights may still limit the exercise of rights on the basis of the principle of good faith.[202] It has been rightly expressed that:

> Be that as it may, where a duty of good faith is recognized and redress granted for its violation, there is at least an implied recognition that the abuse of a right is an actual wrong since, in essence, such an abuse is necessarily a violation of the overriding obligation of good faith.[203]

1.131 The above submission may be illustrated in cases of abusive discharge of at-will employees under US law, where courts rely on the obligation to act in good faith to preclude the abusive dismissal of at-will employees. In *Fortune v National Cash Register Co*, the employer dismissed a sales representative after the employer received a 5 million dollar order procured by the sales representative. The employer exercised his right to dismiss the sales representative to avoid granting him a bonus commission. The Court found that the termination was contrary to the implied covenant of good faith and fair dealing which applied to all contracts, and thus constituted a breach of the contract.[204] In civil legal systems, the same result may be achieved by applying the principle of abuse of rights.[205]

1.132 Moreover, courts often engage in an analysis or reasoning which greatly parallels that of abuse of rights. In one case regarding an employee that was dismissed because he filed a case against the employer, the Court noted that while dismissing employees at-will is a recognized legal right, it should not be used for a 'purpose ulterior to that for which the right was designed'.[206]

1.133 The obligation to act in good faith was used by US courts in a manner similar to that of abuse of rights to address the issue of abusive exercise of discretion as well. In the case of *Tymshare v Covell*, the employer had the right to keep a portion of sales representatives' earnings in a fund. These earnings were calculated on the basis of a quota that could be changed by the employer at any time at their sole discretion. The Plaintiff submitted that the employer's decision to retroactively change the

[202] Herch Lauterpacht, *The Development of International Law by the International Court* (Cambridge University Press 1982) 163–64; Annekatrien Lenaerts, 'The General Principle of the Prohibition of Abuse of Rights: A Critical Position on Its Role in a Codified European Contract Law' (2010) 18 European Review of Private Law 1145–46.

[203] Litvinoff (n 50) 1661.

[204] *Fortune v National Cash Register Co*, 364 NE 2d 1251 (Mass 1977), 1252–53.

[205] *Clark v Glidden Coating & Resins*, 666 F Supp 868 (ED La 1987); *Sanborn v Oceanic Contractors Inc*, 448 So 2d 91 (La 1984).

[206] *Smith v Atlas Off-Shore Boat Services Inc*, 653 F 2d 1057 (5th Cir 1981), 1062; Perillo (n 148) 56–57.

quota after the Plaintiff's termination was in bad faith. While the employer argued that the exercise of such discretionary power was not affected by his motives, even if he acted unreasonably, the Court found that it did not mean that it could be used 'for any reason whatsoever, no matter how arbitrary or unreasonable'.[207] The Court further noted that a permissible act may constitute a contractual breach if performed in bad faith.

Similarly, in *Daitch Crystal v Neisloss*, a lease agreement granted the tenant the right to operate a supermarket in a shopping centre. A dispute then arose after the landlord attempted to build a supermarket on an adjacent land for a competitor. The Court found that the landlord breached the lease agreement. The Court recognized that it was not empowered to make a new contract between the parties, however, it emphasized that 'in every contract there exists an implied covenant of good faith and fair dealing'.[208] Scholars have noted that the Court did not rely on the terms of the lease, but had applied the principle of good faith to limit an abuse of right.[209] 1.134

Based on the above, it is submitted that while there is no overarching general principle of abuse of substantive rights in the common law, the latter has devised and applied different rules and principles to avert manifest abuse and unfairness. This is particularly conspicuous under US law. By and large, these rules/principles operate in a manner similar to abuse of rights and achieve the same purpose. 1.135

2. Procedural abuse: abuse of process

The right to bring legal action in court is a sacred right expressed in most constitutions.[210] Nevertheless, one who uses this right for a purpose other than that contemplated by the law or to harm the other litigant, commits a tort of abuse of process,[211] which is nothing short of an abuse of a procedural right.[212] 1.136

[207] *Tymshare Inc v Covell*, 727 F 2d 1145 (DC Cir 1984).

[208] *Daitch Crystal Dairies v Neisloss*, 190 NYS2d 737 (App Div 1959), aff'd mem, 167 NE 2d 643 (NY 1960), cited in Perillo (n 148) 76.

[209] Perillo (n 148) 76.

[210] Ascensio (n 118) 765.

[211] *Attorney General v Barker* [2000] 1 FLR 759; *Sheets v Teddy's Frosted Foods Inc*, 427 A 2d 385, 387 (Conn 1980); John D Lawson, 'The Action for the Malicious Prosecution of a Civil Suit' (1882) 30 The American Law Register 353, 365–66.

[212] Robert Kolb, 'General Principles of Procedural Law' in Andreas Zimmermann and others (eds), *The Statute of the International Court of Justice: A Commentary* (Oxford University Press 2006) 831; Eric De Brabandere, '"Good Faith", "Abuse of Process" and the Initiation of Investment Treaty Claims' (2012) 3 Journal of International Dispute Settlement 619; Catala and Weir (n 29) 225–26; Mayrand (n 21) 999; Chris Brunner, 'Abuse of Rights in Dutch Law' (1977) 37 Louisiana Law Review 729, 743–45; Yuval Shany, *The Competing Jurisdictions of International Courts and Tribunals* (Oxford University Press 2003) 256; Robert Kolb, *The International Court of Justice* (Hart Publishing 2013) 947; Walton (n 25) 508; Nathan Tamblyn, 'Lawful Act Conspiracy: Malice and Abuse of Rights' (2013) Singapore Journal of Legal Studies 158, 166; Tania Voon, Andrew Mitchell, and James Munro, 'Legal Responses to Corporate Manoeuvring in International Investment Arbitration' (2014) 5 Journal of International Dispute Settlement 41, 61; Ascensio (n 118) 764–65; *Abaclat v Argentine Republic*, ICSID Case No ARB/07/5, 647, Decision on Jurisdiction and Admissibility of 4 August 2011.

1.137 The courts' inherent power/jurisdiction to preclude the abuse of procedural rights has long been established in the common law[213] to maintain the integrity of the legal system.[214] In 1885, Lord Blackburn noted:

> [F]rom early times (I rather think, though I have not looked at it enough to say, from the earliest times) the Court had *inherently* the right to see that *its process was not abused* by a proceeding *without reasonable grounds*, so as to be vexatious and harassing – the Court had the right to protect itself against such an abuse.[215] (Emphasis added)

1.138 The principle of abuse of process is an intrinsic part of the common law.[216] The principle's interrelation to the broader principle of abuse of rights is acknowledged by scholars, and is evident by its terminology, function, and application.

1.139 Abuse of process generally denotes the use of procedural rights for a purpose other than that for which such procedural rights were established,[217] and applies to 'all categories of cases in which the processes and procedures of the court, which exist to administer justice with fairness and impartiality, may be converted into instruments of injustice or unfairness.'[218] Section 682 of the Restatement (Second) of Torts defines abuse of process as follows:

> One who uses a legal process, whether criminal or civil, against another primarily to accomplish a purpose for which it is not designed, is subject to liability to the other for harm caused by the abuse of process.[219]

1.140 The above demystification of the principle is consistent with that found in other common law jurisdictions. Thus, in Canada and Australia the principle is said to operate to preclude any abuse that violates the principles of fairness and justice and that may bring the administration of justice into disrepute.[220]

1.141 Similar to the operation of abuse of rights, abuse of process is not restricted to rigid categories or defined circumstances, but its application is warranted whenever the factual matrix of the case reveals unfairness, unreasonable conduct, or injustice.[221] It similarly limits the abuse of any procedural right and is not limited to a category of rights. As highlighted by the California Court of Appeal: 'The term "process" as used in the tort of abuse of process has been broadly interpreted to encompass the entire range of procedures incident to litigation.'[222]

[213] MS Dockray, 'The Inherent Jurisdiction to Regulate Civil Proceedings' (1997) 113 Law Quarterly Review 120, 123.
[214] Mark Crosswhite, 'Abuse of Process and Malicious Prosecution in Alabama' (1987) 38 Alabama Law Review 99, 99.
[215] *Metropolitan Bank v Pooley* [1885] 10 AC 210, 220.
[216] In England, the courts' inherent power in this regard is stipulated in rule 3.4 of the English Civil Procedure Rules.
[217] Tobi Goldoftas, 'Abuse of Process' (1964) 13 Cleveland-Marshall Law Review 163, 163; Kolb (n 212) 831; Gaillard (n 5) 34; Gaffney (n 68) 516; *Rosen v American Bank of Rolla*, 627 A 2d 190 (Pa Super Ct 1993).
[218] Peter Barnett, *Res Judicata, Estoppel, and Foreign Judgments* (Oxford University Press 2001) para 6.06; *Walton v Gardiner* [1993] 177 CLR 378, 395 (Australia).
[219] Section 682 of the Restatement (Second) of Torts (1977).
[220] *Toronto City v C.U.P.E.* [2003] 3 SCR 77; *R v Scott* [1990] 3 SCR 979, 1007; *Rogers v The Queen* [1994] HCA 42.
[221] *Ashmore v British Coal Corp*, [1990] 2 QB 338; Lord Justice Maurice Kay, *Blackstone's Civil Practice 2013* (13th edn, Oxford University Press 2012) para 33.12.
[222] *Younger v Solomon*, 38 Cal App 3d 289, 296 (1974); *Rosen v American Bank of Rolla*, 627 A 2d 190, 192 (Pa Super Ct 1993).

Courts have occasionally expressed the opinion that restricting the application of abuse of process to fixed categories is unwise, and that it should be left as a broad tool to be applied by courts when warranted.[223] As stated by the English Court of Appeal in the case of *Ashmore v British Coal Corp*: **1.142**

> A litigant has a right to have his claim litigated, provided it is not frivolous, vexatious or an abuse of the process. What may constitute such conduct must depend on all the circumstances of the case; the categories are not closed and considerations of public policy and the interests of justice may be very material.[224]

It functions in a manner that ameliorates the rigidity of the common law and maintains the fairness and reasonableness of procedures.[225] In elaborating abuse of process, the House of Lords (now the Supreme Court) noted: **1.143**

> It concerns the inherent power which any court of justice must possess to prevent *misuse of its procedure* in a way which, *although not inconsistent with the literal application of its procedural rules, would nevertheless be manifestly unfair to a party to litigation before it*, or would otherwise bring the administration of justice into disrepute among right-thinking people. The circumstances in which abuse of process can arise are very *varied* [. . .]. It would, in my view, be most unwise if this House were to use this occasion to say anything that might be taken as limiting to fixed categories the kinds of circumstances in which the court has a duty (I disavow the word discretion) to exercise this salutary power.[226] (Emphasis added)

Its application in the common law resembles the application of abuse of rights to limit abuse of procedural rights in civil legal systems.[227] Typically, courts engage in a balancing process of the competing interests,[228] and tend to find an abuse on the basis of objective criteria, mainly relying on the purpose for which the right was exercised and the reasonableness of exercising the right in question.[229] **1.144**

Thus, as noted by one scholar, abuse of process is considered to be synonymous with the principle of abuse of right and its gist is 'the misuse or misapplication of process which would be justified in itself for an end other than that which it was designed to accomplish'.[230] **1.145**

As stated by the English Court of Appeal, in a case that involved proceedings brought to harass the opponent: **1.146**

[223] *Hunter v Chief Constable of the West Midlands* [1982] AC 529, 536.
[224] *Ashmore v British Coal Corp* [1990] 2 QB 338, 348.
[225] Barnett (n 218) paras 6.03–6.06.
[226] *Hunter v Chief Constable of the West Midlands* [1982] AC 529, 536.
[227] Audley Sheppard, 'Res Judicata and Estoppel' in Bernardo M Cremades and Julian DM Lew (eds), *Parallel State and Arbitral Procedures in International Arbitration* (ICC Institute of World Business Law 2005) 236–7.
[228] *Johnson v Gore Wood & Co*, [2002] 2 AC 1: 'whether an action was an abuse of process [. . .] should be judged broadly on the merits taking account of all the public and private interests involved and all the facts of the case'.
[229] *Broxton v McClelland and Another* [1995] EMLR 485, 496–98.
[230] Iluyomade (n 30) 58–59.

> A claimant's motive for asserting a legal right was irrelevant. Accordingly, the institution [of] proceedings with an ulterior motive was not of itself enough to constitute an abuse of process. An action was only an abuse if the court's processes were being misused to achieve something not properly available to the claimant in the course of properly conducted proceedings.[231]

1.147 An interesting application of abuse of process pertains to the issue of *res judicata*, whereby the principle is utilized to remedy the rigidity of the triple identity test, and is known in English law as the 'rule in *Henderson v Henderson*'.[232] In this case, the Court held that parties were required to bring forward their *whole* case, and that the Court would not 'permit the same parties to open the same subject of litigation in respect of matter[s] which might have been brought forward as part of the subject in contest, but which was not brought forward, only because they have, from negligence, inadvertence, or even accident, omitted part of their case'.[233] The crux in the rule in *Henderson* was the element of reasonableness required by the parties when bringing an action before the Court.[234]

1.148 Accordingly, courts establish an abuse of process where a procedural right is exercised for a purpose other than that for which the right was granted,[235] or where bringing the claim is unreasonable.[236]

1.149 On a related note, the application of abuse of process confers wide discretionary power upon courts who are bestowed with the role of balancing of interests in order to determine if there is any abuse. Thus, even if the conditions of its application are satisfied, courts may still find no abuse given the competing interests at stake. To that effect, in the case of *Attorney General v Barker*, the Court noted that:

> Whether, where the condition is satisfied, the court will exercise its discretion to make an order, will depend on the *court's assessment of where the balance of justice lies*, taking account on the one hand of a citizen's prima facie *right to invoke the jurisdiction of the civil courts* and on the other the need to provide members of the public with *a measure of protection against abusive and ill–founded claims*.[237] (Emphasis added)

1.150 Scholars acknowledge that abuse of process is an application of the principle of abuse of rights.[238] While the existence of a functional equivalent to abuse of rights is

[231] *Wallis v Valentine* [2002] EWCA Civ 1034, [2003] EMLR 8.

[232] This is also applied in Australia and Canada: 'Interim Report: "Res Judicata" and Arbitration' (International Law Association, Berlin 2004) 8; Paul M Perell, 'Res Judicata and Abuse of Process', (2001) 24 Advocates Quarterly 189, 192–93; *Toronto (City) v Canadian Union of Public Employees* [2003] SCJ No 64 (Sup Ct); *Danyluk v Ainsworth Technologies Inc* [2001] 2 SCR 460, 2001 SCC 44, para 18; *Port of Melbourne Authority v Anshun Pty Ltd* (1981) 147 CLR 589 (Australian High Court); *Johnson v Gore Wood & Co* [2002] 2 AC 1, where the House of Lords noted that the *Henderson* Rule falls under the ambit of abuse of process.

[233] *Henderson v Henderson* [1843] 3 Hare 100, 67 ER 313, 319.

[234] The criterion applied by the court was 'reasonable diligence' of the party. ibid; *Fidelitas Shipping Co Ltd v V/O Exportchleb* [1966] 1 QB 630, 640.

[235] *Goldsmith v Sperrings Ltd and Others* [1977] 1 WLR 478, 489; Goldoftas (n 127) 163.

[236] *Jameel v Dow Jones and Co Inc* [2005] EWCA Civ 75, [2005] QB 946; *Henderson v Henderson* [1843] 3 Hare 100, 67 ER 313, 319; *Fidelitas Shipping Co Ltd v V/O Exportchleb* [1966] 1 QB 630, 640.

[237] *Attorney General v Barker* [2000] 1 FLR 759.

[238] Kolb (n 212) 831.

controversial in relation to substantive rights, all main systems, including the common law systems, 'apply or, at least are willing to recognize, some kind of 'abuse of rights' rule in relation to the exercise of rights during adjudication'.[239] As rightly stated by Gaillard: 'while common law systems do not recognize any general principle of abuse of rights, English courts have long upheld their inherent jurisdiction to sanction a party's exercise of its procedural rights in an abusive manner'.[240]

Similarly, after confirming that the principle of abuse of rights also operates in the common law in the form of different torts, Charles Kotuby and Luke Sobota noted that: **1.151**

> Almost universally, then, parties must not be allowed to abuse the legal process so as to harm or harass others – in other words, to invoke a 'right, power, or competency whose form or purpose is not consistent with the purposes of the right, power, or competency concerned, for instance, if it is exercised for the purpose of evading an . . . obligation or obtaining an undue advantage.[241]

The view that abuse of process is a clear manifestation of abuse of rights is not limited to English law, but is also recognized in other common law systems. For example, in the US, scholars note that abuse of process is a 'narrowly circumscribed version of the doctrine of abuse of rights',[242] and in Australia it is acknowledged that the tort of abuse of process is 'the clearest illustration in our law of what civilians call an "abuse of right" '.[243] **1.152**

Finally, it is worth mentioning that other torts found in the common law also function in a manner similar to abuse of procedural rights, including the tort of malicious prosecution under English and US law.[244] **1.153**

As provided by the English Supreme Court, the tort of malicious prosecution requires providing proof that the defendant was actuated by malice, that he had no reasonable and probable cause for bringing the claim, and that the claimant suffered damages.[245] Thus, whilst the tort of abuse of process mainly rests on the ulterior purpose of exercising the right (deviation of purpose), the tort of malicious prosecution appears to emphasize the element of malice, which may be inferred objectively from the lack of probable/reasonable cause.[246] **1.154**

[239] Shany (n 212) 256.
[240] Gaillard (n 5) 33.
[241] Kotuby and Sobota (n 176) 110–11.
[242] Perillo (n 148) 64.
[243] John Fleming, *The Law of Torts* (8th edn, The Law Book Company 1992) 623.
[244] Section 382 of the Restatement (Second) of Torts (1965); Gaillard (n 5) 33; Lawson (n 211) 365–66.
[245] *Willers v Joyce* [2016] UKSC 43, 52–56, where the English Supreme Court confirmed that claims for malicious prosecution of civil proceedings can be brought under English law, and noted that the 'ingredients of the tort of malicious prosecution were that the injury had been suffered in consequence of the malicious use of legal proceedings brought without a reasonable basis'; *CFC 26 Ltd v Brown Shipley and Co Ltd* [2016] EWHC 3048 (Ch); *Crawford Adjusters (Cayman) Ltd v Sagicor General Insurance (Cayman) Ltd* [2013] UKPC 17. Unlike abuse of process, the tort of malicious prosecution also requires the termination of the original proceedings in the plaintiff's favour; Goldoftas (n 217) 164; Crosswhite (n 214) 120.
[246] Devine (n 29) 167–169; Crosswhite (n 214) 110 and 113; *SS Kresge Co v Ruby*, 348 So 2d 484, 489 (Ala 1977); *Juman v The Attorney General of Trinidad and Tobago and Another* [2017] UKPC 3, providing that the element of malice may be implied from gross negligence.

1.155 That said, it is submitted that both torts are manifestations of the broader principle of abuse of rights and demonstrate the different criteria of abuse: malice, reasonableness, and deviation of purpose.

1.156 Just as the case in relation to the abuse of rights, where an abuse of process is established, courts will intervene to put an end to it by, for example, staying the legal process, and if harm is already caused, courts will grant damages to the aggrieved.[247]

IV. Abuse of Rights in International Law

1.157 This section examines whether the principle of abuse of rights is part of international law.

1.158 Prior to embarking on an analysis of how courts and tribunals have utilized and applied the principle to prevent the abuse of different rights under international law, it seems in order to first provide a succinct overview of the principle's recognition as reflected by prominent scholars.

A. Abuse of Rights is Part of International Law

1.159 Owing to the principle's wide acceptance in national legal systems and the potent interests it aims to uphold, decision makers and prominent scholars have long considered abuse of rights to be part of international law, either as a general principle of international law or part of customary international law.[248]

1.160 The recognition and application of abuse of rights as part of international law is frequently premised and grounded on Article 38 of the Statute of the ICJ which refers to the general principles of law recognized by civilized nations as a source of law.[249]

1.161 In 1920, when the Advisory Committee of Jurists was drafting Article 38 of the Statute of the Permanent Court of International Justice ('PCIJ'), the Italian member of the committee (Arturo Ricci-Busatti), referred to the principle of abuse of rights as an epitome of 'general principles of law'.[250]

1.162 The possibilities of the application of the principle of abuse of rights in relations among States are manifold. As noted by Lauterpacht: 'there is no legal right, however well established, which could not, in some circumstances, be refused recognition on the ground that it has been abused'.[251] Thus, a range of rights are susceptible to being abused, may

[247] *Goldsmith v Sperrings Ltd and Others* [1977] 1 WLR 478, 489.
[248] Kotuby and Sobota (n 176) 108.
[249] Iluyomade (n 30) 53.
[250] Permanent Court of International Justice: Advisory Committee of Jurists, 'Procès-verbaux of the Proceedings of the Committee, June 16th-July 24th 1920, with Annexes' (The Hague: Van Langenhuysen Brothers 1920) 314–15 and 335.
[251] Lauterpacht (n 21) 164.

fall within the purview of the principle, and may trigger its application. The following are some examples:

The principle may be applied to determine questions relating to the interference with, or diversion of, waters of rivers flowing from one State to another. Thus, it is generally said that States should not abuse their rights in this regard, and that they have an obligation to refrain from any unwarranted interference with the flow of a river to the detriment of another State.[252] **1.163**

The right to expel foreigners is fully held by every State and is deduced from its very sovereignty. The position that a State has an unfettered right to expel aliens at its absolute discretion without just cause is recognized by some writers. However, courts and tribunals recognize that the State's right is not absolute, and emphasize that the right of expulsion can be exercised only in extreme instances, in the manner least injurious to the alien, and sufficient reasons must be advanced.[253] Lauterpacht recognized that the principle of abuse of rights is often applied in substance in order to draw the precise line of demarcation: **1.164**

> The conspicuous feature of these awards is the view that the undoubted right of expulsion degenerates into an abuse of rights whenever an alien who has been allowed to take up residence in the country, to establish his business and set up a home, is expelled without just reason, and that such an abuse of rights constitutes a wrong involving the duty of reparation.[254]

Similarly, although the right of a State to close its ports to foreign commerce is unequivocal, it is generally held that the unreasonable exercise of such right, without giving proper notice particularly to those frequently admitted to these ports, may constitute an international wrong establishing a duty of compensation.[255] **1.165**

A State's right to grant its nationality to individuals and its entitlement to the recognition by other States of that nationality is generally recognized only if it represents a genuine connection between the individual and the State granting its nationality. As shall be outlined below, the principle of abuse of rights is sometimes used by international courts and tribunals to ascertain the existence of a genuine bond of nationality between a State and an individual that confers upon the State the right to put forward an international claim on his behalf. **1.166**

Another right conferred by international law that may trigger the application of abuse of rights pertains to the right of a State to make use of its own territory. Although the State's right is recognized, it must refrain from acting in a manner prejudicial to the interests of other States. Thus, the State exercising its right must protect other States **1.167**

[252] Lauterpacht (n 190) 300.
[253] See the *Boffolo Case (of a general nature), Italian-Venezuelan Commission*, Reports of International Arbitral Awards (1903) vol X, 534.
[254] Lauterpacht (n 190) 297.
[255] ibid 297–98.

against any injurious acts from individuals within its territory. For example, as provided by one tribunal: 'No State has the right to use or permit the use of its territory in such a manner as to cause injury by fumes in or to the territory of another or to the properties or persons therein'.[256] In commenting on this decision Bin Cheng noted that the Tribunal 'struck a proper balance between a State's rights and obligations. Any overstepping of this limit would constitute an abuse of right'.[257]

1.168 A reference to the importance of abuse of rights in the context of the regime of the high seas is found in the 1953 Report of the International Law Committee which was submitted to the General Assembly. The Commission adopted a number of articles covering the basic aspects of the international regulation of fisheries. Pursuant to Article 3, States are under an obligation to accept, upon their nationals, any system of regulation of fisheries in any area of the high seas which an international authority, created within the framework of the UN, shall prescribe as being essential for the purpose of protecting the fishing resources against waste or extermination.

1.169 The Commission acknowledged that the principle of abuse of rights comprises the legal basis for the general rule formulated in Article 3 and noted the following:

> The Commission, in adopting the articles, was influenced by the view that the prohibition of abuse of rights is supported by judicial and other authority and is germane to the situation covered by the articles. A State which arbitrarily and without good reason, in rigid reliance upon the principle of the freedom of the seas, declines to play its part in measures reasonably necessary for the preservation of valuable, or often essential, resources from waste and exploitation, abuse a right conferred upon it by international law. The prohibition of abuse of rights, in so far as it constitutes a general principle of law recognised by civilised States, provides to a considerable extent a satisfactory legal basis for the general rule as formulated in article 3.[258]

1.170 It is further accepted that the principle applies not only to prevent the abuse of substantive rights, but also applies to preclude the abusive exercise of procedural rights. Thus, whilst a State has the right of access to an international court, the Court shall refrain from exercising its jurisdiction over the State or dismiss the claims as inadmissible, if the State abuses its procedural rights.[259] As rightly provided by Robert Kolb:

> Abuse of procedure a special application of the prohibition of abuse of rights, which is a general principle of international law as well as in municipal law. It consists of the

[256] The *Trail Smelter Case* (United States, Canada), (1949) Reports of International Arbitral Awards, (1941) vol III, 1905–82, Award of 11 March 1941.

[257] Cheng (n 122) 130.

[258] International Law Commission, 'Report of the International Law Commission Covering the Work of its Fifth Session' UN Doc A/CN.4/76, 1 June–14 August 1953, in Ybk of the International Law Commission 1953 (United Nations 1959) vol 2, para 100.

[259] Yuka Fukunaga, *Abuse of Process under International Law and Investment Arbitration* (2018) 33 ICSID Review 181, 184.

> use of procedural instruments or rights by one or more parties for purposes which are alien to those for which the procedural rights were established.[260]

As shall be discussed later, the importance of the principle of abuse of rights in international law can also be deduced from its recognition in international legal instruments such as the United Nations Convention on the Law of the Sea[261] and the European Convention for the Protection of Human Rights and Fundamental Freedoms.[262] **1.171**

Moreover, the view that the principle of abuse of rights is a potent principle of international law has been incessantly confirmed by prominent international law jurists. **1.172**

Accordingly, Hersch Lauterpacht noted that abuse of rights is a paramount principle of international law and is considered one of the basic elements of the international law of torts.[263] **1.173**

The renowned Bin Cheng mentioned the principle of abuse of rights as a general principle of international law and confirmed its acceptance by international courts and tribunals: **1.174**

> The principle of good faith which governs international relations controls also the exercise of rights by States. The theory of abuse of rights (*abus de droit*), recognised in principle both by the Permanent Court of International Justice and the International Court of Justice, is merely an application of this principle to the exercise of rights.[264]

Another scholar confirmed that the prohibition of abuse of process, which is inferred from the more general principle of good faith, is grounded in international law, specifically as a general principle of law in the meaning of Article 38 of the Statute of the ICJ.[265] **1.175**

To the same effect, Michael Byers also noted that owing to its widespread existence in national legal systems, states, judges, arbitrators, and scholars consider 'abuse of rights to be part of international law, whether as a general principle of law or as part of customary international law'.[266] **1.176**

Andreas Ziegler and Jorun Baumgartner recognized that the obligation to act in good faith is part of international law as a general principle of law and referred to abuse of rights as a particularization of the principle of good faith. They noted that: **1.177**

> Known in civil law jurisdictions as the abuse of rights doctrine, properly speaking and in common law jurisdictions as a specific application of torts law, scholarship and

[260] Robert Kolb, '*General Principles of Procedural Law*' in Andreas Zimmermann and others (eds), *The Statute of the International Court of Justice: A Commentary* (2nd edn, Oxford University Press 2012) para 49.
[261] Articles 294.1 and 300 of the United Nations Convention on the Law of the Sea (1982).
[262] Articles 17 and 35.3 of the European Convention for the Protection of Human Rights and Fundamental Freedoms (1953) (as amended in 1998).
[263] Lauterpacht (n 190) 303 and 306.
[264] Cheng (n 122) 121.
[265] Ascensio (n 118) 765–66.
[266] Byers (n 4) 397.

international jurisprudence seem to overwhelmingly accept it as a general principle of law or as part of customary international law.[267]

1.178 Another scholar who examined the status of the principle on the international level and considered the practice of international courts and tribunals submitted that:

> The decisions of some international tribunals and the practice of a number of states reveal that the principle of abuse of right has become accepted as part of international law and that states may, and often do, invoke the principle as the basis of an international claim. There is no substantial reason to exclude the application of the principle from international law; the extensive nature of the power and discretion of states and their often asserted freedom to exercise these rights as they see fit in an increasingly interdependent world makes the need for the application of the principle of abuse of right even more desirable.[268]

1.179 Additionally, others have confirmed that the principle comprises a potent principle limiting the exercise of rights conferred by international law and that it is applicable in international arbitration:

> [T]he principle constitutes a general principle of law and therefore applies to investment arbitration conducted under an investment agreement, regardless of an express agreement between the parties as to the applicable law. The right to investment arbitration given to an investor by an investment agreement is inherently subject to limitations under rules and principles of international law.[269]

1.180 In the context of the WTO, Mitchell provided that the principle of abuse of rights can be applied under the WTO Tribunal's jurisdiction. He also confirmed that it stems from the broader principle of good faith, it is a well-recognized general principle of international law, and is 'necessary to prevent the judicial character of WTO Tribunals from being abused by Members'.[270]

1.181 Similar to the question of abuse under municipal laws, international law relies on and endorses different criteria of abuse. Particularly, it is said that international law prohibits any malicious or unreasonable exercise of right, and forbids the evasion of a rule of law, a contractual or a treaty obligation under the guise of an alleged exercise of right.[271]

1.182 The balancing factor, or the reasonableness criterion, has been particularly emphasized by prominent scholars, including Bin Cheng, who noted that:

[267] Zeigler and Baumgartner (n 189) 30–31.
[268] Iluyomade (n 30) 72.
[269] Fukunaga (n 259) 185.
[270] Andrew Mitchell and David Heaton, 'The Inherent Jurisdiction of WTO Tribunals: The Select Application of Public International Law Required by Judicial Function' (2010) 31 Michigan Journal of International Law 561, 609, and 618.
[271] Cheng (n 122) 122–23.

It follows from this interdependence of rights and obligations that rights must be reasonably exercised. The reasonable and bona fide exercise of a right implies an exercise which is genuinely in pursuit of those interests which the right is destined to protect and which is not calculated to cause any unfair prejudice to the legitimate interests of another State, whether these interests be secured by treaty or by general international law. The exact lining dividing the right from the obligation, or, in other words, the line delimiting the rights of both parties is traced at a point where there is a reasonable balance between the conflicting interests involved.[272]

B. The Practice of International Courts and Tribunals

International courts and tribunals have referred to and applied the principle of abuse of rights on several occasions to preclude the abuse of different substantive and procedural rights. **1.183**

Despite the general acceptance of the principle as discussed above, it is not clear under what circumstances the use of the right in question constitutes an abuse. Accordingly, it is important to refer to and examine the practice of judicial and quasi-judicial bodies that applied, or considered applying, the principle of abuse of rights. **1.184**

Given that numerous investment arbitral awards are carefully examined and analysed in other sections, these awards shall not be discussed in this section. **1.185**

The following overview of cases is important in order to determine if the principle is recognized as part of international law; demonstrate different rights susceptible of being abused; pinpoint the high threshold applied; and ascertain the principle's conditions of application and the criteria used to establish an abuse. **1.186**

1. ICJ and PCIJ

Abuse of rights appears to have secured some measure of recognition on the part of the International Court of Justice ('ICJ') which has had several occasions to refer to the principle in its judgments. Although neither the ICJ Statute nor the ICJ Rules explicitly provide for the principle of abuse of right, its application to the merits and to the procedures is recognized owing to the perception that it constitutes a 'general principle of law' as per Article 38(1)(C) of the ICJ Statute.[273] **1.187**

From a practical perspective, the application of abuse of rights to preclude the abusive exercise of procedural rights may seem questionable given that, hitherto, the ICJ did not apply the principle in the context of procedural rights. However, it is to be highlighted that the ICJ did not explicitly or implicitly reject the principle's application. It **1.188**

[272] Cheng (n 122) 131–32.
[273] Fukunaga (n 259) 183.

merely provided on several occasions that the principle's conditions of application were not fulfilled. As rightly articulated by Kolb:

> The Court, however, has never found the conditions for an application of the principle to be fulfilled. But it did not reject the concept as such; it merely affirmed that its application was not warranted in the cases under consideration.[274]

1.189 The application of the principle has the effect of limiting a State's access to the Court in disregard to the jurisdiction which has been established by consensus between the disputing parties. Given that the right to access the Court is a sacred right, it should only be overridden in exceptional circumstances, where the damage resulting from the exercise of jurisdiction is manifest and unequivocal.[275]

1.190 A prudent reading of a number of the decisions that relied on or referred to the principle of abuse of rights confirms that the principle is an intrinsic part of international law. Furthermore, for the determination of an abuse of rights the question of subjective fault and intention is not necessarily of importance. It is rather advocated that the potency of the principle emanates from the desire to prevent an unfair exercise of rights; or an exercise of right for a purpose other than that for which the right was established.[276]

1.191 In the seminal case of *Barcelona Traction*, the ICJ considered the issue of piercing the corporate veil for the purpose of diplomatic protection of shareholders. The Government of Belgium brought a claim against Spain on behalf of its nationals, who owned shares in the Canadian corporation Barcelona Traction.

1.192 Although the ICJ rejected the Belgian Government's claim, the Court emphasized the importance of the abuse of rights principle as a protective measure to remedy unfairness and endorsed the 'deviation of purpose' as a criterion of abuse. The Court provided that requirements of fairness and equity may mandate that the corporate veil be pierced in cases of an abuse of right, particularly whereby the legal personality has been used for a purpose other than that for which it was originally intended to serve.

1.193 The Court explicitly provided that:

> Forms of incorporation and their legal personality have sometimes not been employed for the sole *purposes they were originally intended to serve*; sometimes the corporate entity has been unable to protect the rights of those who entrusted their financial resources to it; *thus inevitably there have arisen dangers of abuse, as in the case of many other institutions of law.* Here, then, as elsewhere, the law, confronted with economic realities, has had to provide protective measures and remedies in the interests of those within the corporate entity as well as of those outside who have dealings with it: the law has recognized that *the independent existence of the legal entity cannot be treated as an absolute.* It is in this context that the process of 'lifting the corporate

274 Kolb (n 260) para 40.
275 Fukunaga (n 259) 186.
276 Lauterpacht (n 190) 294–95.

veil' or 'disregarding the legal entity' has been found justified and equitable in certain circumstances or for certain purposes. The wealth of practice already accumulated on the subject in municipal law indicates that the veil is lifted, for instance, *to prevent the misuse of the privileges of legal personality, as in certain cases of fraud or malfeasance, to protect third persons such as a creditor or purchaser, or to prevent the evasion of legal requirements or of obligations.* [...] In accordance with the principle expounded above, the process of lifting the veil, being an exceptional one admitted by municipal law in respect of an institution of its own making, *is equally admissible to play a similar role in international law.* It follows that on the international plane also there may in principle be special circumstances which justify the lifting of the veil in the interest of shareholders.[277] (Emphasis added)

Furthermore, Judge Ammoun explicitly referred to the principle of abuse of rights as a general principle of international law: **1.194**

> Abuse of right, like denial of justice, is an international tort, contrary to the opinion which the Spanish Government seems to espouse. This is enshrined in a general principle of law which emerges from the legal systems of all nations.[278]

Another example illustrating the relevance of the abuse of rights principle in international law is the recent case of *Equatorial Guinea v France*. The relevant facts may be briefly recalled. A judicial investigation was conducted before the French courts concerning the misappropriation of public funds, including questions of how the son of Equatorial Guinea's president, Teodoro Nugema Obiang Mangue, acquired a luxury building in Paris, which was confiscated in 2012 after a finding that 'the building had been wholly or partly paid out of the proceeds of the offences under investigation'.[279] **1.195**

Obiang was made Second Vice-President of Equatorial Guinea in charge of defence and security in May 2012, and Equatorial Guinea argued that the confiscation of this building was improper as Obiang enjoyed diplomatic immunity and the residence was diplomatic property. **1.196**

In its Preliminary objections, France argued that the Court lacks jurisdiction on the grounds that Equatorial Guinea's claims amounted to an abuse of process. France submitted that Equatorial Guinea's application constituted an abuse of process 'because it was submitted in the manifest absence of any legal remedy and with the aim of covering abuses of rights committed in other respects'.[280] **1.197**

Whilst the majority did not hold that an abuse of process was established, the Court clearly recognized the principle and considered its application to prevent the abuse of *substantive* and *procedural* rights. However, the Court emphasized that the application **1.198**

[277] *Barcelona Traction, Light and Power Co, Ltd (Belgium v Spain)*, ICJ Judgment of 5 February 1970, paras 56–58.
[278] ibid, Separate Opinion of Judge Ammoun, 324.
[279] The case of *Immunities and Criminal Proceedings (Equatorial Guinea v France)*, Decision on the Preliminary Objections of 6 June 2018, [2016] ICJ Rep 1148, para 28.
[280] ibid para 141.

of the principle is only warranted in *exceptional* circumstances. To that end, the Court noted that:

> An abuse of process goes to the procedure before a court or tribunal and can be considered at the preliminary phase of these proceedings. In this case, the Court does not consider that Equatorial Guinea, having established a valid title of jurisdiction, should be barred at the threshold without clear evidence that its conduct could amount to an abuse of process. Such evidence has not been presented to the Court. It is only in exceptional circumstances that the Court should reject a claim based on a valid title of jurisdiction on the ground of abuse of process. The Court does not consider the present case to be one of those circumstances.
>
> As to the abuse of rights invoked by France, it will be for each Party to establish both the facts and the law on which it seeks to rely at the merits phase of the case. The Court considers that abuse of rights cannot be invoked as a ground of inadmissibility when the establishment of the right in question is properly a matter for the merits. Any argument in relation to abuse of rights will be considered at the stage of the merits of this case.[281]

1.199 Moreover, Judge Donoghue disagreed with the majority's narrow definition of abuse of rights and abuse of process, and opined that the Court should have found the Application inadmissible on the basis of the abuse of process principle:

> Despite conclusive evidence of the character of the conduct in which the Applicant engaged as a predicate for its assertion of rights in this Court, the Court allows the case to proceed to the merits, as if this is yet another disagreement about the nuances of the regime of diplomatic immunity. To preserve the integrity of its judicial function, I believe that the Court should not have allowed itself to be used to further this effort by the Applicant. It should instead have upheld the third preliminary objection [abuse of process]. Accordingly, I dissent.[282]

1.200 In the case of *Nottebohm (Liechtenstein v Guatemala)*, the Court clearly acknowledged that the principle is part of international law and delineated the conditions of its application. Liechtenstein claimed restitution and compensation from the Government of Guatemala on the ground that the latter had acted towards Friedrich Nottebohm, a citizen of Liechtenstein, in a manner contrary to international law.

1.201 The Court held that Liechtenstein's claim was inadmissible on grounds relating to Mr Nottebohm's nationality. It was acknowledged that the grant of nationality is entitled to recognition by other States only if it represents a genuine connection between the individual and the State granting its nationality. The existence of a genuine bond of nationality between a State and an individual confers upon the State the right to put forward an international claim on his behalf. Such bond was not established in this case. Mr

[281] ibid paras 150–51.
[282] ibid para 19.

Nottebohm, a German national, settled in Guatemala in 1905 and continued to reside there. After the beginning of the Second World War, he obtained Liechtenstein nationality and returned to Guatemala.

Owing to the fact that Mr Nottebohm's nationality was not based on any genuine prior **1.202**
link with Liechtenstein, and the sole object of his naturalization was to enable him to acquire the status of a neutral national in time of war, the Court held that Liechtenstein was not entitled to bring an international claim on his behalf against Guatemala.

In relation to an argument made on the basis of abuse of rights, Judge Read recognized **1.203**
the application of the principle in international law and emphasized the principle's conditions of application: it presupposes: (1) the existence of a right; (2) the abuse of that right; (3) and that the abuse of the right in question caused damage to the State invoking the principle. He noted:

> Abuse of right is based on the assumption *that there is a right to be abused.* In the present case it is based upon the assumption that Liechtenstein had the right under international law to naturalize Mr. Nottebohm, but that, in view of the special circumstances and the manner in which the right was exercised, *there was an improper exercise of the right* - an exercise so outrageous and unconscionable that its result, i.e. the national status conferred on Mr. Nottebohm, could not be invoked against Guatemala. The doctrine of abuse of right cannot be invoked by one State against another unless the State which is admittedly exercising its rights under international law *causes damage to the State invoking the doctrine.*[283](Emphasis added)

In the *Anglo-Norwegian Fisheries* case, Norway enacted a decree by which it reserved **1.204**
certain fishing grounds located off its northern coast for the exclusive use of its own fishermen. The question before the ICJ was whether this decree, which laid down a method for drawing the baselines from which the width of the Norwegian territorial waters had to be calculated, was valid under international law.

The ICJ held that neither the method nor the actual baselines stipulated under the 1935 **1.205**
Decree were contrary to international law and noted that:

> The base-line has been challenged on the ground that it does not respect the general direction of the coast. It should be observed that, however justified the rule in question may be, it is devoid of any mathematical precision. In order properly to apply the rule, regard must be had for the relation between the deviation complained of and what, according to the terms of the rule, must be regarded as the general direction of the coast. Therefore, one cannot confine oneself to examining one sector of the coast alone, *except in a case of manifest abuse*; nor can one rely on the impression that may be gathered from a large scale chart of this sector alone. In the case in point, the divergence

[283] The Case of *Nottebohm (Second Phase), (Liechtenstein v Guatemala)*, Judgment of 6 April 1955, [1955] ICJ Rep 37, Dissenting Opinion of Judge Read.

> between the base-line and the land formations is not such that it is a distortion of the general direction of the Norwegian coast.[284] (Emphasis added)

1.206 In the separate opinion of Judge Alvarez, he provided that the sovereignty of States is limited not only be the rights of other States but also by other rules and principles of international law such as the principle of abuse of rights.[285]

1.207 The theoretical significance of the principle has been referred to in other judgments and advisory opinions. For example, Judge Alvarez highlighted that any misuse or abuse of rights by a State is generally prohibited and used the right of passage as an example:

> A State may remain within the limits of its right—for instance, a right of passage—and yet may abuse this right if it take advantage of the passage to obtain information on the natural resources, strategic bases, fortifications, etc., of the State through which the passage takes place.[286]

1.208 More importantly, Judge Alvarez then confirmed that abuse of rights is an accepted principle in international law and provided that the ICJ should embrace it and further develop it owing to the fundamental interests it endeavours to advance.[287]

1.209 Similarly, Judge Weeramantry referred to abuse of rights as a 'well-established area of international law' when discussing sustainable development and its role in the resolution of environmentally related disputes.[288]

1.210 Abuse of rights appears to have secured some measure of recognition on the part of the PCIJ as well. In the case of *Certain German Interests in Polish Upper Silesia*, one of the issues before the Court related to Germany's powers in Upper Silesia during the period between the effective date of the Treaty of Versailles and the transfer of sovereignty to Poland. The PCIJ limited the right of Germany to dispose of certain assets by affirming that in the case of an abuse of rights the transfer or alienation of assets would amount to a violation of international law.

1.211 Furthermore, the Court confirmed that any abuse of right cannot be presumed, but must be adequately proved by the party invoking the application of the principle. The Court held that:

> Germany undoubtedly retained until the actual transfer of sovereignty the right to dispose of her property, and only a misuse of this right could endow an act of alienation with the character of a breach of the Treaty; such misuse cannot be presumed,

[284] See the *Fisheries Case (United Kingdom v Norway)*, Judgment of 18 December 1951, [1951] ICJ Rep 141–42.
[285] ibid 152, Individual Opinion of Judge Alvarez.
[286] See Competence of the General Assembly for the Admission of a State to the United Nations, Advisory Opinion of 3 March 1950, Dissenting Opinion by Judge M Alvarez, 15.
[287] ibid.
[288] See *Case Concerning the Gabčíkovo-Nagymaros Project (Hungary v Slovakia)*, Judgment of 25 September 1997, [1997] ICJ Rep 88, Separate Opinion of Vice-President Weeramantry, at 95.

> and it rests with the party who states that there has been such misuse to prove his statement.[289]

The PCIJ confirmed the possible application of the principle if proven by the party invoking it in its decision in the *Case of Free Zones of Upper Savoy and the District of Gex*. The Court suggested that if a State attempts to avoid its contractual obligations by resorting to measures having the same effect as the specifically prohibited acts, an abuse of rights would result: **1.212**

> A reservation must be made as regards the case of abuses of a right, since it is certain that France must not evade the obligations to maintain the zones by erecting a customs barrier under the guise of a control cordon. But an abuse cannot be presumed by the Court.[290]

Based on the above, although it is clear that the practice of the ICJ reveals the recognition and importance of the principle of abuse of rights in the context of international law, it reflects a restrictive application of the principle where it applies only in cases of manifest abuse. **1.213**

2. Iran-US Claims Tribunal

The principle of abuse of rights has been invoked on several occasions before the Iran-US Claims Tribunal. In this regard, the principle has been particularly invoked in relation to questions of nationality to preclude the admissibility of certain claims. **1.214**

In applying the principle, it seems that the Tribunal examines the conduct of the parties in order to ascertain if there is an abuse. It is of particular importance to note that the Tribunal primarily looks into the reasonableness of claimants' conduct and the purpose of exercising their right to renounce and/or acquire a specific nationality. If it becomes clear that such right is exercised for the purpose of obtaining an unfair advantage, or to obtain a right that it should have been barred from obtaining, an abuse of right might be established. **1.215**

The following three cases clarify that the principle of abuse of rights is recognized and regularly applied by the Iran-US Claims Tribunal and further pinpoint the circumstances that warrant its application. **1.216**

In the case of *James M Saghi v the Government of the Islamic Republic of Iran*, one of the Claimants had renounced his Iranian nationality when he was 18 years old, and later re-acquired it for the sole purpose of purchasing shares in a company that he believed could be owned only by Iranian nationals. **1.217**

[289] *Case Concerning Certain German Interests in Polish Upper Silesia (Germany v Poland)* PCIJ Rep Series A No 7, Judgment of 25 May 1926, 30.

[290] See the *Case of Free Zones of Upper Savoy and the District of Gex (France v Switzerland)*, PCIJ Series A/B No 46, Decision of 7 June 1932, 167.

1.218 The Tribunal refused to sanction or uphold this egregious conduct and applied the caveat to deny recovery for the expropriated shares on the ground that to do otherwise 'would permit an abuse of right'.[291]

1.219 Similarly, in the case of *Rouhollah Karubian v the government of the Islamic Republic of Iran*, Karubian was born in Tehran in 1912 and permanently resided in the United States in 1948, becoming a naturalized US citizen in 1954. However, between 1957 and 1973, he relied on his retained Iranian nationality to speculate on the Iranian real estate market, purchasing several parcels of undeveloped land.

1.220 The Respondent argued that the claims should be barred 'by principles of clean hands, estoppel, good faith and abuse of rights which operate in international law'. The Tribunal endorsed the Respondent's position and noted:

> The Tribunal must therefore assume that the Claimant purchased all the properties that are subject of these Claims in his capacity as an Iranian national after he had acquired United States nationality. He now claims in respect of those properties as a national of the United States. If the Tribunal were to allow him to recover against the Respondent in these circumstances, it would be permitting an abuse of right.[292]

1.221 Finally, in the case of *Frederica Lincoln Riahi v the Government of the Islamic Republic of Iran*, the Tribunal examined whether the Claimant's acquisition of real estate in Iran as an Iranian national and her subsequent claim before the Tribunal as a US national constituted an abuse of right. The Respondent advocated that general principles of international law such as the principle of abuse of rights is relevant to ascertain whether the caveat bars the claims on the merit. The Respondent submitted that the principle should apply to preclude claims arising of rights retained or acquired in violation of Iranian law.

1.222 In dismissing part of the Claimant's claims, the Tribunal held:

> Applying the rules established by the precedents of the Tribunal as discussed in the preceding paragraphs, the Tribunal holds, somewhat similar to its holding in Karubian, that the right to acquire real property in Iran by contract, apart from certain limited exceptions not relevant here, is a benefit reserved for Iranian nationals. The Claimant acquired the ASP Apartment by using the only possible nationality that she could invoke for purchasing that apartment, i.e. her Iranian nationality. Now she claims the same ownership right against the Government of Iran as a United States national. Allowing the Claimant to recover against the Respondent in this situation would be to permit an abuse of right.[293]

[291] The case of *James M Saghi v the Government of the Islamic Republic of Iran*, Case No 298, Award No 544-298-2, of 22 January 1993, Iran-US Claims Tribunal, vol 29 (Cambridge University Press 2000) 39–40.
[292] The case of *Rouhollah Karubian v The Islamic Republic of Iran*, Case No 419, Award No 569-419-2 of 6 March 1996, Iran-US Claims Tribunal, vol 32 (Cambridge University Press 2001) 40, para 161.
[293] The case of *Frederica Lincoln Riahi v The Government of the Islamic Republic of Iran*, Case No 485, Award No 600-485-1 of 27 February 2003, Iran-US Claims Tribunal, vol 37 (Cambridge University Press 2006) para 278.

Moreover, in his separate opinion. Mr Noori opined that the A18 caveat is rooted in a number of well-established and settled principles of international law that include the principles of good faith and abuse of right. He recognized that abuse of rights has been consistently upheld in a number of awards and then noted that 'there is no doubt that the principle of abuse of rights is a principle of international law'.[294] **1.223**

Based on the above, it appears evident that tribunals often apply the principle to bar a party from denying or alleging certain facts or courses of action owing to that party's previous conduct, in application to the established maxim *venire contra factum proprium*. **1.224**

3. WTO Tribunals

Abuse of rights has also been applied by the World Trade Organisation ('WTO') panels and WTO Appellate Body to prevent the abusive interpretation and application of treaty rights.[295] **1.225**

Article XX of the General Agreement on Tariffs and Trade ('GATT') on General Exceptions lays out a number of specific instances in which WTO members may be exempted from GATT rules. For example, paragraphs (b) and (g) of Article XX allow WTO members to adopt policy measures that are inconsistent with GATT disciplines, but necessary to protect human, animal, or plant life or health, or relating to the conservation of exhaustible natural resources. **1.226**

However, these measures should not be imposed to achieve any other purpose. The chapeau to Article XX stipulates that these measures should not apply in a manner that would constitute a disguised restriction on international trade. Scholars, as well as the WTO Appellate Body, have construed this to be a manifestation of the principle of abuse of rights.[296] **1.227**

In the case of *United States Import Prohibition of Certain Shrimp and Shrimp Products*, the Tribunal applied the principle and provided that any abuse of GATT Article XX (on General Exceptions)[297] is tantamount to an abuse of right and thus a violation of the treaty. The Tribunal explicitly stipulated that: **1.228**

> The chapeau of Article XX is, in fact, but one expression of the principle of good faith. This principle, at once a *general principle of law and a general principle of international law, controls the exercise of rights by states. One application of this general principle, the application widely known as the doctrine of abus de droit*, prohibits the abusive exercise

[294] The case of *Frederica Lincoln Riahi v The Government of the Islamic Republic of Iran*, Case No 485, Award No 600-485-1, Concurring and Dissenting Opinion of Assadollah Noori of 18 September 2003, Iran-US Claims Tribunal, vol 37 (Cambridge University Press 2006) para 41 and footnote 71.

[295] *Brazil-Retreaded Tyres*, WT/DS332/AB/R, WTO Appellate Body Report, 17 December 2007, 224–26; Todd Weiler, *The Interpretation of International Investment Law: Equality, Discrimination and Minimum Standards of Treatment in Historical Context* (Martinus Nijhoff 2013) 306.

[296] For example, see Kotuby and Sobota (n 176) 109.

[297] Article XX provides that Member States have the right to exceptionally take certain measures as long as they are not applied arbitrarily or in a discriminatory manner.

of a state's rights and enjoins that whenever the assertion of a right 'impinges *on the field covered by [a] treaty obligation, it must be exercised bona fide, that is to say, reasonably*.' (Emphasis added)[298]

1.229 This decision confirms the potency of abuse of rights in international law and sheds light on the criterion of abuse endorsed and applied by the Tribunal. As apparent from the decision, the Tribunal provided that finding an abuse requires a delicate exercise of marking the line of equilibrium between the competing rights and interests of the Member States in order to assess the abusive nature of the measure applied.[299]

1.230 Thus, it appears evident that the Tribunal endorsed the criterion of reasonableness in order to assess the existence of an abuse. This was also confirmed in other cases decided by the Appellate Body of the WTO.[300]

V. Conclusion

1.231 The omnipresence of the principle of abuse of rights in civil legal systems is evident. The above review testifies that civil legal systems endorse a general principle of abuse of rights. While it originated in, and was limited to, the sphere of property law, now it is endorsed as a principle with general application.[301] Thus, the generality of the principle, as required in general principles of law, is to a certain extent satisfied.[302]

1.232 However, a review of the discussed legal systems conveys that such ubiquity of the principle does not necessarily reflect a uniform legal basis of the principle's existence, or a uniform method of how it is utilized to prevent an abuse of right.

1.233 Its scope of application seems rather indefinite. Some legal systems have explicitly spelled out the conditions *sine qua non* for its application. This approach is arguably advantageous as it may assist the courts in their determination of an abuse of right. Other laws preferred to merely indicate that an abuse of right is prohibited, leaving it to the decision maker to establish guidelines and criteria of what constitutes abuse.

1.234 Finally, the legal basis upon which abuse is established may differ depending on the scope of abuse of rights in the respective law. Some systems use the principle to preclude any form of abuse, whereas other systems may invoke the broader principle of good faith to tackle different forms of abuse.

1.235 Despite such variation, it seems plausible to infer that all reviewed systems have intrinsic rules to preclude the abusive exercise of any right (substantive or procedural).

[298] Decision rendered by the WTO Appellate Body in the case of *United States—Import Prohibition of Certain Shrimp and Shrimp Products* (12 October 1998) WT/DS58/AB/Rpara 158.
[299] ibid, para 159.
[300] WTO Appellate Body in the case of *United States—Standard for Reformulated and Conventional Gasoline and Like Products of National Origin* (WT/DS2/AB/R) (1996) 35 ILM 603, 626.
[301] Walton (n 172) 87; Walton (n 25) 505
[302] Lauterpacht (n 190) 300–05.

In relation to the common law, the principle's application to limit abuse of procedural rights appears conspicuous. As to substantive abuse, while it appears that the common law is more restrictive in its limitation on rights, certain principles may operate as a qualification/limitation to the exercise of rights. As such, it is submitted that under common law, abuse of rights does not generally give rise to a cause of action unless it falls under the scope of a pre-existing tort. 1.236

On a different note, many advocate that the common law is influenced by international law and generally accepted principles.[303] As stated by Lord Denning in the case of *Trendtex*: 'the rules of international law, as existing from time to time, do form part of our English law'.[304] Given that abuse of rights is generally considered part of international law, and has emerged as a general principle of law as shall be discussed later,[305] it is submitted that such recognition may bring the principle of abuse of rights into the common law.[306] 1.237

303 See Michael Kirby, 'The Growing Impact of International Law on the Common Law' (2012) 33 Adelaide Law Review 7, 11–12, and 15; Malcolm N Shaw, *International Law* (6th edn, Cambridge University Press 2008) 138.

304 *Trendtex Trading Corporation v Central Bank of Nigeria* [1977] QB 529, 554.

305 Lauterpacht (n 190) 300–06; Byers (n 4) 397.

306 It is worth mentioning that the United Kingdom argued for the application of abuse of rights in the Fisheries arbitration case. *United Kingdom v Iceland*, Memorial of the Merits of the Dispute submitted by the Government of the United Kingdom [1973] ICJ Pleadings 267, paras 153–54; Byers (n 4) 397.

2

Commentary on the Principle: Conditions of Application and Limitation

I. Introduction

A review of the application of abuse of rights in the above-mentioned legal systems makes it feasible to draw the conditions *sine qua non* for its application. Such a review equally confirms that legal systems apply different criteria to establish an abuse of right.[1] **2.01**

In this section one shall endeavour to distil the concept of abuse of rights to its essential elements. This shall be undertaken by shedding light on: (II) the conditions necessary for its application; and the principle's areas of concern (III). **2.02**

In doing so, one aims to examine general convergence in relation to the elements of the principle, delineate any limitations or challenges in its application (in its conditions or as a result of its application), and highlight responses to such challenges prior to seeking its introduction/application as a general principle in international arbitration. **2.03**

In discussing the conditions of application, including the different criteria adopted to establish an abuse of right, the limitations of each criterion are to be examined. It shall be submitted that focusing on the 'balancing factor' criterion (reasonableness) qualifies as the most solid and sound criterion of abuse. **2.04**

While focus remains on the legal systems reviewed above, one endeavours to refer to a wider range of laws in order to suggest further consensus in relation to certain issues regarding the principle's conditions and its application. **2.05**

[1] Irina Petrova, 'Stepping on the Shoulders of a Drowning Man" The Doctrine of Abuse of Right as a Tool for Reducing Damages for Lost Profits: Troubling Lessons from the Patuha and Himpurna Arbitrations' (2004) 35 Georgetown Journal of International Law 455, 463.

II. Conditions of Application

2.06 An examination of the principle's application reveals that there is consensus among the different laws on the principal elements of abuse of rights.

2.07 Precisely, the application of abuse of rights assumes the existence of an acknowledged legal right (A); and that such right ceases legal protection given that it has been abused by the right holder (B).

2.08 Moreover, the act in question must have caused harm to the other party. The damage or loss sustained may be material or moral damages.[2] Once a court is satisfied that an abuse is established, it will either award damages to the aggrieved party, or will grant specific performance, i.e. order the right-holder to refrain from, or cease, the abusive action.[3]

A. The Existence of a Legal Right

2.09 Abuse of rights presumes the existence of a right and presupposes that the conduct/act in question is exercised within the formal limits of the right.[4]

2.10 This condition raises three issues that merit clarification. It merits a brief outline on: (1) the definition and concept of a 'right'; (2) the meaning of acting within the formal limits of a right; as well as elaborating (3) the different rights covered by the principle of abuse of rights.

1. The definition of a right in the context of abuse of rights

2.11 Much has been said regarding the definition and scope of a right.[5] On the one hand, Bernhard Windscheid, influenced by the writings of Savigny, advocated an individualistic perception of a right and emphasized the superiority of the will.[6] According to this

[2] Elspeth Reid, 'Abuse of Rights in Scots Law' (1998) 2 Edinburgh Law Review 129, 131; Babatunde O Iluyomade, 'The Scope and Content of a Complaint of Abuse of Right in International Law' (1975) 16 Harvard International Law Journal 47, 75; *Cementownia SA v Republic of Turkey*, ICSID Case No ARB (AF)/06/2, Award of 17 September 2009, para 171 where the Tribunal acknowledged the possibility of awarding moral damages in cases of abuse of rights.

[3] Julio Cueto-Rua, 'Abuse of Rights' (1975) 35 Louisiana Law Review 965, 991; Article 7.2 of the Spanish Civil Code.

[4] AN Yiannopoulos, 'Civil Liability for Abuse of Right: Something Old, Something New . . . ', (1994) 54 Louisiana Law Review 1195, 1195; Alexandre Kiss, 'Abuse of Rights' in Rudolf Bernhardt (ed), *Encyclopedia of Public International Law* (North-Holland 1992) vol 1, para 2; Gianluigi Palombella, 'The Abuse of Rights and the Rule of Law' in András Sajó (ed), *Abuse: The Dark Side of Fundamental Rights* (Eleven International 2006) 9–10; Iluyomade (n 2) 48.

[5] For a detailed account of the different definitions of a 'right', see Roscoe Pound, 'Legal Rights' (1915) 26 International Journal of Ethics 92.

[6] Bernhard Windscheid, '*Lehrbuch Des Pandektenrechts*' (1862), cited in Anna Di Robilant, 'Abuse of Rights: The Continental Drug and the Common Law' (2010) 61 Hastings Law Journal 687, 670; 670; Robert Alexy, 'Individual Rights and Collective Goods', in Carlos Nino (ed), *Rights* (New York University Press 1992) 164; David M Rabban, *Law's History: American Legal Thought and the Transatlantic Turn to History* (Cambridge University Press 2013) 112 (discussing Savigny's theory that possession is 'protected as a manifestation of individual will, the intent to hold property against the world'); Roscoe Pound, 'The Scope and Purpose of Sociological Jurisprudence' (1911) 25 Harvard Law Review 140, 143.

view, a right is regarded as the sphere of the right holder's absolute and unlimited will. Windscheid provided that a right 'assigns each individual the sphere in which his will posits law for all other individuals; if the individual is not respected in this sphere, he may complain to the state'.[7]

The above ideology of rights corresponds to the 'will theory of rights' advocated by Hart,[8] whereby he viewed legal rights in terms of the law granting the right holder the 'exclusive control, more or less extensive, over another person's duty'.[9] To Hart, the conception of rights is significantly individualistic, as he believed that the purpose of rights is to foster the individual autonomy.[10] 2.12

This depiction of rights serves to grant the right holder the ultimate possible scope for free action.[11] However, it is very individualistic, formal, and fails to take into consideration the social needs, purpose of rights, or the ends aimed at by conferring rights.[12] Thus, such an individualistic conception of rights would not accommodate the principle of abuse of rights, as the latter draws clear limitation to one's exercise of his subjective rights and advocates that one's freedom is limited by the rights and interests of others.[13] It has been stated that an 'utterly individualistic notion of right, as the one maintained by Windscheid, leaves no room for abuse of right'.[14] 2.13

On the other hand, Rudolph von Jhering, who was regarded as one of the most reputable legal scholars in the nineteenth century, equated rights to individual interests.[15] To this school of legal thought, a right denotes an *interest*, recognized and protected by the law to fulfil a certain purpose:[16] 'power allocated for the purpose of satisfying interests worth protecting'.[17] According to Jhering, perceiving a right in an abstract way, 2.14

[7] Helge Dedek, 'From Norms to Facts: The Realization of Rights in Common and Civil Private Law' (2010) 56 McGill Law Journal 77, 99, citing Bernhard Windscheid, *Die Actio des römischen Civilrechts, vom Standpunkte des heutigen Rechts* (Julius Buddeus 1856) 3.

[8] Herbert Adolphus Hart, '*Essays on Bentham* (Oxford University Press 1982) 181–82.

[9] ibid 183.

[10] In this regard, Hart equates the right holder to a *sovereign*. ibid; William E Edmundson, *An Introduction to Rights* (2nd edn, Cambridge University Press 2012) 98.

[11] The definitions given by Savigny, Kant, and Puchta in Pound (n 6) 143.

[12] NM Korkunov, *General Theory of Law*, English Translation by W. G Hastings, (2nd edn, The Macmillan Company 1922) 107–08; James Harrington Boyd, 'Socialization of the Law' (1917) 22 American Journal of Sociology 822, 824.

[13] see Michael Byers, 'Abuse of Rights: An Old Principle, A New Age' (2002) 47 McGill Law Journal 389, 397; John H Crabb, 'The French Concept of Abuse of Rights' (1964) 6 Inter-American Law Review 1, 8.

[14] Yiannopoulos (n 4) 1195, footnote 114.

[15] Rudolph V Jhering, *Geist des römischen Rechts auf den verschiedened Stufen seiner Entwicklung* (5th edn, Leipzig 1906) Part 3, 339, cited in Alexy (n 6) 164; John H Hallowell, *The Decline of Liberalism as an* Ideology (Kegan Paul, Trench, Trubner & Co Ltd 1946) 65.

[16] Hasso Hofmann, 'From Jhering to Radbruch: On the Logic of Traditional Legal Concepts to the Social Theories of Law to the Renewal of Legal Idealism' in Damiano Canale, Paolo Grossi, and Hasso Hofmann (eds), *A History of the Philosophy of Law in the Civil Law World, 1600-1900* (Springer 2009) 307; Pound (n 6) 143; René David, 'The Legal Systems of the World: Their Comparison and Unification' in *International Encyclopaedia of Comparative Law* (Martinus Nijhoff 1975) vol 2, 22; Cueto-Rua (n 3) 99–96; Hofmann (n 16) 308; Iredell Jenkins 'Rudolf Von Jhering' (1961) 14 Vanderbilt Law Review 169, 172.

[17] Rabban (n 6) 111–12.

without looking at the social purpose behind conferring it upon the right holder, materially defies 'social reality'.[18]

2.15 Defining rights in terms of securing the interests socially accepted and legally protected also corresponds to Bentham[19] and MacCormick's[20] perception of rights, namely the 'benefit theory of rights'.[21] The 'interest' or 'benefit' theory of rights has been criticized by some legal jurists in terms of failing to carefully define interests.[22] Despite such criticism, such understanding of rights influenced many scholars, including Roscoe Pound[23] and David Lyons, who advocated that this conception of rights has universally superseded the rather individualistic and abstract ideology of rights.[24]

2.16 A prudent reading of the *interest theory* of 'rights' implies that if there is no interest, or such interest is not a legitimate one reflecting an acknowledged purpose, there is no right.[25]

2.17 One is persuaded to endorse this definition of rights as it clearly illustrates the rationale of abuse of rights. It defines rights in terms of interests/benefits and acknowledges that each right is conferred upon an individual by the legal authority to fulfil a certain purpose.[26] It is submitted that defining rights in terms of interests legally protected and acknowledging that rights are conferred upon individuals for the satisfaction of a certain purpose 'sets outer limits for the exercise of rights'.[27]

2.18 Thus, acknowledging interests as the ultimate idea behind rights, and subsequently, placing emphasis on social or collective interests rather than individual interests, led to introducing and accepting the principle of abuse of rights.[28] Roscoe Pound declared

[18] ibid 106. Moreover, it is submitted that the 'will theory' has serious flaws in explaining duty rights, inalienable rights, and rights of children. George W Rainbolt, *The Concept of Rights* (Springer 2006) 34–38; Corsin Bisaz, *The Concept of Group Rights in International Law: Groups as Contested Right-Holders, Subjects and Legal Persons* (Nijhoff 2012) 14; Hallowell (n 15) 63–65.

[19] Edmundson (n 10) 97; Jeremy Bentham 'Of Laws in General', in H.LA Hart (ed), *The Works of Jeremy Bentham* (Athlone Press 1970); Jeremy Bentham, *An Introduction of the Principles of Morals and Legislation* (Athlone Press London 1970) 206; Joseph Raz's definition of rights in Joseph Raz, *The Morality of Freedom* (Oxford University Press 1986) 166.

[20] Neil MacCormick, 'Rights in Legislation', in PMS Hacker and J Raz (eds), *Law, Morality and Society, Essays in Honour of H. L. A. Hart* (Oxford University Press 1977) 189.

[21] Amongst the other related definitions of rights is that of *Regelsberger* where rights denote the authority of the will that is recognized by the law for the satisfaction of certain interests. Ferdinand Regelsberger and George S. Maridakis, *General Principles of the Law of Pandects* (1935) 99 translated and cited in Yiannopoulos (n 4) 1195, footnote 114.

[22] Korkunov (n 12) 112–15; James Gordley, *The Jurists: A Critical History* (Oxford University Press 2013) 289.

[23] Rabban (n 6) 107.

[24] Pound (n 6) 143; David Lyons, 'Rights, Claimants, and Beneficiaries' (1969) 6 American Philosophical Quarterly 173. However, other authors have attempted to defend the 'will theory' of rights. Paul Graham, 'The Will Theory of Rights: Defence' (1996) 15 Law and Philosophy 257.

[25] Jenkins (n 16) 172; Neil Duxbury, 'Jhering's Philosophy of Authority' (2007) 27 Oxford Journal of Legal Studies 23, 32–33. It has been submitted that the law does not protect any interest, but only interests that the right holder is ought to have according to the legislator or the legal authority conferring the right in question. Bisaz (n 18) 15.

[26] Pound (n 6) 140–41.

[27] Yiannopoulos (n 4) 1195, footnote 114.

[28] Roscoe Pound calls this stage the 'socialisation of law' in Roscoe Pound, 'The End of Law as Developed in Legal Rules and Doctrines' (1914) 27 Harvard Law Review 195, 226.

that this ideology of rights has led legal systems to limit the exercise of property rights and prohibit the anti-social and/or the abusive exercise of rights.[29]

Moreover, this description of rights greatly resembles that of Josserand who provided, in the context of abuse of rights, that: **2.19**

> [R]ights are bestowed by the State on a human being taking into consideration the satisfaction of his interests, not any interest, but legitimate interests [. . .] when the holder of the right exercises his right without any interest, or for the satisfaction of an illegitimate interest [. . .] that it can be said that he abuses and therefore ceases to have the power to request the protection of the law.[30]

Based on the above, understanding the ideology of rights as a power conferred by the legal authority upon the right holder, to advance legally protected *interests* in order to satisfy a certain purpose, seems to be the best depiction of rights that can accommodate the essence of the principle of abuse of rights.[31] As stated by the prominent Bin Cheng: **2.20**

> [E]very right is the legal protection of a legitimate interest. An alleged exercise of a right not in furtherance of such interest, but with the malicious purpose of injuring others can no longer claim legal protection of the law. Malitiis non est indulgendum [malice must not be indulged].[32]

2. An act within the formal limits of the right

Abuse of rights presupposes that the act in question is done within the formal limits of a given right. This necessarily excludes from the ambit of abuse of rights two types of conduct often confused with abuse of rights: acts done *without* a right, and acts in *excess* of the scope of the right. **2.21**

Where an individual's action is undertaken without a right, this is purely an illicit act, or an ultra vires, but not an abuse of a right; it is impossible to speak of an abuse of a right which does not exist.[33] **2.22**

Additionally, where the conduct of an individual deviates from the official limits of a right and demonstrates conduct outside or in excess of the scope of the right, this is simply an excessive act: acts beyond the boundaries of the right, but not an abuse of the right.[34] A contrario, abuse of rights is an act done *within the formal limits* of a **2.23**

[29] ibid.

[30] Louis Josserand, *De L'esprit des droits et de leur relativité: Théorie dite de l'abus des droits* (2nd edn, 1939) 388 cited and translated in Cueto-Rua (n 3) 996.

[31] Yiannopoulos (n 4) 1195, footnote 114.

[32] Bin Cheng, *General Principles of Law as Applied by International Courts and Tribunals* (Cambridge University Press 2006) 122.

[33] Cueto-Rua (n 3) 983; FP Walton, 'Motive as an Element in Torts in the Common and in the Civil Law' (1909) 22 Harvard Law Review 505, 501.

[34] David Angus, 'Abuse of Rights in Contractual Matters in the Province of Quebec' (1962) 8 McGill Law Journal 150, 151; DJ Devine, 'Some Comparative Aspects of the Doctrine of Abuse of Rights' (1964) Acta Juridica 148.

right, but fails to enjoy legal protection given the circumstances in which the right was exercised.[35]

2.24 If one enjoys a *pedestrian* path easement over another's land,[36] and if the easement right holder decides to drive his *car* across the property, this is not an abuse of right, but is rather an act in *excess* of, and outside the scope of, the right. The right is defined and qualified and does not include the right to use an automobile. Thus, such conduct simply demonstrates acts beyond the boundaries of the right and may comprise a different tort, such as trespass.[37] Moreover, it is not an abuse of right if the individual does not have the right to enter onto the adjoining property in the first place (does not enjoy a pedestrian path easement in the first place).

2.25 A contrario, if the right holder exercised his right within its formal limits albeit unreasonably, or for a purpose other than that for which the right was granted, this may constitute an abuse. For example, if the right holder constantly walked across the property for no legitimate or serious reason, other than to annoy the neighbours or to harass them, this may qualify as an abuse of right.[38]

2.26 The above distinction reveals that the scope of application of abuse of rights as opposed to excessive acts may depend on the nature and the limitation/qualification imposed on the right in question. Rights that are defined in general terms, conferred in an abstract manner, and do not have a priori statutory or judicial qualification may be more subject to the possibility of being abused. For such rights, the principle serves as a tool to introduce a posteriori judicial qualification.[39] On the other hand, acts done outside of, or in excess of, the scope of rights seem to relate more to rights that are carefully defined and qualified.[40] Thus, abuse of rights enables the decision maker to articulate more detailed rules, or qualifications, with regard to a right conferred in general terms.[41]

2.27 The presumption that one must have a right in order to speak of an abuse of rights is often emphasized by scholars and courts/arbitral tribunals.[42] This is fortified by the

[35] Cueto-Rua (n 3) 983; Angus (n 34), 151.
[36] Crabb (n 13) 11.
[37] ibid.
[38] ibid.
[39] Palombella (n 4) 11.
[40] Crabb (n 13) 17; Kazuaki Sono and Yasuhiro Fujioka, 'The Role of the Abuse of Right Doctrine in Japan' (1975) 35 Louisiana Law Review 1037, 1046–47; Palombella (n 4) 11; Soliman Morcos, *Al Wafi Fi Sharh Al Qanun Al Madani (A Treatise on the Explanation of the Civil Code)* (1988 edn) vol 2, 355. This conclusion is further manifested by the fact that civil legal systems, as well as international law, often confer rights in general terms and thus embrace the principle of abuse of rights, unlike common law systems where rights are rather defined and qualified, and hence it is usually provided that an abuse of rights principle is not necessary. Pierre Catala and John A Weir, 'Delict and Torts: A Study in Parallel, Part II' (1964) 38 Tulane Law Review 221, 237–38.
[41] Sono and Fujioka (n 40) 1046–47.
[42] Robert Biever, 'Speech' in Council of Europe, *Abuse of Rights and Equivalent Concepts: The Principle and its Present Day Application* (Strasbourg 1990) 21; Eric De Brabandere, '"Good Faith", "Abuse of Process" and the Initiation of Investment Treaty Claims' (2012) 3 Journal of International Dispute Settlement 619–20; Yiannopoulos (n 4) 1195; Petrova (n 1) 469; George A Rosenberg, 'The Notion of Good Faith in the Civil Law of Quebec' (1960) 7 McGill Law Journal 2, 21; *ConocoPhillips v The Bolivarian Republic of Venezuela*, ICSID Case No ARB/07/30, Decision on Jurisdiction and the Merits of 3 September 2013, para 273; *Chevron Corporation (USA) and Texaco Petroleum Company (USA) v The Republic of Ecuador*, UNCITRAL, PCA Case No 34877, Interim Award of 1 December 2008, para 137.

case of *State Bank of Commerce v Demco of Louisiana*,[43] which pertained to lender liability. In this case, an officer of the lending institution had written a letter pertaining to the debtor and sent it to a third party. The debtor filed a case and sought damages given that the letter caused injury to his business and to his reputation. The Court refused to apply abuse of rights given that the lending institution (State Bank) did not have the right to send this letter in the first place, and thus it was futile to speak of an abuse of rights.[44]

3. Rights susceptible to abuse

A review of the different civil legal systems testify to the historic evolution of abuse of rights. While it first began operating in the domain of property law,[45] its scope and reach then extended to all legal matters, and it became established that there is a general principle of abuse of rights that limits the abusive exercise of any right.[46] **2.28**

Thus, the scope of abuse of rights includes both substantive[47] and procedural rights.[48] **2.29** It is interesting to note a Dutch case that involved the question of whether the right to appeal was abusive.[49] In this case, a husband had appealed against a decree of separation. It was provided that the husband had no serious interest in appealing the decree, but appealed for the purpose of harming his wife. The husband's attorney served the writ of appeal late in order to prevent the wife from cross-appealing the separation decree. According to Dutch law, if such appeal was allowed, the wife would have been precluded from the alimony. The Court found that this procedural right has been exercised for a purpose other than that for which it was granted and was exercised without a legitimate interest.[50]

Moreover, it is submitted that any right is susceptible to being abused.[51] In this regard, **2.30** one partially disagrees with the distinction made by Josserand and the consequences

[43] *State Bank of Commerce v Demco of Louisiana*, 483 So 2d 1119 (La App 5th Cir 1986).

[44] ibid 1122.

[45] Albert Mayrand, 'Abuse of Rights in France and Quebec' (1974) 34 Louisiana Law Review 994.

[46] *Hero Lands Co v Texaco, Inc*, 310 So 2d 93, 99 (La 1975); Walton (n 33) 505; Byers (n 13) 392; Catala and Weir (n 40) 222–25; Cueto-Rua (n 3) 967.

[47] *Sanborn v Oceanic Contractors, Inc*, 448 So 2d 91 (La. 1984); Glenda Redmann, 'Abuse of Rights: An Overview of the Historical Evolution and the Current Application in Louisiana Contracts' (1987) 32 Loyola Law Review 946, 964; *Kawaguchi v Mizunoya*, 24 Minshu 2015 (Sup Ct, 11 Dec 1970); *Obonai v Orizume Sangyo Co*, 19 Minshu 2212 (Sup Ct, 21 Dec 1965) cited in Sono and Fujioka (n 40) 1044–45 (applying abuse of rights in contractual disputes in Japan).

[48] Yasuhei Taniguchi, 'Good Faith and Abuse of Procedural Rights in Japanese Civil Procedure' (2000) 8 Tulane Journal of International and Comparative Law 167, 173–75; Walton (n 33) 508; Vera Bolgar, 'Abuse of Rights in France, Germany, and Switzerland: A Survey of a Recent Chapter in Legal Doctrine' (1975) 35 Louisiana Law Review 1015, 1033; Byers (n 13) 392; Catala and Weir (n 40) 225; Cueto-Rua (n 3) 967; Mayrand (n 45) 999 (regarding French law and law of Quebec); Chris Brunner, 'Abuse of Rights in Dutch Law' (1977) 37 Louisiana Law Review 729, 743–45 regarding Dutch law; Devine (n 34) 154; Egyptian Court of Cassation, Session held on 27 February 2012, Challenge No 266, Judicial Year 71; Egyptian Court of Cassation, Session held on 13 February 2010, Challenge No 3317, Judicial Year 67; Egyptian Court of Cassation, Session held on 26 May 2004, Challenge No 5036, Judicial Year 72; Egyptian Court of Cassation, Session held on 4 May 1999, Challenge No 4464, Judicial Year 68.

[49] HR 26 June 1959, NJ 1961, No 553 cited in Brunner (n 48) 743.

[50] Brunner (n 48) 743.

[51] This equally applies to any arbitration-related right: ICC Case No 13209/DK/RCH of 25 November 2005, referred to in Wilske (2009a), (n 59) 207; *Phoenix Action v The Czech Republic*, ICSID Case No ARB/06/5, Award of

he reached based on such distinction. According to Josserand, certain rights may be regarded as absolute rights.[52]

2.31 Absolute rights are those sacrosanct rights that are conferred by the law upon the individual to be exercised without any limitation. Absolute rights, according to Josserand, are not susceptible of being abused given that the interests of the society lies in the uncontrolled exercise of those rights. A parents' right to oppose their child's marriage was often referred to as the epitome of an absolute right.[53]

2.32 However, it is difficult to identify a set of legal rights that are not susceptible to being subject to statutory/judicial qualifications and limits, or not susceptible to abuse.[54]

2.33 In this regard, while Josserand expressly provides that the right of a parent to oppose a child's marriage is the epitome of absolute rights, this submission is rather questionable given that there are cases, including a case examined by Josserand himself, where it was held that the father's refusal of his son's marriage was abusive.[55] Accordingly, the sanctity of rights and absolutism theory may appear vacuous in content.

2.34 Rather than advocating the existence of absolute rights, it is submitted that a more coherent conclusion would be that rights which are carefully defined, limited, and qualified in their scope are less susceptible to abuse,[56] and that certain rights may have thus far successfully resisted being subject to an abuse test.[57]

2.35 Abuse of rights is not limited to private rights, but also applies to prevent the abuse of public law rights.[58] In an arbitration held under the auspices of the Cairo Regional Centre for International Commercial Arbitration ('CRCICA'), the application of abuse of rights in administrative law and to administrative contracts was addressed.[59] An administrative contract was concluded for the provision of paper for printing from an

15 April 2009, para 107; ('every rule of law includes an implied clause that it should not be abused'); *Philip Morris Asia Limited v The Commonwealth of Australia*, PCA Case No 2012-12, Award on Jurisdiction and Admissibility of 17 December 2015, under UNCITRAL Rules, para 404; Karel Daele, *Challenge and Disqualification of Arbitrators in International Arbitration* (Kluwer Law International 2012) 103–04; Christoph Brunner, 'Note—Federal Supreme Court, 28 April 2000' (2000) 18 ASA Bulletin 566, 576.

[52] Harold C Gutteridge, 'Abuse of Rights' (1935) 5 Cambridge Law Journal 22, 28
[53] ibid; Morcos (n 40) 354.
[54] Paolo Grossi, 'Legal Absolutism and Private Law in the XIX Century' in Alessandro Pizzorusso (ed), *Italian Studies in Law* (Martinus Nijhoff 1994) 8 ('the absolutist house of cards crudely appeared as what in large part it had really been: an intelligent, very clever fiction'; Morris R Cohen, 'On Absolutisms in Legal Thought' (1936) 84 University of Pennsylvania Law Review 681; Catala and Weir (n 40) 235; Crabb (n 13) 16–18.
[55] *B v C*, Lyon, 23 January 1907, Dalloz 1908.2.73, note Josserand, Sirey 1909.2.310, cited in Crabb (n 13) 16; Walton (n 33) 507–08.
[56] Joseph M Perillo, 'Abuse of Rights: A Pervasive Legal Concept' (1996) 27 Pacific Law Journal 37, 48–9.
[57] Crabb (n 13) 16.
[58] It is submitted that abuse of rights is an intrinsic part of administrative law: the concept of *détournement de pouvoir*. Mayrand (n 45) 1002 citing Josserand, *De L'esprit des Droits Et De Leur Relativité* (2nd edn, 1939), ('when a public administrator commits a distortion (or misuse, "détournement") of power, it is also at the same time an abuse of right for which he is liable, with only this difference that the abuse concerns a right related to the public function and not to a private function.').
[59] *Two African printing companies v An African printing authority*, Final Award, CRCICA Case No 154 of 2000, 3 August 2000, in MEI Alam Eldin (ed), *Arbitral Awards of the Cairo Regional Centre for International Commercial Arbitration II* (Kluwer Law International 2003) 45–50.

Asian company. Pursuant to the contract, Claimants were required to issue a letter of guarantee of 5 per cent of the value of products to be reduced after each shipment. The Respondent then requested a new letter of guarantee of 20 per cent of the value of one of the shipments. Although this was not stipulated in the contract, Claimants submitted it. A *force majeure* existed due to the civil war that occurred in the country of the Asian company. The Respondent claimed the value of the two letters of guarantee did not pay the price of other shipments and started another procurement. Claimants initiated arbitration proceedings.

The arbitral Tribunal, sitting in Egypt and applying Egyptian law, recognized first that all contracts, civil and administrative, are subject to the principle of good faith. Furthermore, the Tribunal provided that the Respondent had breached the good faith principle and had abused its rights.[60] In reaching this conclusion, the Tribunal relied on several judgments of the Egyptian Administrative Courts (State Council), whereby abuse of rights was applied to administrative contracts to limit the abusive exercise of rights by administrative authorities. **2.36**

The principle is recognized as a general principle of international law,[61] and has been used to limit the abuse of rights under public international law, such as: the right to expel aliens, the State's right to close its ports to foreign commerce, to assess the reasonableness of the discretionary power of States, and to the question of interference with or diversion of waters of rivers that flows from one State to another.[62] **2.37**

The principle similarly applies to limit the abusive exercise of rights conferred upon the courts/arbitrators.[63] **2.38**

In the ICSID case of *Saipem SpA v Bangladesh*, the Tribunal had to examine whether the Bangladesh Court committed an abuse of rights. The Bangladesh Court exercised its right of supervisory jurisdiction over an ICC arbitral Tribunal and decided to revoke the Tribunal's authority. Upon examining the factual matrix of the case, the ICSID Tribunal found that such decision lacked any sound legal or factual grounds.[64] After acknowledging that national courts may have the right to revoke arbitral tribunals' authority in cases of misconduct, the Tribunal found that such discretionary power has been exercised for reasons other than that for which they were conferred. The Tribunal stated: 'the standard for revocation used by the Bangladesh courts and the manner in which the judge applied the standard to the facts indeed constituted an abuse of right.'[65] **2.39**

[60] ibid 46.

[61] Charles T Kotuby and Luke A Sobota, *General Principles of Law and International Due Process* (Oxford University Press 2017) 108.

[62] Hersch Lauterpacht, *The Function of Law in the International Community* (Oxford University Press 2011) 297–99.

[63] Award in *Saipem SpA v Bangladesh*, ICSID Case No ARB/05/7 of 30 June 2009, paras 149–61; Taniguchi (n 48) 174.

[64] *Saipem SpA v Bangladesh* (n 63) paras 154–55.

[65] ibid para 159.

2.40 In conclusion, while one acknowledges that certain rights may have not, hitherto, been subject to the principle of abuse of rights, it is submitted that this emanates from the view that such rights have been:

> [A]lready modified by exclusions embracing most of those factors that would otherwise have been looked upon as abuses. That doesn't amount to much of an absolute right if its absoluteness depends on conceding in advance those things that would be most liable to be condemned as abuses, whereby doing those things then falls into the category of excesses [excessive use of right or acts beyond the scope of a right] rather than abuses.[66]

B. Abuse of the Right

2.41 The second condition for the principle's application is that the right holder must have exercised his right in an abusive manner. However, for this condition to be fulfilled, one must determine what conduct/behaviour constitutes an abuse. In other words, courts need certain criteria to determine whether one's conduct is abusive.

2.42 Courts do not generally rely on one test. They endorse a number of different tests/criteria and establish abuse if any of the tests is fulfilled.

2.43 That said, an abuse of right is established if one of the following criteria is fulfilled: (1) exercise of the right with an intent to harm; (2) exercise of the right for a purpose other than that for which it was granted; (3) if the right holder could not reasonably have decided to exercise it, given the disparity between the interests pursued and the potential harm caused thereby; or (4) exercise of the right contrary to the principle of good faith.[67]

2.44 In this next section, the different criteria applied by courts shall be examined. In doing so, emphasis will be given to the interrelation between the different criteria and any limitations associated thereto.

1. Exercise of the right with an intent to harm

2.45 Abuse is established if the right holder exercises the right for the purpose of harming another individual. This demonstrates the classic form of conduct tainted with abuse.[68]

[66] Crabb (n 13) 17.

[67] Cueto-Rua (n 3) 985–1003; Yiannopoulos (n 4) 1180; Perillo (n 56) 47; James C Exnicios, 'Abuse of Rights: An Overview of the Historical Evolution and the Current Application in Louisiana Contracts' (1987) 32 Law Review 946, 946–49.

[68] Mayrand (n 45) 994 and 1000; Article 226 of the German Civil Code; Article 833 of the Italian Civil Code; Article 1295.2 of the Austrian Civil Code; Article 7 of the Spanish Civil Code; *Colmar*, 2 May 1855, DP 1856.2.9, 10, cited in Cueto-Rua (n 3) 965; Crabb (n 13) 13; *Illinois Central Gulf RR v International Harvester Co*, 368 So 2d 1009 (La 1979); Egyptian Court of Cassation, Session held on 4 April 1985, Challenge No 1244, Judicial Year 54; Article 30 of the Kuwaiti Civil Code.

This criterion of abuse is endorsed by most laws that acknowledge the principle.[69] Legal systems that adopt a restrictive approach to abuse of rights, such as Germany[70] and Italy,[71] tend to limit the principle's application to rights exercised for the purpose of inflicting harm on another individual. **2.46**

In relation to rights that are exercised for more than one purpose, it is the predominant view that abuse is still established based on this criterion if the primary purpose/motive for exercising the right was to inflict harm.[72] **2.47**

This criterion entails a subjective test and may thus comprise an intricate criterion of abuse; one which is problematic from a pure evidentiary legal stance.[73] To that end, Julio Cueto-Rua rightly stipulates that: **2.48**

> Whoever seeks recovery of damages caused by abusive use of rights and has to prove the presence of the intent to harm faces the troublesome question of producing clear evidence of a psychological process. This difficulty may defeat the aims which the doctrine of abuse of rights has sought to achieve.[74]

The subjective criterion of an intent to harm has the advantage of a definitive test of abuse. It is definitive from a theoretical legal stance in terms of carefully drawing a line between acts that are abusive and acts that are not, by limiting the latter by proof of malice.[75] However, as articulated by Gutteridge, the fact that it primarily relies on investigating a psychological element (motive), as well as introducing a largely ethical component in the evaluation of the act in question, may render it ineffective.[76] **2.49**

The same conclusion has been reached by Pierre Catala and John Weir, where they provided that proving the: **2.50**

> Such a malicious intention must be proved, however, and this may present a difficult problem for the plaintiff. As questions of intention belong to the category of inward mental and emotional processes, there is no means of establishing with scientific accuracy the defendant's ill will or malice (apart from his own admission or pentothal).[77]

[69] Cueto-Rua (n 3) 991; Crabb (n 13) 13; French *Cour d'Appel de Montpellier*, 1e Chambre section c2, 21 October 2015, No de RG: 14/06363; French *Cour de Cassation*, Civ 1re, 24 June 2015, no 14-17795.

[70] Article 226 of the German Civil Code.

[71] Article 833 of the Italian Civil Code limits the abuse of rights principle to the malicious intention of the right holder. Similarly, it is often stated that Austrian courts tend to limit the application of the principle to cases of malicious intention. Joseph Voyame, Bertil Cottier, and Bolivar Rocha, 'Abuse of Right in Comparative Law' in 'Abuse of Rights and Equivalent Concepts: The Principle and Its Present Day Application' (Proceedings of the 19th Colloquy on European Law, Luxembourg, 6–9 November 1989) (Council of Europe 1990) 28–30.

[72] This is the case in French law, Swiss law, Louisiana law, and Egyptian law. *Affaire Clément-Bayard*, Req, 3 August 1915, DP III.1917.1.79, cited in Cueto-Rua (n 3) 981; Crabb (n 13) 13; Bolgar (n 48) 1033 and 1036; *Trushinger v Pak*, 513 So 2d 1151, 1154 (La 1987); *Ballaron v Equitable Shipyards, Inc*, 521 So 2d 481 (La 1988); Abd El-Razzak El Sanhouri, *Al Wasit Fi Sharh Al Qanun Al Madani (A Treatise on the Explanation of the Civil Code)* (Cairo 2010 edn) vol 1, 757–59.

[73] Catala and Weir (n 40) 224; B Edmeades, 'Abuse of Rights' (1978) 24 McGill Law Journal 136, 137–38; Cueto-Rua (n 3) 988.

[74] Cueto-Rua (n 3) 995, footnote 92.

[75] Rosenberg (n 42) 21; Gutteridge (n 52) 25.

[76] Gutteridge (n 52) 26.

[77] Catala and Weir (n 40) 224–25.

2.51 This difficulty is evident in the context of international arbitration, where parties allege an abuse of right but tribunals do not find an abuse for the lack of proof of an intention to cause harm.[78] In this regard, in the case of *Saluka Investments v the Czech Republic*,[79] the Respondent claimed that in initiating the arbitral proceedings, the Claimant had ulterior motives. Specifically, it was alleged that bringing the proceedings was abusive since its purpose was to take advantage of the delay which would take place during the arbitration, and take advantage of the running of the statute of limitation to prevent the Respondent State from bringing civil or criminal actions.[80] While acknowledging that the existence of such an ulterior motive may be abusive, the Tribunal held that such an allegation is unsubstantiated as no proof of malice had been provided.[81]

2.52 The difficulty in applying a purely subjective criterion of abuse is further fortified by the fact that German courts rarely rely on section 226 of the German Civil Code, which expressly adopts the intent to harm as the criterion of abuse,[82] to the extent that some hold it inoperative.[83] A contrario, courts tend to rely on sections 242 and 826 of the Code pertaining to acts contrary to good faith and acts exercised in a manner *contra bonos mores*, given that the latter provisions comprise an objective test of abuse and do not require proof of malice.[84]

2.53 It is worth noting that some scholars provide that an exercise of the right without a legitimate or serious interest is another, stand-alone, criterion of abuse.[85] While one does not attempt to refute this, it seems that the 'legitimate or serious interest' criterion rather comprises an objective imperative indicium used by courts to prove and determine an intent to harm.[86] To that effect, it has been rightly stated that 'the *objective* test of a person not deriving any benefit from the act serves as a *presumption* for the existence of the malicious intention'.[87] (Emphasis added).

2.54 Accordingly, it is submitted that embracing such an indicium is an attempt to deviate from the extreme subjective nature of the intent to harm criterion, given its inherent perplexities from an evidentiary point of view. In this regard, it seems that:

[78] *Atlantic Triton Company Limited v People's Revolutionary Republic of Guinea*, ICSID Case No ARB/84/1, Award of 21 April 1986, 3 ICSID Reports 13; Hervé Ascensio, 'Abuse of Process in International Investment Arbitration' (2014) 13 Chinese Journal of International Law 763, 770.

[79] *Saluka Investments BV v The Czech Republic*, UNCITRAL Partial Award, registered by the Permanent Court of Arbitration of 17 March 2006.

[80] ibid para 184.

[81] ibid para 236.

[82] Reinhard Zimmermann and Simon Whittaker, *Good Faith in European Contract Law* (Cambridge University Press 2000) 694, note 145; Cueto-Rua (n 3) 995, footnote 92.

[83] Gutteridge (n 52) 37.

[84] Zimmermann and Whittaker (n 82) 694, note 145; Cueto-Rua (n 3) 995, footnote 92.

[85] Cueto-Rua (n 30) 992.

[86] Viktor Knapp, *International Encyclopedia of Comparative Law* (Springer 1983) Part I, Chapter 2, 110; JE Scholtens, 'Abuse of Rights' (1958) 75 South African Law Journal 39, 43; Brunner (n 48) 739; Gutteridge (n 52) 32; Rosenberg (n 42) 21–22.

[87] Scholtens (n 86) 43; Amos and Walton, *Introduction to French Law* (3rd edn, Oxford University Press 1967) 219.

> Plaintiffs have been *rescued from this difficulty* [proving an intent to harm] by the judges who, starting from the facts of the case, *presume an intention to cause damage.* In this inquiry, *there is one very weighty piece of evidence: the lack of any real interest or benefit for the defendant.* Where the author of an act which harms his neighbor has acted without seeking any material advantage for himself, without deriving any personal benefit from his action, one is justified in supposing that he was inspired by the sole motive of causing damage to another person. This complete absence of any motive of material self-interest for the performance of the harmful act, *allows the court to deduce* as a psychological certainty (though not a scientific one) the existence of an intention to cause harm.[88] (Emphasis added).

Thus, the legitimate/serious interest indicium has been adopted by the courts as a presumption of malice and may comprise a rule of evidence: *res ipsa loquitur.*[89] This conclusion can be equally inferred from the decisions of the courts where evincing an intent to harm is often presumed where it is shown that there is no serious or legitimate interest on the part of the right holder.[90] **2.55**

For example, in the French *Saint Galmier* case,[91] which involved adjacent springs yielding mineral water, where an owner of one of the springs installed and operated a pump which greatly diminished the water yielded from the adjacent spring owned by another individual. The Plaintiff requested the Court to order the Defendant to reduce the operation of the installed pump. Despite the Defendant's assertion that he was merely exercising his right, the Court provided that the right holder cannot exercise his right if it is exclusively inspired by an intent to inflict harm on another.[92] While there was no proof of malice, the Court inferred such intention from the fact that the Defendant obtained no serious benefit from his act.[93] **2.56**

This is also the case in the Egyptian jurisprudence, where malice is established if it is proven that the right holder has no legitimate or serious interest in exercising the right in question.[94] In this regard, the Egyptian Court of Cassation often provides that an exercise of a right is abusive where the right holder exercises it with an intent to harm, which is established if the right is exercised with no serious or legitimate interest.[95] The term 'which is established only if the right is exercised with no serious or **2.57**

[88] Catala and Weir (n 40) 224–25.

[89] *Res ipsa loquitur* entails an evidentiary rule where a plaintiff establishes a *rebuttable presumption* of fault/negligence on the part of the defendant/right holder. Catala and Weir (n 40) 225.

[90] Amos and Walton (n 87) 220.

[91] *Saint Galmier* case, Lyon, 18 April 1856, DP 1856.2.199 cited in Robilant (n 6) 69–70; Cueto-Rua (n 30) 965–66; French *Cour de Cassation*, Civ 3re, 8 October 2015, no 14-16216.

[92] Cueto-Rua (n 3) 965–66.

[93] Gutteridge (n 52) 33.

[94] Explanatory Memorandum of the Egyptian Law No 131 of 1948 Promulgating the Civil Code, 32–33; Sanhouri (n 72) 759–60; Morcos (n 40) 371.

[95] Egyptian Court of Cassation, Session held on 9 February 2012, Challenge No 15906, Judicial Year 80; Egyptian Court of Cassation, Session held on 26 May 2004, Challenge No 5036, Judicial Year 72; Egyptian Court of Cassation, Session held on 22 April 2003, Challenge No 2633, Judicial Year 72; Egyptian Court of Cassation, Session held on 4 May 1999, Challenge No 4464, Judicial Year 68; Egyptian Court of Cassation, Session held on 13 July 1999, Challenge No 2886, Judicial Year 68.

legitimate interest' is regularly found in the rulings of the courts, and clearly testifies to the fact that the serious/legitimate interest test is used by courts merely as an indicium of malice, rather than as a stand-alone criterion of abuse.

2.58 Accordingly, the criterion of intent to harm and that of serious and legitimate interest are not necessarily separate, but are greatly intertwined from a practical point of view.[96]

2. Exercise of the right for a purpose other than that for which it was granted

2.59 This criterion of abuse is of concrete importance as its rationale and application differed over time. This variation helps elucidate and depict the transformation of abuse of rights: from having a clear social perception (preserving the interests of the society and/or State), to emphasizing its corrective role in balancing the competing/conflicting interests of the parties.

2.60 During the nineteenth century, abuse of rights was of potency in French law as a response to the then rampant absolutism of possessive individualism.[97] The individualistic school of legal thought was vehemently attacked, and it was submitted that legal rights are not absolute; they are conferred on an individual to achieve a certain purpose. Defying the said purpose renders the exercise of a right abusive.[98] To that effect, some provided that 'to abuse a right is to proceed, intentionally or unintentionally, against the purpose of the institution of which one has misunderstood the finality and the function'.[99] Thus, a functional and teleological approach to rights has emerged, where rights are exercised in accordance with their function.

2.61 Accordingly, this criterion of abuse presupposes that rights do not exist in a vacuum or in stasis; they are conferred upon the right holder for a specific social purpose, and the exercise of the right is merely a means to satisfy such prescribed purpose. If the holder of the right derogates from the very purpose of its existence, it may be abusive given the factual matrix of the case.[100]

[96] In this regard, Amos and Walton noted that 'in practice, the [courts] do not search for the *subjective* intention to do harm, but *infer* that from the commission of acts consistent with no other intention' (Emphasis added): Amos and Walton (n 87) 220.

[97] Post the French revolution, the political-social philosophy of liberalistic individualism was prevalent. According to this, individual interests prevailed over the collective interests of the community, as an individual was perceived as the supreme entity. Individuals were immune from any responsibility for damages caused in the exercise of rights. András Sajó, *Abuse: The Dark Side of Fundamental Rights* (Eleven International Publishing 2006) 29; Bolgar (n 48) 1016–17; Crabb (n 13) 5 and 18; Reid (n 2) 133.

[98] VE Greaves, 'The Social-Economic Purpose of Private Rights: Section 1 of the Soviet Civil Code. A Comparative Study of Soviet and Non-communist Law' (1935) 12 New York University Law Quarterly Review 433–44.

[99] Louis Josserand, *De I 'esprit des droits et de leur Relativité: Théorie dite dès l'Abus des Droits* (2nd edn, 1925), cited in James Gordley, 'The Abuse of Rights in the Civil Law Tradition' in Rita de la Feria and Stefan Vogenauer (eds), *Prohibition of Abuse of Law: A New General Principle of EU Law?* (Hart Publishing 2011) 36; Shael Herman, 'Classical Social Theories and the Doctrine of "Abuse of Right"' (1977) 37 Louisiana Law Review 747, 754.

[100] Walton (n 33) 501; Josserand (n 30) 1001; *Prest v Petrodel Resources Ltd* [2013] 2 AC 415, 17, providing that abuse of rights in the civil legal systems extends not just to the illegal and improper invocation of a right, but also to its use for a purpose other than that for which it exists; *Barcelona Traction (Belgium v Spain)* [1970] ICJ 39, Judgment of 5 February 1970) 56; *Travelers Indemnity Co v Hunt*, 371 So 2d 342 (La Ap 4th Cir), *writ denied*, 374 So 2d 657 (1979), 343–44; Exnicios (n 69) 963–64.

Moreover, according to this criterion, rights are conferred upon individuals for the satisfaction of certain ends, which do not necessarily benefit the right holder, but more importantly, benefit the whole society.[101] That said, one submits that this social emphasis of the criterion demonstrates that the role of abuse of rights was to prioritize the interests shared by the society, rather than the interests of another individual. To that end, in defining abuse based on this criterion, it was submitted that abuse of rights is inspired from 'clearly social conceptions',[102] and that a right has: 2.62

> [A] function to perform in its *social* setting, and must be considered in relation to the needs and rights of *society* at large. The key to interpreting rights is to place them in their social milieu, and as so placed, determine what rationally must be their function or range of functions. If the right is being exercised for a purpose at variance with the nature and function of the right, then there is abuse and resulting liability.[103] (Emphasis added).

Emphasis on the social element of abuse of rights was clearly evident in the Soviet Code of 1923, which was prefaced by a clause that read: 'civil rights are protected by the law except in those cases in which they are exercised in a sense contrary to economic and social purposes.'[104] 2.63

This implies an overly socialist approach/conception of rights which, arguably, may not reconcile with the currently prevailing economic and/or political environment. Moreover, delineating the social purpose and the function of the right in question is not an easy task. Such difficulty is confirmed by the fact that some legal systems opted to totally abandon the 'purpose of the right' as a criterion of abuse. In this regard, Egyptian law and French law appear to be good epitomes to illustrate this issue. 2.64

A review of the legislative history of abuse of rights under Egyptian law demonstrates that, in codifying the criteria of abuse, the Egyptian legislator has considered, and deliberately refrained from referring to: the social purpose of the right.[105] In setting this criterion aside, the Egyptian legislator acknowledged its theoretical flaws and its practical pitfalls. 2.65

From a purely theoretical stance, it seems difficult to carefully ascertain the precise socio-economic function of each right. The limitation of the social purpose criterion is further manifested in its implementation.[106] Given its inherently broad terms and its relative nature, the social purpose test bears undeterminable variable parameters, as 2.66

[101] Bolgar (n 48) 1018; Gutteridge (n 52) 27–28; Crabb (n 13) 18; Byers (n 13) 393; Robilant (n 6) 93–94.
[102] Crabb (n 13) 18.
[103] ibid 19–20.
[104] Greaves (n 98) 454; Byers (n 13) 393; Article 30 of the Kuwaiti Civil Code.
[105] The legislative history of Article 5 of the Egyptian Civil Code testifies to that effect. Prior to opting for the 'legitimate interest' criterion, the social purpose criterion was considered: Explanatory Memorandum of the Egyptian Law No 131 of 1948 Promulgating the Civil Code, 33. However, some judges refer to the social purpose criterion in applying abuse of rights: Egyptian Court of Cassation, Session held on 27 February 2005, Challenge No 871, Judicial Year 74.
[106] Morcos (n 40) 348; Sanhouri (n 72) 762–63.

it primarily relies on an individual assessment of each decision maker.[107] This may be precarious as it may shift the prevalent role of courts/tribunals, from merely applying the law to capriciously affecting its creation. Thus, it arguably defies the legal certainty needed in a criterion of abuse.

2.67 A similar approach has been taken in French law. While it was the predominant view that the social function of rights constitutes a criterion of abuse under French law,[108] it is often advocated that this is no longer the case. Pirovano, who carefully examined the decisions of French courts in this regard, concluded that the social purpose criterion, as developed by Josserand, is not generally accepted by the courts.[109] In his view, determining the social function of rights may be a difficult matter to be left to judicial discretion, given that it comprises a political question which the decision maker is not well-prepared to decide.[110]

2.68 This approach is shared by other prominent scholars, who submit that the social purpose criterion is difficult to identify.[111] To that effect, Gutteridge provided that:

> It may perhaps also be observed that a rule which leaves it to the discretion of a judge to determine the social or economic purpose of a statute, is open to grave objection. The political prejudices of the individual cannot fail to tincture his interpretation of a rule of this kind, and no judge should be placed in the invidious position of being compelled to adjudicate in such circumstances.[112]

2.69 Moreover, the social element of this criterion is difficult to grasp and appears to lack juridical explanation. It affords no explanation as to why an anti-social exercise of right is deemed unlawful.[113] Notwithstanding the above, the 'purpose of the right' criterion remains applicable in a number of legal systems. For example, Article 281 of the Greek Civil Code emphasizes the social function of the right, as it states that 'the exercise of a right is prohibited where it manifestly exceeds the bounds of good faith, morality or the economic or social purpose of that right'.[114] Additionally, Article 124 of the Lebanese Civil Code of Obligations stipulates that an exercise of a right is abusive if it exceeds the aim on account of which such right was conferred.[115] Similarly, Article 1071 of the Argentine Civil Code provides that:

[107] Sanhouri (n 72) 762–63; Morcos (n 40) 348.

[108] Cueto-Rua (n 30) 1001–02.

[109] Pirovano, 'La fonction sociale des droits: Réflexions sur le destin des théories de Josserand', in Recueil Dalloz Sirey, sec Chronique 67, 70 (1972), cited and translated in Cueto-Rua (n 3) 1001–02.

[110] ibid; Reid (n 2) 137; Greaves (n 98) 464.

[111] WT Tête, 'Tort Roots and Ramifications of the Obligations Revision' (1987) 32 Loyola Law Review 47, 81–3; Catala and Weir (n 40) 230; Cueto-Rua (n 3) 1002; Mayrand (n 45) 1000.

[112] Gutteridge (n 52) 42.

[113] Cheng (n 32) 131.

[114] Article 281 of the Greek Civil Code, translated in Case C-367/96 *Alexandros Kefalas and Others v Elliniko Dimosio (Greek State) and Organismos Oikonomikis Anasygkrotisis Epicheiriseon AE (OAE)* [1998] ECR I-02843, para 12.

[115] Article 124 of the Lebanese Civil Code.

> the regular exercise of one's right or the performance of a legal obligation cannot make illicit any act. The law does not protect the abusive exercise of rights. Such will be considered the exercise which is contrary to the ends which [the law] took into account when they [the rights] were recognized [. . .].[116]

The Belgian law also endorses the purpose of the right amongst the criteria of abuse.[117] Finally, this is fortified by the Louisiana jurisprudence which often refers to rights exercised for a purpose other than that for which it was granted, as a clear application of abuse of rights.[118]

However, from a practical stance, it appears that in applying this criterion some courts do not necessarily engage in a detailed analysis of the social and/or economic purpose of the right. A contrario, reference is often made to the general purpose of the right conferred and focuses on the reasonableness of the act in question, without any explicit reference to, or analysis of, the social-economic purpose.[119] This conclusion may be inferred from decisions rendered by the Louisiana courts. **2.70**

The case of *Travelers Indemnity Co v Hunt*[120] involved an indemnity agreement whereby Hunt (the Appellant) was obliged to indemnify Travelers Indemnity Company (the Appellee), in consideration for their agreement to provide bonds pertaining to construction works done by another party. The Appellant's contractual obligation pertained to indemnification against any claim relating to the issuance of the bonds. The contract granted the Appellee the 'exclusive right to determine for itself and the Indemnitors whether any claim or suit brought against the Company or the Principal upon any such bond shall be settled or defended and its decision shall be binding and conclusive upon the Indemnitors'.[121] **2.71**

Proceedings were initiated by the Appellee to recover certain legal fees that it incurred as a result of defending claims related to the issuance of the bonds. Given that the attorney's fees amounted to 10,140.00 US Dollars, while the value of that claim was only 2,184.23 US Dollars (the case was heard by the District Court, Court of Appeals, and Supreme Court), the Appellant argued that the Appellee could have decided to settle rather than incurring all such legal costs. **2.72**

[116] Article 1071 of the Argentine Civil Code; Cueto-Rua (n 3) 997; Article 7 of the Spanish Civil Code and Article 1185 of the Venezuelan Civil Code.

[117] Voyame, Cottier, and Rocha (n 71) 34; Michelangelo Temmerman, 'The Legal Notion of Abuse of Patent Rights', NCCR Trade Regulation, Working Paper No 2011/23, 6.

[118] *Trushinger v Pak*, 513 So 2d 1151, 1154 (La 1987); *Ballaron v Equitable Shipyards, Inc*, 521 So. 2d 481 (La 1988); *Ouachita National Bank in Monroe v Palowsky*, 554 So 2d 108 (La 1989); *Addison v Williams*, 546 So 2d 220 (La 1989); *Fidelity Bank and Trust Co v Hammons*, 540 So 2d 461 (La 1989); *210 Baronne St Ltd Partnership v First Nat'l Bank of Commerce*, 543 So 2d 502, 507 (La App 4th Cir), *writ denied*, 546 So 2d 1219 (1989).

[119] Article 30 of the Kuwaiti Civil Code stipulates that an abuse is established where the right is exercised for a purpose other than that for which it was granted or if the right holder deviates from the *social function* of the right in question. Notwithstanding the reference to the social purpose of the right, Article 30 goes on to provide certain examples of abusive conduct, that is, where a right is exercised with no legitimate interest; if exercised maliciously; if exercised unreasonably; or if the damage caused *exceeds the normal or reasonable harm* that may be endured.

[120] *Travelers Indemnity Co v Hunt*, 371 So 2d 342 (La App 4th Cir), *writ denied*, 374 So 2d 657 (1979).

[121] ibid 343.

2.73 The Court acknowledged that such contention pertained to the principle of abuse of rights. It then provided that determining if there was an abuse in this case depended on the examination of the purpose for which the right is granted: 'If the holder of the right exercises the right for a purpose other than that for which the right was granted, the right may have been abused.'[122] Rather than mentioning any social or economic purpose of the contractual right in question, the Court merely attempted to investigate whether the right was exercised solely to benefit the right holder, the Appellee, or to defend the interests of the Appellant.[123] In its decision, the Court stated that:

> We therefore find that the appeal of the adverse judgment by Travelers did not constitute an abuse of a right. The evidence simply does not indicate that Travelers pursued this litigation for *its own purposes* while misleading appellants as to the ultimate cost, but rather that the actions of appellants' attorney left Travelers *with no other choice* than to appeal. The trial judge ruled in accordance with the evidence and we affirm.[124] (Emphasis added).

2.74 The right in question relates to the right to decide whether to defend or settle the claim. That said, it appears evident that the Court did not necessarily engage in any detailed analysis of the social and/or economic function of the contractual right. Moreover, it is submitted that the decision of the Court and its rationale primarily rested on the element of reasonableness of the conduct in question. In its decision, the Court relied on: (a) whether the Appellee exercised its contractual right to merely advance its interests or with regard to the interests of the Appellant; and (b) if there was an alternative option for the Appellee or whether this constituted the only, or most, effective option.

2.75 This case is also interesting in conveying that even when examining the purpose of the right in question, courts often focus on the *individual* interests of the *parties*, rather than examining any interests of the *society*. This may demonstrate that while the application of this criterion was originally perceived as a tool to protect the interests of the society, it now focuses on balancing the competing interests of the individuals.[125]

2.76 The case of *Illinois Central Gulf RR v International Harvester Co*[126] further evinces the above submission. This case pertained to a lease agreement that provided that the lessee may not sublet the leased premises without the written consent of the lessor. Harvester requested Illinois Central's permission to sublease the premises, however, Illinois Central refused. Notwithstanding such refusal, Harvester sub-leased the premises. After unsuccessful negotiations, Illinois Central initiated proceedings and alleged that Harvester violated the lease contract by subletting the premises. Harvester contended

[122] ibid 343–44.
[123] ibid.
[124] ibid 344.
[125] George M Armstrong and John C LaMaster, 'Retaliatory Eviction as Abuse of Rights: A Civilian Approach to Landlord-Tenant Disputes' (1986) 47 Louisiana Law Review 1, 18.
[126] *Illinois Central Gulf RR v International Harvester Co*, 368 So 2d 1009 (La 1979).

that the lessor's exercise of its right to withhold its consent was tantamount to an abuse of rights.[127]

After acknowledging the 'purpose of the right' as a criterion of abuse,[128] the Court examined whether the lessor's right to withhold its written consent was exercised for a purpose other than that for which it was granted. The Court provided that: 2.77

> We cannot say that Illinois Central exercised its right to withhold consent to a sublease for a purpose other than that for which it was granted. *The record is devoid of evidence of the parties' intention in placing the clause in the leases.* It cannot be assumed that the lessor merely sought by the clause to protect itself against an objectionable subtenant. The parties likely would have limited the interdiction to subleases with objectionable sublessees if this had been the lessor's only concern.[129] (Emphasis added).

This decision testifies to the fact that: (a) the Court did not undertake a scrupulous analysis of the purpose of the right; and (b) the Court's perception and understanding of the 'purpose of the right' criterion was to examine the interests of the individuals and not that of the society. The Court's only proof that there was no deviation of the right's purpose, was that there was no evidence of the parties' intention of placing the clause in the lease agreement. 2.78

In the case of *Modernfold (Bas St-Laurent) Ltée v New Castle Products*[130] the Canadian Court decided that the use of a contract for purposes other than those envisaged by the contracting parties constituted an abuse of right. In that case, abuse was established given that the manufacturer ended his exclusive distribution contract with his agent for the sole purpose of earning the profits for himself.[131] This decision further confirms that courts tend to focus on the individual interests of the parties, rather than examining any social interests. In deciding the purpose of the contract, the Court focused on the common intention of the parties. 2.79

The above demonstrates that applications of abuse of rights is generally concerned with balancing the interests of individuals, rather than focusing on the social purpose of rights. This is consistent with French law, where it is submitted that the 'notion of abus de droit in French Law is a doctrinal expression symbolizing a balance of private interests'.[132] 2.80

It is worth mentioning that the purpose of the right criterion is regularly used by the Court of Justice of the European Union ('CJEU') to determine if there is an abuse of right in matters of the European Union ('EU') law.[133] In the case of *Emsland-Stärke* 2.81

[127] ibid 1013.

[128] ibid 1014. In doing so, the Court referred to 1000–03 of Julia Cueto-Rua's article which pertains to the criterion of 'social purpose of the right': Cueto-Rua (n 3) 1000–03.

[129] ibid 1015.

[130] *Modernfold (Bas St-Laurent) Ltée v New Castle Products (Canada) Ltd* [1973] CS 220.

[131] ibid.

[132] Devine (n 34) 158.

[133] It is worth mentioning that abuse of rights is recognized by the CJEU as a *general principle of EU law*: Case C-321/05 *Hans Markus Kofoed v Skatteministeriet* [2007] ECR I-5795, para 38; Annekatrien Lenaerts, 'The General

GmbH v Hauptzollamt Hamburg-Jonas,[134] a German company transported goods to Switzerland for the sole purpose of benefiting from an export refund provided for in another legislation. Upon doing this, the German company returned the goods to Germany and still requested the export refund. The CJEU acknowledged that this conduct constituted an abuse of rights. In its decision, the CJEU provided that a 'finding of an abuse requires, first, a combination of objective circumstances in which, despite formal observance of the conditions laid down by the Community rules, the purpose of those rules has not been achieved'.[135]

2.82 Accordingly, it is submitted that this criterion was first adopted to link the exercise of a right to the right's social and economic purpose, and to give the principle a social dimension: evaluating the interests of the right holder against the interests of the community.[136] However, one submits that due to its practical difficulty, the application of this criterion now does not necessarily have a social element, but is rather applied to determine if the exercise of the right was reasonable by examining the legal purpose of the right (such as the common intention of the parties of the contract or the purpose of a treaty),[137] and the interests of the individuals implicated in the dispute.[138]

3. The unreasonable exercise of the right: the balancing factor

2.83 Rights must be exercised reasonably. The exercise of a right is unreasonable where the right holder exercises it with minimal serious or legitimate interest,[139] or where there is disparity between the benefit(s) and prejudice(s) resulting from the exercise of the right.[140]

2.84 The author opts for the term 'balancing factor' as investigating the degree of reasonableness of a given interest requires a prudent investigation of all other relevant interests and balance them in order to determine whether the exercise of the right in question is abusive.

Principle of the Prohibition of Abuse of Rights: A Critical Position on Its Role in a Codified European Contract Law' (2010) 18 European Review of Private Law 1121, 1138.

[134] Case C-110/99 *Emsland-Stärke GmbH v Hauptzollamt Hamburg-Jonas* [2000] ECR I-1569,

[135] ibid para. 52.

[136] In this formulation of abuse of rights, it applied to benefit the society and not necessarily to benefit the individual. Gutteridge (n 52) 27–28 ('Law is brought into being for the benefit of the community and not for the advantage of the individual'); Greaves (n 98) 464.

[137] Yael R Borman, 'Treaty Shopping Through Corporate Restructuring of Investments: Legitimate Corporate Planning or Abuse of Rights?' (2011) 24 Hague Ybk of International Law 359, 368–370; *Phoenix Action v The Czech Republic*, ICSID Case No ARB/06/5, Award of 15 April 2009, para 142; Ascensio (n 78) 780.

[138] Tête (n 111) 70–71.

[139] *Karaha Bodas Co v Perusahaan Pertambangan Minyak Das Gas Bumi Negara*, 364 F 3d 274 (5th Cir 2004), ('An action violates abuse of rights doctrine if [. . .] the action is totally unreasonable given the lack of any legitimate interest in the exercise of the right and its exercise harms another'); Gutteridge (n 52) 32.

[140] Edmeades (n 73) 138; Perillo (n 56) 47; Lauterpacht (n 62) 303–04, providing that abuse is established, not because of the intention, but because the interests injuriously affected are more important; Kiss (n 4) para 4; CJEU, 23 March 2000, Case C-373/97 *Diamantis* [2000] ECR I-1705, para. 43; Ernest J Weinrib, *Corrective Justice* (Oxford University Press 2012) 112–15, discussing that courts may award damages in lieu of an injunction on the basis of abuse of rights. If monetary compensation is adequate for the plaintiff, while issuing an injunction would be oppressive to the defendant and the plaintiff would derive no substantial benefit therefrom, courts may apply abuse of rights to *balance the competing interests* and reach equipoise (remedial fairness).

This conforms to the 'interest theory' of rights, which entails that disputes generally comprise different competing interests, and the State/decision maker must engage in an equipoise in order to 'select what interests it regards as most worth of protection'.[141] **2.85**

The balancing factor presupposes that reasonableness and unrestricted egoism are antinomies. If a reasonable person, acting in the same circumstances, envisages or expects that his/her exercise of right may cause serious damage to another individual, reason and sensibility mandates the right holder to refrain from exercising the right in such a manner.[142] However, if one envisages that damages may in fact occur, and accepts these damages to achieve one's own interests, this may defy reasonableness and constitute an abuse of right.[143] Applying this criterion of abuse relies on examining the act in question based on the reasonable man construct.[144] **2.86**

If the depiction of rights as legally protected interests is acknowledged, adopting the balancing factor renders the principle of abuse of rights a tool that seeks to maintain a fair balance between the respective interests of the parties. It is appropriate to refer here to the renowned Bin Cheng who illustrated this in the context of international law, so he is quoted *in extenso*: **2.87**

> The theory of abuse of rights, while protecting the legitimate interests of the owner of the right, imposes such limitations upon the right as will render its exercise compatible with [. . .] the legitimate interests of the other contracting party. Thus a fair balance is kept between the respective interests of the parties and a line is drawn delimiting their respective rights. Any overstepping of this line by a party in the exercise of his right would constitute a breach of good faith, an abuse of right, and a violation of his obligation.[145]

(i) The balancing factor is an effective criterion of abuse

The effectiveness of this criterion emanates from the fact that: (1) it covers certain applications of abuse of rights which may not necessarily be covered if other criteria are adopted; (2) it is widely used in different legal systems; (3) it encompasses other criteria; (4) it is widely used by arbitral tribunals when applying abuse of rights as a general principle of law; and (5) it comprises an objective standard of abuse. **2.88**

Firstly, courts may establish an abuse of right despite the fact that *no fault* has been committed or proven. As previously mentioned, courts may extend the principle to **2.89**

[141] Boyd (n 12) 824; Pound (n 5) 104; A Javier Trevino, *Classic Writings in Law and Society* (2nd edn, Transaction Publishers 2011) 89–90; Michael Willrich, *City of Courts: Socializing Justice in Progressive Era Chicago* (Cambridge University Press 2003) 109; Gordley (n 22) 289; Brunner (n 48) 731; Morcos (n 40) 372–73.

[142] Reid (n 2) 137; Sanhouri (n 72) 760–61.

[143] Japanese case of *Mitamura v Suzuki*, 26 Saiko Saibansho minji hanreishu 1067 (Sup Ct, 27 June 1972), cited in Sono and Fujioka (n 40) 1037.

[144] Yiannopoulos (n 4) 1182.

[145] Cheng (n 32) 129.

such cases given the gravity of damages caused to an individual from the exercise of a right, despite the fact that the right holder is not at fault.[146]

2.90 The French Court of Cassation rendered a decision expressly adopting such an extensive application of abuse of rights.[147] In this case, the construction of buildings had caused damage to a neighbour who subsequently sought compensation. The French Court of Appeal dismissed the case and held that in the absence of any fault proven against the right holder, the Court cannot order compensation based on abuse of rights. However, the Court of Cassation vacated the decision and ruled that the right holder may be held liable, notwithstanding the absence of fault, if the harm caused exceeds the normal or reasonable harm that may be endured by neighbours.[148] While it may appear that such extension of abuse of rights primarily pertains to the right of property or ownership, scholars submit that this was only the starting point of the principle's extension to cases where no fault has been committed.[149]

2.91 It is worth mentioning that this is also the case under Shari'a law, where the predominant view is that the intention of the right holder is irrelevant and that the principle is primarily concerned with the gravity of damages caused as a result of the exercise of the right.[150]

2.92 While this extensive application of the principle must be used with great caution, one submits that all other criteria of abuse fail to justify this outcome. If one presumes that no fault has been committed by the right holder, how can one establish an abuse of rights based on malice, deviation of the purpose of the right or bad faith? That being said, adopting the balancing factor allows courts to extend the application of abuse of rights to cases where no fault was committed.[151]

2.93 Moreover, in certain cases, abuse of rights may be used by courts to create a *new* contractual right/obligation rather than merely ameliorate the harshness of an *existing* right/obligation (the curative role of abuse of rights). In these instances, the principle appears in its most extensive reach and acts more as a sword than a shield. In the

[146] In some cases, damages are granted even though the right holder is held to not have committed any fault, given the harm caused to another individual as a result of the exercise of the right. Mayrand (n 45) 1000–02; Crabb (n 13) 19–20; Reid (n 2) 131. Article 63 of the Qatari Civil Code provides that abuse may also be established if the exercise of right causes uncommon extravagant harm/damage to another person.

[147] *Epoux Vullion v Société immobilière Vernet- Christophe Subsequent Developments*, JCP 1971 2 16781, translated by Tony Weir.

[148] ibid.

[149] Mayrand (n 45) 1000–02, where similar cases in French law and Quebec law are provided.

[150] Nabil Saleh, 'The Role of Intention (Niyya) Under Saudi Arabian Hanbali Law' (2009) 23 Arab Law Quarterly 347, 349–50; Sobhi Mahmassani, *The General Theory of the Law of Obligations and Contracts under Islamic Jurisprudence* (Beirut 1972) 35–55.

[151] *Himpurna California Energy Ltd v PT PLN (Persero)*, Ad-hoc arbitration under UNCITRAL rules, Final award of 4 May 1999, (2000) XXV Ybk Commercial Arbitration 11; *Patuha Power Ltd (Bermuda) v PT (Persero) Perusahaan Listruik Negara (Indonesia)* (1999) 14 Mealey's Int'l Arb Rep B-1, B-44, where the Tribunal used the criterion of reasonableness to establish an abuse of right given the unreasonable amount of damages sought by the Claimants, despite the fact that the Claimants were not acting in bad faith.

Canadian case of *Posluns v Enterprises Lormil Inc*,[152] a contract of lease was concluded whereby the lessee had a right to use the leased premises to serve a limited list of food. The lessor then decided to open a competing restaurant, which served some of the listed food in the same shopping mall. The contract did not contain any provision restricting the lessor from doing this. In an action regarding the payment of the rent, the lessee invoked abuse of rights and successfully argued that reasonableness mandates that a guarantee of exclusivity be implicitly read into the contract.[153] One submits that the balancing factor covers the curative role of abuse of rights. If one uses the criterion of malice, proving it does not necessarily justify adding or implying a new contractual provision to remedy the victim of abuse. Similarly, the derogation of the purpose as a criterion fails to substantiate the outcome of the decision in *Posluns*. If the parties freely chose not to have a guarantee of exclusivity, it seems logical to presume that he who invokes the absence of such provision is not deviating from the purpose of his contractual right, but is rather abiding by it.

Secondly, it is submitted that this criterion has gained the widest support in national legal systems,[154] and is also endorsed by the CJEU as part of EU law and in international law.[155] **2.94**

As previously mentioned, Article 5 of the Egyptian law explicitly endorses the balancing factor and provides that an exercise of right is abusive 'if the interests pursued are of minor importance, so that they are manifestly disproportionate to the harm caused to others'.[156] **2.95**

This is consistent with the position taken in the Netherlands and Quebec. Article 13.2 of the Civil Code of the Netherlands stipulates that abuse of rights is established where the right holder could not reasonably have decided to exercise it, given the disproportion between the interests pursued and the harm caused thereby.[157] Similarly, Article **2.96**

[152] Quebec Superior Court in *Posluns v Enterprises Lormil Inc* [1990] Quebec 200-05-001584-858, JE 90-1131 (CS), cited in Rosalie Jukier, 'Banque Nationale du Canada v. Houle (S.C.C.): Implications of an Expanded Doctrine of Abuse of Rights in Civilian Contract Law' (1992) 37 McGill Law Journal 221, 235.

[153] ibid.

[154] Bolgar (n 48) 1027–28; Brunner (n 48) 731; *Trushinger v Pak*, 513 So 2d 1151, 1154 (La 1987); *Ballaron v Equitable Shipyards, Inc*, 521 So 2d 481 (La 1988); *Ouachita National Bank in Monroe v Palowsky*, 554 So 2d 108 (La 1989); *Addison v Williams*, 546 So 2d 220 (La 1989); *Fidelity Bank and Trust Co v Hammons*, 540 So 2d 461 (La 1989); *210 Baronne St Ltd Partnership v First Nat'l Bank of Commerce*, 543 So 2d 502, 507 (La App 4th Cir), *writ denied*, 546 So 2d 1219 (1989); *Des Cheneaux v Morin Inc* (1987), 20 QAC 157; *Caisse populaire de Baie St-Paul v Simard*, Sup Ct Saguenay, No 24005000043845, 9 September 1985; *Banque Nationale du Canada v Houle* [1990] 3 SCR 122; Egyptian Court of Cassation, Session held on 24 March 1991, Challenge No 1238, Judicial Year 56; Egyptian Court of Cassation, Session held on 4 April 1985, Challenge No 1244, Judicial Year 54; Sanhouri (n 72) 760–61; Morcos (n 40) 372–73; Article 3.13 of the Dutch Civil Code; Article 7 of the Spanish Civil Code; ICC Case No 12456 of 2004, in Jean-Jacquez Arnaldez, Yves Derains and Dominique Hascher (eds), *Collection of ICC Arbitral Awards 2008-2011* (Kluwer Law International 2013) 826; Nicholae Gradinaru, 'Abuse of Rights' (2012) 4 Contemporary Readings in Law and Social Justice 1010, 1011, (discussing the law of Romania); Betul Tiryaki, 'The Legal Results of the Abuse of Rights in Case of Contradiction to the Formal Rules of Contracts' (2008) 1 Ankara Bar Review 30, 36, (discussing Turkish law); Article 30 of the Kuwaiti Civil Code.

[155] Case C-373/97 *Diamantis* [2000] ECR I-1705, para 43; Cheng (n 32) 129; Ascensio (n 78) 764–65.

[156] Article 5 of the Egyptian Civil Code.

[157] Article 13.2 of the Netherlands Civil Code of 1992, translated in Byers (n 13) 395; Netherland's Supreme Court in *Kuipers v De Jongh*, HR April 17, 1970, NJ 1971, no 89, translated in Brunner (n 48) 739.

7 of the Quebec Civil Code provides that rights exercised unreasonably constitute an abuse of right.[158]

2.97 This proportionality test is precisely what the balancing factor entails. According to this criterion, abuse is not defined by an inflexible or rigid criterion, but by a careful examination of the factual matrix of the case, and by balancing all competing interests.[159]

2.98 Other laws do not explicitly refer to the balancing factor. However, a comparative synthesis of most laws, including those examined above, reveals that the balancing factor comprises an effective criterion of abuse, depicts the rationale of the principle, and constitutes the core of all other criteria. Albert Mayrand rightly stated that the 'theory of the abuse of rights is penetrating our law through the combined action of the legislators and of the tribunals. It promotes the idea of reasonableness without which justice would disagree with the law: *summum jus, summa injuria*'.[160]

2.99 As previously mentioned, the element of reasonableness is neither peculiar to, nor inconsistent with, French law.[161] In measuring the degree of reasonableness, courts take into consideration the interests served by the right's effectuation and the damage caused by the exercise of the right as shall be discussed below.

2.100 The Egyptian eminent scholars, El Sanhouri and Morcos, confirm that this criterion depicts the rationale of abuse of rights.[162] Finding an abuse of right depends on the degree of reasonableness of the conduct in question, which is determined upon the balancing of the competing interests of the right holder and the interests of the other individual(s).[163] To that effect, Morcos rightly stated that in all cases where abuse is established (regardless of which criterion is used to establish an abuse), courts engage in a process of balancing the competing interests, and finding an abuse entails that the interests of those who oppose the exercise of the right were more important to uphold.[164] This depicts that the balancing factor, by infusing the element of reasonableness, comprises the *raison d'être* and the basis of abuse of rights.

2.101 A case in Argentina demonstrates that the court may bar one from exercising his right if such an exercise is unreasonable or may cause greater damage to the other individual.[165] The case involved a potential buyer interested in acquiring two adjacent apartments in a building. Between both apartments there was an internal corridor, which was not owned by anyone, but was to be used by all owners of the building. The

158 Article 7 of Quebec Civil Code, translated in Byers (n 13) 395.

159 *Higgins Oil and Fuel Co v Guaranty Oil Co*, 145 La 233, 82 So 206 (1919), 211; Greaves (n 98) 441; Yiannopoulos (n 4) 1182.

160 Mayrand (n 45) 1012–13.

161 Devine (n 34) 157; French *Cour de Cassation*, Civ 2e, 13 November 2015, no 13-28180 discussed below; Reid (n 2) 137; but cf Knapp (n 86) 111.

162 Morcos (n 40) 375; Sanhouri (n 72) 756–61.

163 ibid; Egyptian Court of Cassation, Session held on 26 October 2008, Challenge No 15487, Judicial Year 77, applying the balancing factor to determine if the initiation of proceedings were abusive.

164 ibid.

165 Case of Diario La Ley, 22 October 1974, Case No 71031, cited in Cueto-Rua (n 3) 993.

seller told the potential buyer that he might use part of the corridor to enhance the communication between both apartments. Following such representation, the buyer bought both apartments. Based on Argentinian law, the ownership is transferred to the buyer once a formal deed is signed before the notary, and the particulars and extent of the ownership rely on the information stated in the deed. There was no mention in the deed in relation to the use of the corridor. Following the sale, the buyer modified part of the corridor and thereafter, other owners of the building brought a suit against him on the grounds that they had a right to use the corridor. While it remains evident that the buyer had no right to modify the corridor to benefit his apartments, and the owners did possess the right to use it, the Court analysed the interests at stake; it provided that while such modification is important to the buyer, it does not cause any serious damage to the other owners. The Court concluded that while the other owners had the right to use the full corridor, it would be an abuse of rights given that, unlike the buyer, the other owners did not have a serious interest in exercising their right.

In Germany, courts use the test of reasonableness to establish whether there is an abuse of rights. It is provided that the 'notion of reasonableness implies a reasonable use of rights. The reasonable man would not carry a legal interest to an extreme. The reasonable man test is, therefore, employed by judges as a means against abuse of rights'.[166] **2.102**

The test of reasonableness as a criterion of abuse is neither peculiar to, nor inconsistent with, Louisiana law,[167] where it is often held that analysing 'a claim of abuse of rights requires a careful balancing of competing policies'.[168] Moreover, it is submitted that the balancing process is utilized by the courts irrespective of the criterion upon which they base their decisions on claims of abuse of rights.[169] **2.103**

Belgian law similarly recognizes the principle of abuse of rights as an application of the general principle of good faith.[170] In relation to the criteria of abuse, it is well acknowledged that reasonableness, and balancing of the competing interests, comprises a criterion of abuse.[171] In defining abuse of rights, Belgian courts often provide that it is an exercise of a right in a manner that a prudent person would not undertake.[172] In **2.104**

[166] Willi E Joachim, 'The "Reasonable Man" in United States and German Commercial Law' (1992) 15 Comparative Law Ybk of International Business 341, 354.

[167] *State Ex Rel Bailey v City of W Monroe*, 418 So 2d 570 (La.1982).

[168] Armstrong and LaMaster (n 125) 16.

[169] *Travelers Indemnity Co v Hunt*, 371 So 2d 342 (La App 4th Cir), *writ denied*, 374 So 2d 657 (1979) 343–44, as previously mentioned, while this case pertained to the 'purpose of the right' as a criterion of abuse, the decision of the Court and its rationale were primarily premised on the element of reasonableness of the conduct in question; *McCastle v Rollins Envtl Serv*, 456 So 2d 612, 618 (La 1984); *Equipements Select Inc v Banque Nationale du Canada*, Sup Ct Québec, No 20005003613820, 18 November 1986 translated in *Banque Nationale du Canada v Houle* [1990] 3 SCR 122, 41, where the Court applied the 'reasonableness' test, even though it based its decision on bad faith as a criterion of abuse: 'a thorough analysis of the facts of those cases indicates that reasonableness was a determinative factor of "bad faith" or "malice"'.

[170] Article 1134.3 of the Belgian Civil Code; Temmerman (117) 6.

[171] Voyame, Cottier, and Rocha (n 71) 34; Zimmermann and Whittaker (n 82) 521.

[172] Belgian Court of Cassation, 8 February 2001 (AC 2001, no 78); Belgian Court of Cassation, 1 February 1996 (AC 1996, no 66); Belgian Court of Cassation, 21 June 2000 (AC 2000, no 392); Belgian Court of Cassation, 11 June 1992 (AC 1991–92, no 534); Belgian Court of Cassation, 10 September 1971 (AC 1972, 42), cited in Temmerman (n 117) 7.

applying abuse of rights, the Belgian Court of Cassation often holds that an exercise of a right is deemed abusive where it appears that the right was exercised without a reasonable interest, which is established if there is disparity between the interests which are served by the exercise of the right and the interests which could be damaged as a result of such exercise.[173]

2.105 It is interesting to note a case decided by the Canadian Supreme Court that dealt with abuse of rights and the criterion of reasonableness. The case pertained to a bank's right to take possession and liquidate the company's held assets.[174] In this case, the Court scrupulously examined the principle of abuse of rights in the Canadian jurisprudence, evaluated the different criteria adopted by the courts in contractual and extra-contractual matters, and concluded that the objective criterion of reasonableness was suitable in determining an abuse of rights. Applying the law of Quebec, the Court stated that:

> The time has come to assert that malice or the absence of good faith should *no longer* be the exclusive criteria to assess whether a contractual right has been abused [. . .] there can no longer be a debate in Quebec law that *the less stringent standard of 'the reasonable exercise' of a right*, the conduct of the prudent and reasonable individual, as opposed to the more stringent test of malice and the absence of good faith, can ground liability resulting from an abuse of contractual rights.[175] (Emphasis added).

2.106 In South Africa, it is acknowledged that the criterion used to find an abuse of rights is reasonableness. In doing so, South African courts consider other elements including the existence of malice, legitimate/serious motive, and the damages suffered by the exercise of the right.[176]

2.107 Moreover, the balancing factor is not peculiar to the common law's depiction of abuse.[177] The English case of *Jameel v Dow Jones* illustrates this submission. The Claimant brought defamation proceedings in relation to an alleged defamatory internet article that had been accessed by five people. The Court dismissed the claim and, upon considering all the competing interests, decided that the claim constituted an abuse of process. Precisely, the Court applied the criterion of reasonableness. The Court engaged in a balancing process between one's right of freedom of expression under the European Convention on Human Rights and the protection of one's reputation. Given

[173] Belgian Court of Cassation, 18 June 1987 (AC 1986–87, 1441); Belgian Court of Cassation, 19 September 1983 (A.C., 1983–1984, 53–54), cited in Temmerman (n 117) 7.
[174] *Banque Nationale du Canada v Houle* [1990] 3 SCR 122, 3–4.
[175] ibid 44–45.
[176] *Gien v Gien*, 1979 (2) SA 1121 (South Africa); Reid (n 2) 151.
[177] *Attorney General v Barker* [2000] 1 FLR 759, where the Court noted: 'The hallmark of a vexatious proceeding is in my judgment that it has little or no basis in law (or at least no discernible basis); that whatever the intention of the proceeding may be, its effect is to subject the defendant to inconvenience, harassment and expense *out of all proportion to any gain likely to accrue to the claimant*; and that it involves an abuse of the process of the court, meaning by that a use of the court process for a purpose or in a way which is significantly different from the ordinary and proper use of the court process.

the minimal damage caused by the publication, the Court found the claim unreasonable, disproportional, and thus constituted an abuse of process.[178]

Thirdly, not only does the balancing factor depict the basis of abuse of rights but it is submitted that this criterion is sufficiently broad to encompass the other criteria as well. This causes the other criteria to become imperative factual elements; indices, which assist courts/tribunals in establishing whether the exercise of right was reasonable.[179] **2.108**

In relation to the exercise of a right with an *intent to inflict harm*, this falls under the ambit of the unreasonable exercise of rights. If an exercise of a right is abusive where there is disparity between the interests and harm caused, the exercise of a right to merely inflict harm is, a fortiori, abusive given that the malicious intent is neither a legitimate nor a serious interest.[180] **2.109**

A contextual analysis of the different competing interests at stake must be conducted in order to establish abuse. Whilst such analysis is not necessary where the right holder has no legitimate or serious interest at all, it is indispensable in cases where the right is exercised for a pretext of a fictitious or minimal interest that is outweighed by the harm caused. **2.110**

In this regard, cases that involve a *mixture of motives* do not seem to be challenging if courts adopt the balancing factor. Where a right holder is driven by plurality of motives, some legitimate or serious, such as to seek an economic advantage, (as was the case in the *affaire Clément-Bayard*), the balancing factor enables decision makers to examine all the particulars of the case, any motives associated with the exercise of the right, and decide if the conduct in question is unreasonable. As stated in the *affaire Clément-Bayard*, the Court found an abuse given that the right holder expected the possible damages that may occur, accepted such damages, with the purpose of reaching his ends on capitalizing his profits, to the detriment of *Clément-Bayard*. In reaching its decision, it seems palpable that the Court indirectly adopted the balancing factor. While a legitimate motive existed, and the right holder was not acting directly to cause harm to another, the analysis of the competing interests at stake revealed to the Court that the predominant motive was an illegitimate one and the exercise was unreasonable. **2.111**

Additionally, in relation to the exercise of a right for a purpose other than that for which it was granted, this also falls under the ambit of the balancing factor and constitutes an *indicium* to assist courts in finding an abuse. Measuring the reasonableness of the act in question necessarily entails an investigation of the purpose of the exercise of the right and how it impacted others.[181] The leading Japanese case of *Mitamura v Suzuki* clearly **2.112**

[178] *Jameel v Dow Jones and Co Inc* [2005] EWCA Civ 75, [2005] QB 946.

[179] Ascensio (n 78) 780–81, providing that an 'intent to harm' should not be a condition, but 'it should be assessed by tribunals in connection with other criteria—objective ones').

[180] Walton (n 33) 502; Cueto-Rua (n 3) 995–96; *Milward v Glaser* (1949) 4 SA 931 (South African case providing that malice necessarily means that the exercise of the right was unreasonable); Reid (n 2) 151.

[181] Crabb (n 13) 22; Morcos (n 40) 375; Armstrong and LaMaster (n 125) 18.

illustrates the interrelation between the balancing factor and the social purpose of the right in question.[182] In this case, the Japanese Supreme Court held that:

> In all cases a right must be exercised in such a fashion that the result of the exercise remains within a scope judged *reasonable* in the light of the prevailing *social conscience*. When a conduct by one who purports to *have* a right to do so fails to show *social reasonableness* and when the consequential damages to others exceed the limit which is generally supposed to be borne in the social life, we must say that the exercise of the right is no longer within its permissible scope. Thus, the person who exercises his right in such a fashion shall be held liable because his conduct constitutes an abuse of right.[183] (Emphasis added).

2.113 This is further confirmed by the decision of the Supreme Court of Canada where it was explicitly stated that the criterion of reasonableness may 'encompass a number of situations, including the use of a contract for purposes other than the ones contemplated by the parties'.[184]

2.114 In 2015, the French Court of Cassation applied the balancing factor. The Court also implicitly demonstrated how the balancing factor may operate by encompassing other criteria of abuse as factual indices. The case[185] pertained to a mortgage debt assignment agreement concluded between MP (assignee) and FGI (assignor) whereby the latter transferred to the former its entitlement to the debt it had towards SCI (the real estate promoter of the mortgaged building). The initial creditor of SCI was not the assignor but a bank that later assigned its debt to FGI. The assignee attempted to exercise its seizure right against the residents of the building. The Court of Appeal nullified the seizure procedures on the basis that they constituted an abuse of right. The French Court of Cassation reiterated the Court of Appeal's findings and concluded that there was an abuse of right.

2.115 The Court held that the right of seizure conflicts with real-estate property right which is a constitutional right. Accordingly, it may not be invoked unless properly exercised.

2.116 In assessing the proportionality and reasonableness of the seizure procedures, one submits that the Court considered the intention of exercising the right and the purpose of the assignment agreement. The Court deduced that an intent to inflict harm motivated the assignee to attempt the seizure procedures. The Court highlighted the presence of a dispute between the assignee and the residents of the building in relation to the former's easement of a right of way. The Court concluded that the presence of such a dispute was the primary reason behind the seizure proceedings. The assignee's intention to cause harm was also deduced from the correspondences issued by the assignee's counsel, which included explicit terms referring to the assignee's intention of revenge.

[182] Byers (n 13) 393.
[183] Sono and Fujioka (n 40) 1037.
[184] *Banque Nationale du Canada v Houle* [1990] 3 SCR 122, 57.
[185] French *Cour de Cassation*, Civ 2e, 13 November 2015, no 13-28180.

Thus, the Court explained that the assignee concluded the assignment agreement on its 'subsidiary' intention and that the recovery of the debt was only a pretext advanced by the assignee to justify the seizure procedures. **2.117**

Further, the Court implicitly considered the deviation of purpose criterion. The court emphasized that the purpose of exercising the seizure proceedings attempted by the assignee greatly differed from the parties' common intention (purpose shared by the parties when concluding the assignment agreement).[186] **2.118**

This reflects the balancing process required by courts. The Court considered the weight of property rights, together with the fact that the assignee had exercised the right of seizure to inflict harm, and had deviated from the common intention of the parties at the time of concluding the agreement. Based on all of this, the Court concluded that this constituted an abuse of right. **2.119**

Based on the above, it is submitted that defining abuse in terms of reasonableness effectively includes all the other 'criteria' as factual elements to measure the degree of reasonableness. As stated by Bin Cheng:[187] **2.120**

> [R]ights must be *reasonably* exercised. The *reasonable* and bona fide exercise of a right implies an exercise which is genuinely in *pursuit of those interests which the right is destined to protect* and which is *not calculated to cause* any *unfair prejudice* to the *legitimate interests* of another [. . .]. The exact line dividing the right from the obligation, or, in other words, the line delimiting the rights of both parties is traced at a point where there is a *reasonable balance between the conflicting interests involved.* This becomes the limit between the right and obligation, and constitutes, in effect, the limit between the respective rights of the parties. The protection of the law extends as far as this limit [. . .]. Any violation of this limit constitutes an abuse of right and a breach of the obligation - an unlawful act.[188] (Emphasis added).

It becomes clear that embracing the balancing factor as a criterion of abuse enables decision makers to take into consideration whether the right holder exercised the right: (1) with an intent to harm; (2) with legitimate and serious interests; or (3) against the purpose intended by the right. Thus, it is more accurate to state that the balancing factor comprises *the* criterion of abuse, and that all other 'criteria' comprise sub-factors, *indices*, to be used and investigated as factual elements in order to measure the degree of reasonableness of the right in question.[189] **2.121**

Fourthly, a review of the principle's application as a general principle of law, as shall be discussed below, reveals that arbitral tribunals do not restrict themselves to a strict criterion of abuse but rather assess all the factual matrix of the case and often endorse the **2.122**

[186] ibid.
[187] It is to be noted that Bin Cheng's statement relates to the principle of abuse of rights in the context of international law.
[188] Cheng (n 32) 131–32.
[189] Ascensio (n 78) 780–81.

balancing factor. As provided by one tribunal, the criterion of abuse should strike a fair balance between the need to safeguard one's rights and the need to deny protection to abusive conduct.[190]

2.123 In the recent case of *Teinver and Autobuses v Argentine*,[191] the investors claimed that the host State abused its right in starting criminal investigations. The Claimants alleged that the State had threatened criminal prosecution to the Claimants and their legal representatives for their role in the arbitration, and used the State media to disseminate inflammatory statements about the Claimants and their legal counsel. In the Claimants' view, these abusive actions were motivated by the State's attempt to aggravate the dispute, to mount a smear campaign before the arbitral Tribunal, to prevent the enforcement of the Tribunal's eventual award, and to undermine the integrity of the arbitration, and thus constituted 'an abuse of Argentine's domestic criminal process for the purpose of avoiding the payment of compensation required under international law for the admitted expropriation of Claimants' investments in Argentine'.[192] The Respondent asserted that such claims were unsubstantiated, and that without concrete evidence of abuse, provisional measures could not be justified.[193]

2.124 The Claimants' adoption of the balancing factor to prove an abuse of right, as well as its application by the Tribunal is conspicuous. The Claimants based their claim of an abuse of the State's rights on that their request to suspend the criminal proceedings would not unreasonably burden the State: 'While Claimants would suffer irreparable harm if the provisional measures are not granted, Respondent would not incur any meaningful harm'.[194] This reflected an explicit application of the balancing factor. As shall be mentioned, an imperative element of the balancing factor is that courts/tribunals should also investigate/consider the personal interests of the parties by conducting a *comparative impairment test*: comparing the gravity of damages between the parties and the benefits potentially realized from the exercise of the right.[195]

2.125 Similarly, in deciding that there was no abuse of rights and rejecting the Claimants' request, the Tribunal first acknowledged that the State had a sovereign right to conduct criminal investigations. However, it was also recognized that if such right was abused, provisional measures may be granted, as well as a potential award for damages. The Tribunal balanced the above considerations against the fact that the remaining step in the arbitration proceedings was the rendering of the award, and concluded that there

190 *Renée Rose Levy and Gremcitel SA v Republic of Peru*, ICSID Case No ARB/11/17, Award of 9 January 2015, para 185.

191 *Teinver SA, Transportes de Cercanias SA and Autobuses Urbanos del Sur SA v The Argentine Republic*, ICSID Case No ARB/09/1, Decision on Provisional Measures of 8 April 2016.

192 ibid paras 74–76, 101, and 131.

193 ibid para 115.

194 ibid para 108.

195 Morcos (n 40) 375; Mayrand (n 45) 1000–02; Crabb (n 13) 19–20; *Epoux Vullion v Société immobilière Vernet- Christophe Subsequent Developments*, JCP 1971. 2. 16781, translated by Tony Weir; Netherland's Supreme Court in *Kuipers v De Jongh*, H.R. April 17, 1970, N.J. 1971, no. 89, translated in Brunner (n 48) 739.

was no pending harm from any abuse.[196] However, the Tribunal found that using the media to publicize the dispute was abusive as it had aggravated the dispute, and thus a provisional measure ordering the Respondent to refrain from the aggravation of the dispute in this regard was issued.[197]

In another case, *Quilborax v Bolivia*, the Claimants requested provisional measures ordering the Respondent to discontinue criminal proceedings relating to the arbitration.[198] It was the Claimants' submission that the State abused its right to investigate criminal behaviour, as it used its right solely to influence the current arbitration, as an abusive tactic to avoid the arbitration on the merits, and to force the Claimants to give up their claims.[199] **2.126**

The Tribunal noted that Bolivia had an inherent right to conduct criminal investigations. The Tribunal then highlighted that this right was *not* absolute, could be abused, and must be balanced against the Claimants' right to pursue the arbitration, and to have their claims fairly considered.[200] By balancing Bolivia's interest to pursue criminal investigations against the Claimants' interest in resolving their dispute before the Tribunal, and their right to have access to evidence and the integrity of the evidence (the criminal proceedings had a material effect on potential witnesses), the Tribunal found that there was an abuse and issued provisional measures. It is of particular interest to note that the Tribunal also considered and balanced the potential harm caused by the exercise of right, and concluded that: 'the harm that such a stay would cause to Bolivia is proportionately less than the harm caused to Claimants if the criminal proceedings were to continue'.[201] This is an explicit application of the reasonableness criterion of abuse. **2.127**

The proposition that arbitral tribunals generally adopt the balancing factor to establish any abuse of right is further fortified if one recognizes cases where arbitrators have considered the conduct of the aggrieved party, and whether it was also tainted with any abuse.[202] As mentioned earlier, the evaluation of the conduct of the aggrieved party should be taken into consideration when assessing the existence of abuse. The fact that tribunals rightly consider the reasonableness of the aggrieved party's conduct as well confirms that reasonableness comprises the *raison d'être* of the principle's foundation and that it is an effective criterion of abuse. No other criteria justifies considering the conduct of the aggrieved party in assessing claims of abuse of rights. **2.128**

[196] *Teinver SA, Transportes de Cercanias SA and Autobuses Urbanos del Sur SA v The Argentine Republic*, ICSID Case No ARB/09/1, Decision on Provisional Measures of 8 April 2016, paras 190–91.

[197] ibid para 210.

[198] *Quilborax SA, Non Metallic Minerals SA and Allan Fosk Kaplún v Plurinational State of Bolivia*, ICSID Case No ARB/06/2, Decision on Provisional Measures of 26 February 2010.

[199] ibid para 46.

[200] ibid paras 123 and 148.

[201] ibid para 165.

[202] *Ampal-American Israel Corp et al v Arab Republic of Egypt*, ICSID Case No ARB/12/11, Decision on Jurisdiction of 1 February 2016, para 329.

2.129 Finally, the balancing factor comprises an objective test which enables decision makers to examine one's external behaviour and the particulars of the dispute rather than the never-ending legal quest of fishing in one's internal belief to deduce an intent and to unveil one's veiled will.[203] The corrective role of abuse of rights, to ameliorate the harshness of law, further fortifies that abuse should not necessarily be linked to the state of mind of the right holder, but rather to his/her conduct which reveals his/her interests as opposed to the other conflicting interests at stake.[204] In this regard, it has been stated that:

> [I]t is not the will or intent of the holder of the right that counts, but the results of his acts. In this situation, a *balancing of interests* is necessary for the determination of the questions of the type of redress that should be accorded, namely, an award of damages, restoration of a previous situation, or injunctive relief for the future.[205] (Emphasis added).

2.130 The 'balancing factor' criterion may be seen as a double edged sword: it grants wide discretionary power to courts/tribunals. However, this discretionary power is indispensable for a principle such as the abuse of rights. The very existence of the principle rests on its function as a *corrective* tool, to ameliorate the harshness of positive law. This role primarily relies on the discretionary power of decision makers.

(ii) Applying the balancing factor to find an abuse of rights

2.131 While it is apparent that the balancing factor is generally used, explicitly or implicitly, by courts and arbitrators, there is no guidance on how such a balancing exercise is to be undertaken and how to identify the competing interests involved. However, one does not purport to lay down a strict or rigid path that should be followed by courts/tribunals. A contrario, it is submitted that the application of a principle, which attempts to ameliorate the harshness and inflexibility of the law, should be left as a flexible tool to be utilized by the decision maker given the specificities of the dispute in question.[206] In this regard, it has been rightly stated by Lauterpacht that the 'determination of the point at which the exercise of a legal right has degenerated into an abuse of a right is a question which cannot be decided by an abstract legislative rule, but only by the activity of courts drawing the line in each particular case'.[207]

[203] Walton (n 33) 501; Devine (n 34) 148; O'Sullivan, 'Abuse of Rights' (1955) 8 Current Legal Problems 66; FP Walton, 'Delictual Responsibility in the Modern Civil Law (More Particularly in the French Law) as Compared with the English Law of Torts' (1933) 49 Law Quarterly Review 70, 87–9.

[204] Yiannopoulos (n 4) 1197; Saleh (n 150) 349; Tête (n 111) 79–80.

[205] Yiannopoulos (n 4) 1197; *Higgins Oil & Fuel Co v Guaranty Oil Co*, 145 La 233, 82 So 206 (1919) 211 ('cases like the present one are not to be decided by the application of any broad or inflexible rule, but by a careful weighing of all the circumstances attending them, by diagnosing them'); *Moss v Burke & Trotti, Inc*, 198 La 76, 81, 3 So 2d 281, 283 (1941).

[206] Borman (n 137) 389; *Mobil Corp v Republic of Venezuela*, ICSID Case No. ARB/07/27, Decision on Jurisdiction of 10 June 2010, paras 177 and 184; *Renée Rose Levy and Gremcitel SA v Republic of Peru*, ICSID Case No ARB/11/17, Award of 9 January 2015, para 186; *Transglobal Green Energy LLC and Transglobal Green Panama SA v Republic of Panama*, ICSID Case No ARB/12/28, Award of 2 June 2016, para 118.

[207] Herch Lauterpacht, *The Development of International Law by the International Court* (Cambridge University Press 1982) 162.

Establishing abuse requires courts/arbitrators to deduce whether there exists a 'true conflict' of interests or a 'false conflict'.[208] The extent of 'balancing' of competing interests required will necessarily depend on whether there is a true conflict of interests, or if the appearance of such is false. 2.132

At first, courts need to examine if the act in question is exercised without any legitimate interest, that is, solely to inflict harm to another. If it is proven that the right holder had no other purpose but to inflict harm, abuse is established and there is no need to further investigate or dwell upon the issue.[209] In these cases, it is submitted that the illicit interest to inflict harm vitiates all other interests.[210] Thus, there is no true conflict of interests, as the law does not confer a right to be exercised for an illicit purpose and thus legal protection is extended to the aggrieved by ordering the demolishment and/or compensation for the damages caused.[211] Example of false conflict cases include the case where a party initiates judicial proceedings not to safeguard or enforce a particular right, but solely to damage the reputation of his opponent, to prolong litigation, or to force the adversary to incur legal costs of litigation.[212] It is submitted that in these cases there exists no true conflict of interests and thus, no material balancing of interests is required to establish abuse. 2.133

In the majority of cases it will be difficult to deduce malice given its inherent evidentiary limitation. Furthermore, in most cases, rights are exercised for a multiplicity of purposes, primary and secondary, making it difficult to decide the predominant one. 2.134

In such cases courts/tribunals are required to look further in order to determine if there is an abuse of rights. Courts are to examine all interests at stake. If it is the case that each party has a legitimate interest prescribed by the law and is thus requesting the court's assistance to protect it, this amounts to a case of true conflict of interests, where the courts must utilize the balancing factor to solve it.[213] 2.135

Decision makers are to carefully investigate the competing interests weighing for and against finding an abuse. Some of the interests against finding an abuse may include, inter alia, the interest to give effect to clear legal rules/contractual provisions, and treat it as a decisive reflection of one's rights, to advance legal certainty and security 2.136

[208] The terms 'true conflict' and 'false conflict' are used to differentiate between cases where decision makers are faced with legitimate competing interests that require a balancing exercise to decide which interest(s) ought to be upheld; and cases that involve one-sided acknowledged interests versus illegitimate interest(s), which does not strictly require a balancing exercise.

[209] Catala and Weir (n 40) 225–26.

[210] Cheng (n 32) 122.

[211] Pound (n 28) 228.

[212] Catala and Weir (n 40) 225–26; Nadja Erk, *Parallel Proceedings in International Arbitration: A Comparative European Perspective* (Kluwer Law International 2014) 11; Rosenberg (n 42) 20; H Foster, 'Abuse of Rights—Civil Law—Legal Reasoning: Bradford v Pickles Revisited' (1973) 8 University of British Columbia Law Review 343, 349; Walton (n 33) 508; Nathan Tamblyn, 'Lawful Act Conspiracy: Malice and Abuse of Rights' (2013) Singapore Journal of Legal Studies 158, 166.

[213] ; Pannal A Sanders, '"At Will" Franchise Terminations and the Abuse of Rights Doctrine' (1981) 42 Louisiana Law Review 210, 223, providing that there is often a conflict/tension between several interests and policies in contractual arrangements: ('Security of transactions, freedom of contract, supremacy of the will, and fundamental fairness').

between individuals;[214] the interest of safeguarding autonomy of the will and freedom of contract.[215]

2.137 On the other hand, there are equally potent legal interests including: that a right should be exercised for a legitimate purpose and not comprise an instrument for the promotion of chicanery,[216] the right not to be damaged,[217] the exercise of a right should not deviate from the purpose intended by the law,[218] and the interest of reaching a fair and equitable decision.[219]

2.138 Moreover, an imperative element of the balancing factor is that courts are to also investigate the personal interests of the parties by conducting a comparative impairment test: comparing the gravity of damages between the parties and the benefits potentially realised from the exercise of the right.[220] In a dispute regarding the construction of a garage between the lands of the disputants, the Supreme Court of the Netherlands referred to the principle of abuse of rights and utilized the balancing factor by conducting a comparative impairment test:

> This, however, does not exclude the possibility that De Jongh would have abused her right by demanding the removal of the garage from her land, instead of accepting a reasonable compensation, *in case the loss* Kuipers would suffer by its removal, *considered both independently and in comparison to De Jongh's interests, would be so heavy that De Jongh could not reasonably have decided to exercise her right to demand the removal.* (Emphasis added).[221]

2.139 Based on all the above, which shall be deduced from the factual particulars of the case, decision makers are to decide which interest ought to be legally protected. These interests will necessarily vary from one legal area to another (abuse of contractual terms raises different competing interests from abuse of initiating parallel proceedings) and the weight given to each interest will necessarily differ based on the factual matrix of the case.[222]

2.140 Cases of true conflict dominate the arena of abuse of rights and are manifested in all legal areas. On such account, *exempli gratia*, where a party initiates parallel judicial or arbitral proceedings regarding interrelated issues, his opposing party may argue that such conduct is tantamount to an abuse of right.[223] Given that in many cases the party

[214] *Banque Nationale du Canada v Houle* [1990] 3 SCR 122, 33; Jukier (n 152) 234; Crabb (n 13) 22–23.
[215] Mayrand (n 45) 1004; Jukier (n 152) 233.
[216] Crabb (n 13) 23; Gutteridge (n 52) 22–23.
[217] Glanville L Williams, 'The Foundation of Tortious Liability' (1939) 7 Cambridge Law Journal 111116.
[218] Morcos (n 40) 375; 26; Sono and Fujioka (n 40) 1037; Cheng (n 32) 125.
[219] *Aselford Martin Shopping Centres Ltd v AL Raymond Ltée* [1990] RJQ (CS), 1974–1976, where the Court disregarded an explicit contractual provision on the basis of abuse of rights, and decided that principles such as fairness, justice and equity override the freedom of contract and autonomy of the will, cited in Jukier (n 152) 236–37; *Banque Nationale du Canada v Houle* [1990] 3 SCR 122, 33; Cheng (n 32) 125.
[220] Morcos (n 40) 375; Mayrand (n 45) 1000–02; Crabb (n 13) 19–20; *Epoux Vullion v Société immobilière Vernet- Christophe Subsequent Developments*, JCP 1971 2 16781, translated by Tony Weir; Netherland's Supreme Court in *Kuipers v De Jongh*, HR 17 April 1970, NJ 1971, no 89, translated in Brunner (n 48) 739.
[221] Netherland's Supreme Court in *Kuipers v De Jongh*, HR April 17, 1970, NJ 1971, no 89, translated in Brunner (n 48) 739.
[222] Cheng (n 32) 124–25.
[223] *Lauder v Czech Republic*, UNCITRAL Final Award of 3 September 2001; *CME v Czech Republic*, UNCITRAL Partial Award of 13 September 2001, where abuse of process was argued albeit rejected by the arbitral Tribunal.

who initiates parallel proceedings does so in pursuit of many legal and personal interests, it is submitted that courts may effectively utilize the balancing factor to resolve such complex issues.

In the prevailing normative scenario, some of the interests for initiating the parallel proceedings comprise: forum shopping, to gain certain substantive and/or procedural benefits;[224] cases of pathological jurisdiction or arbitration clauses;[225] for the location of the debtor's assets;[226] as a dilatory tactic,[227] to exert financial pressure or to force a settlement etc.[228] On the other hand, the opposing party also has interests that may comprise, inter alia, the need for procedural harmonization; economy of justice and fairness;[229] aversion of early access to one's arguments in the parallel proceedings in revealing a party's defence strategy; and promoting legal coherence and aversion of conflicting or duplication of awards.[230] 2.141

Courts may effectively use the balancing factor to weigh the relevant competing interests and measure the degree of reasonableness of the act of initiating the parallel proceedings.[231] Evidently, the seriousness and reasonableness of any of the interests stated above will primarily depend on the factual matrix of the case. For example, while forum shopping is not necessarily an illegitimate interest,[232] it may be found unreasonable if the subject matter of the parallel proceedings is greatly intertwined, as in such a case the conundrum of having conflicting judgments/awards regarding intertwined issues is augmented. 2.142

Similarly, cases of abuse of contractual rights may involve a true conflict of interests.[233] In the *Houle* case mentioned above, the Canadian Supreme Court acknowledged that finding an abuse entailed disregarding the autonomy of the will and *pacta sunt servanda*. However, upon examining the competing interests, the Court decided 2.143

[224] Richard Kreindler, 'Parallel Proceedings: A Practitioner's Perspective', in Michael Waibel and Asha Kaushal (eds), *The Backlash against Investment Arbitration* (Kluwer Law International 2010) 128; Erk (n 212) 12–13; Richard Kreindler, 'Arbitral Forum Shopping', in Bernardo M Cremades and Julian DM Lew (eds), *Parallel State and Arbitral Procedures in International Arbitration* (ICC Publishing 2005) 159, 166, and 178; Yuval Shany, *The Competing Jurisdictions of International Courts and Tribunals* (Oxford University Press 2003) 259.

[225] Erk (n 212) 11–12.

[226] Stephen Cromie, *International Commercial Litigation* (2nd edn, Butterworths 1997) 473; Erk (n 212) 11 ('a creditor, by contrast, may be forced to institute parallel proceedings in different jurisdictions if the debtor's assets are situated in different countries').

[227] Parallel proceedings may be initiated as a dilatory tactic in order to gain time and hide one's assets. Erk (n 212) 11

[228] Joseph T McLaughlin, 'Arbitration and Developing Countries' (1979) 13 The International Lawyer 211, 211; Erk (n 212) 11.

[229] Philippe Leboulanger, 'Multi-Contract Arbitration' (1996) 13 Journal of International Arbitration 43, 54–55, and 62–64; Jamie Shookman, 'Too Many Forums for Investment Disputes? (2010) 27 Journal of International Arbitration 361, 362; Erk (n 212) 15.

[230] Shookman (n 229) 362; Leboulanger (n 229) 62–64; Erk (n 212) 15; Gilles Cuniberti, 'Parallel Litigation and Foreign Investment Dispute Settlement' (2006) 21 ICSID Review 381, 414.

[231] Shany (n 224) 258–59, providing that abuse of rights in the context of parallel proceedings enables a balance of interests to determine if the initiation of the parallel proceedings is reasonable or abusive.

[232] Erk (n 212) 12–13; Franco Ferrari, 'Forum Shopping in the International Commercial Arbitration Context: Setting the Stage' in Franco Ferrari (ed), *Forum Shopping in the International Commercial Arbitration Context* (Sellier European Law Publisher 2013) 1–21.

[233] For an analysis of applying abuse of rights on the basis of the proposed balancing factor in the context of landlord–tenant disputes, see Armstrong and LaMaster (n 125) 14–18; *Sté Fiat Auto France v SA Cachia Holding et autres, Recueil Dalloz-Sirey* 1995 J 355, cited in Reid (n 2) 139–40.

that reasonableness, fairness, and reaching an equitable outcome prevailed over the other interests.[234]

2.144 To conclude, the balancing factor requires courts to examine all competing interests involved in the case in order to determine if an abuse of right is established. Such interests will greatly vary depending on the legal dispute and the particulars of each case.

4. The exercise of the right in good faith

2.145 Bad faith as a criterion of abuse raises a number of issues that warrant elaboration. While some legal systems endorse bad faith as a criterion of abuse, such position is questionable given that abuse of rights is an application of the broader concept of good faith.

2.146 Prior to embarking on an analysis of bad faith as a criterion of abuse **(iii)**; and highlighting the interrelation between good faith and abuse of rights **(ii)**; it seems proper to first shed light on the meaning of good faith **(i)**.

2.147 An abridged examination of the meaning of good faith and its relation to the principle of abuse of rights is of paramount importance in order to demonstrate that good faith should not be regarded as a criterion of abuse.

(i) Definition of good faith

2.148 The term 'faith' in the terms 'good faith' or 'bad faith' refers to purpose or intent.[235] Both 'good faith' and 'bad faith' are by definition antonyms, they are inherently two irreconcilable concepts, where the existence of one excludes the existence of the other.[236]

2.149 The principle of good faith is a principle that eludes a priori definition.[237] It is recognized that the meaning of good faith, in domestic or international law, varies with the context.[238] Such confusion is exacerbated when one acknowledges that it may also vary within one legal system.[239] It is often questioned whether the principle is a concept with

[234] A similar conclusion was reached by the Canadian Court in *Drouin v Electolux Canada Ltée* [1988] RJQ 950 (CA); and in *Posluns v Enterprises Lormil Inc* [1990] Quebec 200-05-001584-858, JE 90-1131 (CS), cited in Jukier (n 152) 235–36.

[235] Definition as given by *Black's Law Dictionary* (4th edn, West Publishing Co 1968) 719.

[236] Tête (n 111) 59–60.

[237] *Russel v Russel* [1897] AC 436, providing that terms such as good faith and honesty can be illustrated but not defined.

[238] Richard E Speidel, 'The "Duty" of Good Faith in Contract Performance and Enforcement' (1996) 46 Journal of Legal Education 537, 540; section (205) Restatement (Second) of Contracts, comment (a) (1981); Robert Kolb, Principles as Sources of International Law: With Special Reference to Good Faith' (2006) 53 Netherlands International Law Review 1, 13–14; *Wintershell et al v The Government of Qatar*, Ad hoc award of 1988, (1988) 15 Ybk Commercial Arbitration 30; John Honnold, *Documentary history of the uniform law for international sales: the studies, deliberations, and decisions that led to the 1980 United Nations Convention with introductions and explanations* (Kluwer Law 1989) 298; Michael Bridge, 'Does Anglo-Canadian Contract Law Need a Doctrine of Good Faith?' (1984) 9 Canadian Business Law Journal 385, 407.

[239] Zimmermann and Whittaker (n 82) 690.

a general meaning that applies to different situations that fall within its purview, or if it is more than one concept sharing the same name.[240]

Given its various applications, its hybrid manifestations and its broad scope, it is often said that any definition of the principle of good faith either spirals 'into the Charybdis of vacuous generality or collide with the Scylla of restrictive specificity'.[241] Thus, some argue that it is more efficient to focus on forms and elements of good faith rather than attempt to define it. **2.150**

Similarly, its scope is rather elusive.[242] It is difficult to provide what acts contravene the principle.[243] The difficulty emanates from the fact that the constituents of good faith are various and ambiguous. **2.151**

In attempting to illustrate the concept, some emphasize the subjective element of the principle: the psychological element of investigating one's state of mind.[244] However, the predominant view focuses on objective elements.[245] Thus, it is said that it imposes an obligation of 'playing fairly', 'coming clean', or 'putting one's cards on the table', observing the standards of 'honesty', 'reasonableness', 'a duty of cooperation', and 'protecting reasonable expectations'.[246] In using such terms, it is often said that they are difficult to define which render 'those definitional attempts into mere substitutions of words that fail to provide the clarity warrantedly expected from either a definition or an explanation'.[247] **2.152**

Some argue that good faith means one should not frustrate legitimate and reasonable expectations.[248] **2.153**

[240] Saul Litvinoff, 'Good Faith' (1997) 71 Tulane Law Review 1645, 1649; Robert S Summers, '"Good Faith" in General Contract Law and the Sales Provisions of the Uniform Commercial Code' (1968) 54 Virginia Law Review 199; BJ Reiter, 'Good Faith in Contracts' (1983) 17 Valparaiso University Law Review 705.

[241] Summers (n 240) 206.

[242] Ewan McKendrick, *Contract Law* (9th edn, Palgrave Macmillan 2011) 221–22; Bernardo M Cremades, 'Good Faith in International Arbitration' (2012) 27 American University International Law Review 761, 761; Paul J Powers, 'Defining the Undefinable: Good Faith and the United Nations Convention on the Contracts for the International Sale of Goods' (1999) 18 Journal of Law and Commerce 333, 334.

[243] Reiter (n 240) 706.

[244] Robert Kolb, 'Principles as Sources of International Law: With Special Reference to Good Faith' (2006) 53 Netherlands International Law Review 1, 14.

[245] AS Hartkamp, 'Judicial Discretion under the New Civil Code of the Netherlands' (1992) 40 The American Journal of Comparative Law 551, 554–55; Michael Joachim Bonell, *An International Restatement of Contract Law: The UNIDROIT Principles of International Commercial Contracts* (3rd edn, Transnational Publishers 2005) 131.

[246] *Yam Seng Pte Limited v International Trade Corporation* [2013] EWHC 111 (QB) 121–45; the Australian New South Wales Court of Appeal in *Renard Constructions (ME) Pty v Minister for Public Works* (1992) 26 NSWLR 234; Cremades (n 242) 767–68; Lord Johan Steyn, 'Contract Law: Fulfilling the Reasonable Expectations of Honest Men' (1997) 113 Law Quarterly Review 433, 438–439; Malcolm N Shaw, *International Law* (6th edn, Cambridge University Press 2008) 103–4; *Nuclear Tests Cases* [1974] ICJ Rep 253, 267; E Allan Farnsworth, 'Good Faith Performance and Commercial Reasonableness Under the Uniform Commercial Code' (1963) 30 University of Chicago Law Review 666; Jane Stapleton, "Good Faith in Private Law" (1999) 52 Current Legal Problems 1, 7; Russel A Eisenberg, 'Good Faith under the Uniform Commercial Code—A New Look at an Old Problem' (1971) 54 Marquette Law Review 1; Andrew Terry and Cary Di Lernia, 'Franchising and the Quest for the Holy Grail: Good Faith or Good Intentions' (2009) 33 Melbourne University Law Review 542, 556–69.

[247] Litvinoff (n 240) 1664.

[248] JM Paterson, 'Duty of Good Faith: Does it Have a Place in Contract Law?' (2000) 74 Law Institute Journal 47, 48; Woo Pei Yee, 'Protecting Parties' Reasonable Expectations: A General Principle of Good Faith' (2001) 1 Oxford

2.154 Other scholars argue that good faith has no general meaning, but functions as an 'excluder'; it is a term that is used to exclude conduct tainted with bad faith.[249] However, one cannot accept this definition alone as it turns good faith to a vacuous shell that lacks actual content.[250] Not only does it lack certainty, but it fails to cover important aspects of the duty to act in good faith.

2.155 Good faith entails more than absence of bad faith, it comprises acts and omissions.[251] It presumes a co-operative obligation, an honest and reasonable conduct, and to have regard to the reasonable expectations and legitimate interests of the other party(ies).[252]

2.156 Finally, it is worth noting the definition of good faith adopted in the Restatement (Second) of Contracts. While taking into consideration that the meaning may vary depending on the context in which it is used, it is submitted that good faith:

> [E]mphasizes faithfulness to an agreed common purpose and consistency with the justified expectations of the other party; it excludes a variety of types of conduct characterized as involving 'bad faith' because they violate community standards of decency, fairness or reasonableness. The appropriate remedy for a breach of the duty of good faith also varies with the circumstances.[253]

2.157 The above definition finds a balance between the different views stated above. While it endorsed the 'excluder' view, it also gave effect to other aspects of good faith, namely, preserving the parties' reasonable expectations, and acting reasonably and fairly.

2.158 On a related note, it is submitted that the meaning of the principle of good faith encompasses the prohibition against abuse of rights. In the case of *Yam Seng Pte Limited v International Trade Corporation*, which discussed whether English law does or should recognize a general duty to perform contracts in good faith, Leggatt J emphasized that good faith covered many situations including that a power conferred by a

University Commonwealth Law Journal 195, 223; Pound (n 5) 215; Roscoe Pound, *Jurisprudence* (West Publishing Co 1959) vol 1, 413–15; Steven Burton, 'Breach of Contract and the Common Law Duty to Perform in Good Faith' (1980) 94 Harvard Law Review 369.

[249] Summers (n 240) 199–207; Robert S Summers, 'The General Duty of Good Faith—Its Recognition and Conceptualization' (1982) 67 Cornell Law Review 810, 818–19.

[250] Alan D Miller and Ronen Perry, 'Good Faith Performance' (2013) 98 Iowa Law Review 689, 704.

[251] Harold Dubroff, 'The Implied Covenant of Good Faith in Contract Interpretation and Gap-Filling: Reviling a Revered Relic' (2006) 80 St John's Law Review 559, 594–95; Tête (n 111) 59–60; Roger Brownsword, 'Positive, Negative, Neutral: the Reception of Good Faith in English Contract Law' in Roger Brownsword, Norma Hird, and Geraint Howells (eds), *Good Faith in Contract* (Ashgate 1999) 17; Litvinoff (n 240) 1665; Mohamed S Abdelwahab, 'The Nuts and Bolts of Construction Arbitration in the MENA: Principles and Practice' in Stavros Brekoulakis and David Thomas (eds), *The Guide to Construction Arbitration* (Global Arbitration Review 2017); Michael Bridge, 'Doubting Good Faith' (2005) 11 New Zealand Business Law Quarterly 426, 429.

[252] Anthony Mason, 'Contract, Good Faith and Equitable Standards in Fair Dealing' (2000) 116 Law Quarterly Review 66, 69; J Edward Bayley, 'A Doctrine of Good Faith in New Zealand Contractual Relationships' (Thesis, University of Canterbury 2009) 101–02, providing that there must be a balance between preserving a party's self-interest and giving effect to the other party's reasonable expectations; Brownsword (n 252) 17; E Allan Farnsworth, *Contracts* (2nd edn, Little, Brown and Company 1990) 550–51; Terry and Lernia (n 247) 551–52; Elisabeth Peden, *Good Faith in the Performance of Contracts* (LexisNexis Butterworths 2003) 170; Tête (n 111) 81.

[253] Section 205 of the Restatement (Second) of Contracts, Comment (a), (1981).

contract on one party must be exercised 'for the purpose for which it was conferred, and must not be exercised arbitrarily, capriciously or unreasonably'.[254] In this regard, it appears that the principle of good faith covers different aspects of abuse of rights, that is, that rights must be exercised reasonably and for the purpose for which the right was conferred.[255]

Another attempt to delineate the principle of good faith accentuates that part of the principle's role is seeking to restrain one's pursuit of self-interest where it is unreasonable given the factual matrix of the case.[256] There is no one clear definition of the principle of good faith. It is submitted that the different definitions of the principle encompasses the different aspects of the principle of abuse of rights.[257] **2.159**

(ii) The relation between good faith and abuse of rights

The good faith obligation is both substantive and procedural; it is a general principle explicitly endorsed by most legal systems.[258] It governs the substantive and procedural rights/obligations of the parties.[259] **2.160**

Whilst it is explicitly enshrined in the codes of the civil law jurisdictions, the essence and spirit of the good faith duty arguably constitutes an intrinsic part of the common law legal systems.[260] **2.161**

[254] *Yam Seng Pte Limited v International Trade Corporation* [2013] EWHC 111 (QB) 145; *Abu Dhabi National Tanker Company v Product Star Shipping Limited,* [1993] Ll Rep 397, 404; *Socimer International Bank Ltd v Standard Bank London Ltd* [2008] 1 Ll Rep 558, 575–77; Summers (n 250) 813.

[255] Terry and Lernia (n 247) 560.

[256] Stapleton (n 247) 7; Knapp (n 86) 115.

[257] A right exercised with a malicious intention is contrary to good faith. Litvinoff (n 240) 1665.

[258] Cremades (n 242) 767–69; Edward Thomas, 'Good Faith in Contract: A Non-Sceptical Commentary' (2005) 11 New Zealand Business Law Quarterly 391, 392; Taniguchi (n 48) 173–74; Cairo Court of Appeal, 5 February 2013, Case Nos 35, 41, 44, and 45, Judicial Year 129; Brabandere (n 42) 609; Kuwaiti Court of Cassation, Session held on 12 December 1995, Challenges nos 59, 64, 65, and 72, Judicial Year 1995.

[259] Bernard Hanotiau, 'Complex Multicontract-Multiparty Arbitration' (1998) 14 Arbitration International 369; VV Veeder, 'The Lawyer's Duty to Arbitrate in Good Faith', (2002) 18 Arbitration International 431, 439.

[260] *Interfoto Picture Library Ltd v Stiletto Visual Programmes Ltd* [1989] QB 433 (CA), 439, Lord Justice Bingham: 'English law has, characteristically, committed itself to no such overriding principle but has developed piecemeal solutions in response to demonstrated problems of unfairness'; ICSID Case No ARB/81/1, 25 September 1983, (1985) X Ybk Commercial Arbitration 61, 69, providing that 'estoppel is based on the fundamental requirement of good faith, which is found in all systems of law, national as well as international'; Aubrey Laine Thomas, 'Nonsignatories in Arbitration: A Good-Faith Analysis' (2010) 14 Lewis and Clark Law Review 953, 964, ('The concept of good faith in contractual dealings is pervasive in both common law and civil law systems'); Speidel (n 238) 537; Klaus Peter Berger, 'The International Arbitrator's Dilemma: Transnational Procedure versus Home Jurisdiction: A German Perspective' (2009) 25 Arbitration International 217, 234; W Tetley, 'Good Faith in Contract Particularly in the Contracts of Arbitration and Chartering' (2004) 35 Journal of Maritime Law and Commerce 561, 572, ('equity has played a major role as a stand-in for good faith in English commercial law'); Bonell (2005), (n 245) 130–31; Roy Goode, 'International Restatements of Contract and English Contract Law' (1997) 2 Uniform Law Review 231, 240. In the case of *Yam Seng Pte Limited v International Trade Corporation* mentioned above, the Court provided an extensive explanation of the good faith principle and recognized that it is now endorsed by most common law systems, including the United States, Australia, and New Zealand. After attempting to shed light on the particulars of good faith, Leggatt J concluded that there was nothing foreign to English law in recognizing an implied duty of good faith, and he suggested that the traditional hostility towards the principle of good faith was misplaced, *Yam Seng Pte Limited v International Trade Corporation* [2013] EWHC 111 (QB) 145 and 153. However, this view was later challenged and rebuked by the Court of Appeal in *Mid Essex Hospital Services NHS Trust v Compass Group UK and Ireland Ltd* [2013] EWCA Civ 200; *Bristol Groundschool Ltd*

2.162 Moreover, good faith is considered an inherent part of the *lex mercatoria*,[261] a general principle of law,[262] and is explicitly referred to as a mandatory principle under the UNIDROIT principles of International Commercial Contracts of 2010 ('UNIDROIT Principles'),[263] and under other internationally recognized legal instruments.[264]

2.163 Although the interrelation between the general principle of good faith and abuse of rights is unequivocal,[265] the demarcation between both concepts is not always conspicuous.

2.164 It is submitted that abuse of rights is an application of the principle of good faith and that the latter cannot, therefore, comprise an effective criterion of abuse. This is illustrated by the fact that the principle of good faith is broader than abuse of rights; the latter is confined to the exercise of rights.[266] This submission is strengthened by the views shared by scholars and is recognized by courts and tribunals.

2.165 Given its inherently broad scope, the *bona fides* principle constitutes a standard and a source from which more defined rules and doctrines can be deduced and derived.[267] In this regard, abuse of rights, a principle embodying the element of reasonableness in the exercise of rights,[268] is one of the applications of the *bona fides* principle.[269] This submission does not, however, negate or detract from abuse of rights its current

v Intelligent Capture and others [2014] EWHC 2145 (Ch); *MSC Mediterranean Shipping Company SA v Cottonex Anstalt* [2016] EWCA Civ 789, para 45.

261 Thomas E Carbonneau, 'A Definition of and Perspective upon the Lex Mercatoria Debate' in Thomas E Carbonneau (ed), *Lex Mercatoria and Arbitration: A Discussion of the New Law Merchant* (Kluwer Law International 1998) 17; *Phoenix Action Ltd v Czech Republic*, ICSID Case No ARB/06/5, Award of 15 April 2009, para 107; ICC Case No 3131 of 1979, (1984) IX Ybk Commercial Arbitration 109; Tetley (n 261) 591–92, 596; ICC Case No 5721 of 1990, in Yves Derains, Sigvard Jarvin, and JJ Arnaldez (eds), *ICC Arbitral Awards 1986-1990* (ICC Publications 1994) 404–05; Filip De Ly, *International Business Law and Lex Mercatoria* (North Holland 1992) 264; Lorena Carvajal Arenas, 'Good Faith in the *Lex Mercatoria*: An Analysis of Arbitral Practice and Major Western Legal Systems' (PhD Thesis, University of Portsmouth 2011).

262 Bonell (n 245) 142; Klaus Peter Berger, *The Creeping Codification of the Lex Mercatoria* (Kluwer Law International 1999) 165; Shaw (n 247) 103–04; UNCITRAL Arbitral Award, Case No SCH-4318, 15 June 1994, applying the prohibition of *venire contra factum proprium* as an application of good faith as a general principle of law; ICJ case of *Certain Norwegian Loans (France v Norway)*, Separate Opinion of Judge Sir Hersch Lauterpacht [1957] ICJ Rep 9, 53; Franco Ferrari, 'The CISG's Interpretative Goals, Its Interpretative Method and Its General Principles in Case Law (Part II)' (2013) 13 Internationales Handelsrecht 181, 190; John O'Connor, *Good Faith in International Law* (Dartmouth Publishing Co 1991) 2; Robert Kolb, 'Principles as Sources of International Law: With Special Reference to Good Faith' (2006) 53 Netherlands International Law Review 1, 17; Ascensio (n 78) 765.

263 Article 1.7 of the UNIDROIT Principles of 2010. ('(1) Each party must act in accordance with good faith and fair dealing in international trade. (2) The parties may not exclude or limit this duty').

264 Article 7.1 of the United Nations Convention on Contracts for the International Sale of Goods; Article 3 of the Directive on Unfair Terms in Consumer Contracts 1993; Article 31(1) of the Vienna Convention on the Law of Treaties 1969.

265 Litvinoff (n 240) 1660.

266 Rosenberg (n 42) 17.

267 Shaw (n 247) 103; Litvinoff (n 240) 1652; Tetley (n 261) 566; Robert Kolb, 'Principles as Sources of International Law: With Special Reference to Good Faith" (2006) 53 Netherlands International Law Review 1, 17–19; O'Connor (n 263) 124; Anthony D'Amato, 'Good Faith', in Rudolf Bernhardt (ed), *Encyclopaedia of Public International Law* (Elsevier 2003) vol 2, 599.

268 Mayrand (n 45) 1012–13.

269 Cheng (n 32) 121; Andreas Zeigler and Jorun Baumgartner, '*Good faith as a General Principle of (International) Law*' in Andrew Mitchell and others (eds), *Good Faith and International Economic Law* (Oxford University Press 2015) 30; *Phoenix Action Ltd v Czech Republic* ICSID Case No ARB/06/5, Award of 15 April 2009, para 107; Brabandere (n 42) 618–20; Cremades (n 242) 768–769; Lauterpacht (n 207) 163–64; Taniguchi (n 48) 174; Lenaerts (n 133) 1146–45; Shany (n 224) 256; Carvajal Arenas (n 262) 99; Tania Voon, Andrew Mitchell, and James Munro, 'Legal Responses to Corporate Manoeuvring in International Investment Arbitration' (2014)

legal standpoint in many jurisdictions as an autonomous principle with its own specific contours and concerns.[270] Both concepts are not redundant,[271] but are rather supplementary.[272]

The relationship between the two concepts is clear under Egyptian law, as well as other laws in the MENA region.[273] The Egyptian Court of Cassation has explicitly provided that good faith encompasses the prohibition against abuse of rights.[274] **2.166**

Such correlation between good faith and abuse of rights is not merely an important theoretical observation, but has serious practical ramifications. The perception that a general principle of good faith embodies the prohibition against abuse of rights indicates that jurisdictions that do not explicitly endorse abuse of rights may still limit the exercise of rights on the basis of the principle of good faith.[275] **2.167**

An example of this is found in US law which recognizes the principle of good faith. In this regard, it has been stated that good faith acts as a safety valve 'to which judges may turn to fill gaps and qualify or limit rights and duties otherwise arising under rules of law and specific contract language'.[276] **2.168**

The UNIDROIT Principles clearly recognize that abuse of rights is an application of the broader principle of good faith. The Principles, after providing the overarching principle of good faith, go on to demonstrate certain rules/doctrines that fall within the purview of good faith, including abuse of rights.[277] It is of particular interest to note that the provision regarding abuse of rights was originally intended as a separate provision under the Principles, but it was decided to locate it under the good faith principle, as one of its important applications.[278] Such recognition of the relation between both concepts under the Principles is further confirmed by scholars.[279] **2.169**

In the case of *Abaclat and Others v Argentine Republic*, the arbitral Tribunal discussed the relationship between the principle of good faith and abuse of rights, and expressed **2.170**

5 Journal of International Dispute Settlement 41, 61; Ascensio (n 78) 777; Robert Kolb, 'Principles as Sources of International Law: With Special Reference to Good Faith' (2006) 53 Netherlands International Law Review 1, 19.

[270] Zimmermann and Whittaker (n 82) 676.

[271] Anthony D'Amato, 'Good Faith' in Rudolf Bernhard, (ed), *Encyclopedia of Public International Law* (North-Holland 1995) vol 2, 600; Patricia Birnie and Alan Boyle, *International Law and the Environment* (Oxford University Press 1992) 126.

[272] Byers (n 13) 411.

[273] Abdelwahab (n 252).

[274] Egyptian Court of Cassation, Hearing session of 27 April 2006, Challenge No 3473, Judicial Year 75.

[275] Lauterpacht (n 207) 163–64; Lenaerts (n 133) 1146–45; Litvinoff (n 240) 1661

[276] Summers (n 250) 812; Dubroff (n 252) 570; David Stack, 'The Two Standards of Good Faith in Canadian Contract Law' (1999) 62 Saskatchewan Law Review 201, 210–11; Arthur Hartkamp, 'The Concept of Good Faith in the UNIDROIT Principles for International Commercial Contracts' (1995) 3 Tulane Journal of International and Comparative Law 65, 65–6; but see MP Ellinghaus, 'In Defense of Unconscionability' (196978 Yale Law Journal 757, 779–80, using unconscionability to reach the same result.

[277] Comment 2 to Article 1.7 of the UNIDROIT Principles of 2010, which provides that a typical example of behaviour contrary to the principle of good faith and fair dealing is abuse of rights.

[278] International Institute for the Unification of Private Law, Report by the Working Group for the Preparation of Principles of International Commercial Contracts, 6 June 2003, 58–60; Bonell (n 245) 58.

[279] Bonell (n 245) 133.

that abuse of rights was a fundamental principle applicable in investment law as a manifestation of the principle of good faith.[280]

2.171 The WTO decision in the case of *United States Import Prohibition of Certain Shrimp and Shrimp Products* further illustrates the relationship between abuse of rights and the principle of good faith.[281] In this case, the Tribunal explicitly stipulated that:

> The chapeau of Article XX is, in fact, but one expression of the principle of good faith. This principle, at once a *general principle of law and a general principle of international law*, controls the exercise of rights by states. *One application of this general principle, the application widely known as the doctrine of abus de droit*, prohibits the abusive exercise of a state's rights and enjoins that whenever the assertion of a right "impinges on the field covered by [a] treaty obligation, *it must be exercised bona fide, that is to say, reasonably*. (Emphasis added).[282]

2.172 Whether abuse of rights can always be perceived as an application of the principle of good faith necessarily depends on one's definition of good faith. If one purports to endorse a broad definition of good faith, including standards such as fairness and reasonableness,[283] then it is submitted that the prohibition against abuse of rights is nothing but a manifestation of the principle of good faith.

(iii) Good faith as a criterion of abuse

2.173 As previously mentioned, good faith is sometimes used as a test to determine if there is an abuse of rights.[284]

2.174 However, the particulars of what constitutes an abuse based on the principle of good faith is not clear. In many instances, it appears that the criterion of good faith is not a stand-alone criterion, but is rather an emulation of one of the other criteria of abuse.

2.175 In a case involving the liability of a member of a limited liability company, the German court acknowledged the validity of the company, but held that it would be contrary to the principle of good faith, and thus an abuse of right, if it upheld the separation of the assets of the company from its members given the circumstances of the case. In justifying its decision, the Court held that it would be contrary to, and a deviation from, the purpose of the law, if such separation was upheld.[285] It seems palpable that

[280] *Abaclat and Others v Argentine Republic*, ICSID Case No ARB/07/5, Decision on Jurisdiction and Admissibility of 4 August 2011, para 646.

[281] Decision rendered by the WTO Appellate Body in the case of *United States—Import Prohibition of Certain Shrimp and Shrimp Products* (12 October 1998) WT/DS58/AB/R; Andrew D Mitchell, 'Good Faith in WTO Dispute Settlement' (2006) 7 Melbourne Journal of International Law 339, 371.

[282] ibid para 158.

[283] By and large, it is submitted that all definitions of good faith pertain to the notion of reasonableness, honesty and fairness. Mason (n 253) 69; Adam Wallwork, 'A Requirement of Good Faith in Construction Contracts?' (2004) 20 Building and Construction Law 257; Australian case of *Burger King Corp v Hungry Jack's Pty Ltd* [2001] NSWCA 187, (21 June 2001, where the Court applied the principle of good faith to limit the party's exercise of its rights; Elisabeth Peden, 'When Common Law Trumps Equity: The Rise of Good Faith and Reasonableness and the Demise of Unconscionability', The University of Sydney, Legal Studies Research Paper No 06/57 (2006) 2.

[284] Cueto-Rua (n 3) 996.

[285] Judgment of 29 November 1956, 22 BGHZ 226, 230 (1957) translated and cited in Bolgar (n 48) 1029–30.

although the Court's ruling is based on the 'deviation from the purpose' criterion, it is disguised and cloaked under the principle of good faith.

Similarly, Swiss courts often rely on good faith to establish an abuse of right. In doing so, decisions of Swiss courts, in essence, rely on other criteria of abuse. For example, Swiss courts have found an abuse of rights based on the criterion of good faith, where legal institutions are used for a purpose contrary to that prescribed by the law;[286] and in another case, it was held that the decisions of the general assembly of a corporation are abusive if such decisions were against the interests of the minority and do not serve a serious interest to the majority.[287] Here again, it is evident that while the decisions establishing an abuse relied on the principle of good faith, abuse was actually premised either on the reasonableness of the act in question (disparity between the interests) or that of the purpose of the law. **2.176**

Additionally, in discussing abuse of rights under Swiss law, A Von Tuhr wrote: **2.177**

> The exercise of rights, as the law indicates, is subject to the postulates of good faith, that is to say, those exigencies should be respected which are proper of the circumstances, and that the holder of the right, correctly behaving, *owes to the interests of the other party*. Otherwise, he will be responsible for an abuse of right, and will not be protected by the law; the abusive exercise of a right is an illicit act and obliges him to redress the damages caused thereby.[288] (Emphasis added).

Again, the criterion of good faith appears as a general constraint rather than a defined or a clear criterion of abuse. More precisely, it seems to be synonymous to the notion of reasonableness in the exercise of rights. Thus, in jurisdictions where the law does not explicitly endorse specific criteria of abuse, as in the case of Swiss law[289] and German law,[290] courts tend to rely on the general notion of good faith to find an abuse of right. **2.178**

In discussing good faith as a criterion of abuse, it has been provided that it is premised on the rules of positive morality and elementary fairness.[291] In adopting the good faith criterion, it appears that decision makers are expected to determine if there is an abuse based on moral norms and their perceived sense of fairness.[292] Given that good and bad are relative concepts, adopting such an open-ended test of abuse may cause serious prejudice to individuals. It invites decision makers to resort to their personal preferences when determining whether a right should be protected or sacrificed.[293] Thus, given its **2.179**

[286] BGE 94.1.659, Journal des Tribunaux 216 (1970); BGE 86.2.417 (1961), Journal des Tribunaux 325 (1961), cited in Bolgar (n 48) 1036.

[287] BGE 95.2.157 (1970), Journal des Tribunaux 344 (1970), cited in Bolgar (n 48) 1036.

[288] A Von Tuhr, *Tratado De Las Obligaciones*, 270 (1934), translated in Cueto-Rua (n 3) 998.

[289] Given that the Swiss legislator linked abuse of rights with the principle of good faith, this explains the regular reference to good faith in cases of abuse, despite the fact that examining the rulings in these cases demonstrate that the decisions are generally premised on more specific criteria, such as the deviation of purpose.

[290] As previously mentioned, the restrictive approach of the German Civil Code reflected in Article 226 explains why German courts tend to rely on the broader principle of good faith stipulated under Articles 242 and 826.

[291] Cueto-Rua (n 3) 996–97.

[292] Litvinoff (n 240) 1650.

[293] Crabb (n 13) 22–23; Litvinoff (n 240) 1661.

inherently broad terms, one submits that the good faith criterion bears undeterminable variable parameters, which fails to make it a sound criterion of abuse.[294]

2.180 It is important to note that by challenging the effectiveness of good faith as a criterion of abuse, one does not attempt to disregard the importance and indispensability of the principle of good faith to the principle of abuse of rights. For some legal systems, as in the case of Germany, good faith is regularly used by courts to sanction the abusive exercise of rights given the inherent narrow terms of section 226 of the German Civil Code, and to prevent dealing with its evidentiary limitation.[295] In this regard, it has been rightly stated that section 242 of the German Civil Code has played a pivotal role in limiting the exercise of rights.[296]

2.181 In a case study prepared by *Reinhard Zimmermann* and *Dirk Verse*,[297] the case pertained to a lessee who had to pay a monthly rent amounting to DM 1,000. However, given that the lessee regarded this amount to be excessive, he only paid DM 900. While the lessor did not protest, three years later he requested the lessee to pay the remaining amount for the previous three years. This case study pertained to what may be called 'sitting on one's rights'. After acknowledging that the lessee cannot succeed on grounds of waiver or modification of contractual terms, it was stated that he may have a claim on the basis of abuse of rights: '[l]oss (Verwirkung) in these kind of cases is based upon an abuse of right in the specific form of *venire contra factum proprium*. It constitutes a sub-category of behaviour not in accordance with the requirements of good faith'.[298]

2.182 This case is of interest as it (a) shows how German courts may use the broad principle of good faith to limit the unreasonable exercise of rights; (b) provides evidence that abuse of rights is an application of the principle of good faith; and (c) demonstrates that the prohibition against inconsistent conduct is perceived as a manifestation of abuse of rights.

III. Abuse of Rights: Areas of Concern

2.183 The application of abuse of rights raises certain issues that warrant clarification. A review of its scope reveals its elasticity and extensiveness. As previously mentioned, there is no substantive or procedural right that may not a priori be brought within the purview of the principle's operation.[299] This comprehensiveness, while not worrying, calls

[294] Joseph Thompson, 'Good Faith in Contracting: A Sceptical View' in Angelo Forte (ed), *Good Faith in Contract and Property Law* (Hart Publishing 1999) 75.

[295] BGH, 29 April 1959, BGHZ 30, 140; Steven Reinhold, 'Good Faith in International Law', Bonn Research Papers, Paper No 2/2013, 3; Zimmermann and Whittaker (n 82) 694; also in Belgium, while limitation on the exercise of rights is based on abuse of rights, the Belgian Supreme Court held that in cases of contractual rights, abuse is established on the basis of good faith. Belgian Supreme Court, 19 September 1983, Bull Cass, 1983–1984, 52, RDC, 1984, 276; Belgian Supreme Court, 18 June 1987, RW, 1987–1988, 503, JT, 1988, 8, cited in De Ly (n 262) 154–55.

[296] Cremades (n 242) 773; Zimmermann and Whittaker (n 82) 24–25; Berger (n 261) 233; Joachim (n 166) 354.

[297] Zimmermann and Whittaker (n 82) 515–16.

[298] ibid 516; Berger (n 261) 233.

[299] Lauterpacht (n 62) 312–13.

for additional prudence from courts and tribunals as its misuse may undermine substantial legal interests.[300]

At the outset, one must note that an abuse of right cannot be presumed by courts/tribunals, but must be proved by the party.[301] This is also the same in international law.[302] In the *Case Concerning certain German Interests in Polish Upper Silesia*, the Permanent Court of International Justice ('PCIJ') held: 'such misuse [abuse of right] cannot be presumed, and it rests with the party who states that there has been such misuse to prove his statement'.[303] **2.184**

Given that it is a deviation from clear legal rules, and imposes a limitation/restriction on rights *ex post facto*, some argue that abuse of rights defies the necessary legal certainty required in business transactions.[304] Understandably, the more legal rules can be a reflection of one's rights and duties, the more legal certainty is achieved. In this regard, in the *RomPetrol* case, the arbitral Tribunal stated that it would 'have great difficulty in an approach that was tantamount to setting aside the clear language agreed upon by the treaty Parties in favour of a wide-ranging policy discussion'.[305] **2.185**

The principle's possible defiance of legal certainty does not, however, appear to be compelling criticism of abuse of rights. Any equitable principle, such as abuse of rights, may introduce some uncertainties to the law.[306] Also, while legal certainty is a virtue, it should not be overstated in the face of reaching an equitable and fair outcome: **2.186**

> Certainty should not be over-valued. Rules which aim to be too prescriptive in order to promote certainty will often fail to do justice to unique circumstances that might require unique solutions. Certainty is always opposed to flexibility. The latter is also a value often supported in isolation.[307]

Moreover, such uncertainty is no different than applying any general principle of law, which also introduces uncertainty.[308] That said, adopting an objective criterion of **2.187**

300 Georg Schwarzenberger, 'Uses and Abuses of the "Abuse of Rights" in International Law' (1956) 42 Transactions of the Grotius Society, Problems of Public and Private International Law 147, 152; Tête (n 111) 78.

301 Byers (n 13) 399; Lauterpacht (n 207) 163.

302 Kiss (n 4) para 33.

303 See *Case Concerning Certain German Interests in Polish Upper Silesia (Germany v Poland)* PCIJ Rep Series A No 7, Judgment of 25 May 1926, 30; *Case of the Free Zones of Upper Savoy and the District of Gex (France v Switzerland)* PCIJ Rep Series A/B No 46, 167.

304 Catherine LaLumiere, 'Speech', in Council of Europe '*Abuse of Rights and Equivalent Concepts: The Principle and its Present Day Application*' (Proceedings of the 19th Colloquy on European Law, Luxembourg, 6–9 November 1989) (Strasbourg 1990) 12; Petrova (n 1) 481.

305 *RomPetrol Group NV v Romania*, ICSID Case No ARB/06/03, Decision on Preliminary Objections on Jurisdiction and Admissibility of 18 April 2008, 85. However, there are investment arbitration cases which demonstrate that tribunals are willing to prohibit the abuse of the arbitral process and to preclude bad faith conduct, despite of the express terms of a treaty/contract. *Gustav F W Hamester GmbH & Co KG v Republic of Ghana*, ICSID Case No ARB/07/24, Award of 18 June 2010, 123–124; *Libananco Holding Ltd v Turkey*, ICSID Case No ARB/06/8, Decision on Preliminary Issues of 23 June 2008, 78; *Millicom International Operations BV and Sentel GSM SA v Republic of Senegal*, ICSID Case No ARB/08/20, Decision on Jurisdiction of 16 July 2010, 84; Voon, Mitchell, and Munro (n 270) 63–64.

306 Perillo (n 56) 96.

307 Jeffrey Waincymer, 'Promoting Fairness and Efficiency of Procedures in International Commercial Arbitration—Identifying Uniform Model Norms' (2010) 3 Contemporary Asia Arbitration Journal 32.

308 Foster (n 212) 352.

abuse, such as the balancing factor, relatively limits much of the uncertainties associated with abuse of rights.[309] This was similarly adopted in relation to the notion of public policy which equally bears undeterminable variable parameters.[310]

2.188 What is being argued here is not an open-ended application of abuse of rights with no restraints. Rather, one posits that a reasonable balance should be found: where one should be able to ascertain his/her respective rights/obligation by examining the legal instrument in question (law/contract/treaty); however, one must additionally recognize that such rights are not absolute, but must be exercised reasonably.[311]

2.189 Moreover, as the principle's application arguably encroaches on individual rights, some scholars criticize that its application confers a wide discretionary power upon courts/arbitrators, contravenes the notion of laisser-faire, and possibly invites a high degree of judicial law making.[312]

2.190 While this critique seems logical, it is not directed against the principle per se, but rather demonstrates uncertainty about the possible misuse of the principle given its broad scope and its reliance on the determination of the decision maker rather than on strict codified rules. It must be pinpointed that 'any judicial or arbitral decision, as a human activity, has a strong discretionary content subject to personal valuation'.[313] The discretionary power granted to decision makers in applying abuse of rights is not greater than that conferred in relation to established principles and overarching notions such as good faith, reasonableness,[314] and public policy.[315] To that effect, it is stated that the discretionary power granted to courts in applying abuse of rights 'is obviously the same with the criteria of fault, proper conduct and good faith. Yet experience shows that the judges show no tendency whatever to make bad use of the powers which they have been given in this area'.[316]

[309] Tête (n 111) 79–80; Cueto-Rua (n 3) 999; Gutteridge (n 52) 27.

[310] Public policy was first assessed subjectively: *Besant v Wood*, [1879] 12 Ch 605, 620 ('public policy must be, to a certain extent, a matter of individual opinion'). This was criticized and an objective standard was then established: PE Nygh, *Foreign Status, Public Policy and Discretion* (1964) 12 International and Comparative Law Quarterly 39, 51; *Boys v Chaplin*, [1971] AC 356, 378; *Fender v St. John-Mildmay*, [1938] AC 1, 12; *Louks v Standard Oil Co*, 224 NY 99, 111, 120 NE 198 202 [1918], referred to in Lawrence Collins, *Dicey and Morris on the Conflict of Laws* (13th edn, Sweet & Maxwell 2000) vol 1, 81 ('the courts are not free to refuse to enforce a foreign right at the pleasure of judges, to suit the individual notion of expediency or fairness'); Explanatory Memorandum of the Egyptian Law No 131 of 1948 Promulgating the Civil Code, (vol 2), 223, providing that public policy should be based on objective criteria.

[311] Crabb (n 13) 22–23.

[312] Gutteridge (n 52) 40.

[313] Cremades (n 242) 785.

[314] EP Belobaba, 'Good Faith in Canadian Contract Law' in *Special Lectures of the Law Society of Upper Canada, Commercial Law: Recent Developments and Emerging Trends* (Toronto, De Boo 1985) 77–78; Crabb (n 13) 23; Zimmermann and Whittaker (n 82) 689–99; George P Fletcher, 'The Right and the Reasonable' (1985) 98 Harvard Law Review 949, 943–50.

[315] Kojo Yelpaala, 'Restraining the Unruly Horse: The Use of Public Policy in Arbitration, Interstate and International Conflict of Laws in California' (1989) 2 The Transnational Lawyer 379, 380–81, and 394; Nygh (n 311) 49–50; *Russ v Russ* [1962] 3 WLR 930, 939, regarding the courts' discretionary power not to apply the *lex domicilii* on grounds of public policy.

[316] Knapp (n 86) 118.

Accordingly, rather than criticizing the discretionary power upon which abuse of rights relies, it seems necessary to focus on the calibre of the judge/arbitrator upon whom the law confers discretionary power to decide many factual and legal intrinsic issues: **2.191**

> But no formula, however wisely drafted, can control the exercise of judicial discretion under the rubric of 'good faith' or 'abuse of right' independent of the character of the judge. If 'what good faith requires' is the conduct of a just man in the circumstances, the judge must himself be a just man in order to determine it. Therefore the maintenance of the highest caliber of the judiciary becomes increasingly important as the discretion of the judge is broadened [. . .].[317]

The legal certainty desired in business transactions can be maintained, and the discretionary power granted can be confined, if one acknowledges that decision makers need not to apply the principle except in cases of flagrant abuse.[318] **2.192**

To conclude, abuse of rights—as all equitable principles—grants a broad discretionary power to decision makers. It must therefore be applied with utmost prudence and should rely on objective criteria to preclude any prejudice as a result of the personal preferences of the courts/arbitrators. Decision makers must resort to, and utilize, the principle in exceptional circumstances where abuse is flagrant. **2.193**

However, one need not to introduce an inflexible criterion to preclude the principle's misapplication.[319] This would necessarily defy the *raison d'être* of the principle which was created, a fortiori, to ameliorate the rigidity of the law.[320] Abuse of rights is similar, in this regard, to the notion of reasonableness in that: **2.194**

> [N]o set of rules can determine what is reasonable in all situations. Nor does reasonableness lend itself to definitive specification on the basis of custom or of market practices. We do not always know what the reasonable requires, but working with this open-ended concept at the core of our legal system saves us from the constricting effects of positivism.[321]

While the balancing factor proposed in this book equally demands a broad discretionary power vested in the courts/arbitrators, such crucial power is to be confined to the legal particulars and factual matrix of the case, regarding interests emanating from an acknowledged legal relationship between those implicated in the dispute, and is not linked to specific moral norms or beliefs of the decision maker. **2.195**

[317] Tête (n 111) 83.

[318] For example, in relation to investment arbitration disputes, it is generally acknowledged that arbitral tribunals rarely find an abuse of right. Voon, Mitchell, and Munro (n 270) 64–65; *Chevron Corporation (USA) and Texaco Petroleum Company (USA) v The Republic of Ecuador*, UNCITRAL, PCA Case No 34877, Interim Award of 1 December 2008, paras 143 and 146.

[319] Finding an abuse depends on the factual matrix of each case. *Mobil Corp v Republic of Venezuela*, ICSID Case No ARB/07/27, Decision on Jurisdiction of 10 June 2010, paras 177 and 184; Borman (n 137) 389.

[320] Lauterpacht (n 207) 162; Byers (n 13) 406; Robert Kolb, 'Principles as Sources of International Law: With Special Reference to Good Faith' (2006) 53 Netherlands International Law Review 1, 16; Ascensio (n 78) 764–65.

[321] Fletcher (n 315) 980.

2.196 The concerns discussed above call for decision makers to be prudent in resorting to and applying the principle and to avert its misuse.[322]

IV. Conclusion

2.197 To not endorse abuse of rights, jurisdictions would be swimming against the tide.[323]

2.198 In this section, the characteristic elements of abuse of rights were examined. Precisely, based on reviewing its application in a number of legal systems, the principle's conditions of application were discussed, and the primary concerns associated with the principle were also mentioned.

2.199 In doing so, it was clear that the principle assumes the existence of an acknowledged legal right and that such a right ceases legal protection given that it has been abused by the right holder. Upon a discussion on the different tests/criteria regularly used to establish an abuse of right, and based on the inherent limitation of each criterion, it was submitted that the balancing factor constitutes an effective criterion of abuse.

2.200 It is reasonable to submit that there is some sort of general acceptance that any right cannot be unreasonably exercised, and that such unreasonableness is not to be decided by any rigid rule or test, but by a flexible balancing exercise of the existing competing interests involved.[324] This creates a proper limit on each right and further advances 'the smooth and proper functioning of the legal system'.[325]

2.201 The potency of the balancing factor stems from its nature as a device that seeks and maintains a fair balance between the competing interests of the parties involved. While it is submitted that no rigid rules shall be adopted to guide decision makers, the balancing factor should contain sub-factors to guide decision makers. These sub-factors include, inter alia, the indices applied by courts as criteria of abuse (such as existence of malice, the purpose of the right, and legitimate interest). The sub-factors shall also comprise all competing interests at stake, which will necessarily vary from one legal dispute to another. Another sub-factor entails conducting a comparative impairment test to assess the reasonableness of the act in question.

2.202 The universal acknowledgment of this scintillating corrective device in different legal systems begs the question as to whether it can be considered a general principle of law in international arbitration. This is discussed in the next chapter.

322 Lauterpacht (n 207) 164.

323 This statement was used by Leggatt J in the case of *Yam Seng Pte Limited v International Trade Corporation* [2013] EWHC 111 (QB), discussing the common law approach to the principle of good faith.

324 *Tidewater Inc et al v the Bolivarian Republic of Venezuela*, ICSID Case No ARB/10/5, Decision on Jurisdiction of 8 February 2013, para 147.

325 Cheng (n 32) 136.

3

The Nature of Abuse of Rights in International Arbitration

I. Introduction

3.01 Upon acknowledging the importance of abuse of rights in national and international law, it becomes imperative to discern the nature and function of abuse of rights in international arbitration. Thus, in this chapter, one shall discern the legal basis of abuse of rights in international arbitration. In other words, if arbitrators choose to rely on abuse of rights to enforce or refuse the recognition of a given right, do they apply it as a general principle of law or only as part of the applicable national or international law?

3.02 Secondly, if the transnational nature of abuse of rights is acknowledged, it becomes imperative to elucidate how the principle operates in the context of international arbitration; is its application restricted to cases where it is part of the applicable substantive law; or is it regarded as a principle of transnational public policy?

3.03 Many transnational norms and standards that became omnipresent in international legal doctrine and practice are derived from municipal norms and private-law principles.[1] A question raised in this regard is whether the principle of abuse of rights elevates to a transnational principle.

[1] Jaye Ellis, 'General Principles and Comparative Law' (2011) 22 European Journal of International Law 949, 950; Harold C Gutteridge, 'Comparative Law and the Law of Nations' (1944) 21 British Year Book of International Law 1, 1–2; Emmanuel Gaillard, 'General Principles of Law in International Commercial Arbitration—Challenging the Myths' (2011) 5 World Arbitration and Mediation Review 161, 162.

3.04 In order to ascertain the transnational nature of the abuse of rights principle, and whether it comprises a general principle of law, this chapter shall adopt the methodology used in previous chapters, and that is often relied upon in ascertaining general principles of law. In this regard, the criterion mostly used to identify general principles of law, acknowledged and accepted in jurisprudence, is examining the acknowledgment of the principle in different families of legal systems.

3.05 Moreover, one shall also shed light on the perception of the principle of abuse of rights as acknowledged by prominent scholars; as reflected in international legal instruments such as uniform laws; and as applied by arbitral tribunals.[2] This methodology is particularly used in the arena of international arbitration: 'in the arbitration context, the best indication of the acceptance of a proposition as a general principle is its frequent invocation by arbitral tribunals and its recognition by scholars'.[3]

3.06 Analysis of the above shall be attained by examining arbitration doctrine and practice in commercial and investment arbitration. However, emphasis may be given to investment arbitration cases solely for the existence of material to that effect. It is submitted that any conclusion reached in relation to the nature of the principle should extend to, and apply in, international commercial arbitration.

3.07 Prior to discussing the nature of abuse of rights and how it operates as a general principle, it is necessary to elaborate on the meaning of a principle in the context of general principles of law.

II. The Definition of a Principle in the Context of General Principles of Law

3.08 In deciding cases, decision makers may resort to, and rely on, different standards. Some of these function as rules, while others operate as principles. In his seminal work entitled *Taking Rights Seriously*, Ronald Dworkin noted that a *principle* is:

> [A] *standard* that is to be observed, not because it will advance or secure an economic, political, or social situation deemed desirable, but because it is a *requirement of justice or fairness or some other dimension of morality*.[4] (Emphasis added)

3.09 To illustrate the meaning of principles, Dworkin referred to the following example: In the case of *Rigs v Palmer*,[5] an heir named in a will murdered his grandfather for the purpose of receiving the inheritance. The Court first acknowledged that if the provisions of the law regulating the making and effect of wills are interpreted in a strict manner,

[2] Note, 'General Principles of Law in International Commercial Arbitration' (1988) 101 Harvard Law Review 1824–25.

[3] ibid.

[4] Ronald Dworkin, *Taking Rights Seriously* (Bloomsbury 2013) 39.

[5] *Riggs v Palmer*, 115 NY 506, 22 NE 188 (1889), referred to in Dworkin (n 4) 39.

the murderer should receive the property. However, the Court refused to recognize the right to inherit established by the statute and relied on some fundamental legal principles. The Court provided that:

> [A]ll laws as well as all contracts may be controlled in their operation and effect by general, fundamental maxims of the common law. No one shall be permitted to profit by his own fraud, or to take advantage of his own wrong, or to found any claim upon his own iniquity, or to acquire property by his own crime.[6]

This case is of particular importance as it not only demonstrates the meaning of principles, but may also be used to clarify the nature and function of abuse of rights as a legal principle. The case fortified that a *right* conferred by a legal instrument such as a statute or a contract (right to inherit) is not absolute and does not apply irrespective of the circumstances. It may be controlled or modified in light of other broader *principles*. By considering the conduct of the heir, the Court rightly found that giving effect to the right in question would be inequitable. **3.10**

A prudent reading of the above entails that a principle often involves a *broad* standard required by moral norms or other considerations of fairness and justice, and that it may operate to control or modify a given rule.[7] This greatly resembles the nature and function of abuse of rights: a broad principle that has a remedial function[8] formed on moral grounds,[9] as well as on considerations of justice and fairness.[10] It is a principle that operates as a corrective mechanism to soften and ameliorate the rigidity of strict legal rules.[11] It is particularly interesting to note that the principles referred to in the mentioned case partially demonstrate manifestations of the abuse of rights principle. Thus, the principle that 'no one shall be permitted to profit or take advantage of his own wrong' is often perceived as an application of abuse of rights.[12] **3.11**

In drawing a line of demarcation between legal rules and principles, it is rightly noted that unlike rules, a principle does not mandate reaching a particular decision but is to be merely considered in light of other competing principles.[13] In case **3.12**

[6] ibid.

[7] Dworkin (n 4) 39.

[8] Joseph Voyame, Bertil Cottier, and Bolivar Rocha, 'Abuse of Right in Comparative Law' in 'Abuse of Rights and Equivalent Concepts: The Principle and Its Present Day Application' (Proceedings of the 19th Colloquy on European Law, Luxembourg, 6–9 November 1989) (Council of Europe 1990) 48.

[9] James B Ames, 'Law and Morals' (1910) 23 Harvard Law Review 97, 110; Harold C Gutteridge, 'Abuse of Rights' (1935) 5 Cambridge Law Journal 22; the case of *Colmar*, 2 May 1855, DP 1856.2.9, 10, cited in Julio Cueto-Rua, 'Abuse of Rights' (1975) 35 Louisiana Law Review 965; James Gordley, 'The Abuse of Rights in the Civil Law Tradition' in Rita de la Feria and Stefan Vogenauer (eds), *Prohibition of Abuse of Law: A New General Principle of EU Law?* (Hart Publishing 2011) 34; *Illinois Central Gulf RR v International Harvester Co*, 368 So 2d 1009 (La 1979).

[10] Cueto-Rua (n 9) 996–97; *Trushinger v Pak*, 513 So 2d 1151, 1154 (La 1987); *Ballaron v Equitable Shipyards, Inc*, 521 So 2d 481 (La 1988); *Ouachita National Bank in Monroe v Palowsky*, 554 So 2d 108 (La 1989); *Addison v Williams*, 546 So 2d 220 (La 1989); *Fidelity Bank and Trust Co v Hammons*, 540 So 2d 461 (La 1989).

[11] AN Yiannopoulos, 'Civil Liability for Abuse of Right: Something Old, Something New . . . ' (1994) 54 Louisiana Law Review 1173, 1195.

[12] Duarte G Henriques, 'Pathological Arbitration Clauses, Good Faith and the Protection of Legitimate Expectations' (2015) 31 Arbitration International 349, 357.

[13] Dworkin (n 4) 42; Scott J Shapiro, 'The 'Hart-Dworkin' Debate: A Short Guide for the Perplexed', Public Law and Legal Theory Working Paper Series, Working Paper No 77 (2007) 9.

of conflicting principles or interests, it is resolved by choosing the outcome 'supported by the principles that have the greatest aggregate weight'.[14] As expressed by Dworkin:

> [I]t [a principle] states a reason that argues in one direction, but does not necessitate a particular decision [. . .] There may be other *principles* or policies *arguing in the other direction* [. . .] If so, our principle may not prevail, but that does not mean that it is not a principle of our legal *system*, because in the next case, *when these contravening considerations are absent or less weighty, the principle may be decisive*. All that is meant, when we say that a particular principle is a principle of our law, is that the principle is one which officials must take into account, if it is relevant, as a consideration inclining in one direction or another.[15] (Emphasis added)

3.13 This depiction of principles equally confirms and fortifies the nature and function of abuse of rights. As previously mentioned, in determining if there is an abuse of right, courts/arbitrators are to utilize the balancing factor to carefully weigh the competing interests. While some of the mentioned interests and/or principles may direct decision makers in one direction, other competing interests and principles may prevail in other cases, given the different circumstances.

3.14 Having succinctly defined principles, it is important to discuss the meaning of general principles of law. As a term of art, general principles of law may have different meanings and functions.

3.15 General principles of law may be used, specifically in a transnational context, to denote those principles that are rooted in, and accepted by, different legal systems. In this regard, general principles of law function as a conflict of laws method: the non-selection method of conflict of laws or the conflict avoidance method,[16] and reflect principles that are generally acknowledged by different States. Unlike the *lex mercatoria*, which are generated by the community of merchants, general principles of law pertain to principles that originate from, and exist in, national legal systems, and are identified by a comparative law analysis.[17]

3.16 General principles of law may be also viewed as a source of law. This is specifically the case in civil legal systems. Given that case law only enjoys persuasive authority, general principles of law may be used to create legal rules in order to fill a lacuna that exists in statutes and customs.[18] Others advocate that general principles of law constitute guiding principles rather than a source of law as they provide a basis for the establishment of specific legal rules.[19] It appears that general principles of law function in a

[14] Scott J Shapiro, 'The "Hart-Dworkin" Debate: A Short Guide for the Perplexed', Public Law and Legal Theory Working Paper Series, Working Paper No. 77 (2007) 9.
[15] Dworkin (n 4) 42.
[16] Filip De Ly, *International Business Law and Lex Mercatoria* (North Holland 1992) 295 and 476.
[17] Gaillard (n 1) 162.
[18] De Ly (n 16) 194.
[19] ibid 194.

manner that develop legal systems by constantly filling gaps that appear in the decision-making process.[20]

Finally, these principles have an equally important role in international law. Article 38 of the Statute of the ICJ refers to general principles of law as a source for adjudication before the Court. These principles usually denote principles and standards that are derived from the municipal laws of States.[21] James Crawford referred to them as 'principles of municipal jurisprudence, in particular of private law, in so far as they are applicable to relations of States'.[22] **3.17**

III. Abuse of Rights: A General Principle of Law in International Commercial and Investment Arbitration

Owing to the sacrosanct principle of party autonomy in international arbitration, arbitral tribunals generally honour the choice of law chosen by the parties.[23] If parties fail to designate the law to govern the dispute, arbitrators have to ascertain the applicable rules and/or principles.[24] Rather than designating a national substantive law, parties often choose, or the arbitral tribunal may decide,[25] to apply transnational substantive standards or principles to govern their relationship.[26] These a-national principles offer parties the opportunity to subject their contractual relationship to standards that are independent of the particularities of any national legal system and take into consideration the particular needs of international commerce.[27] **3.18**

The possible application of general principles of law, or other a-national rules of law, is fortified by the reference to 'rules of law' that can be found in many modern arbitration **3.19**

[20] ibid 194–95.

[21] Ellis (n 1) 954–55, citing Verdross, 'Les principes généraux du droit dans la jurisprudence internationale' (1935) III *RCADI* 195, 204; De Ly (n 16) 199 (providing that the majority of scholars take a comparative view and hold that Article 38 refers to principles that exist in national legal systems).

[22] James Crawford, *Public International Law* (Oxford University Press 2012) 34–35; Robert Jennings and Arthur Watts, *Oppenheim's International Law* (9th edn, Oxford University Press 1992) vol 1, 29; Alan Redfern and others, *Redfern and Hunter on International Arbitration* (6th edn, Oxford University Press 2015) para 3.134.

[23] Julian DM Lew, Loukas A Mistelis, and Stefan M Kröll, *Comparative International Commercial Arbitration* (Kluwer Law International 2003) 417–18; Note (n 2) 1817; Partial Award on Jurisdiction and Admissibility in ICC Case No 6474 of 1992, (2000) XXV Ybk of Commercial Arbitration 278, 282; Interim Awards and Final Award of 1983, 1984, and 1986 in ICC Case No 4145 of 1983, (1987) XXI Ybk Commercial Arbitration 97, 100.

[24] Linda Silberman and Franco Ferrari, 'Getting to the Law Applicable to the Merits in International Arbitration and the Consequences of Getting it Wrong' in Franco Ferrari and Stefan Kroll (eds), *Conflict of Laws in International Arbitration* (Sellier 2011) 264.

[25] Arbitration Chamber of Paris, Case No 9246 of 1996, (1997) XXII Ybk Commercial Arbitration 28, 31 (where the parties failed to choose an applicable law, and the arbitral tribunal applied the *lex mercatoria*); ICC Case No 6500 of 1992 (1992) 119 Journal du Droit International 1015 (noting that arbitral tribunals may resort to transnational rules where the connecting factors are not capable of being clearly identified) referred to in Emmanuel Gaillard and John Savage (eds), *Fouchard Gaillard Goldman on International Commercial Arbitration* (Kluwer Law International 1999) 879–80.

[26] Lew, Mistelis, and Kröll (n 23) 448–49 and 451; Michael Mustill, 'The New Lex Mercatoria: The Next Twenty-five Years' (1988) 4 Arbitration International 86, 98; Note (n 2) 1819.

[27] ICC Case No 8385 of 1995 (1997) 124 Clunet 1015, 1061–66 <https://www.trans-lex.org/11> accessed 20 February 2019.

statutes and rules.[28] Moreover, it is of particular interest to mention that the ILA adopted a resolution in 1992 noting that awards based on transnational rules and principles, such as general principles of law, are enforceable.[29]

3.20 The recognition and application of general principles of law is neither peculiar to, nor inconsistent with, international arbitral case law.[30] Given that these principles represent an epitome of existing transnational contract law,[31] there are reported cases where arbitrators have applied these principles even without an express reference to them by the parties.[32] The view that arbitrators may resort to general principles of law where parties fail to designate an applicable law is not subject to consensus in arbitration doctrine.[33]

3.21 Ascertaining a new general principle of law necessitates examining the existence of the principle in question in different legal systems of the world. That said, is it necessary that the principle be recognized in all legal systems?

3.22 Such an overly restrictive approach is neither necessary nor practical, as it hinders the arbitrator's ability to resort to a principle found in private law.[34] The method adopted should therefore be ascertaining the prevailing trend within national laws, rather than establish unanimous recognition.[35] To that effect Gutteridge noted:

> It would seem that the more generous of these criteria is to be preferred because to insist on precise similarity of rule in all systems of law would be to demand the

[28] Lew, Mistelis, and Kröll (n 23) 452; Gary B Born, *International Commercial Arbitration* (2nd edn, Kluwer Law International 2014) 2662 ; Article 28 of the UNCITRAL Model Law; Article 27 of the Stockholm Chamber of Commerce of 2017; Article 21 of the ICC Arbitration Rules of 2012; Article 31 of the ICDR Arbitration Rules of 2014; Article 35.1 of the Rules of the Hong Kong International Arbitration Centre of 2013; Article 39.2 of the Egyptian Arbitration law No 27 of 1994; Article 1054 of the Netherlands Code of Civil Procedure of 1986; Article 187.1 of the Swiss Private International Law allows the parties to choose a national substantive law or *other rules of law*. This may be construed to recognize the application of general principles of law, *lex mercatoria*, or uniform international instruments such as the UNIDROIT Principles of International Commercial Contracts; Ole Lando, 'The Lex Mercatoria in International Commercial Arbitration' (1985) 34 International and Comparative Law Quarterly 747, 748; ICC Case No 3380 of 1980, (1982) VII Ybk Commercial Arbitration 116; ICC Case No 3131 of 1979, (1984) IX Ybk Commercial Arbitration 109, 110 (applying *lex mercatoria*); ICC Case No 3540 of 1980, (1982) VII Ybk Commercial Arbitration 124, 128, (applying *lex mercatoria*).

[29] Lew, Mistelis, and Kröll (n 23) 455.

[30] ICC Case No 8385 of 1995, (1997) 124 Clunet 1015, 1061–66 <https://www.trans-lex.org/11> accessed 20 February 2019; ICC Case No 8365 of 1996, in Jean-Jacques Arnaldez, Yves Derains, and Dominique Hascher, *Collection of ICC Arbitral Awards 1996-2000* (Wolters Kluwer 2009) 1078–79; Klaus Peter Berger, *The Creeping Codification of the New Lex Mercatoria* (2nd edn, Kluwer Law International 2010) 108; Klaus Peter Berger, 'The New Law Merchant and the Global Market Place: A 21st Century View of Transnational Commercial Law', <https://www.trans-lex.org/2> accessed 20 February 2019; Michael Joachim Bonell, 'A "Global" Arbitration Decided on the Basis of the UNIDROIT Principles: In re Andersen Consulting Business Unit Member Firms v Arthur Andersen Business Unit Member Firms and Andersen Worldwide Societe Cooperative' (2001) 17 Arbitration International 249, 249; Article 1.101 of the Principles of European Contract Law of 2002.

[31] Lew, Mistelis, and Kröll (n 23) 463.

[32] ICC Case No 9797 of 2000, (2000) 15(8) Mealey's Int'l Arb Rep A1; Bonell (n 30) 249.

[33] Gaillard (n 1) 164–66; Emmanuel Gaillard, 'Transnational Law: A Legal System or a Method of Decision Making' (2001) 17 Arbitration International 59.

[34] Michael Nolan, 'Issues of Proof of General Principles of Law in International Arbitration' (2009) 3 World Arbitration and Mediation Review 505, 510.

[35] Emmanuel Gaillard, *Legal Theory of International Arbitration* (Martinus Nijhoff 2010) 48–52; Emmanuel Gaillard, 'Thirty Years of Lex Mercatoria: Towards the Selective Application of Transnational Rules' (1995) 10 ICSID Review 208.

impossible and so to destroy – or at least, seriously diminish – the value of any resort to private-law sources and analogies.[36]

Thus, prior to finding a general principle of law, and before transposing such a private-law principle to international arbitration, an arbitrator must examine the principle's recognition in different legal systems. This should be no different from the position adopted and applied in international law.[37] Article 38 of the Statute of the ICJ provides that it shall apply 'the general principles of law recognized by civilized nations'.[38] In commenting on this Article, it is widely accepted that the term 'general' denotes the principle's recognition in most, and not all, legal systems, and that for a principle to be elevated to a general principle, its application should not defy the 'fundamental concepts of any of those systems'.[39] **3.23**

It is often held that a given principle is considered a general principle of law. However, it is usually overlooked that the term 'general principle of law' normally denotes *substantive* principles and not *procedural* principles.[40] **3.24**

Given that this book addresses abuse of substantive and procedural rights, it is important to examine whether the abuse of rights principle is considered to be a general principle of substantive law (**A**) within the context of international arbitration, as well as a general principle of arbitral procedure (**B**). **3.25**

One shall then examine whether the principle of abuse of rights enjoys any mandatory nature, that is, if it may apply as a principle of transnational public policy that overrides the applicable law, or if it can only apply as a general principle where arbitrators are entitled to resort to such principles (**C**). **3.26**

A. General Principle of Substantive Law

It is submitted that the principle of abuse of rights has elevated and developed as a general principle of law. As shall be discussed below, this submission is confirmed by the principle's recognition in most national legal systems and in international law; its acceptance as a general principle of law by scholars; and by virtue of its application as a general principle by arbitral tribunals in the domain of national and international law. **3.27**

[36] Gutteridge (n 1) 4–5.

[37] Gaillard (n 35) 48.

[38] Article 38 of the Statute of the International Court of Justice, available at <http://www.icj-cij.org/documents/?p1=4&p2=2> accessed 20 February 2019.

[39] Gutteridge (n 1) 4–5; LC Green, 'Comparative Law as a "Source" of International Law' (1968) 42 Tulane Law Review 61–62 ; Annekatrien Lenaerts, 'The General Principle of the Prohibition of Abuse of Rights: A Critical Position on Its Role in a Codified European Contract Law' (2010) 18 European Review of Private Law 1121, 1124.

[40] Charles Molineaux, 'Applicable law in arbitration: The Coming Convergence of Civil and Anglo-Saxon Law Via Unidroit and Lex Mercatoria' (2000) 1 Journal of World Investment and Trade 127, 130; Matti S Kurkela and Santtu Turunen, *Due Process in International Commercial Arbitration* (2nd edn, Oxford University Press 2010) 5–8.

3.28 Moreover, it was previously mentioned that the equitable nature of the principle as well as the element/criterion of reasonableness is widely acknowledged in the application of abuse of rights in national legal systems. As shall be discussed below, it appears that the equitable character of the principle remains conspicuous in the transnational context where the it is applied as a general principle of law. Furthermore, the criterion of reasonableness emerged as an equally key factor in the transnational application of the principle to limit the abuse of substantive contractual/treaty rights.

3.29 An overview of different legal systems was undertaken to examine the recognition and application of abuse of rights. Such review testified that many legal systems endorse a general principle of abuse of rights.[41]

3.30 It is submitted that the 'general principle of abuse of rights has been applied by the courts in every department of the law',[42] and that 'the prohibition of abuse of rights is a general principle of law. In view of its general recognition by almost all systems of law'.[43] Thus, the generality of the principle, as required in general principles of law, is satisfied.[44]

3.31 Moreover, in discussing the principle's application across diverse legal systems, it was suggested that the criterion of reasonableness (balancing factor) was elevated to a transnational element of the principle. This criterion of the principle has gained the widest support in civil law jurisdictions,[45] is also endorsed by the CJEU as part of EU law and in international law,[46] and is not

[41] FP Walton, 'Delictual Responsibility in the Modern Civil Law (More Particularly in the French Law) as Compared with the English Law of Torts' (1933) 49 Law Quarterly Review 70, 87; Alexandre Kiss, 'Abuse of Rights' in Rudolf Bernhardt (ed), *Encyclopedia of Public International Law* (North-Holland 1992) paras 9 and 34.

[42] FP Walton, 'Motive as an Element in Torts in the Common and in the Civil Law' (1909) 22 Harvard Law Review 501, 505.

[43] Hersch Lauterpacht, *The Function of Law in the International Community* (Oxford University Press 2011) 306.

[44] ibid 300–305.

[45] Vera Bolgar, 'Abuse of Rights in France, Germany, and Switzerland: A Survey of a Recent Chapter in Legal Doctrine' (1975) 35 Louisiana Law Review 1015, 1027–28; Chris Brunner, 'Abuse of Rights in Dutch Law' (1977) 37 Louisiana Law Review 729, 731; *Trushinger v Pak*, 513 So 2d 1151, 1154 (La 1987); *Ballaron v Equitable Shipyards, Inc*, 521 So 2d 481 (La 1988); *Ouachita National Bank in Monroe v Palowsky*, 554 So 2d 108 (La 1989); *Addison v Williams*, 546 So 2d 220 (La 1989); *Fidelity Bank and Trust Co v Hammons*, 540 So 2d 461 (La 1989); *210 Baronne St Ltd Partnership v First Nat'l Bank of Commerce*, 543 So 2d 502, 507 (La App 4th Cir), *writ denied*, 546 So 2d 1219 (1989); *Des Cheneaux v Morin Inc* (1987), 20 QAC 157; *Caisse populaire de Baie St-Paul v Simard*, Sup Ct Saguenay, No 24005000043845, 9 September 1985; *Banque Nationale du Canada v Houle*, [1990] 3 SCR 122; Egyptian Court of Cassation, Session held on 24 March 1991, Challenge No 1238, Judicial Year 56; Egyptian Court of Cassation, Session held on 4 April 1985, Challenge No 1244, Judicial Year 54; Abd El-Razzak El Sanhouri, *Al Wasit Fi Sharh Al Qanun Al Madani (A Treatise on the Explanation of the Civil Code)* (Dar Al Shorouk 2010 edn) vol 1, 760–761; Soliman Morcos, *Al Wafi Fi Sharh Al Qanun Al Madani (A Treatise on the Explanation of the Civil Code)* (Cairo 1988 edn) vol 3, 372–73; Article 3.13 of the Dutch Civil Code; Article 7 of the Spanish Civil Code; ICC Case No 12456 of 2004, in Jean-Jacquez Arnaldez, Yves Derains, and Dominique Hascher (eds), *Collection of ICC Arbitral Awards 2008-2011* (Kluwer Law International 2013) 826; Nicholae Gradinaru, 'Abuse of Rights' (2012) 4 Contemporary Readings in Law and Social Justice 1010, 1011 (discussing the law of Romania); Betul Tiryaki, 'The Legal Results of the Abuse of Rights in Case of Contradiction to the Formal Rules of Contracts' (2008) 1 Ankara Bar Review 30, 36 (discussing Turkish law); Article 30 of the Kuwaiti Civil Code.

[46] Case C-373/97 *Diamantis* [2000] ECR I-1705, para 43; Bin Cheng, *General Principles of Law as Applied by International Courts and Tribunals* (Cambridge University Press 2006) 129; Hervé Ascensio, 'Abuse of Process in International Investment Arbitration' (2014) 13 Chinese Journal of International Law 763, 764–65; Ybk of the International Law Commission, 1075th Meeting (23 June 1970) vol 1 (New York: United Nations, 1971) 185 para 40.

peculiar to the depiction/perception of the exercise of rights under common law.[47]

Based on the above, arbitrators have resorted to the principle of abuse of rights to resolve diverse substantive issues. In doing so, arbitrators have explicitly or implicitly applied it as a general principle of law. Some examples are discussed to illustrate the above. **3.32**

In ICC Case No 3267,[48] the question of whether the termination of an agreement may constitute an abuse of right was raised. The case related to the construction of a building project. The Claimant terminated the contract because of the Respondent's default in the payment terms. The question before the Tribunal was whether the termination of the contract was legitimate. The Claimant sought a declaration that the contract was legitimately terminated and that the issued advanced guarantee and the performance guarantees became extinguished. The Respondent, however, raised a counterclaim and requested a declaration that such termination, and all consequences thereof, was not legitimate: as the termination 'was without a legitimate cause'.[49] **3.33**

There was no explicit choice of the applicable law in the agreements. After considering the terms of the agreement, the Tribunal decided that it would not apply the laws of a specific legal system, but would decide the case with reference to general principles of law. In assessing the abusive nature of the termination, the Tribunal considered the factual matrix of the case, balanced the competing financial and contractual interests at stake, and examined the legitimacy of the termination. The Tribunal decided that the termination did not amount to an abuse of right. In relying on the principle of abuse of rights, the Tribunal explicitly noted that the principle may be applied as part of national law (where the principle is recognized and regulated); as a general principle of law; and in cases where arbitrators are acting as *amiable compositeur*. In the Tribunal's words: **3.34**

> In addition to the power to decide on the dispute before him on the basis of generally accepted legal principles, without being fettered by the technicalities of a particular legal system, the arbitrator sitting as 'amiable compositeur' is entitled to disregard legal or contractual rights of a party when the insistence on such right amounts to an abuse thereof. This authority is of a particular importance in legal systems that have

[47] Ugo Mattei, *Basic Principles of Property Law: A Comparative Legal and Economic Introduction* (Greenwood Press 2000) 149; Reinhard Zimmermann and Simon Whittaker, *Good Faith in European Contract Law* (Cambridge University Press 2000) 696; Anna Di Robilant, 'Abuse of Rights: The Continental Drug and the Common Law' (2010) 61 Hastings Law Journal 687, 698; Michael Byers, 'Abuse of Rights: An Old Principle, A New Age' (2002) 47 McGill Law Journal 389, 410–15; George P Fletcher, 'The Right and the Reasonable' (1985) 98 Harvard Law Review 949, 953; Elspeth Reid, 'Abuse of Rights in Scots Law' (1998) 2 Edinburgh Law Review 129, 134; David Campbell, 'Gathering the Water: Abuse of Rights After the Recognition of Government Failure' (2010) 7 Journal Jurisprudence 487, 523 (providing that the English law of nuisance which is based on a balancing of competing legitimate interests, partially achieves the purpose of abuse of rights); George M Armstrong and John C LaMaster, 'Retaliatory Eviction as Abuse of Rights: A Civilian Approach to Landlord-Tenant Disputes' (1986) 47 Louisiana Law Review 1, 14; William Prosser and others, *Prosser and Keeton on the Law of Torts* (5th edn, West Publishing Co 1984) (noting that unreasonable interference is the basis for the law of nuisance); Andrew D Mitchell, 'Good Faith in WTO Dispute Settlement' (2006) 7 Melbourne Journal of International Law 339, 371.

[48] Partial Award, ICC Case No 3267 of 1979, (1982) VII Ybk Commercial Arbitration 96.

[49] ibid 97.

not developed an extensive theory of 'abuse of right', such as Swiss law under Art. 2 of its Civil Code.[50]

3.35 This case is of particular interest, as it not only proves that abuse of rights was regarded and applied as a general principle of law, but it also revealed that the element/criterion of reasonableness was inherent to the general principle of abuse of rights. The arbitral Tribunal engaged in a balancing exercise to assess if the exercise in question was abusive or reasonable, even though this was not mandated by a specific national law, but as part of the general principles of law.[51]

3.36 The arbitral awards in the cases of *Himpurna California Energy Ltd v PT (Persero) PLN*[52] and *Patuha Power v PT (Persero) PLN*,[53] confirm that the principle of abuse of rights comprises a general principle of law. Although these cases are discussed in subsequent sections, it suffices here to mention that the arbitrators not only acknowledged abuse of rights as a general principle of law, but went further and applied it as a principle of transnational public policy, applicable regardless of the governing *lex causae* or *lex arbitri*.

3.37 The reasonableness, or abusive nature, of terminating agreements was discussed again in ICC Case No 13184 of 2011.[54] In this case, a Mexican company established two entities (the Respondents). The Respondents subsequently concluded contracts with the Claimant (US distributor A) and similar contracts with another distributor (US Distributor B). When concluding the fourth contract with the distributors, the Respondents introduced certain differences in the contract with the Claimant, as they lacked complete faith in the Claimant. These new changes included a right to terminate the contract without a cause and to have a midterm review meeting. Subsequently, the Claimant realized that these differences were introduced only to his contract and not for the US Distributor B. The Respondents then unilaterally terminated their agreements with the Claimant. The Claimant initiated arbitration proceedings alleging, inter alia, that the Respondents abused their right in terminating the agreement and in concealing the differences in the contracts with both the Claimant and the US distributor B. The law applicable to the merits was the CISG and supplemented by Mexican law.

3.38 In dismissing the claim, the arbitral Tribunal recognized that the Respondents acted in bad faith as they misrepresented and concealed the differences in the contracts. However, it was held that such misrepresentation was not relevant to the formation of the contract as it took place after its execution. The Tribunal found that the

50 ibid 105.

51 ibid 105–06.

52 *Himpurna California Energy Ltd v PT PLN (Persero)*, ad hoc arbitration under UNCITRAL rules, Final Award of 4 May 1999, (2000) XXV Ybk Commercial Arbitration 11; Jan Paulsson, 'Unlawful Laws and the Authority of International Tribunals' (2008) 23 ICSID Review Foreign Investment Law Journal 215, 223.

53 *Patuha Power Ltd (Bermuda) v PT (Persero) Perusahaan Listruik Negara (Indonesia)*, (1999) 14 Mealey's Int'l Arb Rep B-1, B-44.

54 *Distributor Z (US) v Company A (Mexico), Subsidiary B (US)*, Final Award, ICC Case No 13184 of 2011, (2011) XXXVI Ybk Commercial Arbitration 96.

Respondents' exercise of their right to terminate the contract did not amount to an abuse of right, given that it was not maliciously exercised, and was exercised for a legitimate and reasonable purpose, because the termination was motivated by commercial considerations.[55] The Tribunal engaged in a balancing process as it weighed the allegation of abuse against the express terms of the contract, and that the Respondents were exercising a contractual right. They also considered the fact that after being made aware of the differences in the agreements, the Claimant did not initiate proceedings, but instead attempted to pursue the preservation of the contractual relationship.[56]

The application of abuse of rights in this case clearly demonstrates the equitable nature of the principle. This is due to the fact that the Tribunal explicitly took into consideration the adage: *he who comes to equity must come with clean hands*, as they considered the conduct of the aggrieved party in evaluating the abusive nature of the termination. However, this case does not necessarily support the proposition that abuse of rights is a general principle of law. The arbitral Tribunal referred to Mexican law and applied the principle as regulated and embodied under Mexican law.[57] This arguably defies the generality and transnational status of the principle particularly given the Tribunal's approach to resort to national law in order to apply abuse of rights. It may be argued, however, that this does not necessarily negate the transnational status of abuse of rights given that: (a) the contract directed the arbitrators to refer to Mexican law if an issue is not covered under the CISG; (b) pursuant to Article 7.2 of the CISG, arbitrators must resort to a specific kind of general principles, that is, 'general principles on which it [the CISG] is based' in matters not expressly covered under the CISG,[58] and, failing to ascertain those principles, arbitrators are to resort to national law;[59] and (c) it is the general practice within the domain of CISG to automatically resort to national law where the issue is not explicitly regulated under the CISG.[60] **3.39**

When arbitrators attempt to identify general principles of law, they often rely on the UNIDROIT Principles, or other transnational principles,[61] as a reflection of those principles.[62] Given that the UNIDROIT Principles may be considered as a restatement of general principles of law,[63] any reference to abuse of rights may prove helpful **3.40**

[55] ibid paras 55–56.

[56] ibid paras 61–62.

[57] ibid paras 55–56.

[58] It is worth mentioning that some scholars hold the view that the prohibition against abuse of rights, as an application of the broader concept of good faith, is considered a general principle upon which the CISG is based as per Article 7.2: Jorge O Alban, 'The General Principles of the United Nations Convention for the International Sale of Goods' (2012) 4 Cuadernos de Derecho Transnacional 165, 167, note 7.

[59] Article 7.2 of the United Nations Convention for the International Sale of Goods 1980.

[60] Camilla B Andersen, 'General Principles of the CISG—Generally Impenetrable?' in Camilla B Andersen and Ulrich G Schroeter (eds), *Sharing International Commercial Law across National Boundaries* (Wildy, Simmonds and Hill 2008), 16–17.

[61] In this regard, the principles identified by Professor Klaus-Peter Berger and published by the Center for Transnational Law, equally comprise a restatement of general principles of law. Jeffrey Waincymer, 'Promoting Fairness and Efficiency of Procedures in International Commercial Arbitration—Identifying Uniform Model Norms' (2010) 3 Contemporary Asia Arbitration Journal 25, 49. These principles include the principle of abuse of rights: the TransLex-Principles available at <https://www.trans-lex.org/principles/of-transnational-law-(lex-mercatoria)> accessed 20 February 2019.

[62] Redfern and others (n 22) para 3.171; Molineaux (n 40) 130.

[63] Redfern and others (n 22) para 3.178.

in this regard. The UNIDROIT Principles clearly recognize that abuse of rights is a general principle of law, as an application of the broader principle of good faith and fair dealing.[64] The Principles, after providing the overarching principle of good faith and fair dealing, go on to demonstrate certain manifestations and narrower general principles that fall within the purview of good faith and fair dealing, including abuse of rights.[65] It is of particular interest to note that the provision regarding abuse of rights was originally going to be a separate provision under the Principles, but it was decided to locate it under the good faith principle, as one of its important applications.[66]

3.41 The transnational nature of abuse of rights may also be deduced from its recognition in other international legal instruments. Article 300 of the United Nations Convention on the Law of the Sea recognizes a general principle of abuse of rights: 'States Parties shall fulfil in good faith the obligations assumed under this Convention and shall exercise the rights, jurisdiction and freedoms recognized in this Convention in a manner which would not constitute an abuse of right'.[67]

3.42 Moreover, Article 17 of the European Convention for the Protection of Human Rights and Fundamental Freedoms of 1953, as amended in 1998, also includes a general provision on abuse of rights.[68]

3.43 Applying the general principle of abuse of rights as part of the UNIDROIT Principles is also reflected in arbitral decisions. Moreover, the element of reasonableness and endorsing the balancing factor is equally palpable in the application of abuse of rights from the standpoint of the UNIDROIT Principles. Thus, in ICC Case No 8547 of 1999,[69] a dispute arose out of a sale contract. Article 15 of the contract provided that any claim in relation to the quantity and quality of the products must be communicated within fifteen days upon arrival and was to be considered only against presentation of supporting documents issued by a neutral surveyor within thirty days of arrival. The law applicable to the contract was the Hague Convention of 1964 and supplemented by the UNIDROIT Principles. The buyer (the Respondent) received bad quality goods and informed the Claimant. However, the Claimant did not take any steps to remedy this.

3.44 While acknowledging that the Respondent failed to abide by the requirements of Article 15 in case of non-conformity, the arbitral Tribunal provided that the strict adherence to this Article by the Claimant constituted an abuse of right. In the words of the Tribunal:

[64] Michael Joachim Bonell, '*The UNIDROIT Principles in Practice*', (2nd edn, Transnational Publishers 2006) 84.

[65] Comment 2 to Article 1.7 of the UNIDROIT Principles of 2010 provides that abuse of rights is a typical example of behaviour contrary to the principle of good faith and fair dealing.

[66] International Institute for the Unification of Private Law, Report by the Working Group for the Preparation of Principles of International Commercial Contracts, 6 June 2003, 58–60; Michael Joachim Bonell, *An International Restatement of Contract Law: The UNIDROIT Principles of International Commercial Contracts* (3rd edn, Transnational Publishers 2005) 58.

[67] Article 300 of the United Nations Convention on the Law of the Sea 1982.

[68] Article 17 of the European Convention for the Protection of Human Rights and Fundamental Freedoms of 1953 (as amended in 1998).

[69] ICC Case No 8547 of 1999, in Albert Jan van den Berg (ed), (2003) XXVIII Ybk Commercial Arbitration 27–38.

> The arbitral tribunal is convinced of the non-conformity of the goods [. . .] The strict adherence to the requirement of provision No. 15 now by claimant amounts to an abuse of rights [. . .] If claimant could rely on this provision, defendant would have lost any rights in regard to the non-conformity. It is relevant that according to defendant, claimant did have the opportunity to examine the goods.[70]

The corrective function of abuse of rights, and the element of fairness advanced by its application, appears conspicuous in this case. The principle was used to cure unfairness as a result of the rigidity of a contractual right, the strict adherence to which would have been greatly damaging to one of the parties. The Tribunal weighed the competing interests: those of legal certainty and the principle of *pacta sunt servanda*, against fairness and the fact that the goods were not in conformity with the quality agreed upon. The Tribunal emphasized the element of fairness and decided that setting aside the requirements of Article 15 is the *only way* the Respondent can have a claim regarding the non-conformity.[71] **3.45**

The universal status of the abuse of rights principle is also recognized in international law jurisprudence and practice. It is recognized and applied as a general principle of law.[72] It was mentioned by Bin Cheng as a general principle of law applied by international courts and tribunals.[73] James Crawford similarly referred to the principle of abuse of rights as an epitome of the general principles of law.[74] Moreover, in emphasizing the universality of the principle, Sir Hersch Lauterpacht examined the existence of abuse of rights in major legal systems and advocated that, notwithstanding the divergent terminology employed by different systems, 'there is inherent in every system of law the general principle of prohibition of abuse of rights'.[75] **3.46**

The above is confirmed by the practice of international courts and tribunals. In the seminal *Barcelona Traction* case, the ICJ referred to abuse of rights as: 'enshrined in a general principle of law which emerges from the legal systems of all nations'.[76] **3.47**

As a general principle of law, abuse of rights is applied in the context of myriad legal matters, ranging from limiting the host State's sovereign authority to the preclusion of the abusive interpretation of treaty rights.[77] The application of abuse of rights is **3.48**

[70] ibid para 19.
[71] ibid.
[72] Kiss (n 41) paras 9 and 34; Ascensio (n 46) 765–66; Yuka Fukunaga, *Abuse of Process under International Law and Investment Arbitration* (2018) 33 ICSID Review 181, 183.
[73] Cheng (n 46) 121.
[74] Crawford (n 22) 36.
[75] Lauterpacht (n 43) 305–06.
[76] *Barcelona Traction Case* [1970] ICJ 324, Separate Opinion of Judge Ammoun; Jerome B Elkind, *Interim Protection: A Functional Approach* (Martinus Nijhoff Publishers 1981) 5.
[77] Todd Weiler, *The Interpretation of International Investment Law: Equality, Discrimination and Minimum Standards of Treatment in Historical Context* (Martinus Nijhoff 2013) 306; the *Lalanne and Ledour Case*, Reports of International Arbitral Awards (1903–1905) vol X, 17–18; the *Trail Smelter Case* (United States, Canada), Reports of International Arbitral Awards (1941), vol III, 1965; *ADC Affiliate Limited and ADC & ADMC Management Limited v The Republic of Hungary*, ICSID Case No ARB/03/16, Award of the Tribunal, 2 October 2006, paras 423–24.

particularly evident in investment disputes. One scholar advocated that most international investment law disputes before arbitral tribunals could be resolved by the 'repudiation of abuses of right'.[78] Thus, the Tribunal in the case of *Phoenix v The Czech Republic* recognized that abuse of rights constituted a general principle of law,[79] and stipulated that 'nobody shall abuse the rights granted by treaties, and more generally, every rule of law includes an implied clause that it should not be abused'.[80]

3.49 As previously mentioned, abuse of rights has also been applied as a general principle of law by the WTO panels and WTO Appellate Body to prevent the abusive interpretation and application of treaty rights.[81] In the case of *United States Import Prohibition of Certain Shrimp and Shrimp Products*, the Tribunal applied the principle and provided that any abuse of GATT Article XX (on General Exceptions)[82] was tantamount to an abuse of right and thus a violation of the treaty. The Tribunal explicitly stipulated that:

> The chapeau of Article XX is, in fact, but one expression of the principle of good faith. This principle, at once a *general principle of law and a general principle of international law, controls the exercise of rights by states. One application of this general principle, the application widely known as the doctrine of abus de droit*, prohibits the abusive exercise of a state's rights and enjoins that whenever the assertion of a right 'impinges on the field covered by [a] treaty obligation, *it must be exercised bona fide, that is to say, reasonably*. [. . .]. (Emphasis added)[83]

3.50 This decision not only confirms the nature of abuse of rights, but it also strengthens the above proposition regarding the universal/transnational status of the element of reasonableness in the context of abuse of rights. The Tribunal noted that finding an abuse requires marking the line of equilibrium between the competing rights and interests of the Member States in order to assess the abusive nature of the measure applied.[84] This was also confirmed in other cases decided by the Appellate Body of the WTO.[85]

3.51 Finally, it is worth mentioning that abuse of rights is also recognized by eminent scholars and by the CJEU as a general principle of EU law. It is often held that the principle was transposed to EU law by virtue of its recognition by the Member States and its application by the CJEU:

[78] Weiler (n 77) 305.
[79] *Phoenix Action v The Czech Republic*, ICSID Case No ARB/06/5, Award of 15 April 2009, paras 106–07.
[80] ibid paras 107–08.
[81] *Brazil-Retreaded Tyres*, WT/DS332/AB/R, WTO Appellate Body Report, 17 December 2007, 224–26; Weiler (n 77) 306.
[82] Article XX provides that Member States have the right exceptionally to take certain measures as long as they are not applied arbitrarily or in a discriminatory manner.
[83] Decision rendered by the WTO Appellate Body in the case of *United States—Import Prohibition of Certain Shrimp and Shrimp Products* (12 October 1998) WT/DS58/AB/R, para 158.
[84] ibid para 159.
[85] WTO Appellate Body in the case of *United States—Standard for Reformulated and Conventional Gasoline and Like Products of National Origin* (WT/DS2/AB/R) (1996) 35 ILM 603, 626.

> [T]he principle amounts to a general principle of Union law. First, a common concept of abuse of rights exist in the legal traditions of the Member States. Second, the European Court of Justice (ECJ) has gradually built a Union concept of abuse of rights.[86]

Notwithstanding the above, some question the transnational nature of abuse of rights. Whilst acknowledging that many scholars and courts/tribunals advocate the generality and universality of the principle, Gutteridge noted that this is questionable given that the principle remains in a formative stage, is rejected by England and Italy, and that it may be used by debtors to evade their obligations.[87] **3.52**

One does not concur with the reasons mentioned by Gutteridge, and therefore, with his conclusion questioning the transnationality of the principle. The principle of abuse of rights has unequivocally developed since these particular concerns were raised.[88] Moreover, not only is the principle currently recognized and accepted in Italy,[89] but as it was previously mentioned, English law endorses equivalent principles and standards that function in a similar manner and achieve the same purpose as the aims of abuse of rights.[90] Finally, while one acknowledges that the principle's utilization may allow one to evade from its obligation, it was previously highlighted that the principle must be applied with utmost prudence and that decision makers must resort to, and utilize it in exceptional cases where abuse is flagrant. **3.53**

B. General Principle of Arbitral Procedure

A specific procedural principle may also become a general procedural principle if it is recognized and accepted in many legal systems and constantly upheld in international arbitral practice.[91] **3.54**

In this section, abuse of rights as a general procedural principle in international arbitration shall be discussed. **3.55**

One shall, first, succinctly highlight the possible application of general, or transnational, principles of procedure in international arbitration (1); and subsequently discuss the status of abuse of rights (2). **3.56**

[86] Lenaerts (n 39) 1121; Case C-321/05 *Hans Markus Kofoed v Skatteministeriet* [2007] ECR I-5795, para 38.
[87] Gutteridge (n 1) 7.
[88] The concerns shared by Gutteridge were raised in 1944.
[89] Article 833 of the Italian Civil Code recognizes the *aemulatio* principle.
[90] Lenaerts (n 39) 1125.
[91] Rudolf B Schlesinger, 'Research on the General Principles of Law Recognised by Civilized Nations' (1957) 51 the American Journal of International Law 734, 736.

1. The application of transnational principles of procedure in international arbitration

3.57 The recognition and application of transnational procedural principles is neither peculiar to, nor inconsistent with, international arbitration law and practice.[92] The Institute of International Law adopted a resolution in 1989, which provided that:

> *[T]he parties have full autonomy* to determine the procedural [. . .] rules and principles that are to apply in the arbitration [. . .] these rules and principles may be derived from different national legal systems as well as from *non-national sources* such as principles of international law, *general principles of law* [. . .].[93] (Emphasis added)

3.58 Thus, it is widely acknowledged that there are transnational procedural rules and principles in international arbitration.[94]

3.59 Arbitral procedures are generally subject to the sacrosanct principle of party autonomy.[95] Thus, they are governed by the procedural framework adopted by the parties.[96] This framework comprises the rules of law of the arbitration statute designated by the parties or the rules of law determined by the arbitrators, the pre-established arbitration rules (those of an institution or ad-hoc), and any applicable international convention.[97]

3.60 However, owing to the *non-comprehensive* nature of the aforementioned procedural framework, lacunas exist that need to be supplemented.[98] In this context, it is submitted that an autonomous set of transnational or general principles have emerged, and continue to emerge, in international arbitration in order to ensure the administration of arbitral justice.[99]

[92] It is submitted that while English law does not generally recognize the theory of delocalization of arbitration, it recognizes the existence and application of transnational procedural principles in international arbitration: Stewart C Boyd, 'The Role of National Law and the National Courts in England' in Julian DM Lew (ed), *Contemporary Problems in International Arbitration* (Springer 1987) 160; Martin Hunter and Anthony C Sinclair, 'Aminoil Revisited: Reflections on a Story of Changing Circumstances' in Todd Weiler, *International Investment Law and Arbitration: Leading Cases from the ICSID, Nafta, Bilateral Treaties and Customary International Law* (Cameron May 2005) 355.

[93] Article 6 of the Resolution adopted by the International Law Institute, 'Arbitration between States, State Enterprises, or State Entities, and Foreign Enterprises', Session of Santiago de Compostela, 1989, available at <http://www.idi-iil.org/app/uploads/2017/06/1989_comp_01_en.pdf> accessed 03 November 2019.

[94] Fabricio Fortese and Lotta Hemmi, 'Procedural Fairness and Efficiency in International Arbitration' (2015) 3 Groningen Journal of International Law 110, 114–15; Gabrielle Kaufmann-Kohler, 'Globalization of Arbitral Procedure' (2003) 36 Vanderbilt Journal of Transnational Law 1313, 1320–22; Anna Mantakou, 'General Principles of Law and International Arbitration' (2005) 58 RHDI 419; Klaus Peter Berger, 'The International Arbitrator's Dilemma: Transnational Procedure versus Home Jurisdiction: A German Perspective' (2009) 25 Arbitration International 217.

[95] Daniel Girsberger and Nathalie Voser, *International Arbitration: Comparative and Swiss Perspectives* (3rd edn, Kluwer Law International 2016) para 889.

[96] Gaillard and Savage (n 25) 633.

[97] Gary B Born, *International Commercial Arbitration* (2nd edn, Kluwer Law International 2014) 1528–29; William Park, 'The Procedural Soft Law of International Arbitration: Non-Governmental Instruments' in Loukas Mistelis and Julian DM Lew (eds), *Pervasive Problems in International Arbitration* (Kluwer Law International 2006) 141.

[98] Lew, Mistelis, and Kröll (n 23) 524; Park (n 97) 143 and 148.

[99] Stavros Brekoulakis, 'International Arbitration Scholarship and the Concept of Arbitration Law' (2013) 36 Fordham International Law Journal 745, 777–82; Henri Alvarez, 'Autonomy of International Arbitration Process' in Loukas Mistelis and Julian DM Lew (eds), *Pervasive Problems in International Arbitration* (Kluwer Law International 2006) 119; Fortese and Hemmi (n 94) 114–15; Kurkela and Turunen (n 40) 8–9; Hans Smit, 'Proper Choice of Law and the Lex Mercatoria Arbitralis' in Thomas E Carbonneau (ed), *Lex Mercatoria and Arbitration: A Discussion of the New Law Merchant* (Juris Publications 1990) 59.

The extent of the role played by such generally accepted procedural principles is not subject to consensus in arbitration practice and jurisprudence. This variation emanates from the different conceptions and representations of international arbitration, that is, the extent of its autonomy from national legal systems.[100] 3.61

In arbitration doctrine, international arbitration is mainly represented either as: a component of the national legal order of the place of arbitration (*monolocal* or *territorial* vision);[101] anchored in a plurality of national legal systems (*Westphalian* or *pluralistic* vision); or as an autonomous legal order (*transnational* vision).[102] The aforementioned representations differ in that: the monolocal view advocates that the source of legitimacy is the law of seat of arbitration, the Westphalian view considers that international arbitration's legitimacy stems from the acknowledgment of such legitimacy by a number of legal systems; and according to some scholars, the transnational view advocates that the source of legitimacy is the collective acknowledgment by the community of nations as reflected in international instruments and practices.[103] 3.62

Based on the above, while some limit the application of such principles to situations where the parties agree to endorse them, and some advocate their application where there is a gap in the otherwise applicable arbitration rules and the law of the seat,[104] others advocate the necessity to grant greater weight to transnational principles as their application is a reflection of the consensus of nations, which is consistent with their transnational conception of international arbitration.[105] The latter school of thought asserts that whenever the issue is not regulated under the arbitration rules, transnational norms and principles should apply.[106] 3.63

Unlike domestic arbitration which is often conducted on the basis of rules and principles similar to judicial procedures, international arbitration is arguably a stand-alone mechanism that operates in a separate sphere from the particularities of parochial national laws and courts.[107] It is peripatetic, given that it often permeates two or more different jurisdictions, it involves an international dispute between parties, and is decided 3.64

[100] Emmanuel Gaillard, 'International Arbitration as a Transnational System of Justice' in Albert Jan van den Berg (ed), *Arbitration—The Next Fifty Years* (Kluwer Law International 2012) 66.

[101] Francis A Mann, 'The UNCITRAL Model Law—Lex Facit Arbitrum' in Pieter Sanders (ed), *International Arbitration: Liber Amicorum for Martin Domke* (Martinus Nijhoff 1967) 159–61, reprinted in (2014) 2 Arbitration International 241, 244–45 (providing that every arbitration is subject to a specific system of national law which should be the law of the arbitral seat).

[102] Gaillard (n 35); Jan Paulsson, 'Arbitration Unbound: Award Detached from the Law of its Country of Origin' (1981) 30 International and Comparative Law Quarterly 358, 362; for a critique of the mentioned theories of international arbitration, see Jan Paulsson, 'Arbitration in Three Dimensions', LSE Legal Studies Working Paper No 2/2010.

[103] Gaillard (n 100) 67–8; but cf W Michael Reisman and Brian Richardson, 'Tribunals and Courts: An Interpretation of the Architecture of International Commercial Arbitration' in Albert Jan van den Berg (ed) *Arbitration —The Next Fifty Years* (Kluwer Law International 2012) 17–18 (who discusses the transnational view as a rejection of national legal systems).

[104] Georgios Petrochilos, *Procedural Law in International Arbitration* (Oxford University Press 2004) 174–76.

[105] Gaillard (n 100) 69–70.

[106] Julian DM Lew, 'Achieving the Dream: Autonomous Arbitration' (2006) 22 Arbitration International 179, 181.

[107] ibid 202.

by arbitrators from different parts of the globe. Parties opt for international arbitration to avoid the application of national legal procedures that may not be fit for international disputes.[108]

3.65 Moreover, the place of arbitration usually designated by the parties should not be perceived as an unequivocal reflection of the parties' will to subject their arbitration to the rules of procedure of the country of the seat.[109] As advocated by Professor Julian Lew, arbitration is a *sui juris* mechanism, invariably governed by *a-national* or transnational norms and internationally accepted procedural principles, and that national laws have no interest to govern international arbitral procedures.[110] It may be argued that there is a transnational arbitral order whereby general principles of law serve as its *lex arbitri*.[111]

3.66 Advocating the transnational conception of international arbitration, or the existence of an autonomous arbitral legal order, is also of paramount importance to the study of abuse of rights as a transnational principle in international arbitration. This is particularly given that this view accepts that the convergence of national legal principles, as well as emergence of principles constantly applied by international arbitrators, allows the identification of transnational principles[112] such as abuse of rights.

3.67 In this regard, it is submitted that international arbitration should not be restricted by the application of parochial national rules of procedure, but should rather be conducted in accordance with principles that are universally or generally accepted as suitable for the administration of international arbitration. This is particularly the case where the governing arbitration rules are silent or not explicit regarding the matter in question.

3.68 However, it is suggested that the application of transnational principles is of paramount importance and remains inevitable notwithstanding which conception of international arbitration is endorsed.[113] This is precisely the case given the incomprehensiveness of the various established arbitration rules, as well as modern arbitration statutes, and

[108] Jan Paulsson, 'Delocalisation of International Commercial Arbitration: When and Why it Matters' (1983) 32 International and Comparative Law Quarterly 53, 59–60; Lew (n 106) 179–80.

[109] Petrochilos (n 104) para 1.46; Gaillard and Savage (n 25) 635–36; Lew (n 106) 202; Renata Brazil-David, 'Harmonization and Delocalization of International Commercial Arbitration' (2011) 28 Journal of International Arbitration 445, 445, and 455; Paulsson (n 108) 54; Paulsson (n 102) 7–8; *General National Maritime Transport Co v Société Gotaverken Arendal AB*, Paris Court of Appeal, Decision of 21 February 1980 (1981) 20 ILM 884, (where the French Court held that the arbitral proceedings were delocalized despite the fact that the parties chose Paris as the seat of arbitration); and *Societe AKSA SA v Société Norsolor SA*, Paris Court of Appeal, Decision of 9 December 1980, (1981) 20 ILM 887 (recognizing the delocalization of international arbitration and advocating the irrelevance of the seat of arbitration); but cf *Bank Mellat v Helliniki Techniki SA* [1984] QB 291, 301; *Naviera Amazonica Peruano SA v Compania Internacional de Seguros del Peru* [1988] 1 Lloyd's Rep 116, 120 (both English decisions rejecting the delocalization theory and emphasizing the arbitral seat's role).

[110] Lew (n 106) 180–81, 195–96; Kohler (n 94) 1318–20.

[111] Paulsson (n 102) 381.

[112] Gaillard (n 35) 104–05; Brekoulakis (n 798) 777–79.

[113] Gabrielle Kaufmann-Kohler, 'Identifying and Applying the Law Governing the Arbitration Procedure—The Role of the Law of the Place of Arbitration' in Albert Jan van den Berg (ed), *Improving the Efficiency of Arbitration Agreements and Award: 40 Years of Application of the New York Convention*, ICCA Congress Series No. 9 (Kluwer Law International 1999) 354; Gaillard (n 35) 99–100; Paulsson (n 108) 57.

the few mandatory rules found in such statutes.[114] Thus, it is submitted that arbitrators must continuously *strive* to ascertain and apply *generally accepted procedural principles*.[115] This is noted by one author who emphasizes the role of the *lex arbitri*:

> [I]t is only recently that arbitrators have started to fill gaps in arbitration rules by relying upon general rules of procedure adopted in the practice of international tribunals or generally accepted in the laws of states. This is, doubtless, the right approach – again, within the bounds of the *lex arbitri*.[116]

The legal basis for applying transnational procedural principles, and its source of legitimacy, is evidenced by the fact that most modern arbitration statutes and arbitration rules grant the arbitrators, in the absence of parties' choice, the power to conduct the arbitral procedures in light of the principles and rules of law they deem appropriate.[117] **3.69**

The above submission is also confirmed by the practice of arbitrators. For example, in an arbitration initiated under the Arbitration Rules of the Geneva Chamber of Commerce and Industry that took place in Switzerland. The dispute was between an Italian company and a German company. The issue raised before the arbitral Tribunal was whether the Tribunal could order security for costs. The issue was not covered under the Geneva Rules or the Swiss Private International Law Act. The Claimant maintained that the Tribunal lacked the authority to issue such security given that the prevailing view in Switzerland was that courts and arbitrators should not order security for costs. The arbitral Tribunal first provided that Article 182(2) of the Swiss Private International Law Act granted it the autonomy to determine the arbitral procedures. The Tribunal provided that international arbitration was not restricted to the particularities of Swiss law, and it then established its authority to order security for costs by considering the prevailing general principles applied by other tribunals in international arbitration.[118] **3.70**

Another particularly interesting example of the above is reflected in the well-known case of *Dallah v Pakistan*. In this case, Dallah, a Saudi trading group, won an ICC arbitration seated in Paris against Pakistan. Given that the contract was concluded between Dallah and a Pakistani trust created by Pakistan, which was later dissolved, the issue raised before the Tribunal was if the contract and the arbitration clause extended to the Government of Pakistan. Dallah requested the application of Saudi law and Pakistan requested Pakistani law to decide on this procedural issue. The arbitral Tribunal held **3.71**

[114] Park (n 97) 143.
[115] Petrochilos (n 104) para 5.16.
[116] ibid para 5.22.
[117] Article 1509 of the French Arbitration Law of 2011; Article 182 of the Swiss Private International Law Act; Article 25 of the Egyptian Arbitration Law No 27 of 1994; section 4 of the English Arbitration Act of 1996; Article 17 of the UNCITRAL Arbitration Rules (2013); Article 19 of the ICC Rules of Arbitration of 2012; Article 23 of the Stockholm Chamber of Commerce of 2017; Article 44 of the ICSID Convention (1965); Gaillard and Savage (n 25) 635–50; Fernando Mantilla-Serrano, 'Towards a Transnational Procedural Public Policy' (2004) 20 Arbitration International 333, 336; Karl-Heinz Böckstiegel, 'Major Criteria for International Arbitrators in Shaping an Efficient Procedure', in ICC Bulletin Special Supplement, *Arbitration in the Next Decade* (1999) 50.
[118] *A SpA v B AG*, Decision of 25 September 1997 (2001) 19 ASA Bulletin 745, para 8.

that the question should be decided in light of general or transnational procedural principles:

> Judicial as well as Arbitral case law now clearly recognise that, as a result of the principle of autonomy, the rules of law, applicable to an arbitration agreement, may differ from those governing the main contract, and that, in the absence of specific indication by the parties, such rules need not be linked to a particular national law [. . .] but may consist of those *transnational general principles* which the Arbitrators would consider to meet the fundamental requirements of justice in international trade.[119] (Emphasis added)

3.72 Finally, in the leading case of *Dow Chemical v Isover-Saint-Gobain*,[120] the issue before the Tribunal was whether the arbitration clause may extend to a non-signatory entity part of the group of companies. Arbitration proceedings were initiated in Paris on the basis of an ICC arbitration clause. The Defendant raised a jurisdictional challenge providing that the Tribunal had no jurisdiction in relation to the non-signatory subsidiary and the non-signatory parent company. The arbitral Tribunal issued an interim award rejecting the Defendant's jurisdictional challenge and upholding its jurisdiction based on the 'group of companies doctrine'. In doing so, the Tribunal noted that the ICC Rules grant it the power to decide such procedural questions without referring to any specific national law.[121]

3.73 It appears that the theoretical foundation of the group of companies doctrine, as stated by the arbitral Tribunal and nurtured by the French Court, was based on transnational principles, the *lex mercatoria*, and usages of international trade. It was explicitly held that, owing to the *autonomous* nature of the arbitration clause, and in application to the overarching principle of separability, the arbitral Tribunal should not be restricted to a given national law when deciding such procedural matters. A contrario, it was held that ICC Rules allowed the application of transnational principles of international commerce or the *lex mercatoria* to such issues including, inter alia, the possible extension of the arbitration clause.[122] The Tribunal is free to opt for such principles as long as no principle or any rule of international public policy is infringed.[123]

3.74 In the absence of a contrary choice made by the parties, the autonomy granted to arbitrators by virtue of all modern arbitration laws and rules may, therefore, allow arbitrators to refer to and apply transnational principles of arbitral procedure.[124]

[119] *Dallah Real Estate and Tourism Holding Company v The Ministry of Religious Affairs, Government of Pakistan*, [2010] UKSC 46, para 33. It should be noted that the UK Supreme Court refused to enforce the award.

[120] ICC Case No 4131 of 1982, *Dow Chemical v Isover-Saint-Gobain*, (1984) IX Ybk Commercial Arbitration 131.

[121] Interim Award, ICC Case No 4131 of 1982, *Dow Chemical v Isover-Saint-Gobain*, (1984) IX Ybk Commercial Arbitration 131, 133, but cf *Peterson Farms, Inc v C & M Farming Ltd* [2003] EWHC 2298 (Comm) 44–5.

[122] ibid.

[123] ibid 137.

[124] Gaillard and Savage (n 25) 649–50; Kohler (n 94) 1323; ICC Partial Award in Case No 14208/14236 of 2013, (2013) 24 ICC International Court of Arbitration Bulletin 62.

2. Abuse of rights is a generally accepted procedural principle in international arbitration

In the first chapter, the analysis of abuse of rights under various legal systems revealed that there is a general recognition of abuse of procedural rights.[125] It was demonstrated that the different legal systems either rely on the principle of abuse of right, or on abuse of process (under common law),[126] which is a manifestation of abuse of rights,[127] to limit the abuse of procedural rights.[128] The principle of abuse of rights is also sometimes raised before the ICJ to preclude the abuse of procedural rights under international law.[129] **3.75**

The transnational nature of abuse of rights, in the context of procedural rights, does not only stem from its recognition in the different legal systems, but may also be deduced from its recognition in international legal instruments; its recognition by prominent scholars; and by its constant application, as such, by international courts and tribunals in order to limit procedural abuse. **3.76**

The UNIDROIT Principles of Transnational Civil Procedure comprise a statement of internationally accepted procedural principles dealing with international disputes. The Principles, which may extend to the sphere of international arbitration unless incompatible thereto,[130] also endorsed the prohibition of abuse of procedural rights as a principle of a transnational nature.[131] **3.77**

Similar provisions can be found in other international conventions. For example, Article 294.1 of the United Nations Convention on the Law of the Sea provides that: **3.78**

> A court or tribunal provided for in article 287 to which an application is made in respect of a dispute referred to in article 297 shall determine at the request of a party, or may determine *proprio motu*, whether the claim constitutes an abuse of legal process

[125] Article 32.1 of the French Code of Civil Procedure provides that one who acts in a dilatory or abusive manner may be ordered to pay a civil fine and to the reparation of damages.

[126] For an analysis of the recognition of the principle of abuse of process as an application of abuse of rights in the common law systems (Canada, Australia, England and Wales, and the United States), see John P Gaffney, '"Abuse of Process" in Investment Treaty Arbitration' (2010) 11 Journal of World Investment and Trade 515–17.

[127] *Philip Morris Asia Limited v The Commonwealth of Australia*, PCA Case No 2012-12, Award on Jurisdiction and Admissibility of 17 December 2015, under UNCITRAL Rules, para 554; Eric De Brabandere, '"Good Faith", "Abuse of Process" and the Initiation of Investment Treaty Claims' (2012) 3 Journal of International Dispute Settlement 619.

[128] Robert Kolb, 'General Principles of Procedural Law' in Andreas Zimmermann and others (eds), *The Statute of the International Court of Justice: A Commentary* (Oxford University Press 2006) para 65; Yasuhei Taniguchi, 'Good Faith and Abuse of Procedural Rights in Japanese Civil Procedure' (2000) 8 Tulane Journal of International and Comparative Law 167 (discussing the recognition of abuse of rights to limit abuse of procedural rights in Japan); Michele Taruffo, *Abuse of Procedural Rights: Comparative Standards of Procedural Fairness* (Kluwer Law International 1999) (discussing the recognition of abuse of rights in different legal systems).

[129] *Guinea-Bissau v Senegal*, Case Concerning the Arbitral Award of 31 July 1989, [1991] ICJ Rep 53, 63; Gaffney (n 126) 519–21; Andreas Zimmermann and others, *The Statute of the International Court of Justice: A Commentary* (Oxford University Press 2006) 831 (providing that while the ICJ did not hitherto apply abuse of rights to preclude the abuse of procedural rights, it did not reject its application, but merely never found the principle's conditions of application to be fulfilled).

[130] The American Law Institute, *UNIDROIT Principles of Transnational Civil Procedure* (Cambridge University Press 2006) 17.

[131] Principle 11, ibid 30–31.

or whether *prima facie* it is well founded. If the court or tribunal determines that the claim constitutes an abuse of legal process or is *prima facie* unfounded, it shall take no further action in the case.[132]

3.79 Article 35.3 of the European Convention for the Protection of Human Rights and Fundamental Freedoms of 1953, as amended in 1998, provides that:

> The Court shall declare inadmissible any individual application submitted under Article 34 if it considers that: (a) the application is incompatible with the provisions of the Convention or the Protocols thereto, manifestly ill-founded, or an abuse of the right of individual application.

3.80 It is generally acknowledged by distinguished scholars that abuse of procedural rights constitutes a general procedural principle, owing to the fact that it exists in most, if not all, legal systems as well as under international law.[133] As noted by one scholar: '[abuse of procedural rights] is common to all the major legal systems, and may be properly applied by a tribunal in any legal system, including the international legal system, in the exercise of the tribunal's competence to regulate its own proceedings'.[134]

3.81 The renowned Hersch Lauterpacht examined the existence of abuse of rights in major legal systems and advocated that, notwithstanding the different terminology employed, 'there is inherent in every system of law the general principle of prohibition of abuse of rights'.[135] He rightly noted that the principle of abuse of rights exists in the administration of justice of most systems of law, and indeed that 'there is no legal right, however well established, which could not, in some circumstances, be refused recognition on the ground that it has been abused'.[136]

3.82 In a recently published book on general principles of law, Luke Sobota and Charles Kotuby emphasized that the 'negative corollary of the good faith exercise of a legal entitlement is the universal prohibition on abuse of rights'. They further pinpointed that abuse of rights was recognized and referred to as a general principle of law ever since the term 'general principles' was inserted in the PCIJ Statute. They noted that:

> Since then, numerous judges, arbitrators, and scholars have considered abuse of rights to be part of international law, whether as a general principle of law or as part of customary international law.[137]

[132] Article 294.1 of the United Nations Convention on the Law of the Sea 1982; Article 300 which recognizes a general principle of abuse of rights in relation to the exercise of all rights, substantive and procedural, under the Convention ('States Parties shall fulfil in good faith the obligations assumed under this Convention and shall exercise the rights, jurisdiction and freedoms recognized in this Convention in a manner which would not constitute an abuse of right').

[133] Campbell Mclachlan, *Lis Pendens in International Litigation* (Martinus Nijhoff Publishers 2009) 429–30; Gaffney (n 126) 518; Ascensio (n 46) 765–66; Charles T Kotuby and Luke A Sobota, *General Principles of Law and International Due Process* (Oxford University Press 2017) 108.

[134] Vaughan Lowe, 'Overlapping Jurisdiction in International Tribunals' (1999) 20 Australian Ybk of International Law 191, 202–03.

[135] Lauterpacht (n 43) 305–06.

[136] Herch Lauterpacht, *The Development of International Law by the International Court* (Cambridge University Press 1982) 162–64; Lauterpacht (n 43) 300–05.

[137] Kotuby and Sobota (n 133) 108.

In the context of international arbitration, Yuval Shany noted in relation to procedural rights that by virtue of the 'extensive practice of international bodies and the near consensus in the writing of jurists on the matter, the theory [abuse of rights] can probably be viewed as [. . .] a general principle of law'.[138] 3.83

Professor Jan Paulsson similarly acknowledged that it constitutes a general procedural principle and emphasized its transnational nature: '[I]t may be confidently said that the principle of abuse of rights (*abus de droit, Rechtsmissbrauch*) is universal.'[139] 3.84

Professor Rudolf Dolzer also confirmed that the principle of abuse of rights is a general principle of law and should apply in international arbitration to prevent the abuse of the arbitral system: 'The doctrine of abuse itself is firmly grounded in international arbitration law.'[140] 3.85

Other scholars acknowledge that whilst the arbitral framework does not provide for the principle of abuse of rights, the principle is common in national legal proceedings in civil and common legal systems, and thus, it constitutes a general procedural principle common to all legal systems.[141] 3.86

Similarly, Andreas Zimmermann also confirmed that abuse of procedural rights is a general principle of law under international law as well as under municipal laws: 3.87

> [Abuse of process is] a special application of the prohibition of abuse of rights, which is a general principle of international law as well as in municipal law. It consists of the use of procedural instruments or rights by one or more parties for purposes which are alien to those for which the procedural rights were established.[142]

While the principle is constantly applied by arbitrators and international courts as discussed below, some have questioned the normative basis of its application.[143] Scepticism regarding the application of abuse of rights in international arbitration emanates from the fact that the framework of arbitration, comprising national arbitration laws, institutional rules, and any applicable convention, does not recognize or provide for the abuse of rights principle.[144] 3.88

[138] Yuval Shany, *The Competing Jurisdictions of International Courts and Tribunals* (Oxford University Press 2003) 257.

[139] Jan Paulsson, 'The Expectation Model' in Yves Derains and Richard H Kreindler (eds), *Evaluation of Damages in International Arbitration* (Kluwer Law International 2006) 73–74.

[140] Expert Opinion of Professor Rudolf Dolzer, in the case of *Hulley Enterprises, Yukos Universal and Veteran Petroleum v The Russian Federation*, of 20 October 2015, paras 164, 166, 320, 321.

[141] Brabandere (n 127) 618–19.

[142] Zimmermann and others (n 129) 831.

[143] Ascensio (n 46) 782–83; *Wasteful Management Inc v United Mexican States*, ICSID Case No ARB(AF)/00/3, Decision on Preliminary Objections Concerning the Previous Proceedings of 26 June 2002, para 49.

[144] Brabandere (n 127) 621. Equally, the Statute of the ICJ does not provide for the application of abuse of rights. Gaffney (n 126) 518–19. An exception of this can be found in Article 294 of the United Nations Convention on the Law of the Sea.

3.89 To that end, while the principle has been regularly referred to and applied in international arbitration, tribunals apply the principle without referring to any legal provision/rule in the applicable rules of law as the legal basis for their decisions.[145]

3.90 Questioning the principle's normative basis was manifested in the case of *Rompetrol v Romania*. The Respondent alleged that the proceedings were abusive as they were initiated by the Claimant for the purpose of blocking criminal investigations against the Claimant's shareholders.[146]

3.91 While this issue became moot as the Claimant provided that it did not challenge the criminal investigations but merely the manner in which the investigations were conducted, and thus the Respondent no longer maintained its objection,[147] the case remains interesting as the Tribunal questioned the legal basis of abuse of rights in international arbitration. The Tribunal noted:

> Marshalled as it is as an objection at this preliminary stage, this is evidently a proposition of *a very far-reaching character*; it would entail an ICSID tribunal, after having determined conclusively (or at least prima facie) that the parties to an investment dispute had conferred on it by agreement jurisdiction to hear their dispute, deciding nevertheless not to entertain the application to hear the dispute. Given that an ICSID tribunal, under the Washington Convention as interpreted, is bound to exercise a jurisdiction conferred on it, *so far-reaching a proposition needs to be backed by some positive authority in the Convention itself*, in its negotiating history, or in the case-law under it.[148] (Emphasis added)

3.92 By reviewing the approach employed by arbitral tribunals, it appears that arbitrators resort to abuse of rights and apply it as a general principle of law,[149] and that their power/basis to resort to such principle emanates from their inherent power to regulate, and

[145] *Phoenix Action v The Czech Republic*, ICSID Case No ARB/06/5, Award of 15 April 2009; *Cementownia SA v Republic of Turkey*, ICSID Case No ARB(AF)/06/2, Award of 17 September 2009; *Saipem SpA v Bangladesh*, ICSID Case No ARB/05/7, Award of 30 June 2009, para 161; *Lao Holdings NV v The Lao People's Democratic Republic*, ICSID Case No ARB(AF)/12/6, Decision on Jurisdiction of 21 February 2014; *Gold Reserve Inc v Bolivarian Republic of Venezuela*, ICSID Case No ARB(AF)/09/1, Award of 22 September 2014, paras 231–33; *Philip Morris Asia Limited v The Commonwealth of Australia*, PCA Case No 2012-12, Award on Jurisdiction and Admissibility of 17 December 2015, under UNCITRAL Rules, paras 538–54; *ST-AD GmbH v Republic of Bulgaria*, UNCITRAL, PCA Case No 2011-06, Award on Jurisdiction of 18 July 2013, paras 408–23; *Transglobal Green Energy LLC and Transglobal Green Panama SA v Republic of Panama*, ICSID Case No ARB/12/28, Award of 2 June 2016, paras 100–19.

[146] *The Rompetrol Group NV v Romania*, ICSID Case No ARB/06/3, Decision on Respondent's Preliminary Objections on Jurisdiction and Admissibility of 18 April 2008, para 111.

[147] ibid para 115.

[148] ibid para 115.

[149] ICC Partial Award in Case No 14208/14236 of 2013, (2013) 24 ICC International Court of Arbitration Bulletin 62 (while the contract was governed by the laws of State X, the arbitral tribunal applied *abuse of rights as a transnational principle* of law to pierce the corporate veil and extended the arbitration clause to the non-signatory parent company).

preserve the integrity of, the arbitral procedures, as well as to ensure the good administration of arbitral justice.[150] As articulated by one tribunal:

> Nor does the Tribunal doubt for a moment that, like *any other international tribunal*, it must be regarded as endowed with the *inherent powers required to preserve the integrity of its own process* [. . .]The Tribunal would express the principle as being that parties have an obligation to arbitrate fairly and in good faith and that an arbitral tribunal has the inherent jurisdiction to ensure that this obligation is complied with; *this principle applies in all arbitration*, including investment arbitration, and to all parties.[151] (Emphasis added)

As opposed to the case of applicable substantive law, where arbitrators may often decide on the basis of the law governing the contract, as regards procedure, arbitrators decide under *a-national* procedural rules. These are mainly the rules of the arbitration institution or ICSID Convention. *None* of the provisions in the ICSID Convention, arbitration statutes, or rules provide for the abuse of rights principle, *yet arbitrators rely on it* in order to ensure the good administration of justice. It is in this context that arbitrators function in a manner to preserve the integrity of the arbitral process and that a general principle of abuse of rights has emerged owing to the dire need to safeguard the arbitral process, enhance the fairness and efficiency of the proceedings, and ensure the overall administration of arbitral justice. **3.93**

In many instances, arbitrators explicitly refer to abuse of rights as a general principle of law and apply it to a myriad of procedural arbitration-related rights.[152] However, it is argued that even where arbitrators do not refer to it as a general principle of law, the way they utilize the principle in the context of the current legal framework of arbitration provides material evidence that the principle constitutes a general principle of arbitral procedure. **3.94**

In the case of *Mobil Corporation, Mobil Cerro et al, v Bolivarian Republic of Venezuela*, the Respondent claimed that the Exxon Mobil's corporate restructuring through the creation of a Dutch holding company 'constituted an abuse of right',[153] and thus requested the Tribunal to decline jurisdiction under the BIT. The arbitral Tribunal first acknowledged the principle of abuse of rights as a general principle of law and explicitly **3.95**

[150] Chester Brown, *A Common Law of International Adjudication* (Oxford University Press 2007) 245; Gaffney (n 126) 521; Martins Paparinskis, 'Inherent Powers of ICSID Tribunals: Broad and Rightly So' in Ian Laird and Todd Weiler (eds), *Investment Treaty Arbitration and International Law* (Juris 2011) 16 <https://ssrn.com/abstract=1876705> accessed 20 February 2019; Chester Brown, 'The Relevance of the Doctrine of Abuse of Process in International Adjudication' (2010) 7 Transnational Dispute Management 1, 6–12; 'Interim Report on "Res Judicata" and Arbitration' (International Law Association, Berlin 2004) 8; Ascensio (n 46) 783; Utku Topcan, 'Abuse of the Right to Access ICSID Arbitration' (2014) 29 ICSID Review 627, 633; *Legality of Use of Force (Serbia and Montenegro v Belgium)*, Separate Opinion of Judge Higgins, [2004] ICJ Rep 279, para 10; *Hunter v Chief Constable of the West Midlands* [1982] AC 529, 536.

[151] *Libananco Holdings Co Limited v Republic of Turkey*, ICSID Case No ARB/06/8, Decision on Preliminary Issues, 23 June 2008, para 78.

[152] *Orascom TMT Investments Sàrl*, ICSID Case No ARB/12/35, Award of 31 May 2017, para 541.

[153] *Mobil Corp v Republic of Venezuela*, ICSID Case No ARB/07/27, Decision on Jurisdiction of 10 June 2010, para 167.

provided that *all systems of law*, whether domestic or international, adopt the principle of abuse of rights, or similar concepts, to preclude the misuse of the law.[154]

3.96 In applying abuse of rights, the Tribunal recognized that the corporate planning and treaty shopping, even if aimed to gain access to arbitration, could be either legitimate or an abuse of right depending on the factual matrix of the case. Given that the dispute was *foreseeable* to the Respondent, as complaints were sent *prior* to the restructuring, and the Respondent replied to such complaints, the Tribunal drew a distinction between *pre-existing* disputes at the time of the corporate structuring and *future* disputes. It was held by the Tribunal that Claimants' restructuring of their investments to protect such investments and gain access to ICSID was 'a perfectly legitimate goal as far as it concerned future disputes'. A contrario, in relation to the pre-existing disputes, it was held that restructuring of investments to gain access to ICSID constituted an abuse of right.[155]

3.97 The above depiction of the abuse of rights principle was subsequently confirmed in the case of *Pacific Rim Cayman LLC v The Republic of El Salvador* and in the case of *ConocoPhillips*, where the arbitrators provided that the principle of abuse of rights was universal owing to its recognition in all domestic legal systems and under international law, in order to preclude procedural misconduct and the misuse of law.[156]

3.98 In the ICSID case of *Cementownia v Turkey*, the Claimant initiated arbitration against Turkey alleging that the latter had taken measures against two companies which the Claimant asserted to have acquired a percentage of their shares. The Claimant alleged that the Respondent had breached its duties under the applicable Energy Charter Agreement. However, in their last submissions, both parties requested the arbitral Tribunal to dismiss the case. The Claimant requested the dismissal based on its lack of standing to sue. While it alleged that it acquired a shareholding interest in the two companies, it asserted that it could not prove such acquisition, and thus requested the dismissal of the claim but without prejudice. On the other hand, the Respondent requested an award that dealt with the issue of the Claimant's standing to sue, as well as dismissing the claim with prejudice and an award of damages and costs in its favour.[157]

3.99 In its request for damages and costs, the Respondent argued that the arbitral proceedings were initiated solely to inflict harm on Turkey.[158] After acknowledging that the Claimant had brought the arbitration proceedings in bad faith, the Tribunal provided that this conduct violated the general principle of abuse of rights.[159] The Tribunal also

[154] ibid paras 169–72.

[155] ibid paras 204–06.

[156] *Pacific Rim Cayman LLC v The Republic of El Salvador*, ICSID Case No ARB/09/12, Decision on Jurisdiction of 1 June 2012, para 2.44; *ConocoPhillips v The Bolivarian Republic of Venezuela*, ICSID Case No ARB/07/30, Decision on Jurisdiction and the Merits of 3 September 2013, paras 273–74;

[157] *Cementownia SA v Republic of Turkey*, ICSID Case No ARB(AF)/06/2, Award of 17 September 2009, para 109.

[158] ibid para 165.

[159] ibid paras 153–59 and 170.

held that the Claimant abused its rights throughout the proceedings by engaging in dilatory tactics and procedural misconduct, including several requests of time extension, change of its legal counsel, and finding a new legal representation, constantly changing its prayers for relief, and increasing the costs of the arbitration.[160] Finally, while explicitly acknowledging that 'compensation for moral damages may indeed aim at indicating a condemnation for abuse of process',[161] the Tribunal decided to sanction the Claimant and to make him bear all costs related the proceedings.

Another case that confirms that the principle of abuse of rights functions as a transnational principle in international arbitration that is applied to ensure the good administration of justice is the case of *Saipem v Bangladesh*. **3.100**

In this case, a contract was concluded between Saipem, an Italian company, and Petrobangla, a State-owned company of Bangladesh. The contract was for building a gas pipeline in Bangladesh. It was governed by Bangladeshi law and contained an ICC arbitration clause.[162] After building the gas pipeline, Petrobangla refused to pay the retention money agreed upon in the contract. Saipem initiated ICC arbitration in Bangladesh. During the arbitration proceedings, Petrobangla made a number of procedural requests regarding the conduct of the proceedings, which were rejected by the arbitral Tribunal. Consequently, Petrobangla decided to resort to the courts in Bangladesh, notwithstanding the arbitration clause and the pending arbitration proceedings, and requested the revocation of the authority of the ICC Tribunal and also requested an injunction restraining Saipem from the ICC proceedings. The court of Dhaka in Bangladesh confirmed Petrobangla's allegation of arbitrators' misconduct, decided to revoke the ICC Tribunal's authority, and issued the injunction. The ICC Tribunal continued and rendered an award on the merits which found Petrobangla liable.[163] **3.101**

In a request to set aside the award before the Court in Bangladesh, the Court held that: 'there is no Award in the eye of the law, which can be set aside [. . .] A non-existent award can neither be set aside nor can it be enforced'.[164] **3.102**

Based on the above, Saipem relied on the BIT between Italy and Bangladesh and initiated ICSID arbitration proceedings. In resorting to the Bangladeshi Court and hindering the ICC arbitration proceedings, Saipem claimed that its right to arbitrate and its rights determined by the ICC award comprise investments that were expropriated.[165] The ICSID Tribunal held that Saipem's investment reflected in the ICC award was expropriated, and that Bangladesh had abused its rights. **3.103**

[160] ibid para 158.
[161] ibid para 171.
[162] *Saipem SpA v Bangladesh*, ICSID Case No ARB/05/7, Award of 30 June 2009, paras 7–10.
[163] ibid paras 31–50.
[164] Ruth Teitelbaum, 'Case Report on Saipem v Bangladesh' (2010) 26 Arbitration International 313, 314; *Saipem SpA v Bangladesh*, ICSID Case No ARB/05/7, Award of 30 June 2009, para 50.
[165] *Saipem SpA v Bangladesh*, ICSID Case No ARB/05/7, Decision on Jurisdiction of 21 March 2007, para 122.

3.104 The ICSID Tribunal examined the factual matrix of the case and the procedural orders rendered by the ICC Tribunal and found that such a decision lacked any sound legal or factual grounds.[166] After acknowledging that national courts may have the right to revoke arbitral tribunals' authority in cases of misconduct, and that courts are bestowed with a discretionary power in this regard,[167] the Tribunal found that such a discretionary power had been exercised for a purpose other than that for which it was conferred. In establishing abuse of rights, the Tribunal did not rely on any positive legal rule found under the arbitration rules or the ICSID Convention, but rather relied on the *transnational* status of abuse of rights and that it functions to ensure the good administration of justice.[168] The Tribunal stated that:

> [T]he Tribunal is of the opinion that the Bangladeshi courts exercised their supervisory jurisdiction for an end which was different from that for which it was instituted and thus violated the *internationally accepted principle of prohibition of abuse of rights*.[169] (Emphasis added)

3.105 In the case of *Renco Group v Peru*, the Tribunal considered the application of the principle of abuse of rights to determine whether Peru's conduct with respect to the late raising of its waiver objection constituted an abuse of rights. In discussing the principle, the Tribunal noted that:

> The abuse of rights doctrine is an aspect of the principle of good faith and is a well-established general principle of international law. The doctrine has been cited and applied on numerous occasions by international courts and tribunals.[170]

3.106 In addition, in the cases of *Himpurna California Energy Ltd v PT (Persero) PLN*[171] and *Patuha Power v PT (Persero) PLN*,[172] the Tribunal applied the principle of abuse of rights on the issue of request and quantification of damages. The Tribunal confirmed that abuse of rights was a universal principle of law, that it constituted a general principle of law, and provided that it must apply, notwithstanding the applicable rules of law.[173]

3.107 Finally, in the case of *Caratube International Oil LLP and Mr Hourani v Republic of Kazakhstan*, the Respondent argued that owing to its status as a general principle of

[166] ibid para 155.
[167] ibid para 159.
[168] ibid para 149.
[169] *Saipem SpA v Bangladesh*, ICSID Case No ARB/05/7, Award of 30 June 2009, para 161.
[170] *Renco Group v Republic of Peru*, ICSID Case No UNCT/13/1, Partial Award on Jurisdiction of 15 July 2016, para 175.
[171] *Himpurna California Energy Ltd v PT PLN (Persero)*, ad hoc arbitration under UNCITRAL rules, Final Award of 4 May 1999, (2000) XXV Ybk Commercial Arbitration 11; Jan Paulsson, 'Unlawful Laws and the Authority of International Tribunals' (2008) 23 ICSID Review Foreign Investment Law Journal 215, 223.
[172] *Patuha Power Ltd (Bermuda) v PT (Persero) Perusahaan Listruik Negara (Indonesia)* (1999) 14 Mealey's Int'l Arb Rep B-1, B-44.
[173] *Himpurna California Energy Ltd v PT PLN (Persero)*, ad hoc arbitration under UNCITRAL rules, Final Award of 4 May 1999, (2000) XXV Ybk Commercial Arbitration 11, 91–92.

law, the principle should apply to preclude the abusive initiation of multiple proceedings. The Respondent argued that the Claimants had abused the international arbitration system by engaging in an improper claim-splitting and by bringing repetitive claims that could have been brought in one proceeding.[174] Claimants argued that the Respondent failed to prove that the principle of abuse applied to preclude multiple proceedings and that there was no basis for its application.[175]

Although the Tribunal did not find the circumstances of the case to constitute an abuse of right,[176] it explicitly endorsed the possible application of the principle in the context of multiple proceedings and referred to the legal bases for its application. The Tribunal held that: 3.108

> [T]he Parties do not seem to dispute the general premise that the abuse of process doctrine may be applied by international tribunals in order to preserve the integrity of the tribunal and avoid the abuse by one party of the arbitral procedure. [. . .] the Tribunal agrees that the general principle of the prohibition of abuse of process *applies in the context of multiple proceedings* before international tribunals. [. . .] the Respondent has invoked as legal bases for the application of the abuse of process doctrine, inter alia, Article 41 of the ICSID Convention (according to which the Tribunal is the judge of its own jurisdiction) and Article 44 of the ICSID Convention (which grants broad procedural powers to the Tribunal to conduct the arbitration proceedings). Moreover, the Respondent has invoked several *general principles on international law*, such as the principles of good faith and *the prohibition of abuse of right.* In the opinion of the Tribunal, the application of the abuse of process doctrine may be based on the Tribunal's *power to determine the conduct of the arbitration proceedings* and the principles regarding the Parties' *general obligation to participate in the proceedings in good faith and not abuse the rights granted to them*, for example the right to rely on an arbitration agreement to commence an arbitration.[177] (Emphasis added)

The above confirms the status of abuse of rights as a general principle of law.[178] It is submitted that the rising phenomenon of abuse in international arbitration urged arbitrators to find a curative tool that tackles the different forms of abuse that take place during arbitral proceedings. This growing conundrum undermines the status of the international arbitral system as a fair and effective means to settle international disputes.[179] As a result, a general principle of abuse of rights has emerged in international arbitration to tackle different forms of procedural abuse. This submission is corroborated by the principle's wide recognition as a general procedural principle by distinguished 3.109

174 *Caratube International Oil LLP and Mr Devincci Salah Hourani v Republic of Kazakhstan*, ICSID Case No ARB/13/13, Award of 27 September 2017, paras 334–35.

175 ibid para 353.

176 ibid para 381.

177 ibid paras 372 and 376.

178 Nolan (n 34) 505, (providing that transnational principles are resorted to where there is no adequate rule in the applicable law).

179 Emmanuel Gaillard, 'Abuse of Process in International Arbitration' (2017) 32 ICSID Review 17.

scholars, and owing to its constant application to limit the abuse of different arbitration related rights.[180]

3.110 Nothing in the legal framework of international arbitration precludes arbitrators from resorting to and applying abuse of rights. As previously mentioned, most, if not all, modern arbitration statutes, institutional rules, as well as the ICSID Convention, grant arbitrators wide powers to regulate the proceedings, to safeguard the integrity of the arbitral system, and to ensure the good administration of arbitral justice. In order to achieve this, most laws and rules grant arbitrators the right to resort to generally accepted legal principles to decide procedural issues. Whilst it is true that the current commercial/investment arbitral framework does not provide a positive legal rule relating to abuse of rights, the above discussion demonstrates that arbitrators have frequently resorted to the principle of abuse of rights to limit procedural abuse and misconduct in international arbitration. In doing so, arbitrators perceive and apply abuse of rights as a general principle of law.[181] In resorting to abuse of rights, tribunals often base its application on the tribunal's inherent power to safeguard the integrity and fairness of the proceedings, and to ensure the good and fair administration of justice.[182]

C. Is It an Overriding Principle of Law?

3.111 The above confirms the proposition that abuse of rights is applied as a general substantive and procedural principle of law. A rational corollary of this entails that arbitrators are to apply the principle of abuse of rights either as part of the applicable national law (subject to the principle's scope of application and national characteristics under the national law) or as a transnational principle where arbitrators are entitled to resort to general principles of law, that is, where parties refer to transnational standards, or in the absence of a choice.[183]

3.112 The only exception to this is if the principle in question constitutes an overriding principle or a principle of transnational public policy. This is due to the fact that despite the application of any principles or rules of law (national or a-national), certain principles of transnational public policy remain applicable.[184]

[180] *Transglobal Green Energy LLC and Transglobal Green Panama SA v Republic of Panama*, ICSID Case No ARB/12/28, Award of 2 June 2016, para 102 (noting that there is a line of consistent decisions regarding objections to jurisdiction based on abuse of rights).

[181] Topcan (n 849) 627.

[182] ibid, 628–29 and 633; Paparinskis, (n 849); *Mobil Corp v Republic of Venezuela*, ICSID Case No ARB/07/27, Decision on Jurisdiction of 10 June 2010, para. 184; *Wasteful Management Inc v United Mexican States*, ICSID Case No ARB(AF)/00/3, Decision on Preliminary Objections Concerning the Previous Proceedings dated 26 June 2002, para 48.

[183] Alan Redfern and Martin Hunter, *Law and Practice of International Commercial Arbitration* (Sweet & Maxwell 1986) 76; Note (n 2) 1820 ('When the parties clearly designate the substantive law of a particular jurisdiction, there is little room for the application of general principles of law'); Waincymer (n 51) 49; Gaillard (n 1) 163.

[184] Alexis Mourre, 'Arbitration and Criminal Law: Reflections on the Duties of the Arbitrator' (2006) 22 Arbitration International 95, 116; Gaillard and Savage (n 25) 860.

This is consistent with uniform principles found in international legal instruments such as Article 1.103 of the Principles of European Contract law[185] and Article 1.3 of the UNIDROIT Principles.[186] 3.113

In this regard, where parties designate a choice of law or rules of law, and where the principle of abuse of rights is not part of the designated rules of law, are arbitrators still entitled to resort to the principle of abuse of rights as a matter of transnational public policy? 3.114

In this context, it is worth mentioning that transnational, or truly international public policy, denotes those 'fundamental rules of natural law; principles of universal justice; jus cogens in public international law; and the general principles of morality accepted by what are referred to as "civilised nations" '.[187] 3.115

In its Interim and Final Reports on Public Policy as a Bar to Enforcement of International Arbitral Awards, the ILA acknowledged that abuse of rights is a 'fundamental principle of law',[188] and recommended that it be considered a principle of international public policy. The Report first pinpointed that international public policy denotes those fundamental substantive and procedural principles, which pertain to justice and morality, that ought to be protected by the State even if the State is not concerned with or directly connected to the dispute.[189] The Report then mentioned the prohibition of abuse of rights as an epitome of those fundamental principles of international public policy.[190] 3.116

One need not emphasize the value of ILA reports, the level of sophistication of their content, and the international stature of ILA committee members. Indeed, such reports depict best practices and prevailing approaches to the issues scrutinised thereunder. 3.117

The above depiction of abuse of rights as a principle of transnational public policy is not peculiar or alien to the views of scholars and established practices of distinguished 3.118

[185] Article 1:103 of the Principles of European Contract Law: 'Effect should nevertheless be given to those mandatory rules of national, supranational and international law which, according to the relevant rules of private international law, are applicable irrespective of the law governing the contract', <http://www.jus.uio.no/lm/eu.contract.principles.parts.1.to.3.2002/1.103.html> accessed 20 February 2019.

[186] Article 1.3 of the UNIDROIT Principles: 'nothing in these Principles shall restrict the application of mandatory rules, whether of a national, international or supranational origin, which are applicable in accordance with the relevant rules of private international law'; Comment 4 of Article 1.4 of the UNIDROIT Principles of 2010.

[187] Pierre Mayer and Audley Sheppard, 'Final ILA Report on Public Policy as a Bar to Enforcement of International Arbitral Awards' (2003) 19 Arbitration International 249, 259; Pierre Lalive, 'Transnational (or Truly International) Public Policy and International Arbitration' in Pieter Sanders (ed), *Comparative Arbitration Practice and Public Policy in Arbitration* (Kluwer Law International 1987) 295; Martin Hunter and Gui Conde E Silva, 'Transnational Public Policy and its Application in Investment Arbitrations' (2003) 4 The Journal of World Investment 367, 368; Bernard Hanotiau and Olivier Caprasse, 'Public Policy in International Commercial Arbitration' in Emmanuel Gaillard and Domenico Di Petro (eds), *Enforcement of Arbitration Agreements and International Arbitral Awards: The New York Convention in Practice* (Cameron May 2008) 794–96.

[188] International Law Association, *Interim Report on Public Policy as a Bar to Enforcement of International Arbitral Awards* London Conference (2000), Part I.V.B.2.a., 20.

[189] Mayer and Sheppard (n 187) 255.

[190] ibid 255.

arbitrators.[191] As one scholar noted in the context of the public policy exception under the New York Convention:

> The courts generally have construed this public policy exception narrowly, drawing a clear distinction between domestic and international public policy [. . .]. The provision's requirements will only be satisfied where the most basic of notions of morality and justice are infringed. Examples of the interests protected by international public policy are the efforts to combat drug smuggling, child pornography, bribery, corruption [. . .] the prohibition of the abuse of rights, and the protection of the incapacitated.[192]

3.119 While arbitral awards dealing with the mentioned enquiry are indeed scarce, some cases may be mentioned to elucidate the issue.

3.120 It is well-acknowledged that a form of State manoeuvre that may constitute an abuse of right is the principle of *ex re sed non ex nomine* (evasion of the law); where a State manipulates and abuses its regime or domestic procedures to evade its obligations.[193] Thus, where a State, or a State-owned entity, agrees to refer a given dispute to international arbitration, the principle of abuse of rights may operate, as a principle of transnational public policy, to preclude the State from relying on its national law to evade arbitration.[194]

3.121 In the case of *Benteler v Belgium*, the principle was applied to prevent such abusive conduct, and was described as a fundamental rule 'the observance of which is *obligatory* in international arbitration'.[195] Similarly, in the case of *Millicom and Sentel v Republic of Senegal*, the Tribunal provided that it was an established principle in international arbitration that a State was precluded from relying on its domestic law to avoid arbitration or its capacity to arbitrate. The Tribunal further confirmed that this comprises a principle of *transnational public policy*.[196] A similar decision was rendered in ICC Case No 1939 of 1971, where the Tribunal also held that the international community could not sanction the abusive conduct of States or State-owned entities that attempted to evade their obligations by relying on their laws, and that such conduct was contrary to

[191] Stavros Brekoulakis, 'Transnational Public Policy' (forthcoming Article), (providing that the prohibition of abuse of rights constitutes a transnational public policy principle); Karl-Heinz Böckstiegel, *Arbitration and State Enterprises: Survey on the National and International State of Law and Practice* (Kluwer 1984) 25; Gaillard (n 179) 34, (discussing its mandatory nature in relation to substantive and procedural matters); Swiss Federal Tribunal, dated 8 March 2006, in the case of *Tensaccia SPA v Freyssinet Terra Armata RL*, 4P.278/2005, (2006) 24 ASA Bulletin 550, 553.

[192] Dimitri Santoro, 'Forum Non Conveniens: A Valid Defense under the New York Convention' (2003) 21 ASA Bulletin 713, 721.

[193] Paulsson (n 139) 73; Cheng (n 46) 122; Jan Paulsson, 'May a State Invoke its Internal Law to Repudiate Consent to International Commercial Arbitration? Reflections on the Benteler v. Belgium Preliminary Award', (1986) 2 Arbitration International 90.

[194] Böckstiegel (n 191) 25 and 45; Paulsson (n 139) 73.

[195] Ad-hoc arbitration case of *Benteler v Belgium*, Award of 18 November 1983, (1986) 1 Journal of International Arbitration 184, 188; also referred to in *Himpurna California Energy Ltd v PT PLN (Persero)*, ad hoc arbitration under UNCITRAL rules, Final Award of 4 May 1999, (2000) XXV Ybk Commercial Arbitration 11, 91.

[196] *Millicom and Sentel v Republic of Senegal*, ICSID Case No ARB-08-20, Decision on Jurisdiction of 16 July 2010, para 103(b).

transnational public policy.[197] The depiction of abuse of rights, or *venire contra factum proprium*, as an application thereof, was again used as a principle of transnational public policy in ICC Case No 10947 of 2002.[198]

The arbitral awards in the seminal cases of *Himpurna California Energy Ltd v PT (Persero) PLN*[199] and *Patuha Power v PT (Persero) PLN*,[200] fortify and confirm that the principle of abuse of rights is not only a general principle of substantive and procedural law, but that it may also apply as an overriding principle, notwithstanding the applicable rules of law. **3.122**

In these cases, *Himpurna* and *Patuha*, two subsidiaries of an American company, entered into energy sale contracts with *PLN* (the Indonesian State Electricity Corporation). Pursuant to the contracts, *Himpurna* and *Patuha* were obliged to supply electricity to PLN and invest in wells and other infrastructure. Following the Indonesian financial crisis in 1997, presidential decrees were issued to the effect that *PLN* could not perform its contractual obligations. Accordingly, the investments of *Himpurna* and *Patuha* were suspended. *Himpurna* initiated arbitration proceedings and sought damages of 2.3 billion US Dollars. *Patuha* also relied on its contract and initiated arbitration proceedings and sought 1.4 billion US dollars in damages. Given that both cases are almost identical, except for the amount of damages requested, reference herein below, is made to the *Himpurna* award.[201] **3.123**

Applying Indonesian law, the arbitral Tribunal found that *PLN* was in breach of its contractual obligations, performed the contractual obligations in bad faith, and held that *Himpurna* was entitled to damages, including lost profits. However, in relation to awarding lost profits, the Tribunal limited the amount to less than 10 per cent of the amounts claimed. **3.124**

In reaching its decision regarding the damages, the Tribunal relied on the principle of abuse of rights. The Tribunal explicitly acknowledged that the principle is *universal*, constitutes a *general principle of law*, and ensures the legitimacy of the international arbitral process.[202] Given that Indonesian law does *not* include an express reference to abuse of rights, the Tribunal provided that 'it will apply the principle as an element of *overriding* substantive law proper to the international arbitral process'. Thus, the Tribunal held that: **3.125**

[197] ICC Case No 1939 of 1971, [1973] Review Arbitrage 145, referred to in *Millicom and Sentel v Republic of Senegal*, ICSID Case No ARB-08-20, Decision on Jurisdiction of 16 July 2010, para 103(b).

[198] ICC Case No 10947 of 2002, (2004) 22 ASA Bulletin 308, para 30.

[199] *Himpurna California Energy Ltd v PT PLN (Persero)*, ad hoc arbitration under UNCITRAL rules, Final Award of 4 May 1999, (2000) XXV Ybk Commercial Arbitration 11; Jan Paulsson, 'Unlawful Laws and the Authority of International Tribunals'(2008) 23 ICSID Review Foreign Investment Law Journal 215, 223.

[200] *Patuha Power Ltd (Bermuda) v PT (Persero) Perusahaan Listruik Negara (Indonesia)*, (1999) 14 Mealey's Int'l Arb Rep B-1, B-44.

[201] *Himpurna California Energy Ltd v PT PLN (Persero)*, ad hoc arbitration under UNCITRAL rules, Final Award of 4 May 1999, (2000) XXV Ybk Commercial Arbitration 11, 14.

[202] ibid 91–92.

> In such circumstances, it strikes the Arbitral Tribunal as unacceptable to assess lost profits as though the claimant had an *unfettered right* to create ever-increasing losses for the State of Indonesia (and its people) by generating energy without any regard to whether or not PLN had any use for it. *Even if such a right may be said to derive from explicit contractual terms* [. . .] To extract the full benefit of the hard terms of the ESC with respect to investments not yet made, in a situation where that benefit will clearly exacerbate the already great losses of the co-contractant, *strikes the Arbitral Tribunal as likely to constitute an abuse of right* [. . .] *this is a case where the doctrine of abuse of right must be applied in favour of PLN to prevent the claimant's undoubtedly legitimate rights from being extended beyond tolerable norms.*[203] (Emphasis added)

3.126 This case is of particular interest and importance as it highlights the possible application of the principle of abuse of rights in international arbitration, in relation to the phase of awarding and quantifying damages, not only as a general principle of law, but as an overriding principle of law.[204]

3.127 This may suggest that abuse of rights operates as an overriding principle of law, and is to be given effect irrespective of the governing law and the will of the parties.[205]

3.128 Moreover, a review of the award shows that in endorsing abuse of rights as an overriding substantive and/or procedural principle of law, the underlying criterion arguably adopted by the Tribunal was that of reasonableness and balancing of the competing interests.[206] This further confirms the endorsement of this criterion in the transnational context of abuse of rights. Precisely, the Tribunal's award is premised on the view that an abuse of right may be established, *notwithstanding the absence of fault* on the side of the right holder,[207] given the *unreasonable* amount of damages to the counter party: 'beyond tolerable norms'.[208] This is an application of the balancing factor as stated in the previous chapters: where courts/tribunals find an abuse given the gravity of damages caused to an individual from the exercise of a right, notwithstanding the absence of fault. Moreover, the Tribunal's engagement in the balancing of the competing interests is evident as it found an abuse of right despite the fact that such finding arguably

[203] ibid 90.

[204] Others have also advocated that abuse of rights constitutes a transnational public policy principle: Santoro (n 192) 721: 'Examples of the interests protected by international public policy are the efforts to combat drug smuggling, child pornography, bribery, corruption and other generally condemned practices, as well as the notions of good faith, *pacta sunt servanda*, the prohibition of the abuse of rights, and the protection of the incapacitated'; Gui Conde Silva, 'Transnational Public Policy in International Arbitration' (PhD thesis, Queen Mary University of London 2007) 36–37.

[205] Abdulhay Sayed, *Corruption in International Trade and Commercial Arbitration* (Kluwer Law International 2004) 286 (providing that the application of overriding principles limits the parties' choice).

[206] Similarly, the decision rendered by the WTO Appellate Body in the case of *United States—Import Prohibition of Certain Shrimp and Shrimp Products*, WT/DS58/AB/R, 12 October 1998, para 158, (where the tribunal used good faith as a synonym of reasonableness).

[207] The tribunal acknowledged that the right holder has 'undoubtedly legitimate rights', Irina Petrova, '"Stepping on the Shoulders of a Drowning Man" The Doctrine of Abuse of Right as a Tool for Reducing Damages for Lost Profits: Troubling Lessons from the Patuha and Himpurna Arbitrations' (2004) 35 Georgetown Journal of International Law 455, 456 ('However, *without finding any liability or bad faith* by the project companies, the Arbitral Tribunal awarded less than ten percent of the amount each company had claimed in lost profits').

[208] *Himpurna California Energy Ltd v PT PLN (Persero)*, ad hoc arbitration under UNCITRAL rules, Final Award of 4 May 1999, (2000) XXV Ybk Commercial Arbitration 11, 93.

conflicted with the principles of *pacta sunt servanda*[209] and legal security,[210] which are acknowledged interests in contractual arrangements.

Qualifying abuse of rights as a fundamental overriding principle of law is not subject to unanimity in international arbitration, specifically given its defiance to the overarching principle of *pacta sunt servanda*.[211] The dissenting opinion of arbitrator De Fina further testifies to the mandatory nature of abuse of rights as perceived by the majority, and that it constituted a transnational principle of law. He stipulated: **3.129**

> I am particularly troubled by the *novel proposition* adopted by my colleagues that the claimant's *reliance upon its contractual rights* to establish quantum *amounts to an abuse of rights* thus leading to and permitting a substantial reduction of *what might otherwise be awarded*. My concern is that such a questionable proposition and the manner of its application in this Award *prejudices notions of legal security and basic principles of private law* [. . .] the imposition of a concept described as 'abuse of rights' *in the absence of findings of malicious intent or lack of good faith* on the part of the claimant to further reduce the entitlement to damages is in my opinion an inappropriate and unwarranted penalising of the claimant.[212] (Emphasis added)

Subjecting the application of the principle of abuse of rights to a finding of bad faith or malicious intent testifies to the different perception of the principle between the majority and the dissenting arbitrator, that is, a national principle versus a transnational principle. Given that Indonesian law includes a provision regarding good faith, but does *not* expressly provide for abuse of rights,[213] the dissenting arbitrator opined that abuse of rights can only apply where there is proof of bad faith. On the other hand, the majority perceived and applied the principle as a mandatory transnational principle of law,[214] as (a) they did not restrict themselves to the particularities of Indonesian law; (b) they endorsed the criterion of reasonableness which is *not part* of Indonesian law; (c) the principle was applied to prevent awarding unreasonable damages, notwithstanding the absence of fault, which is an application not found under the applicable **3.130**

[209] Michael Pryles commented on the Tribunal's decision and provided that the decision arguably disregarded the principle of *pacta sunt servanda*: Michael Pryles, 'Lost Profit and Capital Investment' (2007) 1 World Arbitral and Mediation Review 1, 14; Henrik M Inadomi, *Independent Power Projects in Developing Countries: Legal Investment Protection and Consequences for Development* (Kluwer Law International 2010) 259 ('the Himpurna/Patuha tribunals limited the doctrine of *Pacta Sunt Servanda* because full expectation damages would constitute an abuse of right').

[210] The dissenting arbitrator provided that applying abuse of rights prejudices the notion of '*legal security*'. *Himpurna California Energy Ltd v PT PLN (Persero)*, ad hoc arbitration under UNCITRAL rules, Dissenting Opinion of Arbitrator De Fina, (2000) XXV Ybk Commercial Arbitration 13; BIICL, 'Case Note: Karaha Bodas and Himpurna Arbitrations', 6 (2008), at <http://www.biicl.org/files/3931_2000_himpurna_and_karaha_bodas_arbitrations.pdf> accessed 20 February 2019.

[211] Pryles (n 209) 14–15; John Y Gotanda, 'Recovering Lost Profits in International Disputes' (2004) 36 Georgetown Journal of International Law 61, 104–05.

[212] *Himpurna California Energy Ltd v PT PLN (Persero)*, ad hoc arbitration under UNCITRAL rules, Dissenting Opinion of Arbitrator De Fina, (2000) XXV Ybk Commercial Arbitration 11, 108.

[213] Article 1338 of the Indonesian Civil Code.

[214] *Himpurna California Energy Ltd v PT PLN (Persero)*, ad hoc arbitration under UNCITRAL rules, Dissenting Opinion of Arbitrator De Fina (2000) XXV Ybk Commercial Arbitration 11, 91–92.

law; and (d) they went beyond the contract and the positive law; they explicitly endorsed and applied the principle as a general and overriding principle of law.

3.131 On a related note, abuse of rights may in some cases function as a principle of transnational public policy (substantive and procedural) even if not explicitly expressed as one.[215]

3.132 In this regard, it is noteworthy to mention ICC Case No 1803 of 1972[216] where a dispute arose out of a contract concluded between a corporation wholly owned by the Pakistan Government (EBIDC) and a French company (SGTM) regarding the construction of a pipeline for the transport of gas in East Pakistan (which became the Republic of Bangladesh in 1971). The contract was subject to Pakistani law and provided for arbitration in Geneva under the rules of ICC. Upon the failure to settle a claim of 12 million French Francs, arbitration proceedings started in Geneva. The then President of Bangladesh issued a decree establishing a corporation (BIDC) and transferred the shares, board of directors, and employees of EBIDC to BIDC. Additionally, the decree provided that the debts incurred were deemed to have been incurred by BIDC. Finally, the decree provided that any arbitration against EBIDC before the issuance of the order was deemed abated and no award shall be binding or enforceable. Subsequently an order was issued to dissolve EBIDC, and another order dissolving BIDC was issued.

3.133 The arbitral Tribunal agreed to SGTM's request to join the Bangladeshi Government and to the substitution of BIDC for EPIDC to the arbitration. The Tribunal rendered an award to the effect that BIDC and the Government of Bangladesh were jointly and severally liable. In this regard, it is of particular interest to mention that the Tribunal held that:

> Be that as it may, the tenor and intended effect of the Disputed Debts Order is *wholly repugnant to Swiss conceptions of natural justice, fair dealing and the standards of morality binding upon sovereign Governments*. The notion that a debt should become void and indeed non-existent ab initio for no better reason than that the debtor has chosen to put it in dispute *is an extreme example of what natural justice abhors* - the person or the public authority setting itself up as judge of its own cause. The *lex fori* certainly does not require me to recognize and apply the Disputed Debts Order. It is a *flagrant abuse of right* and a measure which is quite irreconcilable with Swiss 'ordre public'; it should not be recognized or applied by any Swiss judge or in any arbitration which is proceeding in Switzerland and is governed by Swiss procedural law.[217] (Emphasis added)

3.134 While the arbitrator's decision was based on Swiss law, being the *lex arbitri*, the decision is instructive on the nature of abuse of rights and its possible status as a principle

[215] Silva (n 204) 135–37.

[216] ICC Case No 1803 of 1972, (1980) V Ybk Commercial Arbitration 177–85.

[217] ibid 181. It should be mentioned that this award was set aside by the *Cour de justice* in Geneva and this was further upheld by the Swiss Federal Supreme Court. The Court provided that the arbitrator lacked the jurisdiction to order the joinder of the Government of Bangladesh and the substitution of BIDC for EPIDC as the former does not exist. *Société des Grands Travaux de Marseille v People's Republic of Bangladesh, Bangladesh Industrial Development Corporation*, Swiss Federal Tribunal, 5 May 1976, (1980) V Ybk Commercial Arbitration 217–19.

of transnational public policy. The conduct of the debtor, constituting abuse of rights, was characterized as contrary to *natural justice, fairness*, and standards of *morality*. These potent interests and norms generally reflect a transnational conception of public policy.[218] Thus, while the arbitrator applied abuse of rights to safeguard the most fundamental Swiss norms of fairness and justice, the reasoning employed seems to reflect transnational public policy.[219]

This is consistent with the views of scholars who view this decision as revealing the interrelation between the principle of abuse of rights and transnational public policy. In commenting on this case, one academic noted that while transnational public policy was not explicitly relied on, it was, nevertheless, applied in essence.[220] **3.135**

Based on the above, abuse of rights is considered a fundamental transnational principle of law. Moreover, some go further and apply it as a principle of transnational public policy. This recognition entails that whenever the conditions *sine qua non* of the principle's application are satisfied, arbitrators are to apply it, notwithstanding the choice of law.[221] In this regard, given the procedural framework of international arbitration, where existing laws and rules grant arbitrators the power to resort to, or abide by,[222] generally accepted procedural principles, and due to the constant application of the principle to prevent abuse of procedural rights, it is submitted that abuse of rights should operate as a principle of transnational public policy to prevent the abuse of arbitration related rights. Thus, it should apply in the context of procedural rights, notwithstanding the applicable rules and the *lex arbitri*. **3.136**

In the context of substantive rights, while one agrees with depicting the principle as fundamental given the potent interests it aims to secure, one cannot, hitherto, stipulate that it comprises an established principle of transnational public policy owing to the immaturity of such proposition. This is particularly the case given that any deviation from the applicable substantive law, *lex causae*, is generally frowned upon as it violates the sacrosanct principle of party autonomy, unless the principle is *clearly* of international public policy.[223] Thus, it is ripe for consideration as a principle of transnational public policy from the perspective of *de lege lata*—but the principle's potency **3.137**

[218] Mayer and Sheppard (n 187) 259; Lalive (n 187) 295; Hunter and Silva (n 187) 368.

[219] ICC Case No 6474 of 1992, (2000) XXV Ybk Commercial Arbitration 279, para 36, (where the Tribunal relied on the broader notion of good faith, as a principle of transnational public policy, to prohibit the State from relying on its own non-recognition by the international community to preclude its obligation to arbitrate. In its reasoning, the Tribunal noted that the 'denial of jurisdiction in the circumstances would be contrary to that clear principle of transnational public policy which is the principle of good faith; it would defeat the legitimate expectations of the Parties to the agreements and finally compel the claimant to go before the Courts of the territory, as suggested by the defendant—all results which do not seem, to say the least, to be in keeping with the requirements of international public policy and of natural justice').

[220] Silva (n 204) 135.

[221] Lew, Mistelis, and Kröll (n 23) 419–20.

[222] Some submit that arbitrators must abide by fundamental general procedural principles in international arbitration: ICC Case No 1512 of 1971, (1976) I Ybk Commercial Arbitration 128, 128.

[223] Gaillard and Savage (n 25) 785 and 841–42; Lew, Mistelis, and Kröll (n 23) 419–20; ICC Case No 1512 of 1971, (1976) I Ybk Commercial Arbitration 128, 129; Gaillard (n 61) 163.

demonstrates its suitability and appropriateness to be elevated to such status, that is, *de lege ferenda*.

3.138 On a different note, from a practical perspective, whether the principle elevates to, and operates as, a principle of transnational public policy in relation to substantive rights is not necessarily material to the outcome of cases, particularly given the omnipresence of the principle in national legal systems and its recognition as a general principle of law. Arbitrators shall apply the principle whenever it is part of the applicable substantive law or as part of the general principles of law where he/she is entitled to apply those principles. However, unlike the principle's application as a general principle of law, applying abuse of rights as a national principle necessitates adhering to its specific scope of application under the relevant applicable law, as outlined in the previous chapters.

IV. Conclusion

3.139 The growing panoply of various forms of abuse that take place during the arbitration proceedings required the international community, and particularly arbitrators, to develop non-classic tools to remedy such procedural misconduct. A scrutiny of the principle's application in international arbitration not only demonstrates the omnipresence of the principle in most legal systems as well as under international law, but provides compelling evidence that a general principle of abuse of rights has emerged in international arbitration.

3.140 A review of different legal systems testify that the principle is recognized as a general substantive and procedural principle of law. This is further confirmed by the views of renowned scholars and by the constant application of abuse of rights as a general principle of law.

3.141 While the principle reflects fundamental interests that decision makers should safeguard and enforce, its depiction as part of transnational public policy is controversial.

3.142 It is one's submission that it should apply as a principle of transnational public policy in relation to procedural rights, given the current arbitral framework that grants arbitrators wide discretionary powers. Thus, it should apply regardless of the *lex arbitri*. However, although the principle is fundamental with regard to substantive rights, it should apply only where the arbitrators are allowed to resort to general principles of law, or as part of the national applicable law.

4

The Application of Abuse of Rights in Arbitration

I. Introduction

Parties resort to arbitration to resolve their disputes efficiently and to obtain a final and enforceable award.[1] Any system of justice, including the arbitration system, is not meant for abuse.[2] Thus, it would be paradoxical to support a mischief that the arbitration system seeks to obviate. This could cast doubts as to the system's efficiency and induce distrust in the system that was formed to accommodate parties' interests and uphold their common intentions. **4.01**

In this regard, it is argued that the principle of abuse of rights is necessary in international arbitration as it ensures the good administration of arbitral justice. **4.02**

As shall be scrutinized below, abuse of rights operates in a manner that: achieves fairness during the arbitration proceedings; incentivizes efficiency; enables arbitrators to reach an equitable and reasonable outcome; and preserves the integrity of the arbitration system. **4.03**

It is submitted that the application of abuse of rights equally serves fundamental interests pertaining to the substantive part of the dispute (such as fairness, reasonableness, **4.04**

[1] Gary B Born, *International Commercial Arbitration* (2nd edn, Kluwer Law International 2014) 73–91.
[2] Hervé Ascensio, 'Abuse of Process in International Investment Arbitration' (2014) 13 Chinese Journal of International Law 763, 765; *Libananco Holdings Co Limited v Republic of Turkey*, ICSID Case No ARB/06/8, Decision on Preliminary Issues of 23 June 2008, para 78.

and equitable outcomes).[3] Thus, in ICC Case No 3276 of 1979, the issue of applying abuse of rights and its connection with the power of arbitrators to decide as *amiable compositeur*, or *ex aequo et bono*, was discussed.[4] In this case, the Tribunal established a connection between equity, fairness, and the exercise of rights. It was provided that considerations of fairness and equity necessitate the prohibition of abuse of rights. More importantly, the Tribunal provided that where the conditions *sine qua non* for the application of abuse of rights are not established (if the exercise of right was not malicious, exercised for a legitimate purpose, and was reasonable), equitable considerations may still preclude the exercise of a right if the consequences of such exercise were not fair.[5]

4.05 However, given that international arbitration is inherently procedural,[6] this section shall mainly examine those arbitration related interests/principles that warrant the application of a general principle of abuse of rights in international arbitration.

4.06 Thus, the aim of this chapter is to demonstrate how the principle of abuse of rights is important for the good administration of justice given its advancement of paramount interests. However, it is acknowledged that the notion of good administration of justice eludes a priori meaning and that its essence is rather undeterminable.

4.07 Accordingly, prior to embarking on how the principle operates to advance the aforementioned interests, it is necessary to first shed light on the notion of good administration of arbitral justice by delineating its relevant constituent elements. Once this is achieved, it becomes possible to examine the interrelation of abuse of rights to, and its effect on, the administration of justice.

II. Good Administration of Arbitral Justice

4.08 As a dispute resolution process, international arbitration operates in accordance with a number of guiding principles. Arbitrators arguably have a fundamental duty to ensure the good administration of arbitral justice.[7]

[3] ICC Case No 8547 of 1999, in Albert Jan van den Berg (ed), (2003) XXVIII Ybk Commercial Arbitration, para 19; ICC Case No 3276 of 1979, in Sigvard Jarvin and Yves Derains, *Collection of ICC Arbitral Awards 1974-1985* (Kluwer Law 1990) 86.

[4] ICC Case No 3276 of 1979, in Sigvard Jarvin and Yves Derains, *Collection of ICC Arbitral Awards 1974-1985* (Kluwer Law 1990) 76–87.

[5] ibid 86.

[6] Alexandre Meyniel, 'That Which Must Not be Named: Rationalizing the Denial of U.S. Courts with Respect to the Group of Companies Doctrine' (2013) 3 The Arbitration Brief 18, 29.

[7] Bernardo M Cremades and David JA Caims, 'Trans-national Public Policy in International Arbitral Decision-making: The Cases of Bribery, Money Laundering and Fraud' in Andrew Berkeley and Kristine Karsten (eds), *Arbitration: Money Laundering, Corruption and Fraud* (Kluwer Law International 2003) 80; William W Park, 'The Four Musketeers of Arbitral Duty: Neither One-For-All nor All-For-One' in Yves Derains and Laurent Lévy (eds), *Is Arbitration only As Good as the Arbitrator? Status, Powers and Role of the Arbitrator* (Kluwer Law International 2011) 26; Philippe Leboulanger, 'Multi-Contract Arbitration' (1996) 13 Journal of International Arbitration 43, 904, arguing that the notion of good administration of justice is not merely an obligation on the part of the arbitrators, but may equally require the assistance of arbitral institutions; Utku Topcan, 'Abuse of the Right to Access ICSID Arbitration' (2014) 29 ICSID Review 627, 633.

Ascertaining the meaning of good administration of arbitral justice is not an easy task. Whilst the term may be used by scholars and arbitrators/judges, there appears to be no clear definition of the notion in arbitration doctrine.[8] **4.09**

The notion is often used to refer to the fairness of the proceedings, considerations of due process/equality, efficiency, and integrity of the arbitral process.[9] These principles are also described as the *magna carta* of international arbitration.[10] The potency of these principles, particularly fairness and due process, stems from the fact that they are deemed the core of procedural guarantees conferred upon the parties, and thus parties cannot waive such procedural guarantees.[11] **4.10**

Filip De Ly held that the notion of good administration of arbitral justice includes the requirements of due process, fairness, and efficiency.[12] Similarly, Philippe Leboulanger noted that good administration of justice is a fundamental principle which aims to secure justice and fairness between the parties, and 'serve procedural efficiency and to save time and costs'.[13] **4.11**

Thus, the notion's importance stems from the vital interests it intends to secure. It is a mandatory principle, part of international public policy, and should not be sacrificed in the face of other potent principles such as party autonomy: **4.12**

> From a procedural viewpoint, the sacrosanct principle of autonomie de la volonté should thus be soothed by mandatory principles such as the proper administration of justice, [. . .] which are part of international public policy as conceived by most national legal systems and by the law of international arbitration.[14]

An outline of the relevant pillars that fall under the umbrella of good administration of arbitral justice shall be provided. These comprise: **(A)** fairness; **(B)** due process; and **(C)** efficiency. This discussion is of potency, as one shall go on to examine how the principle of abuse of rights operates within these pillars and how it advances or affects them. **4.13**

[8] Bernard Hanotiau, Complex Arbitrations, Multiparty, Multicontract, Multi-issue and Class Actions (Kluwer Law International 2005) 47–48; Labinal Case, Paris Court of Appeal, 1st Chambers A, 1993 Review Arbitrage 645, referred to in Bernard Hanotiau 'Problems Raised by Complex Arbitrations Involving Multiple Contracts-Parties-Issues – An Analysis' (2001) 18 Journal of International Arbitration 253, 309; Willian W Park, 'Private Disputes and the Public Good: Explaining Arbitration Law' (2005) 20 American University International Law Review 903, 904.

[9] Park (n 7) 26; Application for Review of Judgment No 158 of United Nations Administrative Tribunal, Advisory Opinion [1973] ICJ Rep 166, 179; Georgios Petrochilos, 'Three Pillars of International Public Policy' in Photini Pazartzis and others (eds), *Reconceptualising the Rule of Law in Global Governance, Resources, Investment and Trade* (Hart Publishing 2016) 317; Thomas W Walde, 'Procedural Challenges in Investment Arbitration under the Shadow of the Dual Role of the State' (2010) 26 Arbitration International 3, 11, and 30.

[10] Petrochilos (n 9) 317; Abba Kolo, 'Witness Intimidation, Tampering and Other Related Abuse of Process in Investment Arbitration' (2010) 26 Arbitration International 43, 61.

[11] SI Strong, 'Limits of Procedural Choice of Law' (2014) 39 Brooklyn Journal of International Law 1027, 1101; Aleksandar Jaksic, *Arbitration and Human Rights* (Peter Lang Publishing 2002) 9.

[12] Filip De Ly, 'Paradigmatic Changes – Uniformity, Diversity, Due Process and Good Administration of Justice: The Next Thirty Years' in Stavros Brekoulakis and others (eds), *The Evolution and Future of International Arbitration* (Kluwer Law International 2016) 37.

[13] Leboulanger (n 7) 54.

[14] ibid 97.

A. Fairness

4.14 Parties principally refer their disputes to international arbitration owing to the presumed advantages and benefits that the arbitration system aspires to offer. Obtaining a fair resolution of the dispute is one of the principal purposes of international arbitration.[15]

4.15 One empirical study[16] found that the majority of arbitration users (81 per cent) rated a 'fair and just result' above all other considerations, including obtaining favourable monetary award.[17] It equally comprises a sacrosanct principle, the satisfaction of which is an integral prerequisite for the good administration of arbitral justice.[18]

4.16 The fairness factor has a substantive as well as a procedural element. Substantive fairness implies receiving the 'right' decision and procedural fairness entails receiving it in the 'right' manner.[19] In this regard, some rightly advocate that regardless of how accurate and fair the substantive outcome is, procedural fairness is of paramount importance: even a good and correct result does not compensate for a bad and unfair procedure'.[20]

4.17 The good administration of arbitral justice requires the highest standard of fairness.[21] Arbitration laws and institutional rules emphasize the duty of arbitrators to provide a fair means for the resolution of the dispute,[22] and that it comprises a fundamental principle of international arbitration.[23] That said, section 1(1)(a) of the English Arbitration Act stipulates that 'the object of arbitration is to obtain the fair resolution of disputes by an impartial tribunal without unnecessary delay or expense'.[24] The French arbitration law equally recognizes the potency of fairness, and provides that it must be honoured by the arbitral tribunal and the parties.[25]

15 William W Park, 'Arbitrators and Accuracy' (2010) 1 Journal of International Dispute Settlement 25, 27; David C Sawyer, 'Revising the UNCITRAL Arbitration Rules: Seeking Procedural Due Process Under the 2010 UNCITRAL Rules for Arbitration' (2011) 1 International Commercial Arbitration Brief 24, 26; Nana Japaridze, 'Fair Enough? Reconciling the Pursuit of Fairness and Justice with Preserving the Nature of International Commercial Arbitration' (2008) 36 Hofstra Law Review 1415, 1415–16.

16 This study was conducted by Richard W Naimark, the Vice President of the American Arbitration Association and Stephanie Keer.

17 Richard W Naimark and Stephanie E Keer, 'International Private Commercial Arbitration: Expectations & Perceptions of Attorneys & Business People' (2002) 30 International Business Lawyer 203, 205.

18 De Ly (n 12) 37–38; Leboulanger (n 7) 89–91.

19 Naimark and Keer (n 17) 205; Japaridze (n 15) 1416; Jeffrey Waincymer, 'Promoting Fairness and Efficiency of Procedures in International Commercial Arbitration – Identifying Uniform Model Norms' (2010) 3 Contemporary Asia Arbitration Journal 25, 31.

20 Fabricio Fortese and Lotta Hemmi, 'Procedural Fairness and Efficiency in International Arbitration' (2015) 3 Groningen Journal of International Law 110, 116; Matti S Kurkela and Santtu Turunen, *Due Process in International Commercial Arbitration* (2nd edn, Oxford University Press 2010) 202–03.

21 Gillian Eastwood, 'A Real Danger of Confusion? The English Law Relating to Bias in Arbitrators' (2001) 17 Arbitration International 287, 290.

22 Section 33(1) of the English Arbitration Act of 1996. It is acknowledged that the primary aim of the ICC Rules is to ensure fairness and efficiency in the dispute resolution process: ICC Rules of Arbitration of 2012 (Foreword); Article 22.4 of the ICC Rules of Arbitration of 2012; Article 14.4 of the LCIA Arbitration Rules of 2014; Article 17.1 of the UNCITRAL Arbitration Rules 2013.

23 De Ly (n 12) 27–28.

24 Section 1(a) of the English Arbitration Act of 1996.

25 Article 1464 of the French Code of Civil Procedure as amended in 2011.

4.18 Whilst the above laws and institutional rules have emphasized the importance of fairness in the conduct of arbitral proceedings, there is no clear guidance on what is considered a violation of fairness or how it relates to other principles such as due process or party autonomy.[26]

4.19 Thus, ascertaining how to achieve the desired fairness, or determining the constituent elements of fairness, remains largely ambiguous.[27] The Oxford English Dictionary defines the term 'fair' as 'acceptable and appropriate in a particular situation', and defines fairness as 'the quality of treating people equally or in a way that is reasonable'.[28] Moreover, the term fair is defined in *Black's Law Dictionary* as 'impartial', 'just', 'equitable' and 'disinterested'.[29]

4.20 It is appropriate to endorse the definition used by Filip De Ly, where he described procedural fairness in the context of arbitration as:

> [R]eferring to standards of *reasonable procedural conduct* which go beyond addressing *frustrating tactics* and also address procedural aspects to be solved on the basis of what *reasonable actors are to expect* from one another and are to comply with.[30] (Emphasis added)

4.21 In this regard, it is asserted that the requirement of procedural fairness encompasses an obligation to: prohibit procedural misconduct (which includes frustrating tactics); preclude any other abuse of right; preserve the integrity of the arbitral process; honour the parties' reasonable expectations; and enhance the efficiency of the proceedings.[31] It is of particular interest to mention that the depiction of fairness, so as to preclude abusive conduct, equally conforms to the requirement of fairness under Shari'a law and is consistent with the arbitral process prescribed thereunder.[32]

4.22 The interrelation between the notion of fairness and the principle of abuse of rights is further fortified by the UNIDROIT Principles, whereby Article 1.7 requires parties to act in good faith and fair dealing, and demonstrates that the prohibition against abuse of rights constitutes a manifestation of good faith and fair dealing.[33] By and large, this conforms to the views advocated by other learned scholars who confirm that abusive

[26] De Ly (n 12) 35.

[27] Sawyer (n 15) 26.

[28] *Oxford Advanced Learner's Dictionary* (7th edn, Oxford University Press 2005) 548–49.

[29] *Black's Law Dictionary* (9th edn, West Publishing Co 2009) 674.

[30] De Ly (n 12) 37.

[31] ibid; Tetley (n 634) 561–63 and 615; Japaridze (n 15) 1434–35, (drawing a clear link between fairness and the duty to act in good faith, and also providing that the notion of fairness encompasses a duty of loyalty). In relation to the meaning of the duty of loyalty, see Larry A DiMatteo and others Lucien Dhooge et al, 'The Interpretive Turn in International Sales Law: An Analysis of Fifteen Years of CISG Jurisprudence' (2004) 34 Northwestern Journal of International Law and Business 299, 316–17: 'According to the principle [loyalty], the parties to a contract have to act in favour of the common goal; *they have to reasonably consider the interests of the other party*'.

[32] Nudrat Majeed, 'Good Faith and Due Process: Lessons from the Shari'a' (200420 Arbitration International 97, 108.

[33] Comment (2) to Article 1.7 of the UNIDROIT Principles of 2010, which provides that a typical example of behaviour contrary to the principle of good faith and fair dealing is abuse of rights.

conduct and delaying tactics are unfair and thus defy the good administration of arbitral justice.[34]

4.23 On a related note, it is suggested that arbitrators' duty to resolve the dispute in a fair manner entails that arbitrators should also preserve the integrity of the arbitral system.[35] Part of the requirement of fairness is that arbitral tribunals not only safeguard and preserve the integrity of the arbitral process 'but also that the arbitrator give the appearance of doing so'.[36] In ascertaining what the duty of upholding fairness and preserving the integrity of arbitration process entail, it is held that it requires that: 'all reasonable efforts must be taken by the arbitrator to prevent delaying tactics, harassment of the parties or other participants, or any other disruption of the arbitration process'.[37]

4.24 Similarly, the notion of fairness in arbitration is interrelated to the desire to reach a just and an equitable procedural outcome,[38] even if such outcome does not conform to strict legal rules.[39] This interrelation is not deduced from a purely lexical stance,[40] but is also perceptible from a practical point of view. Thus, in extending the arbitration clause to a non-signatory, arbitral decisions to that effect are often based on the notion of good administration of justice, as encompassing the requirements of *fairness* and *equity*.[41]

4.25 Given that an escalation of costs or time arguably limits one's access to justice, it is generally acknowledged that fairness in the conduct of arbitral proceedings also requires procedural efficiency.[42] Also, without fairness the arbitral proceedings are hardly efficient.[43] The interrelation between fairness in the conduct of the arbitral proceedings and ensuring an efficient resolution of the dispute is evident under established arbitration laws and rules.[44] Accordingly, the requirement of fairness necessitates resolving the dispute without unwarranted delay or costs.[45]

34 Leboulanger (n 7) 89–92.

35 Richard L Garnett, *A Practical Guide to International Commercial Arbitration* (Oceana Publications 2000) 83; Japaridze (n 15) 1435 and 1437; Henry Gabriel and Anjanette H Raymond, 'Ethics for Commercial Arbitrators: Basic Principles and Emerging Standards' (2005) 5 Wyoming Law Review 453, 458.

36 Gabriel and Raymond (n 35) 458.

37 Garnett (n 35) 83; Gabriel and Raymond (n 35) 458.

38 Waincymer (n 19) 30.

39 Interim Award in ICC Case No 3879 of 1984, (1986) XI Ybk Commercial Arbitration 127; Hanotiau (2005) (n 8) 47–48.

40 As previously mentioned, *Black's Law Dictionary* defines the term 'fair' as: impartial; just; equitable; disinterested: *Black's Law Dictionary* (9th edn, West Publishing Co 2009) 674.

41 Hanotiau (n 8) 47–48; Bernard Hanotiau, 'Consent to Arbitration: Do We Share a Common Vision?' (2011) 27 Arbitration International 539, 554.

42 Fortese and Hemmi (n 20) 116.

43 William Park, 'The Procedural Soft Law of International Arbitration: Non-Governmental Instruments' in Loukas Mistelis and Julian DM Lew (eds), *Pervasive Problems in International Arbitration* (Kluwer Law International 2006) 144.

44 Article 14.4 of the LCIA Arbitration Rules of 2014; Article 17.1 of the UNCITRAL Arbitration Rules of 2013; sections 33(b) and 41(3)(a) of the English Arbitration Act.

45 Japaridze (n 15) 1425 and 1432.

B. Due Process

4.26 Another important aspect of international arbitration and an integral part of good administration of justice is that the arbitral proceedings must comply with the requirements of due process.[46]

4.27 Where parties refer a dispute to international arbitration, they waive their sacrosanct constitutional right to have their dispute resolved before a national court.[47] As this arguably limits one's access to justice, certain paramount procedural standards need to be met by arbitrators.[48]

4.28 It is widely recognized that arbitrators are under an obligation to make every effort to render an enforceable award.[49] For an award to be enforceable, it must comply with the requirements of due process.[50]

4.29 Most arbitration laws and institutional rules include provisions that pertain to the requirements of due process.[51] The notion can comprise different obligations under different national laws. Some laws endorse a broad understanding of due process so as to equate it to the notion of fairness and natural justice.[52] In this regard, one endorses the requirements of due process as those enshrined under international legal instruments. To that effect, Article 18 of the UNCITRAL Model law stipulates that parties shall be treated with equality and given an opportunity of presenting their case.[53] Article 17.1 of the UNCITRAL Arbitration Rules provides that 'the arbitral tribunal may conduct the arbitration in such manner as it considers appropriate, provided that the parties are treated with equality and that at an appropriate stage of the proceedings each party is given a reasonable opportunity of presenting its case'.[54] Finally, Article V(1)(b) of the New York Convention similarly emphasizes that due process encompasses the requirement that parties be given an opportunity to present their case.

4.30 In delineating the rationale of due process, Bernardo Cremades noted that it comprises two fundamental procedural aspects: 'access to justice and reasonableness of the

[46] Kurkela and Turunen (n 20); Article 1510 of the French Law on Civil Procedure as amended in 2011; Robert Pietrowski, 'Evidence in International Arbitration' (2006) 22 Arbitration International 373, 392 (providing that good administration of arbitral justice requires that any document presented by one of the parties be known to the other party(ies) and that the latter should be given an opportunity to discuss it).

[47] Kurkela and Turunen (n 20) 2.

[48] Julian DM Lew, Loukas A Mistelis, and Stefan M Kröll, *Comparative International Commercial Arbitration* (Kluwer Law International 2003) 5–34; Kurkela and Turunen (n 20) 2.

[49] Article 41 of the ICC Rules of Arbitration of 2012; Article 32.2 of the LCIA Arbitration Rules of 2014.

[50] Julian DM Lew, 'Iura Novit Curia and Due Process', Queen Mary University of London, Legal Studies Research Paper No 72/2010, 12; Article V(1)(b) of the New York Convention of 1958.

[51] William Park, 'The Procedural Soft Law of International Arbitration: Non-Governmental Instruments' in Loukas Mistelis and Julian DM Lew (eds), *Pervasive Problems in International Arbitration* (Kluwer Law International 2006) 145.

[52] Gabrielle Kaufmann-Kohler, 'Globalization of Arbitral Procedure' (2003) 36 Vanderbilt Journal of Transnational Law 1313.

[53] Article 18 of the UNCITRAL Model Law as amended in 2006.

[54] Article 17.1 of the UNCITRAL Arbitration Rules of 2013.

proceedings'.[55] Accordingly, due process in international arbitration mandates that arbitral proceedings are fairly conducted; that parties are treated equally; and that they are given a reasonable opportunity to be heard and present their case before an unbiased tribunal.[56]

4.31 Although parties often raise or invoke the due process defence to resist recognition or enforcement of an award, courts rarely find a violation of due process and generally adopt a restrictive approach.[57]

4.32 However, abuse of due process is a growing phenomenon. This denotes the current practice of parties, and their legal counsel, who threaten to invoke the defence of due process whenever their procedural requests are not complied with.[58] This enigma is further fortified by the fact that arbitrators regularly fail to limit such abusive conduct and tolerate requests whenever cloaked under due process, that is, due process paranoia.[59] Thus, whilst the requirements of due process are sacrosanct elements of the administration of justice, recent trends demonstrating its regular abuse do not imply good administration of justice. This is particularly the case given that requirements of due process often conflict with the obligation of procedural efficiency (another element of good administration of justice) as discussed later.

4.33 Arbitral tribunals as well as academics are yet to find a tool or principle to be utilized to balance due process and efficiency. As shall be discussed below, it is posited that the principle of abuse of rights not only advances the aforementioned interests that comprise good administration of justice, but may also operate as the balancing mechanism between due process and efficiency.

C. Efficiency

4.34 In the world of business, prevailing in a given dispute primarily entails advancing the commercial goals of the business, and this often means winning in a timely manner.[60]

[55] Bernardo M Cremades, 'The Use and Abuse of "Due Process" in International Arbitration', Alexander Lecture 2016, 6, <https://arbitrajeraci.files.wordpress.com/2018/07/the-use-and-abuse-of-e2809cdue-processe2809d-in-international-arbitration.pdf> accessed 20 February 2019.

[56] Fortese and Hemmi (n 20) 111–12; Park (n 51) 145; Bernard Hanotiau and Olivier Caprasse, 'Arbitrability, Due Process, and Public Policy Under Article V of the New York Convention' (2008) 25 Journal of International Arbitration 721, 727–28; Article V(1)(b) of the New York Convention of 1958; *Generica Limited v Pharmaceuticals Basics Inc*, United States Court of Appeals, Seventh Circuit, 96-4004, 29 September 1997, (1998) 23 Ybk Commercial Arbitration 1076, 1079.

[57] Hanotiau and Caprasse (n 56) 727–28.

[58] Cremades (n 55); Rémy Gerbay, 'Due Process Paranoia' (Kluwer Arbitration Blog, 6 June 2016) <http://kluwerarbitrationblog.com/2016/06/06/due-process-paranoia/> accessed 20 February 2019.

[59] Queen Mary University of London and PricewaterhouseCoopers LLP, '2015 International Arbitration Survey: Improvements and Innovations in International Arbitration (2015) 10; Gerbay (n 58).

[60] Michael McIlwrath and Roland Schroeder, 'The View from an International Arbitration Customer: In Dire Need of Early Resolution' (2008) 74 Arbitration 3, 3.

Cost and time efficiency are very important features of international arbitration.[61] This is often promoted by advocates and supporters of international arbitration.[62]

In addition, these features are indispensable elements for the good administration of arbitral justice.[63] As stated by one tribunal, procedural economy is required by the good administration of justice.[64] Additionally, as rightly noted by Gabrielle Kaufmann-Kohler: **4.35**

> We live in a time when many complain that justice, be it judicial or arbitral, is *too slow, too expensive*, and too cumbersome. *Furthering the efficiency of dispute settlement can obviously contribute to improving the administration of justice*.[65] (Emphasis added)

Chester Brown equally emphasized the importance of efficiency to ensure the good administration of justice: **4.36**

> One of these is the function of ensuring the proper administration of international justice. This is distinct from the function of settling disputes, in that *it emphasizes the need for effectiveness and efficiency in judicial decision-making*, and it is well established in the jurisprudence of international courts, as well as in the literature.[66] (Emphasis added)

Given its importance for the administration of justice, most arbitration laws and institutional rules provide for and attempt to achieve procedural efficiency.[67] Unwarranted delays not only disrupt the arbitral proceedings, but can have manifest financial **4.37**

[61] Born (n 1) 86; Richard Naimark and Stephanie Keer, 'International Private Commercial Arbitration – Expectations and Perceptions of Attorneys and Business People' in Christopher Drahozal and Richard Naimark (eds), *Towards a Science of International Arbitration: Collected Empirical Research* (Kluwer Law International 2005) 49; Francis Higgins, William Brown and Patrick Roach, 'Pitfalls in International Commercial Arbitration' (1980) 35 The Business Lawyer 1035, 1035; Benjamin G Davis, *Improving International Arbitration: The Need for Speed and Trust, Liber Amicorum Michel Gaudet* (ICC Publishing SA 1998); Curtis E von Kann, *The College of Commercial Arbitrators, Guide to Best Practice in Commercial Arbitration* (Juris Publishing Inc 2006) 3; Rudolf Fiebinger and Christoph Hauser, 'An Arbitrator's View: Can Party Autonomy Hinder Procedural Efficiency' in Nathalie Voser (ed), *10 Years of Swiss Rules of International Arbitration* (JurisNet 2014) 174; Nathan D O'Malley, *Rules of Evidence in International Arbitration: An Annotated Guide* (Informa 2012) 315; David W Rivkin, 'Towards a New Paradigm in International Arbitration: The Town Elder Model Revisited' (2008) 23 Arbitration International 375, 376–77; *Fradella v Petricca*, 183 F 3d 17, 19 (1st Cir 1999); *Folkways Music Publishers, Inc v Weiss*, 989 F 2d 108, 111 (2nd Cir 1993); *Stolt-Nielsen SA v Animalfeeds Int'l*, 130 S Ct 1758, 1775 (US S Ct 2010).

[62] Edna Sussman, 'Why Arbitrate: The Benefits and Savings' (2010) 7 Transnational Dispute Management 2; Thomas Stipanowich, 'Arbitration and Choice: Taking Charge of the "New Litigation"' (2009) 7 DePaul Business and Commercial Law Journal 383; Gary Born, *International Commercial Arbitration: Commentary and Materials* (2nd edn, Kluwer Law International 2001); UNCITRAL Secretariat on the Model Law of 1985 Explanatory Note (with amendments as adopted in 2006) 27; EA Schwartz, 'The Rights and Duties of ICC Arbitrators' in *The Status of The Arbitrator*, ICC Bulletin-Special Supplement (ICC Publishing 1995) 77; M Rasmussen, 'Overextending Immunity: Arbitral Institution Liability in the United States, England, and France' (2003) 26 Fordham International Law Journal 1824, 1834–36.

[63] Leboulanger (n 7) 54, 85, and 92.

[64] *Canfor Corporation v United States of America, Tembec et al v United Stated of America*, (UNCITRAL), Order of the Consolidation Tribunal of 7 September 2005, paras 76 and 183; Ridhi Kabra, 'Has Abaclat v Argentina Left the ICSID with a "Massive Problem?"' (2015) 31 Arbitration International 425, 450.

[65] Gabrielle Kaufmann-Kohler, 'When Arbitrators Facilitate Settlement: Towards a Transnational Standard' (2009) 25 Arbitration International 187, 188.

[66] Chester Brown, 'The Inherent Powers of International Courts and Tribunals' (2005) 76 British Yearbook of International Law 195, 231.

[67] Section 33.1 of the English Arbitration Act of 1996; ICC Rules of Arbitration of 2012 (Foreword); Article 14.4 of the LCIA Arbitration Rules of 2014; Article 17 of the UNCITRAL Arbitration Rules 2013.

implications to the prejudiced party.[68] In some cases, unreasonable delay may lead to financial losses that cannot necessarily be remedied by awarding interest or allocating costs.[69]

4.38 Waste of resources in arbitral proceedings is mostly disadvantageous to the parties (or at least one of them) and to the arbitral tribunal, but is not necessarily inconvenient to legal counsel.[70]

4.39 It is acknowledged that the benefits of arbitration may be thwarted, and administration of justice may be brought into disrepute, unless all those involved in the arbitration process actively cooperate to effectively resolve the disputes in question.[71] Although some arbitration laws and rules endeavour to limit such inefficiency,[72] it is generally acknowledged that such rules are inadequate.[73]

4.40 The arbitration process is failing to accommodate the level of efficiency required by its users.[74] In recent surveys and empirical studies, users have complained primarily because of costs, delays, and procedural misconduct during the arbitration process.[75] This is also the case in relation to investment arbitration proceedings which, according to a recent study, last for an average of 3.6 years.[76] One must add that these concerns are not new. While arbitration users have been expressing their concern for some time,[77] the

[68] Alan Redfern and others, *Law and Practice of International Commercial Arbitration* (4th edn, Sweet & Maxwell 2004) 244; McIlwrath and Schroeder (n 60) 4.

[69] Redfern and others (n 51) 244.

[70] Fiebinger and Hauser (n 61) 175. Costs of legal representation is often the main component of costs in arbitration: Klaus Sachs, 'Time and Money: Cost Control and Effective Case Management' in Julian Lew and Loukas Mistelis (eds), *Pervasive Problems in International Arbitration* (Kluwer Law International 2006) 110–13; ICC Commission Report, 'Decisions on Costs in International Arbitration' (2015) 2 ICC Dispute Resolution Bulletin 3.

[71] Redfern and others (n 51) paras 1–46.

[72] See for example, setting time-limits for rendering an award, as in Article 45 of the Egyptian Arbitration Law; Article 820 of the Italian Law of Civil Procedure; Article 25 of the Ecuadorian Arbitration Law; Article 30.1 of the ICC Arbitration Rules; section 33(1)(b) of the English Arbitration Act.

[73] Redfern and others (n 51) 244; the ICSID Arbitration Rules were amended in 2006 to enhance the efficiency of ICSID arbitration, and it is generally held that the rules did not necessarily succeed in achieving this: Antonio R Parra, 'The 2006 Amendments of the ICSID Arbitration Rules' (2006) German Arbitration Journal (SchiedsVZ) 247, 248; Lars Markert, 'Improving Efficiency in Investment Arbitration' (2011) 4 Contemporary Asia Arbitration Journal 215, 223.

[74] Irene Welser and Susanna Wurzer, 'Formality in International Commercial Arbitration – For Better or for Worse?' in Gerold Zeiler and others (eds), *Austrian Arbitration Yearbook 2008* (Manz'sche Verlags- und Universitätsbuchhandlung 2008); Irene Welser and Christian Klausegger, 'Fast Track Arbitration: Just Fast or Something Different?' in Gerold Zeiler and others (eds), *Austrian Arbitration Yearbook 2009* (Manz'sche Verlags- und Universitätsbuchhandlung 2009) 260; Piero Bernardini, 'International Arbitration: How to Make it More Effective' in Laurent Levy and Yves Derains (eds), *Liber Amicorum En l'Honnour de Serge Lazareff* (ICC Publication 2011); Klaus Peter Berger, 'The Need for Speed in International Arbitration' (2008) 25 Journal of International Arbitration 595, 595; Waincymer (n 19) 45; William K Slate II, 'Cost and Time Effectiveness of Arbitration' (2010) 3 Contemporary Asia Arbitration Journal 185, 186; Jorg Risse, 'Procedural Risk Analysis: An ADR-Tool in Arbitration Proceedings' (2009) Austrian Arbitration Yearbook 461, 461.

[75] Queen Mary University of London and PricewaterhouseCoopers LLP (n 59) 7.

[76] Anthony Sinclair, 'ICSID Arbitration: How Long Does it Take?', (2009) 4 Global Arbitration Review 18, 20; Markert (n 73) 217.

[77] This is demonstrated by the similar results of the surveys conducted in 2006 and in 2015: Queen Mary University of London and PricewaterhouseCoopers LLP, 'International Arbitration: Corporate Attitudes and Practices' (2006) 6; Queen Mary University of London and PricewaterhouseCoopers LLP (n 59) 7.

arbitration community have failed to introduce innovative tools to adequately remedy such problems.[78]

The continuation of this trend, which may further increase due to the complexity of business transactions and the lack of defined rules/principles to limit it, may disincentive users from referring disputes to international arbitration, place distrust in the arbitral system,[79] and question the legitimacy of the arbitration system as a whole.[80] **4.41**

Procedural efficiency, and precluding procedural misconduct and abuse, is directly linked to parties' expectations.[81] Parties are presumed to have agreed to arbitrate in good faith and to avoid tactical manoeuvres that may impede procedural efficiency.[82] **4.42**

III. It Ensures the Administration of Arbitral Justice

It is submitted that the application of abuse of rights is vital to ensure the good administration of arbitral justice.[83] As rightly noted by Peter Barnett, the principle advocates that the exercise of rights should be precluded when necessary 'in the face of unfairness to another party, or to avoid the risk that the administration of justice might be brought into disrepute'.[84] **4.43**

Arbitrators' right/obligation to prevent any abuse of rights emanates from their inherent duty to ensure the good administration of arbitral justice.[85] In this regard, Chester Brown rightly noted: '[a]nother aspect of the administration of international justice is the prevention of any "abuse of process" in international adjudication'.[86] **4.44**

[78] While arbitration institutions introduced rules in an attempt to tackle the cost and delay issues, it seems that they arguably failed to overcome the problem. For example, while fast-track arbitration has been introduced in many arbitration rules to remedy the time and cost issues, it is submitted that the 'vast majority' of users have not taken advantage of such tool. Queen Mary University of London and PricewaterhouseCoopers LLP, '2012 International Arbitration Survey: Current and Preferred Practices in the Arbitral Process', 10–15. Also, fast-track arbitration primarily relies on the will of all those involved to cooperate to speed up the arbitral process. Redfern and others (n 51) 286.

[79] Queen Mary University of London and PricewaterhouseCoopers LLP, 1 (2013) 5; Linda Silberman, 'Report: International Arbitration: Comments from a Critic' (2002) 13 American Review of International Arbitration 9, 9; Fiebinger and Hauser (n 61) 175; Michael Karrer, 'Arbitration Saves! Costs: Poker and Hide and Seek' (1986) 3 Journal of International Arbitration 35; *Blue Tee Corp v Koehring Company and United Dominion Industries, Inc*, 999 F 2d 633, 634 (2nd Cir 1993).

[80] Markert (n 73) 217.

[81] Waincymer (n 19) 35.

[82] ibid.

[83] Brown (n 66) 231; Martins Paparinskis, 'Inherent Powers of ICSID Tribunals: Broad and Rightly So' in Ian Laird and Todd Weiler (eds), *Investment Treaty Arbitration and International Law* (Juris 2011) 16 <https://ssrn.com/abstract=1876705> accessed 20 February 2019; Chester Brown, 'The Relevance of the Doctrine of Abuse of Process in International Adjudication' (2010) 7 Transnational Dispute Management 1, 6–12.

[84] Peter Barnett, *Res Judicata, Estoppel, and Foreign Judgments* (Oxford University Press 2001) para 6.05.

[85] Herch Lauterpacht, *The Development of International Law by the International Court* (Cambridge University Press 1982) 165; Paparinskis (n 83) 16; Andrew Newcombe, 'Investor Misconduct: Jurisdiction, Admissibility or Merits?' in Chester Brown and Kate Miles (eds), *Evolution in Investment Treaty Law and Arbitration* (Cambridge University Press 2011) 194; Chester Brown, *A Common Law of International Adjudication* (Oxford University Press 2007) 245–50; Brown (n 83) 6–12.

[86] Brown (n 66) 231.

4.45 This was confirmed by the House of Lords, now the Supreme Court, in England in the context of subsequent proceedings, where Lord Diplock provided that:

> [T]his is a case about *abuse of the process* of the High Court. It concerns the *inherent power* which any court of justice must possess to prevent misuse of its procedure in a way which, although not inconsistent with the literal application of its procedural rules, would nevertheless be *manifestly unfair* to a party to litigation before it, or would otherwise bring the *administration of justice into disrepute* among right-thinking people.[87] (Emphasis added)

4.46 Similarly, Canadian and Australian courts regularly provide that the principle of abuse of rights operates to prevent unfairness and to ensure the overall administration of justice.[88]

4.47 This function of abuse of rights is also upheld by scholars. Thus, it is often acknowledged that the application of abuse of rights by arbitral tribunals emanates from their duty to ensure the good and fair administration of justice and to preserve the integrity of the arbitral system.[89] Gaillard rightly noted that abuse of rights can 'cause significant prejudice to the party against whom it is aimed and can undermine the fair and orderly resolution of disputes by international arbitration'.[90]

4.48 The International Law Association ('ILA') adopted a report which equally emphasized the role of abuse of rights to ensure the good administration of justice. It noted that the principle should apply:

> [I]f it is necessary for a court to prevent a misuse of its procedure in the face of *unfairness* to another party, *or to avoid the risk that the administration of justice might be brought into disrepute*.[91] (Emphasis added)

4.49 Accordingly, it is submitted that the principle of abuse of rights greatly ensures the good administration of arbitral justice as it operates to enhance the efficiency of the proceedings, safeguards the fairness of the proceedings and the equality between the parties, preserves the integrity of the process, and upholds parties' reasonable expectations.[92]

4.50 It seems in order to examine how the principle assists arbitral tribunals in furthering and advancing those paramount elements of the good administration of justice in the context of international arbitration.

87 *Hunter v Chief Constable of the West Midlands* [1982] AC 529, 536.

88 *Toronto City v CUPE* [2003] 3 SCR 77; *R v Scott*, [1990] 3 SCR 979, 1007; *Rogers v The Queen* [1994] HCA 42; John P Gaffney, '"Abuse of Process" in Investment Treaty Arbitration' (2010) 11 Journal of World Investment and Trade 515–16.

89 Topcan (n 7) 628–29 and 633.

90 Emmanuel Gaillard, 'Abuse of Process in International Arbitration' (2017) 32 ICSID Review 17, 18.

91 'Interim Report on "Res Judicata" and Arbitration' (International Law Association, Berlin 2004) 8.

92 Yasuhei Taniguchi, 'Good Faith and Abuse of Procedural Rights in Japanese Civil Procedure' (2000) 8 Tulane Journal of International and Comparative Law 167 (providing that Japanese law relies on abuse of rights, in the context of substantive and procedural rights, whenever the rigid application of law would contravene the sense of fairness and justice).

However, prior to embarking on this analysis, one shall first shed light on the rising phenomenon of abuse of rights in arbitration. This succinct overview is potent given the recent criticism directed at such growing trends of abuse in arbitration and due to the effect of such abuse on the administration of justice. **4.51**

Moreover, as the different intrinsic elements of the good administration of arbitral justice often compete (fairness, due process, and efficiency), and tribunals frequently sacrifice one element to preserve another, it is important to articulate how the principle may be effective to deal with such tensions. **4.52**

A. The Rising Phenomenon of Abuse of Rights Obstructs the Good Administration of Arbitral Justice

While international arbitration offers the prominent scheme for resolution of transnational commercial and investment disputes, the arbitration community must constantly strive to examine areas of concern. Failing to tackle what may affect the good administration of justice may push users away from international arbitration.[93] **4.53**

Abuse of arbitration related rights is a primary concern shared by arbitration users as it generally frustrates the *raison d'être* of international arbitration: a mechanism that ought to be fair and efficient.[94] As such, abuse of the arbitral process that takes place during the different stages of arbitral proceedings must not be tolerated if the arbitral system is ought to prosper. **4.54**

To that effect, Jan Paulsson rightly observes that: **4.55**

> [A]s a matter of social policy, the monopoly of international arbitration is not necessarily, as I just said, a cause for celebration. It is a phenomenon to be evaluated continuously and critically. Moreover, as a matter of professional pride and self-preservation on the part of those who work in the field of international arbitration, the monopoly status should be a cause for constant concern. *If we do not deliver decent justice, if we do not close the door to abuse, we should understand that sharp reactions are likely – sharp reactions which may harm a very valuable tool.*[95] (Emphasis added)

[93] It is worth mentioning that a study of dispute resolution practices in Fortune 1,000 corporations convey that many large corporations are relying more on mediation and other mechanisms aimed at resolving disputes *informally*, *quickly*, and *inexpensively*: Thomas J Stipanowich and Ryan Lamare, 'Living with ADR: Evolving Perceptions and Use of Mediation, Arbitration, and Conflict Management in Fortune 1000 Corporations' (2014) 19 Harvard Negotiation Law Review 1, 43–44; Siegfried H Elsing, 'Procedural Efficiency in International Arbitration: Choosing the Best of Both Legal Worlds' (2011) German Arbitration Journal (SchiedsVZ) 114, 115; McIlwrath and Schroeder (n 60) 10, ('frustration with the length and expense of the arbitration process is increasingly cited as the rationale for favouring court resolution (or at least for no longer favouring arbitration'); Bernhard F Meyer, 'The Swiss Rules of International Arbitration – Five Years of Experience' in R Füeg (ed) *The Swiss Rules of International Arbitration – Five Years of Experience* (Swiss Chambers' Court of Arbitration and Mediation 2009) 17.

[94] William W Park, *Arbitration of International Business Disputes: Studies in Law and Practice* (2nd edn, Oxford University Press 2012); Gaillard (n 90) 17.

[95] Jan Paulsson,'International Arbitration is Not Arbitration' (2008) 2 Stockholm International Arbitration Review 1, 3.

4.56 Others have gone further and provided that abuse of rights in arbitration not only negatively impacts fairness and justice, but may bring the whole arbitral process to naught:

> The procedural rules of an arbitration will fundamentally influence a perception of both fairness and justice; and a procedure which offends the principles of a fair hearing will not create any confidence that a just result will ensue. *If the system does not afford recourse against procedural abuse such as a breach of natural justice or the perpetration of a fraud it will, in my view, self-destruct.*[96] (Emphasis added)

4.57 Remarking on the rising perplexity of abuse, Gaillard noted:

> Over the past decades, parties to arbitrations and their lawyers have developed *an unprecedented array of procedural tactics designed to undermine and prejudice their opponents and to increase the chances that their claims prevail.* The past five years in particular have witnessed the emergence of litigation strategies of the very worst kind, *which threaten to undermine the reputation of international arbitration as an effective and reliable means of resolving international disputes.*[97] (Emphasis added)

4.58 On a related note, the omnipresence of abusive conduct that arises during arbitral proceedings becomes evident if one examines the growing enigma of procedural inefficiency in arbitration and that such inefficiency may stem from abuse of rights.[98] In any procedural issue that may arise which could hinder the efficiency of the proceedings, a distinction must be drawn between delays and increased costs that emanate as a result of the intricacy of the factual and/or legal aspects of the case,[99] and cases where this is a consequence of procedural misconduct and possible abuse of the arbitration process (unwarranted costs and delays).[100]

4.59 Many arbitration proceedings involve an escalation of costs and unwarranted delays as a result of tactics and procedural misconduct.[101] Whilst parties may submit extensive

[96] Patrick M Lane, 'Dilatory Tactics: Arbitral Discretion' in Albert Jan van den Berg (ed), *Improving the Efficiency of Arbitration Agreements and Awards: 40 Years of Application of the New York Convention* (Kluwer Law International 1999) 425.

[97] Gaillard (n 90) 17.

[98] Sachs (n 70) 113; James Rhodes and Lisa Sloan, 'The Pitfalls of International Commercial Arbitration' (1984) 17 Vanderbilt Journal of Transnational Law 19, 36.

[99] Born (n 1) 87; Michael Kerr, 'International Arbitration v. Litigation', (1980) Journal of Business Law 164; Sachs (n 70) 111–12 Welser and Klausegger (n 74) 259; Sachs (n 70) 114; ICC Commission on Arbitration, 'Techniques for Controlling Time and Costs in Arbitration', ICC Publication No 843 (2007) 15 <http://gjpi.org/wp-content/uploads/icc-controlling-time-and-cost.pdf> accessed 2 February 2019.

[100] L Yves Fortier, 'The Minimum Requirements of Due Process in Taking Measures Against Dilatory Tactics: Arbitral Discretion in International Commercial Arbitration – "A few Plain Rules and a Few Strong Instincts"' in Albert Jan van den Berg (ed), *Improving the Efficiency of Arbitration Agreements and Awards: 40 Years of Application of the New York Convention* (Kluwer Law International 1999) 406; Waincymer (n 19) 45–47.

[101] It is interesting to note that the Chairman of the ICC Court of Arbitration in 2005 provided that the problem of costs and delays in arbitration is primarily caused by the parties' counsels. Sachs (n 70) 113; Higgins, Brown and Roach (n 61) 1042; Rhodes and Sloan (n 98) 36; Michael Hwang, 'Why is There Still Resistance to Arbitration in Asia?' in Gerald Aksen and others (eds), *Global Reflections of International Law, Commerce and Dispute Resolution – Liber Amicorum in Honour of Robert Briner* (ICC 2005) 401–11; Irene Welser, 'Efficiency – Today's Challenge in Arbitration Proceedings' in Christian Klausegger and others (eds), *Austrian Yearbook on International Arbitration 2014* (Manz'sche Verlags- und Universitätsbuchhandlung 2014) 153; Bernard Hanotiau, 'International Arbitration in a Global Economy: The Challenges of the Future' (2011) 28 Journal of International Arbitration 89, 100.

submissions and material for legitimate purposes, such as to substantiate their claims, in other instances parties make excessive submissions and request time extensions 'in a strategic effort to delay the proceedings, and may produce additional information that is nothing more than a "smoke bomb" and is unnecessary for a decision of the case'.[102]

This kind of behaviour is often referred to as a guerrilla tactic, which denotes the abuse of the law or a procedural rule by invoking it for a purpose other than that for which it was prescribed for.[103] **4.60**

Often, parties who have no strong legal argument to prevail in a given case deviate from the conventional way of presenting their claims and any supporting evidence, and resort to such guerrilla tactics to 'gradually, deceitfully and viciously wear down the other party, opposing counsel or the arbitral tribunal'.[104] **4.61**

It is this kind of delay and escalation of costs, as a result of abusive conduct, that is unwarranted and, if left unremedied, may undermine the arbitration mechanism and defeats its 'conventional mode of operation'.[105] **4.62**

The significance of this rising enigma is further fortified by the fact that such abuse is frequently resorted to.[106] Although such abuse can be employed by the claimant, it is often the respondent to a claim who is 'prepared to employ whatever tactics may be available to him to reduce or avoid his prospective liability'.[107] **4.63**

It is said that almost 70 per cent of arbitration practitioners have witnessed such abusive conduct, which undoubtedly leads to waste of resources.[108] It has been rightly provided that international arbitration is becoming plagued by procedural abuse and that parties and their counsels have developed 'strategies of the very worst kind'.[109] **4.64**

102 Welser and Klausegger (n 74) 260.

103 Günther J Horvath and others, 'Categories of Guerrilla Tactics' in Stephan Wilske and Günther J Horvath (eds), *Guerrilla Tactics in International Arbitration* (Kluwer Law International 2013) 5; Stephan Wilske, °Internationalisation of Law' in Arbitration: A Way to Escape Procedural Restrictions of National Law?' in Nedim Peter Vogt (ed), *Reflections on the International Practice of Law: Liber Amicorum for the 35th Anniversary of Bär & Karrer* (Helbing & Lichtenbahn 2004) 259–63; Stephan Wilske, 'Crisis? What Crisis? The Development of International Arbitration in Tougher Times' (2009) 2 Contemporary Asia Arbitration Journal 187, 204.

104 Robert Pfeiffer and Stephan Wilske, 'An Etymological and Historical Overview' in Stephan Wilske and Günther J Horvath (eds), *Guerrilla Tactics in International Arbitration* (Kluwer Law International 2013) 3; Lane (n 96) 424.

105 Pfeiffer and Wilske (n 104) 3; O'Malley (n 61) 315.

106 Edward R Leahy and Kenneth J Pierce, 'Sanctions to Control Party Misbehavior in International Arbitration' (1986) 26 Virginia Journal of International Law 291, 299; Stephan Wilske, 'Cost Sanctions in the Event of Unreasonable Exercise or Abuse of Procedural Rights – A Way to Control Costs in International Arbitration' (2006) SchiedsVZ, 188–91; the ICSID caseload statistics reveals that 1 per cent of proceedings are abusively initiated as they involve claims without legal merit: ICSID caseload statistics (Issue 2016-1), 14; Wilske (2009) (n 103) 204; Nadia Darwazeh and Baptiste Rigaudeau, 'Clues to Construing the New French Arbitration Law' (2011) 28 Journal of International Arbitration 381.

107 Cedric Harris, 'Abuse of the Arbitration Process-Delaying Tactics and Disruptions: A Respondent's Guide' (1992) 9 Journal of International Arbitration 87, 87.

108 Edna Sussman, 'All's Fair in Love and War – Or is it? The Call for Ethical Standards for Counsel in International Arbitration' (2010) 7 Transnational Dispute Management 1, 2.

109 Gaillard (n 90) 17.

4.65 Accordingly, it is advocated that arbitration users' 'discontent aims principally at the abuse of otherwise legitimate procedures'.[110] Without a defined principle tailored to deal with procedural misconduct, abusive tactics may increase and be perceived as standard in arbitral practice.[111]

4.66 Abusive conduct not only affects the procedural efficiency of arbitral proceedings, but may also adversely impact the fairness of the procedure and the quality of the ensuing justice.[112]

4.67 In this regard, the lack of a procedural principle that can limit the abuse of the arbitral process[113] not only fails to incentivize efficiency but also violates the parties' expectations in resolving their disputes effectively and fairly.[114] Finding a principle to preclude and sanction the abuse of arbitration-related rights 'would be serving not only the well-assessed interests and expectations of the parties, but also the integrity of arbitration itself'.[115]

4.68 It is in this context that one considers that the principle of abuse of rights may operate to limit abusive conduct that impedes the integrity and fairness of the arbitration process. The principle of abuse of rights can foster the notion of fairness of the proceedings, eliminate the waste of resources precisely in relation to unwarranted escalation of costs and inordinate delay, and limit procedural misconduct that intends to frustrate the process.

4.69 To that effect, Gaillard acknowledged the dire need for the arbitration community to develop tools/principles that are specifically designed to tackle the abuse of the arbitral process. In considering different tools, he provided that: 'an abuse of rights principle is the most promising tool to tackle the growing instances of procedural misconduct in arbitration'.[116]

4.70 Advocating the application of abuse of rights in arbitration to stabilize the arbitral system is further strengthened by observing that much of the tactics and conduct that renders arbitral proceedings inefficient or unfair largely resembles and correlates to the principle of abuse of rights. These tactics generally comprise procedural rights that appear a fortiori legal and legitimate: 'manoeuvres that may on the surface appear legal',[117] however the party exercises them maliciously, unreasonably, or defeats their purpose.[118]

[110] Park (n 94).

[111] Some scholars have circulated guidelines as to how respondents may abuse the arbitral process: Harris (n 107) 87; Rhodes and Sloan (n 98) 36.

[112] Alexander Price and Stephan Wilske, 'Costs and Efficiency in International Arbitration: The Arbitrators' Toolbox for Achieving the "Ideal"' (2007) 32 DAJV Newsletter 184, 184; Wilske (n 106) 188–91.

[113] Queen Mary University of London and PricewaterhouseCoopers LLP (n 59) 7.

[114] Leahy and Pierce (n 106) 293; Darwazeh and Rigaudeau (n 106) 383.

[115] Wilske (2009) (n 103) 208; Martin Raible and Stephan Wilske, 'The Arbitrator as Guardian of International Public Policy: Should Arbitrators go Beyond Solving Legal Issues' in Catherine A Rogers and Roger P Alford (eds), *The Future of Investment Arbitration* (Oxford University Press 2009) 269.

[116] Margaret Ryan, 'Gaillard on Tackling Abuse of Process', (2015) Global Arbitration Review <https://globalarbitrationreview.com/article/1034630/gaillard-on-tackling-abuse-of-process> accessed 20 February 2019.

[117] Horvath and others (n 103) 4.

[118] ibid 4–5.

B. Abuse of Rights Balances the Competing Interests of the Administration of Justice: Due Process and Fairness versus Efficiency

By its very nature, a strict obedience to the requirements of due process and procedural fairness can be at the expense of procedural efficiency.[119] To that end, it appears that much of the lack of efficiency perceived in arbitral proceedings is partly rooted in the due process paranoia.[120] This clash has been described as the 'the never ending battle between efficiency and due process'.[121] Thus, a question that arises in this context is: what are the limits of due process in arbitration? **4.71**

Parties who opt to abuse the procedural rules in order to derail the arbitral proceedings typically rely on due process provisions as an abusive tactic. For example, they will exploit rules providing that they must be treated fairly and afforded an opportunity to present their case to not comply with procedural orders, request extensions, and make unmeritorious applications.[122] **4.72**

This paradoxical issue may be intensified given that obstinate delays may not only comprise a breach of the arbitrators' duty to speed the process,[123] but may also comprise a claim of denial of justice.[124] **4.73**

Section 33.1 of the English Arbitration Act deals with both issues. Part (a) provides that a tribunal shall act fairly and give each party a reasonable opportunity to present his case; and subsequently, part (b) provides that the tribunal shall adopt procedures that avoid unnecessary delay or expense, so as to provide a fair means of dispute resolution.[125] **4.74**

Thus, arbitral tribunals faced with this issue seem to be caught between *Scylla and Charybdis*, that is, on the horns of a dilemma. While it seems flagrant that obstinate delays and similar abusive tactics retract from the system's efficiency and its fairness, and may constitute a potential denial of justice, an attempt to control such tactics may be a breach of due process. One may go further and argue that a situation may involve **4.75**

[119] Kurkela and Turunen (n 20) 192; Fortese and Hemmi (n 20) 111; Price and Wilske (n 112) 184; Waincymer (n 19) 45–47.

[120] Queen Mary University of London and PricewaterhouseCoopers LLP (n 59) 10.

[121] Fortier (n 100) 397; EDD Tavender, 'Considerations of Fairness in the Context of International Commercial Arbitrations' (1996) 34 Alberta Law Review 509, 512 ('There is indeed a tension or "never-ending battle" between the interests of justice or fairness on the one hand and finality and efficiency on the other.').

[122] Hwang (n 101) 401–11 (providing examples of how parties may abuse their procedural rights to derail the arbitration proceedings); Wilske (2009) (n 103) 203–04.

[123] Philip Fouchard, 'Relationship Between the Arbitrator and the Parties and the Arbitral Institution', in *The Status of the Arbitrator*, ICC Bulletin-Special Supplement (ICC 1995) 12; Fortier (n 100) 403.

[124] AV Freeman, *The International Responsibility of States for Denial of Justice* (Longman 1938) 242–63; Jan Paulsson, *Denial of Justice in International Law* (Cambridge University Press 2005) 177; Andrew Newcombe and L Paradell, *Law and Practice of Investment Treaties: Standards of Treatment* (Kluwer Law International 2009), 239; Redfern and others (n 51) 244; McIlwrath and Schroeder (n 60) 6–7 (providing that in many instances arbitration users decide to settle their disputes because of their frustration with the inefficiency of the arbitration process); *Antoine Fabiani (no 1), France v Venezuela*, 31 July 1905, Reports of International Arbitral Awards, vol X, 117 <http://legal.un.org/riaa/cases/vol_X/83-139.pdf> accessed 15 February 2019.

[125] Section 33.1 of the English Arbitration Act of 1996; Articles 14.4.i and 14.4.ii of the LCIA Arbitration Rules of 2014; Article 17 of the UNCITRAL Arbitration Rules of 2013.

two conflicting due process assertions: unreasonable delay and consequently escalation of costs may equally affect one's access to arbitration, especially financially weaker parties, and thus violate fairness and due process.[126] To that effect, William Park rightly provides that: 'Arbitral case management implicates the delicate counterpoise between efficiency and fairness. One of the arbitrator's most difficult tasks is to strike the right equilibrium'.[127]

4.76 In discussing the tension between due process and efficiency in international arbitration, it has been stated that in 'managing cases, due process needs to be balanced against the arbitrator's duty to ensure the efficient and timely completion of their mandate to resolve the dispute'.[128] Although this accentuates the problem, it does not enunciate which procedural tool may strike that balance. It is often provided that one way of solving this conflict is for arbitral tribunals to use the arbitral discretion bestowed upon them by arbitration laws and rules.[129] Some advocate that 'one reaction to arbitration's protean nature has been an emphasis on broad grants of procedural discretion to the arbitrators'.[130] Again, while it is true that such discretionary power is indispensable, and may constitute the legal basis upon which arbitrators can apply a given rule/principle, it does not provide arbitrators with a principle or rule to use to balance such conflict.

4.77 Without a legal principle that can form the foundation of the tribunal's decision on such issues, arbitrators may still fear their award being set aside. Arbitration users have actually raised this emerging concern. In a recent survey, it has been provided that arbitral tribunals are reluctant to act decisively to maintain the effectiveness of the proceedings, for fear of the award being challenged on grounds of due process.[131]

4.78 Thus, there appears to be a dire need to accommodate those ostensibly bewildering antinomies.[132] This urge stems from the fact that choosing one principle over the other will necessarily be contrary to the parties' expectations and contravenes the needs of commerce.[133] A flexible tool/principle is thus required to strike the right equilibrium and assist tribunals in balancing the competing interests of procedural efficiency and the requirements of due process, in a way that can satisfy both.[134]

4.79 It is in this context that one ventures that this due process paranoia can be remedied by applying the principle of abuse of rights in arbitration. Abuse of rights, with its

[126] Fortese and Hemmi (n 20) 116.

[127] William W Park, *Arbitration of International Business Disputes: Studies in Law and Practice* (Oxford University Press 2006) 48; Alan Redfern and Martin Hunter, *Law and Practice of International Commercial Arbitration* (2nd edn, Sweet & Maxwell 1991) 350.

[128] Fortese and Hemmi (n 20) 116.

[129] ibid 121; Fortier (n 100) 405; Article 19 of the Model Law; Article 17.1 of the UNCITRAL Arbitration Rules; Article 22.2 of the ICC Rules; Article 19.1 of the SCC Rules.

[130] Park (n 127) 459; Price and Wilske (n 112) 187; Fortier (n 100) 396.

[131] Queen Mary University of London and PricewaterhouseCoopers LLP (n 59) 10.

[132] Karl Pornbacher and Alexander Dolgorukow, 'Reconciling Due Process and Efficiency in International Arbitration – The Arbitrator's Task of Achieving The One Without Sacrificing the Other' (2013) Belgrade Law Review 50, 51.

[133] McIlwrath and Schroeder (n 60) 4.

[134] Fortier (n 100) 397.

balancing factor as a criterion of abuse, may strike the balance needed between procedural efficiency, fairness, and due process. It may become the very principle to solve the required balancing process; to limit and trim the horns of due process when inefficiency emanates from abusive conduct.

The conflict between efficiency and due process is reflected in the case of *Caribbean Niquel v Overseas Mining*.[135] It involved a dispute regarding a joint venture to operate a mine. When a dispute arose, one of the parties initiated arbitration proceedings and requested damages on the basis of 'lost profits'. The arbitral Tribunal awarded damages based on the theory of 'lost chance'. The award was then set aside as it violated the parties' right to be heard as it did not give the parties an opportunity to discuss the legal basis for the calculation of damages. The conflict here appears to be that if the Tribunal had granted the parties time to discuss the legal basis of the calculation of damages, this would have necessarily delayed the proceedings, increased the costs, and thus affected the efficiency of the proceedings. **4.80**

In this regard, where abuse of rights is embraced by arbitral tribunals, it shall serve as the decisive factor and aid tribunals in reaching a subtle equilibrium: the right to be heard and present one's case is to be safeguarded as long as it is not abused. In addition, inefficiency should be limited where it emanates from procedural misconduct and tactics, but tolerated when it is vital for the resolution of the dispute. If this is achieved, it is possible to have a relatively efficient management of the arbitral proceedings without risking violating requirements of due process and/or fairness.[136] This would serve the overall requirement of the good administration of arbitral justice. **4.81**

While one shall examine the role of abuse of rights in the good administration of justice as a stand-alone general principle to tackle forms of abuse, it is submitted that the principle may also crystallize its potent manifestations in various specific rules to tackle abuse and to balance the competing interests of the administration of justice as well. **4.82**

An example of this is reflected in the enigma of 'sleeping dog' arbitrations.[137] 'Sleeping dog' arbitrations denote proceedings that have been initiated then halted due to a lack of activity from either the claimant, respondent, or the arbitrator(s).[138] The English Arbitration Act gives the arbitrators the right to terminate the proceedings where there **4.83**

[135] Paris Court of Appeals, *La Societe Commercial Caribbean Niquel v La Societe Overseas Mining Investments Ltd*, 25 March 2010, (1st Chamber), Appeal No 08/23901, confirmed in *La Société Overseas Mining Investments Limited v La Société Commercial Caribbean Niquel*, French *Cour de Cassation*, Civ 1re, 29 June 2011, Arrêt no 785 (10-23.321), cited in Fortese and Hemmi (n 20) 123–24.

[136] It is often held that the clash between inefficiency and due process can only be solved by choosing one over the other: Price and Wilske (n 112) 188; Kann (n 61) (advocating that efficiency is one of the key criteria in the resolution of disputes); Park (n 127), (providing that the prevalence of either principle depends on the stage of the arbitral proceedings).

[137] Thomas Bingham, 'The Problem of Delay in Arbitration' in Julian DM Lew and Loukas A Mistelis (eds), *Arbitration Insights: Twenty Years of the Annual Lecture of the School of International Arbitration, Sponsored by Freshfields Bruckhaus Deringer* (Kluwer Law International 2007) 73.

[138] Gordon Smith, 'Dismissal of Arbitration Proceedings For Want of Prosecution' (2009) 5 Asian International Arbitration Journal 190; *Bremer Vulkan Schiffbau und Maschinenfabrik v South India Shipping Corp* [1981] AC 909, 988.

has been an inordinate and inexcusable delay that may indicate that there can be no fair resolution of the dispute.[139] It is acknowledged that the power of arbitrators to take such measure is a statutory power as it emanates from an explicit provision. However, the principle of abuse of rights arguably forms the legal basis for such a provision and can be further utilized to overcome similar enigmas of procedural abuse in arbitration. To that effect, it is widely acknowledged, at least in the civil legal systems, that this type of procedural misconduct denotes, and falls under the ambit of, the principle of abuse of rights in the specific form of *venire contra factum proprium*.[140]

4.84 As shall be discussed below, in resorting to abuse of rights, tribunals are equipped with a tool that can assist them in discerning the conduct of the parties, and their legal counsels, and take into consideration the motives and purpose of any request that may affect the fairness of the proceedings or hinder the efficient conduct of proceedings. Upon a prudent balance of the competing interests, and based on the factual matrix of the case, arbitrators may determine whether such a procedural request is reasonable (conforming to the requirements of procedural due process) or abusive (mere dilatory tactic).

C. The Application of Abuse of Rights Ensures the Good Administration of Arbitral Justice

4.85 This section endeavours to highlight how the application of abuse of rights in international arbitration serves the administration of justice.

4.86 In doing so, the application of the principle to limit abuse that may take place in relation to three different legal issues that are common in international arbitration is examined: corporate/State manoeuvres to access/block arbitral proceedings, parallel arbitral proceedings; and the extension of the arbitration clause to a non-signatory.

4.87 While the application of abuse of rights advances the administration of arbitral justice in relation to different legal questions as well, for obvious spatial-temporal considerations, one shall examine its effect in relation to these three legal subjects given that they properly illustrate the importance of the principle for the good administration of justice.

4.88 An analysis of the aforementioned legal issues shall be achieved by examining the law and practice of commercial and investment arbitration. Emphasis may be given to investment arbitration materials in relation to some issues (corporate and State manoeuvres and parallel arbitral proceedings) and to commercial arbitration materials

[139] Section 41.3 of the English Arbitration Act 1996.

[140] Reinhard Zimmermann and Dirk A Verse, 'Case 22: Sitting on One's Rights - Germany' in Reinhard Zimmermann and Simon Whittaker, *Good Faith in European Contract Law* (Cambridge University Press 2000) 515–16; Matthias E Storme 'Case 22: Sitting on One's Rights - Belgium', in Zimmermann and Whittaker (n 140) 520–21.

in others (non-signatories). In doing this, one is mandated and restricted by the existence and availability of relevant published materials. However, it is submitted that the principle's operation ensures the administration of arbitral justice in international commercial and investment arbitration.

1. Corporate and State manoeuvres to access or block international arbitration proceedings

As previously mentioned, the inherent duty to preserve the integrity of the arbitral process emanates from the tribunal's responsibility to ensure the good administration of arbitral justice.[141] Arbitral tribunals often apply abuse of rights in order to preserve the arbitral integrity and thus ensure the good administration of justice.[142] **4.89**

One area where the requirements of fairness and the duty to preserve the integrity of the arbitral system have urged arbitrators to apply the principle of abuse of rights pertains to the act of structuring investments and corporate nationality planning for a purpose other than that for which such rights were conferred.[143] **4.90**

The rationale in sanctioning any abuse in such cases emanates from the desire to give 'effect to the object and purpose of the ICSID Convention and [. . .] preserving its integrity'.[144] It is widely acknowledged that the purpose of the ICSID Convention is not to afford protection to nationals against their own State; a contrario, the ICSID system is specifically tailored to resolve disputes between *foreign* investors and States, in order to foster the flow of international capital into the Contracting States.[145] **4.91**

Thus, a regular form of abuse may comprise the act of abusing the structure of a company by altering one of its features enabling it to qualify as an investor or an investment covered by the relevant BIT, not for a commercial activity/purpose but primarily to gain access to arbitration. **4.92**

If abusive conduct in this regard is not restricted, this may defy the good administration of arbitral justice as it may violate the parties' reasonable expectations, undermine the integrity of the arbitral system, and demonstrate that there is no limit to ICSID **4.93**

141 Paparinskis (n 83) 18.

142 *Wasteful Management Inc v United Mexican States II*, ICSID Case No ARB(AF)/00/3, Mexico's Preliminary Objection Concerning the Previous Proceedings, Decision of the Tribunal of 26 June 2002, para 49.

143 Paul Michael Blychak, 'Access and Advantages Expanded: Mobil Corporation v. Venezuela and Other Recent Arbitration Awards on Treaty Shopping' (2011) 4 Journal of World Energy Law and Business 32, 32. It is submitted that this is a primary reason why Venezuela terminated its BIT with the Netherlands: Matthew Skinner, Cameron Miles, and Sam Luttrell, 'Access and Advantage in Investor-State Arbitration: The Law and Practice of Treaty Shopping' (2010) 3 Journal of World Energy Law and Business 260, 276–77; Sergey Ripinsky, 'Venezuela's Withdrawal from ICSID: What it Does and Does Not Achieve', International Institute for Sustainable Development, 13 April 2012 <https://www.iisd.org/itn/2012/04/13/venezuelas-withdrawal-from-icsid-what-it-does-and-does-not-achieve/> accessed: 15 February 2019.

144 *Tokios Tokelės v Ukraine*, ICSID Case No ARB/02/18, Dissenting Opinion of 29 April 2004, para 25; *Mobil Corp v Republic of Venezuela*, ICSID Case No ARB/07/27, Decision on Jurisdiction of 10 June 2010, para 184.

145 International Bank for Reconstruction and Development, 'Report of the Executive Directors on the Convention on the Settlement of Investment Disputes Between States and Nationals of Other States', dated 18 March 1965, section 9; *ST-AD GmbH v Republic of Bulgaria*, UNCITRAL, PCA Case No 2011-06, Award on Jurisdiction of 18 July 2013, para 408.

jurisdiction: any domestic dispute may become international if the domestic company merely incorporates a foreign entity that subsequently acquires the shares of the domestic entity.[146] As stated by one tribunal:

> The Tribunal has come to the conclusion that the Claimant's initiation and pursuit of this arbitration is an abuse of the system of international investment arbitration. If it were accepted that the Tribunal has jurisdiction to decide ST-AD's claim, then any pre-existing national dispute could be brought to an international arbitration tribunal by an 'after the fact' transfer of the national economic interests to a foreign company in an attempt to seek protections under a BIT. Such transfer from the domestic arena to the international scene would *ipso facto* constitute a 'protected investment' – and the jurisdiction of an international arbitral tribunal under a BIT would be virtually unlimited. It is the duty of the Tribunal not to protect such an abusive manipulation of the system of international investment protection. It indeed the Tribunal's view that to accept jurisdiction in this case would go against the basic objectives underlying bilateral investment treaties. The Tribunal has to ensure that the BIT mechanism does not protect investments that it was not designed to protect, that is, domestic investments disguised as international investments or domestic disputes repackaged as international disputes for the sole purpose of gaining access to international arbitration.[147]

4.94 The act of corporate restructure or nationality planning raises different competing interests that may affect the administration of justice. As shall be discussed below, the case law fortifies that abuse of rights may effectively apply in this regard to: ensure procedural fairness; fulfil requirements of due process; safeguard the parties' reasonable expectations; and preserve the integrity of the arbitral process.[148]

4.95 Numerous examples exist to show how arbitral tribunals have applied abuse of rights in such circumstances. There exists some sort of consensus in terms of the essential elements required to find an abuse. The case law demonstrates that while corporate planning is a legitimate right and seeking the substantive and procedural protection afforded by a specific BIT is not abusive per se,[149] it may become abusive if such conduct is unfair,

[146] *Phoenix Action v The Czech Republic*, ICSID Case No ARB/06/5, Award of 15 April 2009, para 43; Skinner, Miles, and Luttrell (n 143) 260–63; John Lee, 'Resolving Concerns of Treaty Shopping in International Investment Arbitration' (2015) 6 Journal of International Dispute Settlement 355, 356, and 360; *Pacific Rim Cayman LLC The Republic of El Salvador*, ICSID Case No ARB/09/12, Decision on Jurisdiction of 1 June 2012, paras 2.37–2.38. On the other hand, some argue that allowing access to ICSID arbitration is not contrary to the parties' expectations, as the treaty in question adopted a broad definition of investor and investment. *Aguas del Tunari SA v Republic of Bolivia*, ICSID Case No ARB/02/3, Decision on Respondent's Objections to Jurisdiction of 21 October 2005, para 332.

[147] *ST-AD GmbH v Republic of Bulgaria*, UNCITRAL, PCA Case No 2011-06, Award on Jurisdiction of 18 July 2013, para 423.

[148] Lee (n 146) 375–76.

[149] Ulrich Klemm, 'Investment Through Third Countries: State Practice and Needs of Investors' (2009) 24 ICSID Review 528, 523; Lee (n 146) 358; Christoph Schreuer, 'Nationality Planning' in Arthur W. Rovine (ed), *Contemporary Issues in International Arbitration and Mediation: The Fordham Papers* (Martinus Nijhoff 2013) 18 and 20; Gus Van Harten, *Investment Treaty Arbitration and Public Law* (Oxford University Press 2008) 115; *HICEE BV v The Slovak Republic*, UNCITRAL Partial Award of 23 May 2011, PCA Case No 2009-11, para 103; *Renée Rose Levy and Gremcitel SA v Republic of Peru*, ICSID Case No ARB/11/17, Award of 9 January 2015, para 184; *Aguas del Tunari SA v Republic of Bolivia*, ICSID Case No ARB/02/3, Decision on Respondent's Objections to Jurisdiction of 21 October 2005, paras 245 and 330.

defies the object and purpose of the BIT, and impedes the integrity of arbitration. In assessing the abusive nature of the conduct in question, the *timing* and *motive/purpose* of the exercise of the right (corporate restructuring) is pivotal.[150] Arbitral tribunals will consider the aforementioned elements as well as other indicative elements that may aid them in discerning the intention of the parties.[151] In other words, abuse of rights is established where a corporate restructuring is 'motivated wholly or partly by a desire to gain access to treaty protection in order to bring a claim in respect of a specific dispute that, at the time of the restructuring, exists or is foreseeable'.[152]

In the seminal case of *Phoenix v Czech Republic*, the dispute involved two Czech companies owned by a Czech national who was embroiled in domestic disputes with the Czech Government. Accordingly, the owner of the companies transferred their ownership to *Phoenix*, an Israeli company owned by members of his family. Two months after the restructuring, the Claimant initiated arbitration proceedings. The Respondent submitted that *Phoenix* was nothing short of an *ex post facto* creation of a sham Israeli company, that this conduct represented an egregious case of treaty shopping, and thus constituted an abuse of rights.[153] **4.96**

The Tribunal found that the investment by *Phoenix* was not made in good faith and constituted an abuse of rights. The Tribunal stipulated that the principle of abuse of rights, which is part of the broader notion of good faith, mandates that parties 'deal honestly and *fairly* with each other, to *represent their motives and purposes truthfully*, and to *refrain from taking unfair advantage*' (emphasis added).[154] **4.97**

Upon acknowledging that the principle may operate to remedy unfairness, the Tribunal engaged in a delicate balancing process of the facts and interests at stake to determine if there was an abuse of right. The Tribunal considered: the timing of the investment; the timing of the claim and the substance of the transaction. These considerations warranted the finding that the main purpose of the investment was an 'attempt to render their purely domestic disputes to the protections of the BIT rather than to conduct business'.[155] The Tribunal concluded that the investment was merely an artificial transaction, the creation of a legal fiction to gain access to ICSID, and that it was made in bad **4.98**

[150] *Autopista Concesionada de Venezuela, CA v Bolivarian Republic of Venezuela*, ICSID Case No ARB/00/5, Decision on Jurisdiction of 27 September 2001, para 126, where it was held that there was no abuse of rights as the restructuring (establishing a US entity) took place eight years before the parties entered into the concession agreement in question, thus the entity was not a shell company; Schreuer (n 149) 34; Diane Desierto, 'Arbitral Controls and Policing the Gates to Investment Treaty Claims against States in Transglobal Green Energy v, Panama and Philip Morris v. Australia' (Blog of the European Journal of International Law, 22 June 2016) 1–2, <http://www.ejiltalk.org/arbitral-controls-and-policing-the-gates-to-investment-treaty-claims-against-states-in-transglobal-green-energy-v-panama-and-philip-morris-v-australia/> accessed 19 February 2019.

[151] Desierto (n 150) 2.

[152] *Philip Morris Asia Limited v The Commonwealth of Australia*, PCA Case No 2012-12, Award on Jurisdiction and Admissibility of 17 December 2015, under UNCITRAL Rules, para 536.

[153] *Phoenix Action v The Czech Republic*, ICSID Case No ARB/06/5, Award of 15 April 2009, para 34.

[154] ibid para 107.

[155] ibid para 141.

faith and constituted an abuse of rights. The Tribunal ordered the Claimant to bear all ICSID costs.[156]

4.99 This case is of significance not only for its application of abuse of rights but for its enunciation that the principle's application advances the notion of good administration of arbitral justice. Parties have a reasonable expectation that the ICSID system is specifically tailored to resolve disputes between foreign investors and States.[157] Thus, it would be unfair, and a violation of the reasonable expectations of the parties, for the arbitral system to afford its protection to such abusive conduct. The principle was effectively applied to safeguard those reasonable expectations and to preserve the integrity of the system.[158]

4.100 The above was reinstated and confirmed in the recent case of *Philip Morris v Australia*.[159] The Respondent claimed that the principle of abuse of rights forbade the Claimant from exercising its right to arbitrate.[160] The arbitral Tribunal held that Claimant's restructure of its investment amounted to an abuse of right as it was exercised for the purpose of gaining access to arbitration and *after* the dispute was *foreseeable*. In clarifying the meaning of foreseeability in the context of abuse of rights, the Tribunal held that foreseeability is established where there is a reasonable prospect that 'a measure which may give rise to a treaty claim will materialise'.[161] Moreover, in relation to the motive and purpose of the restructuring of the investment, the Tribunal acknowledged that abuse was not established if restructuring was motivated for reasons other than bringing a claim. However, it was held that such restructuring was not motivated primarily for tax or other business reasons, but mainly to initiate a treaty claim using an entity from Hong Kong.[162]

4.101 In this regard, the depiction of the principle of abuse of rights as a principle necessary to secure the fairness of the proceedings was unequivocal. Abuse of rights was asserted as a principle that ensures that the exercise of rights is reasonable and fair: 'it should at the same time be *fair* and *equitable* as between the parties and not one which is calculated to procure for one of them *an unfair advantage* in the light of the obligation assumed' (emphasis added).[163] That being said, the Tribunal held that the initiation of arbitration constituted an abuse of rights which rendered the claims raised inadmissible.[164]

[156] ibid paras 143 and 152.

[157] *ST-AD GmbH v Republic of Bulgaria*, UNCITRAL, PCA Case No 2011-06, Award on Jurisdiction of 18 July 2013, para 408; International Bank for Reconstruction and Development, 'Report of the Executive Directors on the Convention on the Settlement of Investment Disputes Between States and Nationals of Other States', dated 18 March 1965, section 9.

[158] *Phoenix Action v The Czech Republic*, ICSID Case No ARB/06/5, Award of 15 April 2009, para 113.

[159] *Philip Morris Asia Limited v The Commonwealth of Australia*, PCA Case No 2012-12, Award on Jurisdiction and Admissibility of 17 December 2015, under UNCITRAL Rules.

[160] ibid para 400.

[161] ibid paras 554 and 569; Desierto (n 150) 1.

[162] *Philip Morris Asia Limited v The Commonwealth of Australia*, PCA Case No 2012-12, Award on Jurisdiction and Admissibility of 17 December 2015, under UNCITRAL Rules, paras 570–84.

[163] ibid para 400.

[164] ibid para 588.

4.102 On a related note, abuse of rights may operate not only as a requirement of fairness, but may be mandated by considerations of due process.[165] The duty that parties must be treated equally is sacrosanct in international arbitration.[166] As rightly pointed out by one scholar, it 'is perhaps the most fundamental rule of due process'.[167] This is included in most arbitration laws and institutional rules.[168]

4.103 In this regard, it is submitted that the equality between the parties may also be thwarted where one party foresees the dispute and subsequently makes an investment in the host State without the latter knowing that such an investment was made solely to gain access to arbitration. This may defy the fairness of the proceedings, infringe upon the equality between the parties, and frustrate their reasonable expectations. As asserted in *Philip Morris*:

> [W]here there is a corporate restructur[ing] in the knowledge of an actual or specific future dispute, and a preconceived BIT claim is then brought, *there is no longer an equality of position* between the investor and the host State, and the *investor benefits from an unfair advantage* [since] the investor invests knowing that it is about to/ready to bring a claim [whilst] [t]he host State admits the investment, *in ignorance* of the investor's intent.[169] (Emphasis added)

4.104 This was similarly upheld in the case of *ConocoPhillips*. While the Tribunal found no abuse of rights given that the restructuring took place *prior* to the foreseeability of the dispute,[170] the potency of abuse of rights to ensure the equality between the parties was acknowledged. The Tribunal explicitly noted that:

> There is jurisdiction only if the parties to the dispute have each consented and *throughout the process each is treated on an equal footing, as indeed the principles of due process and natural justice require*. That equality of position in the present context is, in this Tribunal's view, a further factor supporting the growing body of decisions placing some limits on the investor's choice of corporate form, even if it complies with the relevant technical definition in the treaty text.[171] (Emphasis added)

4.105 Accordingly, it seems that the application of abuse of rights may be necessary not only to restore the fairness of the proceedings and to preserve the integrity of the process,

[165] Thomas W Walde, '"Equalityof Arms" in Investment Arbitration: Procedural Challenges, in Katia Yannaca-Small (ed), *Arbitration Under International Investment Agreements: A Guide to the Key Issues* (Oxford University Press 2010) 162.

[166] Peter Binder, *An International Comparison of the UNCITRAL Model Law on International Commercial Arbitration* (1st edn, Sweet & Maxwell 2000) 124–125; Kurkela and Turunen (n 20) 186–87.

[167] Kurkela and Turunen (n 20) 189.

[168] Article 18 of the UNCITRAL Model Law on International Commercial Arbitration of 1985 (with amendments adopted in 2010).

[169] *Philip Morris Asia Limited v The Commonwealth of Australia*, PCA Case No 2012-12, Award on Jurisdiction and Admissibility of 17 December 2015, under UNCITRAL Rules, para 443.

[170] *ConocoPhillips Petrozuata BV, ConocoPhillips Hamaca BV, ConocoPhillips Gulf of Paria BV and ConocoPhillips Company v The Bolivarian Republic of Venezuela*, ICSID Case No ARB/07/30, Decision on Jurisdiction and the Merits of 3 September 2013, paras 279-280.

[171] ibid para 274.

but also as a requirement of due process.[172] This is just as conspicuous in cases where States exercise their rights, particularly their inherent right to investigate criminal wrongdoing, in a manner that may impede the equality of arms, the fairness and integrity of the proceedings, and undermine the arbitral process.[173]

4.106 From a pure theoretical stance, while States retain an inherent right to investigate and prosecute criminal wrongdoing,[174] concerns raised by investors may appear logical where States use this right for economic or political purposes,[175] or as an abusive tool to pressure,[176] intimidate, or induce investors and to baulk an ongoing arbitration.[177] Such abusive conduct by States may: aggravate the dispute;[178] defy the purpose of the BIT in question;[179] damage the purpose of investment arbitration; breach the requirements of due process; and become a threat to the development of international rule of law.[180] To that effect, it has been rightly stated that 'tribunals must be on guard to discern which requests are legitimate and which requests constitute attempts by investors to use investment arbitration to escape answering legitimate criminal allegations'.[181]

4.107 Again, it seems here that barring any abuse of right emanates from considerations of due process and the desire to preserve the integrity and fairness of the arbitration process.[182]

4.108 Some of the aforementioned considerations were clear in the case of *Libananco Holdings v The Republic of Turkey*, where issues of procedural fairness as well as requirements of due process were raised and considered by the arbitral Tribunal. The Claimant alleged that the commencement of criminal investigations against it breached the equality of arms between the parties and also breached Turkey's obligation to arbitrate fairly and in good faith. During the criminal investigations, it was alleged that there was surveillance

[172] Paparinskis (n 83) 19; Thomas W Walde, '"Equality of Arms" in Investment Arbitration: Procedural Challenges' in Katia Yannaca-Small (ed), *Arbitration Under International Investment Agreements: A Guide to the Key Issues* (Oxford University Press 2010) 162.

[173] Walde (n 172) 162; Sébastien Besson, 'Corruption and Arbitration' in Domitille Baizeau and Richard H. Kreindler (eds), *Addressing Issues of Corruption in Commercial and Investment Arbitration* (Kluwer Law International 2015) 106.

[174] Francisco Orrego Vicuña, 'Regulatory Authority and Legitimate Expectations: Balancing the Rights of the State and the Individual under International Law in a Global Society', ICCA, 15 April 2009 <http://www.arbitration-icca.org/media/0/12224293410150/regulatory_authority.pdf> accessed 19 February 2019.

[175] Ruslan Mrzayev, 'International Investment Protection Regime and Criminal Investigations', (2012) 29 Journal of International Arbitration 71, 72; for example in the famous Yukos arbitration, the Claimant alleged that criminal proceedings were initiated by Russia for, inter alia, economic and political purposes: *Yukos International Ltd (Isles of Man) v The Russian Federation*, PCA Case No AA 227, Interim Award on Jurisdiction and Admissibility of 30 November 2009, 48.

[176] Gaillard (n 90) 27.

[177] Henry G Burnett and Jessica Beess und Chrostin, 'Interim Measures in Response to the Criminal Prosecution of Corporations and Their Employees by Host States in Parallel with Investment Arbitration Proceedings' (2015) 30 Maryland Journal of International Law 31, 32.

[178] *Teinver SA, Transportes de Cercanias SA and Autobuses Urbanos del Sur SA v The Argentine Republic*, ICSID Case No ARB/09/1, Decision on Provisional Measures of 8 April 2016, para 74.

[179] Burnett, Beess und Chrostin (n 177) 53.

[180] Mrzayev (n 175) 82.

[181] Burnett, Beess und Chrostin (n 177) 54.

[182] ibid 52.

and interception of legally privileged communications between the Claimant, its counsel, and witnesses.[183]

The arbitral Tribunal recognized the inherent right of States to conduct criminal investigations. However, such right is not absolute, it must not be abused, and must be exercised with regard to the rights of the other party.[184] It was also mentioned that this brings into question sacrosanct principles such as procedural fairness, the equality of the parties, and their right to seek advice and freely advance their cases.[185] Additionally, while not questioning the assurances given by Turkey's counsel that such information was not revealed to them nor used in this arbitration, the Tribunal noted that 'it is not enough that justice should be done, it must also manifestly be seen to be done'.[186] The Tribunal then ordered the State not to interfere with the preparation of the case in the future. **4.109**

In another case, *Quilborax v Bolivia*, the Claimants requested provisional measures ordering the Respondent to discontinue criminal proceedings relating to the arbitration as it aggravated the *status quo* of the arbitration and jeopardized the procedural integrity of the arbitral proceedings.[187] During the arbitration, the Bolivian Government reviewed Claimants' corporate documentation registered in the Bolivian registry, noted some irregularities, and initiated criminal proceedings alleging the forgery of the documents. As part of the criminal investigation, Bolivia also sequestrated corporate records and interrogated persons related to the Claimants, including their former legal counsel. Thus, it was the Claimants' view that the State abused its right to investigate criminal behaviour, as it used it solely to influence the current arbitration; as an abusive tactic to avoid the arbitration on the merits, and force the Claimants to give up their claims.[188] **4.110**

The Tribunal first acknowledged that Bolivia had a right to prosecute conduct that may constitute a crime. However, the Tribunal emphasized that such a right is not absolute, cannot be abused, and must be balanced against the Claimants' rights to pursue the arbitration, and to have their claims fairly considered.[189] Accordingly, abuse was established primarily to restore and maintain the procedural integrity of the arbitration. By balancing Bolivia's interest to pursue the investigation against the Claimants' fundamental interests in resolving their dispute before the Tribunal, and their right to have access to evidence and the integrity of the evidence (the criminal proceedings had a material effect on potential witnesses), the Tribunal chose the latter rights and issued provisional measures. **4.111**

[183] *Libananco Holdings Co Limited v Republic of Turkey*, ICSID Case No ARB/06/8, Decision on Preliminary Issues of 23 June 2008, paras 48 and 72.
[184] ibid para 79.
[185] ibid para 78.
[186] ibid para 79.
[187] *Quilborax SA, Non Metallic Minerals SA and Allan Fosk Kaplún v Plurinational State of Bolivia*, ICSID Case No ARB/06/2, Decision on Provisional Measures of 26 February 2010.
[188] ibid para 46.
[189] ibid paras 123 and 148.

4.112 One submits that any other conclusion would arguably constitute a breach to the requirements of due process, as the Claimants would be deprived of effectively presenting their case and substantiating their claims.[190]

2. Parallel arbitral proceedings

4.113 The prevailing globalization trends have affected the practice of international arbitration. Accordingly, we have witnessed the development of complex arbitrations, which have now become a feature of international arbitration. The growing intricacy of transnational disputes and arbitral proceedings has brought about a matter that has truly become a global paradox, that is, parallel and overlapping proceedings.[191]

4.114 Parallel proceedings generally denote the case where parties initiate the same or related proceedings before different courts/tribunals.[192] While there is no one definition to describe parallel proceedings, as this may differ from one jurisdiction or treaty to another, one finds it apt to consider the definition adopted by the ILA: proceedings pending before a court/tribunal in which the parties and one or more of the issues are the same or substantially the same as the ones before the tribunal.[193]

4.115 The role of abuse of rights to ensure the administration of justice is also evident in the realm of parallel arbitration proceedings.

4.116 In order to demonstrate how the principle of abuse of rights ensures the good administration of justice in the context of parallel proceedings, it seems necessary to first determine the legal and strategic considerations for pursuing parallel and overlapping proceedings. This succinct determination is vital in the context of abuse of rights and the good administration of justice. It was suggested that the principle of abuse of rights not only ensures the administration of justice, but that it balances the competing interests of the good administration of arbitral justice (fairness, due process, and efficiency). In order to examine the adequacy of this submission, highlighting the competing interests in the context of parallel proceedings warrants a succinct elaboration as it shall appear that while some considerations are reasonable and worth legal protection, other considerations seem rather unfair and abusive specifically when considered in light of the colossal risks involved. Thereafter, the operation of abuse of rights to enhance the administration of justice and its role as a mechanism that balances the competing interests shall be discussed by reviewing and analysing three important cases that dealt with the matter.

[190] It was found that the Respondent obstructed the Claimants' access to evidence and alienated potential witnesses, ibid paras 139–48.

[191] Emmanuel Gaillard and Philippe Pinsolle, 'Advocacy in Practice: The Use of Parallel Proceedings' in Doak Bishop and Edward G. Kehoe (eds), *The Art of Advocacy in International Arbitration* (2nd edn, Juris 2010) 174.

[192] Nadja Erk, *Parallel Proceedings in International Arbitration: A Comparative European Perspective* (Kluwer Law International 2014) 16.

[193] International Law Association, *Final Report on Lis Pendens and Arbitration* (Toronto 2006), paras 5.6 and 5.13; Erk (n 192) 16.

(i) Competing interests in parallel arbitral proceedings

As previously mentioned, a right denotes an interest that is recognized and protected by the law to fulfil a certain purpose.[194] It is well acknowledged that each party in international arbitration pursues his/her interests. It is equally recognized that in any given dispute, there exists parties' diverse competing interests and it is the decision maker's role to resolve such conflict.[195] The paradoxical problem of parallel arbitral proceedings is no exception. It involves a multiplicity of interests that primarily rest on those pursued by the party initiating the parallel proceedings and those of the party(ies) opposing such conduct given the risks and procedural hazards associated thereto. **4.117**

Those competing interests often fall within the ambit of the administration of justice, that is, they involve interests that are part of due process considerations, preserving the integrity of the process, protecting parties' reasonable expectations, and interests that affect the efficiency and fairness of the proceedings. **4.118**

Understandably, parties in arbitration proceedings have conflicting interests. A claimant is usually seeking a fast resolution of the dispute and the respondent may attempt to delay or disrupt the proceedings.[196] That said, parallel court or arbitral proceedings may be initiated primarily as a dilatory tactic.[197] In a case decided by the Swiss Federal Tribunal, a reference was made to a case where a scientist concluded a know-how licence agreement with a Swiss pharmaceuticals company (Company X). The agreement contained an ICC arbitration clause. Subsequently, the scientist transferred his rights and obligations to another company (Company Y). A dispute arose between Company X and Company Y in relation to the payment of royalties. The arbitral Tribunal rendered a partial award recognizing the right of Company Y to receive the royalties and deferred the quantum issue to a subsequent phase. Company X decided to declare that the agreement was void and initiated another parallel arbitration proceedings requesting a declaration that the said agreement was void. The Swiss Federal Tribunal acknowledged the tactical intention for the parallel proceedings, in that it was an invitation to review the merits of the rendered award, and provided that: 'Speaking of claim is questionable when dealing with a mere declaratory relief, the only aim thereof being, other than deferring the outcome of the pending case regarding payment, a case in which the Claimant has lost on the principle of liability.'[198] **4.119**

[194] Julio Cueto-Rua, 'Abuse of Rights' (1975) 35 Louisiana Law Review 965, 995–96; Hasso Hofmann, 'From Jhering to Radbruch: On the Logic of Traditional Legal Concepts to the Social Theories of Law to the Renewal of Legal Idealism' in Damiano Canale, Paolo Grossi, and Hasso Hofmann (eds), *A History of the Philosophy of Law in the Civil Law World, 1600-1900* (Springer 2009) 308; Iredell Jenkins 'Rudolf Von Jhering' (1961) 14 Vanderbilt Law Review 169, 172.

[195] Gebhard Bücheler, *Proportionality in Investor-State Arbitration* (Oxford University Press 2015) 28.

[196] Pfeiffer and Wilske (n 104) 3; Lane (n 96) 424; Harris (n 107) 87.

[197] Gaillard and Pinsolle (n 191) 174; Swiss Federal Tribunal (1st Civil law division), 14 May 2001, *Fomento de Construcciones y Contratas SA v Colon Container Terminal SA*, 19 ASA Bulletin 544 (2001); Erk (n 192) 11.

[198] *X SA v Y. Limited*, 1st Civil Law Court, 4A_210/2008, 29 October 2008, 27 ASA Bulletin 309, 319 (2009), translated in Gaillard and Pinsolle (n 191) 179–80.

4.120 On the other hand, parallel proceedings may be triggered by reasons of securing the opposing party's assets located in different places,[199] or as a tool to multiply one's chances of recovery.[200]

4.121 Parallel arbitral proceedings necessarily increases costs and may accordingly defy the good administration of justice in this regard.[201] Thus, parties may abuse the arbitral system by initiating proceedings as a tool to exert economic pressure on another party.[202]

4.122 On a related note, one of the principal reasons/motives associated with parallel proceedings is forum shopping. It is axiomatic that whenever forum shopping is possible, there may exist an interest in choosing the appropriate regime, arbitral situs, and applicable procedural and substantive rules of law.[203] This is particularly the case where the arbitration agreement does not specify the seat of arbitration, and in multi-contract and multi-party disputes.[204]

4.123 While the above-mentioned discussion reflects the competing interests generally shared and advocated by legal scholars, other interests remain relevant. In this regard, one anticipates other scenarios that do not necessarily imply bad faith or abuse. It is widely acknowledged under many arbitration rules that where the respondent fails to appoint an arbitrator within a specific time frame, the arbitral institution, or another authority, may appoint the arbitrator for the respondent.[205] Also in multi-party or multi-contract disputes, claimant(s) and respondent(s) may have conflicting interests and thus require appointing different arbitrators.[206] Given that party-appointed arbitrators is perceived by many as a sacrosanct right,[207] the claimant/respondent, in the above examples, may initiate parallel arbitral proceedings, not for tactical reasons but for the purpose of safeguarding their right to appoint an arbitrator.[208]

[199] Erk (n 192) 11.
[200] See assertion made by the Respondent in *Ampal-American Israel Corp et al v Arab Republic of Egypt*, ICSID Case No ARB/12/11, Decision on Jurisdiction of 1 February 2016, para 313.
[201] Leboulanger (n 7) 62–63.
[202] Erk (n 192) 11.
[203] Richard Kreindler, 'Arbitral Forum Shopping' in Bernardo M Cremades and Julian DM Lew (eds), *Parallel State and Arbitral Procedures in International Arbitration* (ICC Publishing 2005) 159, 176–78; Bernardo M Cremades and Ignacio Madalena, 'Parallel Proceedings in International Arbitration' (2008) 24 Arbitration International 507, 508.
[204] Kreindler (n 203) 154.
[205] Article 12 of the ICC Rules of Arbitration 2012; Articles 2.4 and 7.2 of the LCIA Rules of Arbitration 2014 ('Failure to deliver a Response within time shall constitute an irrevocable waiver of that party's opportunity to nominate or propose any arbitral candidate'); Articles 4 and 9 of the UNCITRAL Arbitration Rules 2013.
[206] Eric A Schwartz, 'Multi-Party Arbitration and the ICC' (1993) 10 Journal of International Arbitration 5, 9, 14; *Siemens AG and BKMI Industrienlagen GmbH v Dutco Construction Co*, 7 January 1992, Bull Civ 1, no 2, referred to in Hanotiau (n 8) paras 443–45.
[207] Charles N Brower and Charles B Rosenberg, 'Why the Paulsson-van den Berg Presumption that Party-Appointed Arbitrators are Untrustworthy is Wrongheaded' (2013) 29 Arbitration International 7; cf Jan Paulsson, *The Idea of Arbitration* (Oxford University Press 2013) 276–283; Jan Paulsson, 'Moral Hazards in International Arbitration' (2010) 25 ICSID Review 339; Albert Jan van den Berg, 'Dissenting Opinions by Party-Appointed Arbitrators in Investment Arbitration' in Mahnoush Arsanjani and others (eds), *Looking to the Future: Essays on International Law in Honor of W. Michael Resiman* (Brill Academic 2011).
[208] Hanotiau (n 8) paras 381–84 and 443–45; Schwartz (n 206) 5.

Another example is the case where an arbitration clause does not specify the seat of arbitration and the tribunal decides to make the hearings or the seat abroad.[209] In this regard, one of the parties may initiate parallel proceedings in his/her home jurisdiction solely for economic reasons, that is, he/she cannot bear the costs associated with an arbitration held abroad.[210] **4.124**

On the other hand, there are risks, procedural enigmas, and competing interests that may ensue in cases of parallel proceedings. As discussed below, this include, inter alia, maintaining the efficiency of proceedings, cost-effectiveness, upholding parties' common intention, and the need to avoid conflicting decisions. Disregarding such vital interests may pose a serious threat to the stability and integrity of the arbitral system and thus defy the good administration of justice.[211] **4.125**

Allowing abusive parallel proceedings may lead to an escalation of costs and waste of resources.[212] Parties have a right (interest) and an expectation to have an efficient resolution of the dispute.[213] In the case of *SGS Société Générale de Surveillance SA v Islamic Republic of Pakistan*, the Tribunal stipulated that: **4.126**

> It would be wasteful resources for two proceedings relating to the same or substantially the same matter to unfold separately while the jurisdiction of one tribunal awaits determination. No doubt the parties have been put to considerable expense already.[214]

Moreover, the risk of inconsistent decisions is high when considering the continuation of parallel proceedings. The materialization of such a risk is a fissure in the arbitration system and a crisis that has practical legal implications.[215] In this regard, Philippe Leboulanger rightly provided that 'it is inadmissible to have contradicting decisions **4.127**

[209] Article 18 of the ICC Rules of Arbitration 2012; Article 16 of the LCIA Rules of Arbitration 2014; and Article 18 of the UNCITRAL Arbitration Rules 2013.

[210] Kreindler (n 203) 178, (providing that considerations of convenience and cost-effectiveness may be reasons to forum shop); Yuval Shany, *The Competing Jurisdictions of International Courts and Tribunals* (Oxford University Press 2003) 259–60.

[211] August Reinisch, 'International Courts and Tribunals, Multiple Jurisdictions' in Max Planck Encyclopedia of Public International Law, (Oxford University Press 2008), para 16; Leboulanger (n 7) 54.

[212] Stephen Bond, 'Dépeçage or Consolidation of the Disputes Resulting from Connected Agreements: The Role of the Arbitrator' in Bernard Hanotiau and Eric A. Schwartz (eds), *Multiparty Arbitration* (ICC Publications 2010) 43; August Reinisch, 'The Proliferation of International Dispute Settlement Mechanisms: The Threat of Fragmentation vs. the Promise of a More Effective System? Some Reflections From the Perspective of Investment Arbitration' in Isabelle Buffard and others (eds), *International Law between Universalism and Fragmentation* (Martinus Nijhoff 2008) 114; August Reinisch, 'International Courts and Tribunals, Multiple Jurisdictions', in Max Planck Encyclopedia of Public International Law (Oxford University Press 2008) 1.

[213] Michael Pryles and Jeffrey Waincymer, 'Multiple Claims in Arbitration between the same Parties' (2008) 56 <http://www.arbitration-icca.org/media/4/63529655901040/media012223886747020multiple_claims_in_arbitrations_between_the_same_parties.pdf> accessed 26 February 2019.

[214] *SGS Société Générale de Surveillance SA v Islamic Republic of Pakistan*, ICSID Case No ARB/01/13, Procedural Order No 2 of 16 October 2002, 304; Laurent Levy, 'Anti-Suit Injunctions Issued by Arbitrators' in Emmanuel Gaillard (ed), *Anti-Suit injunctions in International Arbitration* (IAI Series on International Arbitration No 2, 2005) 122.

[215] Charles N Brower, Charles H Brower II, and Jeremy K Sharpe, 'The Coming Crisis in the Global Adjudication System', (2003) 19 Arbitration International 415, 424; Audley Sheppard, 'Res Judicata and Estoppel' in Bernardo M Cremades and Julian DM Lew (eds), *Parallel State and Arbitral Procedures in International Arbitration* (ICC Institute of World Business Law 2005) 237; Charles N Brower and Jeremy K Sharpe, 'Multiple and Conflicting International Arbitral Awards' (2003) 4 Journal of World Investment 211.

regarding interrelated disputes, as this may result in actual denial of justice. The splitting of complex disputes leaves the door open to inconsistent decisions and to injustice.'[216]

4.128 The need for procedural harmonization should not only be mandated to prevent conflicting decisions, but also because it is directly linked to parties' expectations.[217] Parties trust international arbitration as an authoritative mechanism to obtain a final and binding determination of their disputes in accordance with their expectations.[218] Parties' legitimate expectations would be thwarted where their arbitral award conflicts with another award, or where the issues resolved in the first arbitration are re-opened in subsequent proceedings.[219] Thus, in *Premium Nafta Products and Others v Fili Shipping Company Limited*, Lord Hoffmann emphasized the need to uphold the commercial purpose of the arbitration clause. The said purpose is, in most cases, to refer all disputes to one tribunal and to avoid the duplication of effort, expense, and possibility of inconsistent decisions associated with parallel proceedings.[220]

4.129 The initiation of parallel arbitral proceedings may also violate the fairness of the proceedings and defy requirements of due process. This is particularly the case in relation to complex disputes that are brought before different tribunals. In such cases, one of the parties may be deprived of his right to fully present his case before the tribunal. An example of this was eloquently described by Leboulanger:

> In some cases, if no link is established between the parallel disputes, the fundamental conditions of a fair trial may not be met, namely when the dispute between the parties involves the *exceptio non adimpleti contractus* principle, for instance when one of the parties refrains from performing its obligations under an agreement, by retaining sums owed, in order to defend its contractual rights, that is, only because the other party did not perform its obligations under another agreement belonging to the same group of contracts [. . .] if the arbitral treatment of the two agreements is split, the defendant might not be able even to raise the argument based on the *exceptio* and consequently may be deprived of its right to present its case in an equal position to the claimant's. The ICC Court should pay particular attention to a situation like this and should not ignore its consequences, which would be contrary to the proper administration of justice. The concept of 'a fair hearing' cannot be overlooked.[221]

4.130 Parallel arbitral proceedings may also lead to inequality between the parties and thus pose a threat to due process. This is particularly the case where a party (an investor) initiates multiple arbitral proceedings through a locally incorporated company and

[216] Leboulanger (n 7) 63.
[217] Gary B Born, *International Commercial Arbitration* (Wolters Kluwer 2009) 1074.
[218] Stavros Brekoulakis, 'Res Judicata and Third Parties' (2005) 16 American Review of International Arbitration 1, 3–4.
[219] ibid 3-4.
[220] *Premium Nafta Products Limited and Others v Fili Shipping Company Limited and Others* [2007] UKHL 40, para 13; Nathalie Voser, '*The* Swiss Perspective on Parties in Arbitration: "Traditional Approach with a Twist Regarding Abuse of Rights" or "Consent Theory Plus"' in Stavros Brekoulakis, Julian DM Lew, and Loukas Mistelis (eds), *The Evolution and Future of International Arbitration* (Kluwer Law International 2016) para 9.21.
[221] Leboulanger (n 7) 90–91.

through direct and indirect shareholders against a State. If different arbitral tribunals are constituted in the multiple proceedings, this means that while the investor has to convince one tribunal in order to prevail in the case, the State may have to refute the claims and prevail before all the other tribunals.[222]

The above analysis reveals that such competing interests may be effectively balanced by resorting to abuse of rights. While the arbitration agreement may grant the parties the right to initiate arbitration proceedings, such right should be exercised reasonably. As shall be discussed below, the element of reasonableness, comprising the crux of the principle of abuse of rights, may assist arbitral tribunals in considering questions arising in the context of parallel proceedings to ensure the good administration of justice. **4.131**

As rightly provided by Bernard Hanotiau: **4.132**

> Arbitral institutions and arbitrators have a *correlative obligation* to make sure that the *duty of good faith* is respected by the parties. Consequently, they should, *by all means within the limits of their rules or prerogatives*, make it *impossible for a party to jeopardize another party's case* by *abusing its rights* and unduly *opposing the conduct of a single arbitration or the joinder of parallel proceedings*. It should, however, never be overlooked that the parties' agreement is paramount: *striking a balance* between this agreement, the duty of the parties to act in good faith, and their right to a *fair trial* [. . .] is one of the most difficult challenges that arbitrators and arbitration institutions face and it is their duty to solve it in the best possible way by all available means.[223] (Emphasis added)

The above was eloquently described by Yuval Shany in the context of parallel and subsequent proceedings, so he is quoted *in extenso*: **4.133**

> If one perceives adjudication before a specific forum and not before other competent courts or tribunals to be excessively burdensome, without there being a legitimate interest justifying litigation before the selected forum, insistence by the applicant upon his or her unilateral choice of forum might be regarded as wholly unreasonable, and therefore an abuse of right. *Such a balance of interests might clearly be in place when the same case is pending or has already been decided by another tribunal.* In these circumstances, compelling the respondent party to litigate the same matter before another court or tribunal would certainly cause significant hardship. At the same time, the applicant does not seem to have a legitimate interest in multiple adjudication since he or she has already had (or will have) their 'day in court'. In other words, the abuse of rights doctrine can serve as an additional justification for the adoption of *lis alibi pendens* and *res judicata* (and also *electa una via*) rules, and perhaps even support a liberal construction of their scope of application, so to encompass closely related multiple

[222] Gaillard (n 90) 24–25.
[223] Hanotiau (n 8) para 235.

proceedings, which are extremely onerous for one party and of relatively little utility to the other party. It might also operate to restrict unjustified claim-splitting tactics.[224]

(ii) Abuse of rights and parallel arbitral proceedings

4.134 Whilst deploying the principle of abuse of rights to limit abusive parallel proceedings is not new, arbitral awards that dealt with this issue are scarce. However, the scarcity in the principle's use in this regard does not negate its importance and effectiveness in ensuring the good administration of justice.[225] Additionally, while the examples discussed below pertain to investment arbitration, there is no reason why the principle may not apply to similar cases in commercial arbitration.[226]

4.135 Three cases shall be examined to shed light on the operation of the principle and its effect on the administration of arbitral justice. As shall be discussed below, in the first case the arbitral tribunal refused to apply the principle of abuse of rights and as a result the administration of justice was seriously brought into disrepute. A contrario, in the second and third cases, requirements of good administration of justice mandated the arbitral tribunals to consider/apply the principle.

4.136 (a) ***CME* and *Lauder* cases** In these cases, the arbitration system enabled the investor to initiate two arbitration proceedings against the same State, in relation to the same dispute, merely for relying on different BITs. The cases pertained to the interference with television broadcasting rights granted by the Government of the Czech Republic to a foreign investor. Mr Ronald Lauder, a US national, invested in the television broadcaster through the company Central European Television which was controlled by the Dutch company, CME, of which Mr Lauder was the majority shareholder. Following allegations of expropriation, violation of the obligation of fair and equitable treatment and others, arbitration proceedings were initiated.[227]

4.137 Mr Lauder, relying on his US nationality, initiated arbitration proceedings against the Czech Republic in London based on the United States-Czech Republic BIT. Subsequently, CME initiated arbitration proceedings against the Czech Republic in Stockholm based on the Netherlands-Czech Republic BIT. Both proceedings related to the *same* dispute and raised the *same* legal questions, in relation to the liability of the Czech Republic.[228]

[224] Shany (n 210) 258–59.

[225] For a recent case, see *Caratube International Oil LLP and Mr Devincci Salah Hourani v Republic of Kazakhstan*, ICSID Case No ARB/13/13, Award of 27 September 2017, paras 372 and 376, where the Tribunal noted that 'the general principle of the prohibition of abuse of process applies in the context of multiple proceedings before international tribunals'.

[226] Gaillard (n 90) 23–24 and 32, (noting that parallel arbitration often takes place in commercial arbitration); Hanno Wehland, *The Coordination of Multiple Proceedings in Investment Treaty Arbitration* (Oxford University Press 2013), para 7.31.

[227] *CME Czech Republic BV v The Czech Republic*, UNCITRAL Arbitration Proceedings, Final Award of 14 March 2003, paras 1–33

[228] Yuval Shany, 'Similarity in the Eye of the Beholder: Revisiting the Application of Rules Governing Jurisdictional Conflicts in the Lauder/CME Cases' in Arthur W Rovine (ed), *Contemporary Issues in International Arbitration and Mediation* (Martinus Nijhoff 2007) 123.

The first constituted arbitral Tribunal sitting in London found that the investor failed to substantiate his claims and thus dismissed the claims.[229] A contrario, the second constituted Tribunal sitting in Stockholm produced an utterly conflicting award, whereby it held that the Czech Republic was liable.[230] **4.138**

The Lauder/CME saga elucidates that the potential pernicious effects of parallel proceedings to the administration of justice are not merely important theoretical observations, but have serious legal ramifications. The fact that the two arbitral Tribunals reached contradictory decisions regarding the same set of facts is rightly described as the *ultimate fiasco* in international arbitration.[231] Reaching conflicting decisions regarding the same legal question thwarts the administration of justice as it defies the rule of law, due process, legal certainty, the efficient administration of justice,[232] and may arguably result in an actual denial of justice.[233] **4.139**

It is argued that abuse of rights may operate in this context to temper and limit the right to initiate parallel proceedings by the requirements of good administration of arbitral justice. That said, the application of the principle of abuse of rights was raised albeit rejected by the arbitral Tribunals.[234] **4.140**

While the Respondent asserted that its application ensured the administration of justice as it eludes the risk of conflicting awards,[235] the Tribunals acknowledged the possibility of conflicting awards but did not apply the principle on the grounds that the causes of action and the claimants were not identical in both proceedings.[236] **4.141**

This case is an epitome of how the application of abuse of rights ensures the good administration of justice, and how failing to apply it (or misapplying it) may bring the administration of justice into disrepute. **4.142**

It is important to note that the decisions rendered by the Tribunals should not be considered a rejection of applying abuse of rights in the context of parallel proceedings. A contrario, the awards recognized the principle, but held that the conditions *sine qua non* for its application were not satisfied. Moreover, the Tribunal also recognized the competing principles/interests of the good administration of justice. Thus, while the Tribunal recognized the escalation of costs, efficiency, and the unfair possibility **4.143**

[229] *Ronald S Lauder v The Czech Republic*, UNCITRAL Arbitration Proceedings, Award of 3 September 2001, 74–75.

[230] *CME Czech Republic BV v The Czech Republic*, UNCITRAL Arbitration Proceedings, Final Award of 14 March 2003, para 620.

[231] Reinisch (n 212) 116.

[232] Robin F Hansen, 'Parallel Proceedings in Investor-State Treaty Arbitration: Responses for Treaty-Drafters, Arbitrators and Parties' (2010) 73 Modern Law Review 523, 529; Leboulanger (n 7) 62–63.

[233] Leboulanger (n 7) 63.

[234] *Ronald S Lauder v The Czech Republic*, UNCITRAL Arbitration Proceedings, Award of 3 September 2001, paras 174–80; *CME Czech Republic BV v The Czech Republic*, UNCITRAL Arbitration Proceedings, Partial Award of 13 September 2001, para 412.

[235] *Ronald S Lauder v The Czech Republic*, UNCITRAL Arbitration Proceedings, Award of 3 September 2001, para 169.

[236] ibid para 177.

of conflicting decisions associated with the continuation of parallel proceedings,[237] it decided that such interests could have been equally protected had the Respondent allowed the consolidation of the proceedings.

4.144 In finding no abuse of rights, both arbitral Tribunals emphasized the fact that the Respondent had refused, on several occasions, to consolidate the proceedings and refused to appoint the same arbitrators in the parallel proceedings.[238] This confirms that remedies based on abuse of rights may depend on the reasonable conduct of the aggrieved party.[239] It is acknowledged that consolidating the parallel proceedings or choosing the same arbitrators in both proceedings may be effective in ensuring the good administration of justice.[240]

4.145 The Tribunals erred in applying the principle of abuse of rights in that they adopted, for its application, the same conditions of the principles of *lis pendens* and *res judicata* (the triple identity test). The Tribunal noted that there was no abuse of right as the Claimants and the causes of action were not identical in both cases.[241] While this may be of relevance in the context of *lis pendens* and *res judicata*,[242] it should not be a *condicio sine qua non* for abuse of rights.[243] On the contrary, the principle of abuse of rights is of greater relevance in relation to proceedings that involve similar, but not identical, parties and causes of action.[244] Additionally, equating abuse of rights to the defences of *lis pendens* and *res judicata*, which are often dismissed unless the 'triple identity' test is satisfied, may encourage the abuse of the arbitral system.[245] Thus, abuse of rights

[237] ibid para 178.

[238] ibid paras 173–78; *CME Czech Republic BV v The Czech Republic*, UNCITRAL Arbitration Proceedings, Partial Award of 13 September 2001, para 412.

[239] Shany (n 228) 126–36; Wehland (n 226) para 7.31; Cremades and Madalena (n 203) 515; Mariel Dimsey, *The Resolution of International Investment Disputes: Challenges and Solutions* (Eleven International Publishing 2008) 94; Charles N Brower and Jeremy K Sharpe, 'Multiple and Conflicting International Arbitral Awards' (2003) 4 Journal of World Investment 211, 216.

[240] Leboulanger (n 7) 85 and 89; *Canfor Corporation v United States of America, Tembec et al v United States of America, and Terminal Forest Products Ltd v United States of America*, UNCITRAL, Order of the Consolidation Tribunal of 7 September 2005, para 131.

[241] *Ronald S Lauder v The Czech Republic*, UNCITRAL Arbitration Proceedings, Award of 3 September 2001, para 177.

[242] Even in the context of *lis pendens* and *res judicata*, recent trends, as endorsed in the ILA Report, encourage a more liberal definition of parties: International Law Association, *Final Report on Lis Pendens and Arbitration* (Toronto 2006) para 5.6. ('The recommendation defined "parallel Proceedings" in terms of parties and issues that are the same or substantially the same, rather than in terms of the triple identity test').

[243] The principle of abuse of rights is not an alter ego of *lis pendens* or *res judicata* but has a different and broader sphere of operation. Wehland (n 226) para 7.31; Brown (n 83) 7; Cremades and Madalena (n 203); Filip De Ly and Audley Sheppard, 'ILA Final Report on Lis Pendens and Arbitration' (2009) 25 Arbitration International 3, 80; Carlos S Anzorena, 'Multiplicity of Claims under BITs and the Argentine Case' (2005) 2(2) Transnational Dispute Management, 25.

[244] *Dallal v Bank Mellat* [1986] QB 441, 452 (where the Court applied the principle of abuse of process even though the case was not identical to the subsequent case, given that the application of abuse of process does not require identical parties, causes of action, and relief, unlike the principle of *res judicata*. The Court stated that: 'the question whether an action is an abuse of the process of the court, although closely related to the question whether or not a defence of res judicata exists, is not the same question. Thus the legal defence may be subject to or circumscribed by strict legal criteria whereas the complaint that an action is an abuse of the process of the court does not solely depend on the availability of such a defence and, therefore, broader criteria can be applied'; Shany (n 210) 259.

[245] Cremades and Madalena (n 203) 538; Ryan (n 116) 5.

should be established, not based on any rigid rules, but by considering all interests involved.[246]

Accordingly, a material impediment to standards of fairness, requirements of due process, and the broader notion of administration of justice materialized in these cases as a result of not applying, or misapplying, the principle of abuse of rights. As rightly recognized by scholars and arbitrators, avoidance of conflicting decisions is a requirement of fairness, due process, and efficiency, and the materialization of such risk is a serious defiance to the administration of justice.[247] **4.146**

(b) *Ampal-American Israel Corp et al v Arab Republic of Egypt* The recent award in the case of *Ampal-American Israel Corp et al v Arab Republic of Egypt*[248] also demonstrates the importance of the principle as a requirement of the good administration of arbitral justice. **4.147**

The case involved the termination of a gas supply purchase agreement made after many interruptions in the gas supply as a result of terrorist activity following the revolution that took place in Egypt in 2011. **4.148**

This dispute gave rise to four parallel commercial and investment arbitrations. Ampal Corporation (a company incorporated under the laws of New York), Mr David Fisher (a national of Germany), and other investors who directly or indirectly own the East Mediterranean Gas company ('EMG'), brought ICSID proceedings against the Arab Republic of Egypt. **4.149**

Other than the ICSID case being discussed, the dispute gave rise to another three arbitration proceedings: an ICC arbitration in Geneva brought by EMG against the Egyptian General Petroleum Corporation ('EGPC') and the Egyptian Natural Gas Holding Company ('EGAS');[249] EGPC and EGAS initiated arbitration proceedings against EMG in Cairo under the auspices of the Cairo Regional Centre of International Commercial Arbitration ('CRCICA');[250] and another parallel investment treaty arbitration under the UNCITRAL Rules brought by a Polish-Israeli national, Yosef Maiman, and three other companies including Ampal's subsidiary, Merhav Ampal Group Ltd.[251] **4.150**

[246] Shany (n 210) 258–59; *Tidewater Inc et al v the Bolivarian Republic of Venezuela*, ICSID Case No ARB/10/5, Decision on Jurisdiction of 8 February 2013, para 147

[247] Kabra (n 64) 450; *Canfor Corporation v United States of America, Tembec et al v United States of America, and Terminal Forest Products Ltd v United States of America*, UNCITRAL, Order of the Consolidation Tribunal of 7 September 2005, para 131.

[248] *Ampal-American Israel Corp et al v Arab Republic of Egypt*, ICSID Case No ARB/12/11, Decision on Jurisdiction of 1 February 2016.

[249] ICC Case No 18215/GZ/MHM (unpublished) referred to in Gaillard (n 90) 17. An award was rendered in this case ordering EGPC and EGAS to pay 1.7 billion dollars to Israeli State-owned corporation (IEC) and an amount of 288 million dollars to EMG. Douglas Thomson, 'Israel Wins Gas Supply Claim Against Egypt', (2015) 1 Global Arbitration Review <http://globalarbitrationreview.com/article/1034988/israel-wins-gas-supply-claim-against-egypt> accessed 15 February 2019

[250] CRCICA Case No 829/2012 (unpublished), referred to in Gaillard (n 90) 17.

[251] Summary of the cases in *Ampal-American Israel Corp et al v Arab Republic of Egypt*, ICSID Case No ARB/12/11, Decision on Jurisdiction on 1 February 2016, paras 10–15.

4.151 Gaillard, who represented the Egyptian State in the arbitrations, noted that the initiation of multiple separate arbitrations was 'archetype of abusive procedural conduct'.[252] To that effect, in the ICSID case, Egypt asserted that the Claimants' claims were inadmissible as they constituted an abuse of right. Egypt further alleged that: parallel proceedings were brought to seek to multiply the chances of recovery; part of the Claimants' claim related to the same 12.5 per cent indirect interest in EMG for which Ampal's subsidiary, Merhav-Ampal, claimed in the parallel proceedings; and that Egypt did not consent to be subject to multiple proceedings.[253] On the other hand, the Claimants asserted that there was no abuse of right given that, inter alia, Egypt refused the consolidation of the parallel proceedings.[254]

4.152 The arbitral Tribunal first recognized the principle of abuse of rights and noted that the existence of four parallel arbitration proceedings, involving the same facts, witnesses and claims, may be abusive.[255] The Tribunal then noted that different investors may pursue multiple claims in different fora, even if such claims arise from the same factual matrix. This is not, per se, abusive. The Tribunal then stipulated that parallel arbitration 'may not be a desirable situation but it cannot be characterised as abusive especially when the Respondent has declined the Claimants' offers to consolidate the proceedings'.[256]

4.153 However, in order to mitigate the risk of contradictory awards and to ensure the good administration of justice, the Tribunal found that there was an abuse of right in relation to a portion of the Claimants' claims. In this regard, the Tribunal found that the Claimant Ampal, which was controlled by Mr Yosef Maiman, advanced its claims in relation to the same 12.5 per cent indirect interest in EMG for which Ampal's subsidiaries claim in the parallel arbitration proceedings. To that effect, it noted:

> [W]hile the same party in interest might *reasonably* seek to protect its claim in two fora where the jurisdiction of each tribunal is *unclear, once jurisdiction is otherwise confirmed, it would crystallize in an abuse of process for in substance the same claim is to be pursued on the merits before two tribunals.*[257] (Emphasis added)

4.154 Given that both Tribunals had decided that they had jurisdiction regarding this portion of the claim, there was no risk of denial of justice and accordingly, the Tribunal ordered *Ampal* to cure the abuse by pursuing this claim only before one Tribunal and withdraw it from the other parallel proceedings to avoid double recovery or conflicting awards.[258]

252 Thomson (n 249) 3.
253 *Ampal-American Israel Corp et al v Arab Republic of Egypt*, ICSID Case No ARB/12/11, Decision on Jurisdiction of 1 February 2016, para 313.
254 ibid para 321.
255 ibid para 328.
256 ibid para 329.
257 ibid para 331.
258 ibid paras 333–34; Sebastian Perry, 'Panel Forbids Duplicate Claims in Egyptian Gas Dispute' (2016) 2 Global Arbitration Review <http://globalarbitrationreview.com/article/1036361/panel-forbids-duplicate-claims-in-egyptian-gas-dispute> accessed 20 February 2019.

This decision confirmed the role of abuse of rights in balancing the competing interests of the good administration of justice. The Tribunal recognized one's right to initiate parallel proceedings and one's right to be heard before the competent tribunal based on the relevant BIT (all requirements of due process).[259] However, these interests were balanced against the Respondent's interests to preclude the escalation of costs, safeguard efficiency, and avoid the risk of inconsistent decisions which greatly affect the fairness of the proceedings and ensuing justice.[260] **4.155**

As previously mentioned, the notion of fairness (as part of the good administration of justice) refers to standards of reasonable procedural conduct.[261] That said, whilst one considers the Tribunal to have embraced an overly narrow application of the principle,[262] it appears that abuse was only partially established and did not apply to preclude the initiation of parallel proceedings in relation to the other claims given the unreasonable conduct of the respondent. The Tribunal considered that the Respondent acted unreasonably in that it: refused the consolidation of the proceedings of the two commercial and two investment proceedings; challenged the appointment of the same arbitrator in the parallel proceedings; and initiated parallel proceedings in Cairo. Thus, it seems that the Tribunal did not ascertain the seriousness of the risks associated with parallel proceedings given the unreasonable conduct of the Respondent.[263] One finds it apt to assert that the conduct of Egypt in refusing to appoint the same arbitrator may be characterized as an abuse of right and conduct which arguably defies the good administration of arbitral justice. As rightly noted by Leboulanger: **4.156**

> But, as all rights are susceptible of abuse, a party may abuse its right to designate an arbitrator. The attitude of a party who refuses to designate the same arbitrator in the parallel arbitral panels might be considered as a violation of its obligation to perform, in good faith, its undertakings assumed under the arbitration clause.[264]

On a related note, whilst the decision in *CME/Lauder* recognized the importance of the conduct of the aggrieved party in assessing the abuse of rights claim, it did not specify that it constituted a condition for the principle's application. This is confirmed by the fact that while Egypt declined the consolidation attempts, the Tribunal still found that a portion of the claim constituted an abuse of rights. One may deduce from this decision that if the claims in the parallel proceedings are, wholly or partly, identical, requirements of good administration of justice mandates finding an abuse of right regardless **4.157**

[259] *Ampal-American Israel Corp et al v Arab Republic of Egypt*, ICSID Case No ARB/12/11, Decision on Jurisdiction of 1 February 2016, paras 321(iv) and 329.

[260] ibid paras 328 and 330–39.

[261] De Ly (n 12) 37.

[262] It is submitted that the principle's application should not generally be limited to this portion of the claim, but should extend to prevent claimants from bifurcating their overlapping claims and pursuing them before different tribunals. This is prejudicial to the other party as it allows claimants to maximize their chances of obtaining a favourable outcome while placing the other party in a disadvantageous, unequal, position. Gaillard (n 90) 25–26.

[263] *Ampal-American Israel Corp et al v Arab Republic of Egypt*, ICSID Case No ARB/12/11, Decision on Jurisdiction of 1 February 2016, para 329.

[264] Leboulanger (n 7) 92.

of the opposing party's conduct. On the other hand, if the issues raised are just similar, the conduct of the aggrieved party becomes instrumental.

4.158 (c) ***Orascom TMT Investments v People's Democratic Republic of Algeria*** In the recent ICSID case of *Orascom TMT Investments v Algeria*,[265] the application of abuse of rights and its proactive role/function in the good administration of arbitral justice was more explicit and illustrative.

4.159 A dispute arose from Orascom's alleged investment to build a mobile telecom network for Algeria. The Claimant alleged that Algeria took measures against it, mainly through tax reassessments, due to a political vendetta against the Claimant's Egyptian controlling shareholder as a result of a policy shift against foreign investment.

4.160 The Respondent alleged, inter alia, that the claims asserted by the Claimant were inadmissible as they were tantamount to an abuse of rights. Mr Sawiris, the Claimant's ultimate shareholder, introduced different arbitrations against the Respondent at different levels of the chain of companies under different BITs. The Respondent submitted that this conduct, aimed at maximizing the chances of success, was unfair and an abuse to the protection offered by Algeria to foreign investors. As stated by the Respondent, the principle of abuse of rights should operate to limit the right of multiple shareholders belonging to the same group to initiate proceedings.[266] The Claimant argued that the principle should not extend to limit parallel arbitral proceedings.[267]

4.161 The arbitral Tribunal found that the Claimant's claims were inadmissible and that the initiation of the proceedings constituted an abuse of rights. Whilst acknowledging that the principle had been mainly applied in cases of restructuring an investment to gain access to arbitration, the Tribunal noted that, as a general principle of law, abuse of rights may equally apply in other areas of arbitration law including in the context of parallel proceedings.[268]

4.162 In delineating the application of the principle in the context of parallel proceedings, the Tribunal noted that an investor who controls several entities may commit an abuse of right where he/she relies on different BITs and seeks to impugn the host state for the same measures and claims for the same damage at different levels of the chain. While recognizing that structuring an investment through layers of corporate entities is a right and can be exercised to pursue legitimate purposes, the Tribunal balanced this against other potent interests of the administration of arbitral justice, namely, fairness, waste of resources, and the possibility of multiple recoveries and conflicting decisions.[269]

4.163 It is of particular interest to note that the Tribunal explicitly considered the decisions rendered in the *CME* and *Lauder* cases mentioned above and acknowledged that the

[265] *Orascom TMT Investments Sàrl*, ICSID Case No ARB/12/35, Award of 31 May 2017.
[266] ibid paras 417–19.
[267] ibid paras 449–50.
[268] ibid paras 540–41.
[269] ibid paras 542–43.

failure to apply abuse of rights in those cases led to the issuance of conflicting awards. Moreover, it is to be mentioned that, unlike the cases mentioned above, there were no offers to consolidate the proceedings in this case, and thus one may deduce that applying abuse of rights was more flagrant as the Respondent did not commit any abuse from his side.[270]

Based on the above, it appears that the application of abuse of rights to ensure the good administration of arbitral justice is unequivocal. The cases referred to above clearly demonstrate how the operation of the principle may effectively ensure the fairness and efficiency of the proceedings while safeguarding the requirements of due process. **4.164**

3. The extension of arbitration clause to a non-signatory

Arbitration is generally consent driven and autonomy oriented. Entering into an arbitration agreement is the crucial *condicio sine qua non* for a party to have a right and/or be compelled to participate in the arbitration process.[271] Accordingly, an arbitration agreement generally only binds its parties in accordance with the sacrosanct principle of 'privity'.[272] **4.165**

Arbitration agreements must comply with certain substantive and formal requirements to be valid. The degree of stringency of such requirements vary from one jurisdiction to another.[273] Such pre-requisites of permitting arbitration emanates from the fact that arbitration was originally seen as an exception to the general sacred right to submit disputes to the competent national court.[274] It is often overlooked that such conditions may seem unfair given that an arbitrator has become, arguably, the 'natural judge' in the international business world and that arbitration has become the ordinary dispute resolution mechanism for cross-border disputes.[275] **4.166**

Notwithstanding the above-mentioned, requirements of good administration of justice, commanded legislators, courts, and arbitral tribunals, in some circumstances, to broaden the definition of a 'party' and the scope of a 'contract' and extend the effect of the arbitration agreement to encompass related contracts and non-signatories to the arbitral proceedings based on divergent doctrines and/or principles.[276] **4.167**

[270] ibid para 547.

[271] Stavros Brekoulakis, *Third Parties in International Commercial Arbitration* (Oxford University Press 2010), para 1.09; Egyptian Supreme Constitutional Court, Session held on 13 January 2002, no 155, Judicial Year 20; Egyptian Supreme Constitutional Court, Session held on 3 July 1999, no 104, Judicial Year 20; Egyptian Supreme Constitutional Court, Session held on 6 November 1999, no 84, Judicial Year 19.

[272] Emmanuel Gaillard and John Savage (eds), *Fouchard Gaillard Goldman on International Commercial Arbitration* (Kluwer Law International 1999) 414.

[273] Born (n 1) 657–58 and 833–34.

[274] Otto Sandrock, 'Arbitration Agreements and Groups of Companies' (1993) 27 The International Lawyer 941, 949–50.

[275] Hanotiau (n 101) 103; Julian DM Lew, *Applicable Law in International Commercial Arbitration: A Study in Commercial Arbitration Awards* (Oceana Publications 1978) 413; Paulsson (n 95) 2.

[276] Stavros L Brekoulakis, '*Arbitration and Third Parties*' (PhD thesis, Queen Mary University of London 2008) 153–54; Paris Court of Appeal, First Chamber, 7 December 1994, Review Arbitrage 2 (1996), 245–49 (relying on the notion of good administration of justice), referred to in Karim Youssef, 'The Limits of Consent: The Right or Obligation to Arbitrate of Non-signatories in Group of Companies' in Bernard Hanotiau and Eric A Schwartz (eds), *Multiparty Arbitration* (ICC Publications 2010) 90.

4.168 Thus, it is well-established that legal mechanisms and principles that aid arbitral tribunals to include non-signatories in international arbitration enhance the efficiency and increase the fairness of the arbitral process:

> As courts traditionally may be restrictive toward inclusion of third parties, Multicontract arbitration leads to efficiency, inclusion of all relevant parties and facts, subsequent improvement in consideration of due process and, ultimately, more fairness in arbitral proceedings.[277]

4.169 The doctrines and principles belying extension are either consent driven or founded on equitable considerations.[278] While inferring consent in the former doctrines is, in many cases, largely specious, consent may be lacking in the latter cases. Accordingly, it seems that the concept of consent, in general, is not able alone to elucidate and vindicate the notion of extension and that there is a dire need for a legal principle to better assist decision makers to join non-signatories to ensure the good administration of arbitral justice.[279]

4.170 It is submitted that the application of abuse of rights to issues of non-signatories is an effective principle utilized by arbitrators to balance the competing interests of fairness, efficiency, and due process, and serves the administration of justice.

4.171 The operation of abuse of rights in the context of extension of arbitration clauses raises an important question regarding the role of the principle. In most mentioned applications of abuse of rights, the principle applied to ameliorate the rigidity and harshness of an already existing legal/contractual right. However, as previously mentioned, the principle of abuse of rights may be used to create a *new* contractual right/obligation to avoid an unfair or an inequitable outcome.[280] In such circumstances, the principle appears in its most extensive reach and acts more as a sword than a shield. It is suggested that the operation of the principle in the context of extension of an arbitration clause comprises an epitome of this as it operates to *establish* jurisdiction against a non-signatory.

4.172 As shall be discussed below, resorting to the principle of abuse of rights is not peculiar to the arbitral practice. The principle has been expressly applied in some instances as the legal basis for the extension of the arbitration clause, and in other cases while not explicitly referred to, the *raison d'être* of abuse of rights remains conspicuous where it has been utilized primarily to preserve the reasonable expectations of the parties and to advance the fairness and efficiency of the proceedings. Whilst most cases referring

277 Japaridze (n 15) 1432.

278 Born (n 1) 1433.

279 Stavros Brekoulakis, 'Parties in International Arbitration: Consent v Commercial Reality' in Stavros Brekoulakis, Julian DM Lew, and Loukas Mistelis (eds), *The Evolution and Future of International Arbitration* (Kluwer Law International 2016) paras 8.10–8.15.

280 Quebec Superior Court in *Posluns v Enterprises Lormil Inc* [1990], Quebec 200-05-001584-858, JE 90-1131 (CS), cited in Rosalie Jukier, 'Banque Nationale du Canada v. Houle (S.C.C.): Implications of an Expanded Doctrine of Abuse of Rights in Civilian Contract Law' (1992) 37 McGill Law Journal 221, 235 (where the court applied the principle of abuse of rights to create a contractual provision of a guarantee of exclusivity which was not part of the contract).

to the principle pertain to the theory of piercing the corporate veil or alter ego, other examples shall outline the applicability of abuse of rights to other cases of extension.

However, prior to embarking on an analysis of how abuse of rights operates to ensure the good administration of arbitral justice in relation to issues of extension, it seems proper to first succinctly examine the relevant competing interests that arise where one requests the extension of the arbitration clause to a non-signatory. By and large, these interests are similar to those mentioned in relation to parallel arbitral proceedings. **4.173**

(i) Competing interests relating to the extension of an arbitration clause

In the context of extension of an arbitration clause to non-signatories, diverse competing interests of the parties exist. It involves a multiplicity of interests that primarily rest on those pursued by the party requesting the extension and those of the party(ies) opposing such extension. These interests often fall within the ambit of the administration of justice, that is, they involve interests that are part of due process,[281] protecting parties' reasonable expectations, and interests of procedural efficiency and fairness of the proceedings.[282] **4.174**

Thus, it is well acknowledged that third-party mechanisms are designed to enhance the procedural harmonization and efficiency of arbitral proceedings. The bifurcation of arbitral proceedings lead to a waste of legal and financial resources.[283] Moreover, such bifurcation may lead to irreconcilable or conflicting decisions regarding the same, or intertwined, matters between interrelated parties which is undesirable and may affect the fairness of the process.[284] **4.175**

However, given that consent often remains an important requirement for extension of an arbitration clause, considerations of justice, equity, and efficiency often compete with consent.[285] Arbitrators often rely on good administration of justice, including the notions of equity, fairness, and that of procedural efficiency in assessing whether to extend an arbitration clause.[286] **4.176**

On the other hand, issues regarding the extension of an arbitration clause and multi-party/multi-contract arbitration may raise questions regarding the equality between the parties, particularly in relation to the appointment of the arbitral tribunal. This **4.177**

281 Yaraslau Kryvoi, 'Piercing the Corporate Veil in International Arbitration' (2011) 1 Global Business Law Review 169, 176.

282 Aubrey Laine Thomas, 'Nonsignatories in Arbitration: A Good-Faith Analysis' (2010) 14 Lewis and Clark Law Review 966, 964; *Grigson v Creative Artists Agency LLC*, 219 F 3d 524, 528 (5th Cir 2000).

283 Bond (n 212) 36.

284 *Alfred McAlpine Construction Limited v Unex Corporation Ltd* [1994] 38 Con LR 63, 77; *Abu Dhabi Gas Liquefaction Co v Eastern Bechtel Corp* [1982] 2 Lloyd's Rep 425, 427 ('It is most undesirable that there should be inconsistent finding by two separate arbitrators on virtually the self-same question, such as causation. It is very desirable that everything should be done to avoid such a circumstance').

285 Youssef (n 276) 71–72.

286 *Westland Helicopters Ltd v Arab Organization for Industrialization, et al*, Interim Award, ICC Case No 3879 of 1984, (1986) XI Ybk Commercial Arbitration 127, 132; Hanotiau (n 8) 47; John M Townsend, 'Non-Signatories and Arbitration' (1998) 3 ADR Currents 19, 23; James M Hosking, 'Non-Signatories and International Arbitration in the United States: the Quest for Consent' (2004) 20 Arbitration International 289, 303.

fundamental interest was illustrated in the well-known *Dutco* case.[287] The dispute involved three parties and the agreement included an ICC arbitration clause providing for the appointment of three arbitrators. While *Dutco* nominated its arbitrator, the other two Respondents were unable to agree on one arbitrator given that their interests were not aligned. However, to avoid the appointment of the arbitrator by the ICC they jointly nominated an arbitrator while reserving their right to challenge that appointment. The Respondents then challenged the award before the French courts. The French Court of Cassation invalidated the award and provided that it violated the principle of equality between the parties. It should be noted that while many have raised some concerns in relation to the *Dutco* decision, lots of arbitral institutions have subsequently amended their rules in order to comply with the principles laid down by the French Court of Cassation.[288]

4.178 Additionally, the question of extension of an arbitration clause may raise other issues of due process. This is particularly evident where one acknowledges the fact that a decision to extend an arbitration clause to a non-signatory results in the latter losing his/her proverbial day in court (deprives the non-signatory of judicial access).[289] Thus, a decision to extend an arbitration clause or to join a non-signatory despite the lack of the latter's clear and unambiguous consent to arbitrate may raise questions regarding requirements of due process and fair trial.[290]

4.179 On a related note, the problem of extension primarily affects the reasonable expectations of parties, the preservation of which is an intrinsic element of the administration of justice.[291] The parties' reasonable expectations may be thwarted where a request of extension is granted or denied depending on the factual matrix of each case. Parties have a legitimate and reasonable expectation to have an efficient resolution of the dispute.[292] Moreover, there is an equally reasonable expectation that arbitral proceedings should be harmonized and not result in any conflicting decisions.[293] It is acknowledged that parties trust international arbitration as a dispute resolution mechanism that can effectively put an end to a given dispute. This expectation may be frustrated where a non-signatory is allowed to bring before another forum a question that has been determined by the arbitrators.[294]

4.180 Another particularly important interest that appears conspicuous in the context of extension of an arbitration clause, and similarly linked to parties' reasonable expectations, is the need to bar one's inconsistent conduct to the detriment of another. Such

[287] Hanotiau (n 8) paras 443–57.
[288] Schwartz (n 206) 16.
[289] William W Park, 'Non-Signatories and International Disputes: An Arbitrator's Dilemma' in Permanent Court of Arbitration, *Multiple Party Actions in International Arbitration* (Oxford University Press 2009) para 1.56; Leboulanger (n 7) 67–68.
[290] Youssef (n 276) 73.
[291] De Ly (n 12) 37.
[292] Pryles and Waincymer (n 213) 56.
[293] Born (n 217) 1074.
[294] Brekoulakis (n 276) 144.

preclusion arguably maintains the fairness of proceedings and ensures the good administration of arbitral justice.[295] As rightly stated by the United States Court of Appeal: 'the legal principle [underlying the theory of equitable estoppel] rests on a simple proposition: it is unfair for a party to rely on a contract when it works to its advantage, and repudiate it when it works to its disadvantage'.[296]

Moreover, it is submitted that safeguarding the parties' reasonable expectations constitutes the main rationale behind many of the arbitration decisions regarding extension of arbitration, despite the fact that arbitrators justify those decisions on other grounds, such as the group of companies. **4.181**

Thus, barring a party from denying or alleging certain facts or course of action owing to that party's previous conduct, which comprises the established maxim, *venire contra factum proprium*, is a fundamental requirement of fairness, is recognized as a general principle of law, and is applied by arbitral tribunals and national courts.[297] While this may be often based on the broader principle of good faith,[298] the principle of abuse of rights equally provides that 'no exercise of rights will be given legal recognition if it is contrary to former conduct'.[299] No system or court should tolerate such conduct in light of the sacred tenet: he who attempts to negate what has been maintained shall be precluded and estopped. **4.182**

As shall be seen below, the principle of abuse of rights is an effective tool utilized by arbitrators to advance, and strike the balance required between, the mentioned interests and to serve the overall administration of justice. It operates in certain cases to prevent material fraud or injustice, and applies in other exceptional cases to safeguard **4.183**

[295] Brekoulakis (n 271) para 4.03 (noting that arbitral *estoppel* emanates from the principle of *venire contra factum proprium* which rests on considerations of fairness and equity).

[296] *American Bankers Insurance Group v Richard F Long and Lillie M Long*, 453 F 3d 623, 627 (4th Cir 2006); *Wachovia Bank, National Association v Schmidt*, 445 F 3d 762, 769 (4th Cir 2006).

[297] Gaillard and Savage (n 272) 820; Born (n 1) 1472–73; Klaus Peter Berger, 'The International Arbitrator's Dilemma: Transnational Procedure versus Home Jurisdiction: A German Perspective' (2009) 25 Arbitration International 217, 233; Klaus Peter Berger, *The Creeping Codification of the Lex Mercatoria* (Kluwer Law International 1999) 221; Park (n 289) para 1.51; Michael Joachim Bonell, *An International Restatement of Contract Law: The UNIDROIT Principles of International Commercial Contracts* (3rd edn, Transnational Publishers 2005) 1343; ICC Case No 12456 of 2004, in Jean-Jacquez Arnaldez, Yves Derains, and Dominique Hascher (eds), *Collection of ICC Arbitral Awards 2008-2011* (Kluwer Law International 2013) 811; ICC Case No 5832 of 1988, in Yves Derains, Sigvard Jarvin, and JJ Arnaldez (eds), *ICC Arbitral Awards 1986-1990* (ICC Publications 1994) 547.

[298] Richard E Speidel, 'The "Duty" of Good Faith in Contract Performance and Enforcement' (1996) 46 Journal of Legal Education 537, 540–01; Bin Cheng, *General Principles of Law as Applied by International Courts and Tribunals* (Cambridge University Press 2006) 141–2.

[299] ICC Case No 7421 of 2010, (2010) 21 ICC International Court of Arbitration Bulletin 64; Vera Bolgar, 'Abuse of Rights in France, Germany, and Switzerland: A Survey of a Recent Chapter in Legal Doctrine' (1975) 35 Louisiana Law Review 1027 (German law), and 1033 (providing that Switzerland applies the abuse of rights principle to bar parties from contradicting their previous conduct); Born (n 1) 1472–73; Edward Baldwin, Mark Kantor, and Michael Nolan, 'Limits of Enforcement of ICSID Awards' (2006) 23 Journal of International Arbitration 1, 18–19; Zimmermann and Verse (n 140) 515–16; Matthias E Storme 'Case 22: Sitting on One's Rights - Belgium', in Zimmermann and Whittaker (n 140) 520–21; Talya Uçaryılmaz, 'Equitable Estoppel and CISG' (2013) 3(2) Hacettepe Hukuk Fak Derg 161, 161–78; ICC Case No 6294 of 1991, 118 Clunet 1050 (1991), 1052, available at: https://www.trans-lex.org/206294 (accessed 10 February 2019); ICC Case No 12456 of 2004, in Jean-Jacquez Arnaldez, Yves Derains, and Dominique Hascher (eds), *Collection of ICC Arbitral Awards 2008-2011* (Kluwer Law International 2013) 826; ICC Interim Award, Case No 10671 of 2000, (2006) Clunet 1417, 1422 <https://www.trans-lex.org/210671> accessed 10 February 2019.

the procedural efficiency of the proceedings and to preserve the parties' reasonable expectations.

(ii) Extension of an arbitration clause on the basis of abuse of rights

4.184 This section examines the application of abuse of rights to decide questions of extension. One shall first highlight that the principle is well-recognized as the legal basis for extension based on the theory of piercing/lifting the corporate veil. Subsequently, it shall be noted that the principle equally applies in other cases of extension to safeguard the parties' reasonable expectations, to ensure the fairness of the proceedings, and to enhance the procedural efficiency of the proceedings.

4.185 **(a) Piercing/lifting the corporate veil** It is widely recognized that in exceptional cases an arbitral tribunal may rely on the principle of abuse of rights to disregard the separate legal personality of an entity and extend the arbitration clause pursuant to the theory of piercing/lifting the corporate veil or the theory of alter ego.[300]

4.186 Extension of an arbitration clause on the basis of piercing the corporate veil is directly linked to the notion of good administration of justice. The *raison d'être* of piercing the corporate veil is the notions of equity and fairness.[301] In demystifying the theory of veil-piercing, it is said that it is 'an equitable remedy aimed to address the abuse of rights and to ensure the exercise of good faith in relation to a body corporate.'[302] Decisions to pierce the corporate veil emanate from the dire need to administer justice by attempting to achieve fairness and reach a reasonable and equitable outcome.[303]

4.187 In this regard, it is well-established that the principle of abuse of rights constitutes the juridical basis for the extension of the arbitration clause on the basis of piercing/lifting the corporate veil.[304] This is the prevailing approach in international law and is not peculiar to national laws.

4.188 On the international-law level, abuse of rights is recognized as the basis for piercing the corporate veil and is applied by the International Court of Justice ('ICJ'). As previously mentioned, in the case of *Barcelona Traction*,[305] the ICJ provided that requirements

[300] Hanotiau (n 8) 79–80 and 98; Albert Badia, *Piercing the Veil of State Enterprises in International Arbitration* (Kluwer Law International 2014) 49–50. Sébastien Besson, 'Piercing the Corporate Veil: Back on the Right Track' in Bernard Hanotiau and Eric A Schwartz (eds), *Multiparty Arbitration* (ICC Publications 2010) 149; Born (n 1) 1433.

[301] Henry W Ballantine, 'Separate Entity of Parent and Subsidiary Corporations' (1925) 14 California Law Review 12, 19; Robert B Thompson, 'Piercing the Corporate Veil: An Empirical Study' (1991) 76 Cornell Law Review 1036, 1045; Richard Ramberg, 'Piercing the Corporate Veil: Comparing the United States with Sweden' (2011) 17 New England Journal of International and Comparative Law 159, 160; *Trustees of the National Elevator Industry Pension v Andrew Lutyk*, 332 F 3d 188, 198 (3rd Cir 2003); *Bridas SAPIC et al v Turkmenistan*, 447 F 3d 411, 420 (5th Cir 2006).

[302] Badia (n 300) 49–50.

[303] ibid 57; *N C Ratiu et al v D P Conway* [2005] EWCA Civ 1302, para 75.

[304] Badia (n 300) 49–50; Voser (n 220) para 9.79; ICC Case No 8163 of 1996, 16(2) ICC Bulletin 78 (2005); *Prest v Petrodel Resources Ltd* [2013] 2 AC 415 17–18 ('Most advanced legal systems recognise corporate legal personality while acknowledging some limits to its logical implications. In civil law jurisdictions, the juridical basis of the exceptions is generally the concept of abuse of rights').

[305] *Barcelona Traction (Belgium v Spain)* [1970] ICJ 39, Judgment of 5 February 1970.

of fairness and equity mandate that the corporate veil may be pierced where the legal personality has been used for a purpose other than that for which it was originally intended to serve.[306] Additionally, the ICJ stipulated that piercing or lifting the corporate veil is warranted, inter alia, to prevent *the misuse of the privileges of the legal personality*, in cases of fraud and malfeasance, and to protect those dealing with the corporate entity.[307]

Similarly, Dolzer submitted an expert opinion in the *Yukos* case before the United States District Court of Columbia and noted that abuse of rights is a general principle of law. Moreover, he recognized that the corporate veil may be lifted under international law in the event of an abuse of right.[308] **4.189**

On the municipal law level, the principle of abuse of rights is of great importance in this regard. In Switzerland, the principle is 'omnipresent and permeates the Swiss legal tradition'.[309] Thus, while Switzerland rejects the notion of group of companies piercing the corporate veil (*Theorie des Durchgriffs*) allows courts and arbitral tribunals to lift and disregard the sacrosanct corporate veil in cases of abuse of rights.[310] **4.190**

In ICC Case No 3879 of 1984, the arbitral tribunal, applying Swiss law, stated that 'equity, in common with principles of international law, allows the corporate veil to be lifted, in order to protect third parties against an abuse which would be to their detriment'.[311] **4.191**

In *Alpha SA v Beta*,[312] the issues of group of companies and piercing the corporate veil were discussed. In this case, the arbitral Tribunal pinpointed that the group of companies doctrine was not recognized under Swiss law.[313] However, the Tribunal decided to pierce the corporate veil in order to bind the non-signatory parent. In reaching its decision, it noted that: **4.192**

> [P]iercing the corporate veil was only warranted where (i) a shareholder had total control over an entity, evinced by insufficient capitalization, confusion in the administration and management, and confusion of assets, and (ii) the totality of circumstances constituted an abuse of rights.[314]

Swiss decisions pertaining to lifting the corporate veil 'are all based on the concept of abuse of rights'.[315] As stated by Poudret: **4.193**

306 ibid para 56.
307 ibid paras 56–58.
308 See Expert Opinion of Professor Rudolf Dolzer in the case of *Hulley Enterprises, Yukos Universal and Veteran Petroleum v the Russian Federation*, 20 October 2015, paras 164–66.
309 Tobias Zuberbühler, 'Non-signatories and the Consensus to Arbitrate' (2008) 26 ASA Bulletin 18, 30–31.
310 Ad-hoc Interim Award, in the case of *FR German Engineering Company v Polish buyer*, 9 September 1983, in Albert Jan van den Berg (ed) (1987) 12 Ybk Commercial Arbitration 63, 72.
311 *Westland Helicopters Ltd v Arab Organization, et al*, Interim Award, ICC Case No 3879 of 1984, (1986) XI Ybk Commercial Arbitration 127, 132.
312 *Alpha SA v Beta and Co State Company of Ruritanian Law*, Ad hoc Award of 1991, 2 ASA Bulletin 202, discussed in Brekoulakis (n 12) para 8.99.
313 Zuberbühler (n 309) 25–26.
314 ibid 29.
315 This is based on Article 2 of the Swiss Civil Code; Ad-hoc Interim Award, in the case of *FR German Engineering Company v Polish buyer*, 9 September 1983, (1987) 12 Ybk Commercial Arbitration 63, 72; Swiss

> Swiss law *ignores the notion of a group of companies* [. . .] and is resolutely committed to the legal independence of the company in relation to its sole shareholder or of the subsidiary in relation to the parent company. *It will only be disregarded in exceptional circumstances*, where the fact of resorting to such a subsidiary to escape one's obligations would amount to fraud or to a *patent abuse of right*.[316] (Emphasis added)

4.194 The above is consistent with the prevailing principles under other national laws. In ICC Case No 5721,[317] the Claimant concluded two sub-contracts with X Egypt, which claimed to be a subsidiary of X USA. The sub-contracts were signed on behalf of X Egypt by Z, the president and a shareholder of X USA. Where a dispute arose, the Claimant brought arbitration proceedings against X Egypt, X USA, and Z. X USA and Z challenged the Tribunal's jurisdiction. The Tribunal found that it had jurisdiction over X USA, given that X Egypt was not a separate legal entity, but was merely a branch office. In assessing whether the arbitration clause should be extended to Z, the arbitral Tribunal looked into Egyptian law, as the substantive law, and Swiss law, as the *lex arbitri*, and held that piercing the corporate veil was warranted in cases of abuse of right.[318]

4.195 Similarly, piercing the corporate veil is possible in Germany in cases of fundamental abuse and misconduct.[319] Accordingly, the Germen Federal Supreme Court provided that the doctrinal foundation of piercing the corporate veil was 'the parent company's abuse of the corporate form'.[320] Equally, French law relies on the principle of abuse of rights to pierce the corporate veil.[321]

4.196 **(b) Other explicit and implicit applications of abuse of rights to preserve the parties' reasonable expectations** The relevance of the principle of abuse of rights in ensuring the good administration of arbitral justice is not limited to cases of lifting/piercing the corporate veil, but is equally extended to other cases of extension. This is primarily the case where the principle operates to safeguard the parties' reasonable expectations.

Federal Tribunal, 24 November 2006, 4C.327/2005; Ad-hoc Award of 1991, in the case of *SA v Alpha Beta & Co*, 10 ASA Bulletin 202, (1992); Swiss Federal Tribunal, 16 October 2003, 22 ASA Bulletin 364, (2004); Andrea Meier, 'Multi-party Arbitrations' in Manuel Arroyo (ed), *Arbitration in Switzerland* (Kluwer Law International 2013) 1330; Bernhard Berger and Franz Kellerhals, *International and Domestic Arbitration in Switzerland* (3rd edn, Stämpfli Publishers 2015) 199, para 571.

[316] Hanotiau (n 8) 79–80 citing JF Poudret, 'L'extension de la clause d'arbitrage: approches francais ET Suisse' (1995) 122 Journal Droit International (Clunet) 893, 913.

[317] ICC Case No 5721 of 1990, in Yves Derains, Sigvard Jarvin, and J.J. Arnaldez (eds), *ICC Arbitral Awards 1986-1990* (ICC Publications 1994) 404–05.

[318] Zuberbühler (n 309) 28–29.

[319] ICC Case No 8163 of 2005, (2010) 16 ICC International Court of Arbitration Bulletin 77; Mohamed S Abdelwahab, 'Extension of Arbitration Agreements to Third Parties: A Never Ending Legal Quest through the Spatial-Temporal Continuum' in Franco Ferrari and Stefan Kröll (eds), *Conflict of Laws in International Arbitration* (Sellier 2010) 161; Klaus J Hopt, 'Legal Elements and Policy Decisions in Regulating Groups of Companies' in Clive M. Schmitthoff and Frank Wooldridge (eds), *Groups of Companies* (Sweet & Maxwell 1991) 104.

[320] René Reich-Graefe, 'Changing Paradigms: The Liability of Corporate Groups in Germany' (2005) 37 Connecticut Law Review 785, 802; Carsten Alting, 'Piercing the Corporate Veil in American and German Law – Liability of Individuals and Entities: A Comparative View' (1995) 2 Tulsa Journal of Comparative and International Law 187, 201.

[321] William W Park, 'Non-Signatories and the New York Convention' (2008) 2 Dispute Resolution International 84, 100.

In such cases, arbitral tribunals sometimes explicitly refer to abuse of rights in extending the arbitration clause to a non-signatory. In other cases, while tribunals do not expressly refer to the principle, the reasoning of the tribunals and the rationale of their decisions evince an implicit application of the principle rather than any other principle/doctrine. **4.197**

In a recent case decided by the Swiss Federal Tribunal,[322] a dispute arose out of three contracts concluded between Party A and Party B, members of a group of companies. Party B initiated arbitration proceedings against Party A. Party A brought counterclaims against Party B and against a non-signatory member of the group, Party C. The arbitral Tribunal decided that it did not have jurisdiction over the non-signatory party. Upon a challenge of the award before the Swiss Federal Tribunal, it partially set aside the award and decided that the arbitral Tribunal should have accepted jurisdiction over the non-signatory Party C. **4.198**

The Swiss Federal Tribunal provided that where there is *confusion* between the activity of the signatory company and the non-signatory company member of the group, it may be justified to ignore the legal independence of the different entities, not necessarily based on the doctrine of piercing the corporate veil, but to preserve the *legitimate expectations* of third parties who relied on the appearance of the non-signatory and believed that the non-signatory was a party to the contract and the arbitration agreement enshrined therein.[323] **4.199**

In partially setting aside the arbitral award, the Swiss Federal Tribunal invoked Article 2 of the Swiss Civil Code which enshrines the principle of good faith and the prohibition against abuse of rights. It provided that, given the conduct of the signatory member and the non-signatory member of the group, Party A could have relied in good faith that the non-signatory was a genuine party. Additionally, the relevant members of the group, and specifically the non-signatory member should have extinguished any doubt and made it crystal clear that the non-signatory did not wish to become a party to the agreement. A contrario, the non-signatory intervened in the performance of the contract and thus *contributed to the confusion* of Party A. The Court decided that the arbitral Tribunal should have extended the arbitration agreement to the non-signatory.[324] **4.200**

This is a clear manifestation of the abuse of rights principle.[325] The Court decided that extension of the arbitration clause was warranted to protect the legitimate and reasonable expectations of the party, which had been created as a result of the non-signatory's conduct, and that the law should not protect the abusive inconsistent conduct of the non-signatory to the detriment of the counter party. **4.201**

[322] Swiss Federal Tribunal, 7 April 2014, 4A_450/2013.
[323] ibid grounds 3.2 and 3.5.5.1.
[324] ibid.
[325] Voser (n 220) paras 9.73-9.74 and 9.80–9.81.

4.202 This case is of particular relevance as it is one of the few cases where the Swiss Federal Tribunal decided to partially set aside an arbitral award. The case represents an abuse of rights analysis in cases *not related* to piercing of the corporate veil. Scholars note that the aforementioned case reflects a novel application of abuse of rights in relation to non-signatories. Precisely, it is submitted that in considering the question of extension of the arbitration clause, abuse of rights may be established to safeguard the reasonable expectations of the party, particularly if the non-signatory creates an appearance of being bound and/or 'based on the creation of confusion between a parent and its daughter companies'.[326]

4.203 On a different note, one posits that the essence of abuse of rights has been implicitly applied in other cases of extension. This is particularly the case in relation to cases falling within the ambit of the group of companies doctrine. A review of the conditions *sine qua non* of the group of companies doctrine, and how arbitrators apply it reveal that the main element justifying extension is not 'implied consent', but rather the generation of an expectation of the party requesting the extension and assessing the reasonableness of such an expectation. This greatly resembles the role and function of abuse of rights as evidenced from the Swiss case discussed above. In this regard, compelling a non-signatory to arbitrate based on its contested or lacking consent is want of legal reasoning, and a fallacy that should not be maintained as it does not advance the good administration of justice.[327] This is succinctly illustrated in the following paragraphs.

4.204 Arbitral tribunals have long used the 'group of companies' doctrine as an indirect criterion for vindicating consent and establishing jurisdiction.[328] However, the leading case of *Dow Chemical v Isover-Saint-Gobain*[329] carefully addressed the doctrine's scope and the necessary conditions for its application.[330] The *Dow Chemical* award

[326] ibid; Stephan Wilske, Laurence Shore, and Jan-Michael Ahrens, 'The "Group of Companies Doctrine" – Where is it Heading?' (2006) 17 American Review of International Arbitration 1, 3.

[327] Parties' intention to arbitrate should only be upheld where there is a 'clear and unmistakable intent by [it] to arbitrate'. *Sarhank Group v Oracle Corporation*, 404 F 3d 657 (2nd Cir 2005); Park (n 321) 86. In some cases, the non-signatory may not even be aware of the existence of the arbitration clause. Thus, it is questionable how one can consent to an unknown fact. Brekoulakis (n 271) para 6.28. Some case law which rely on the non-signatory's active involvement in the performance of the contract as basis for extension reveal that *two presumptions* emanate from the active involvement of the non-signatory: a presumption that the non-signatory is *aware* of the arbitration clause, and a presumption of *acceptance* thereof. Both presumptions lack sound legal basis, fail to ascertain the existence of the parties' consent and their mutual intention to include the non-signatory in the arbitration process, and equally fail to ascertain the non-signatory's consent to be joined in the arbitration proceedings. *Korsnas Marma v Durand-Auzias*, Review of Arbitration (1989); and Court of Cassation, *Alcatel Business Systems, Alcatel Micro Electronics and AGF v Amkor Technology et* al, 11 JCP I 168, (2007), cited in Jean-François Poudret and Sébastien Besson, *Comparative Law of International Arbitration* (2nd edn, Sweet & Maxwell 2007) para 256; Andrea M Steingruber, *Consent in International Arbitration* (Oxford University Press 2012) paras 9.40–9.42.

[328] Brekoulakis (n 271) para 5.04. Whilst the principle gained recognition in France, it has been challenged and set aside, either explicitly or implicitly, by other leading arbitration jurisdictions such as England, Switzerland, and the USA: Alan Redfern and others, *Redfern and Hunter on International Arbitration* (5th edn, Oxford University Press 2009) 102; Born (n 1) 1431; Sarita Patil Woolhouse, 'Group pf Companies Doctrine and English Arbitration Law' (2004) 20 Arbitration International 435, 441.

[329] ICC Case No 4131 of 1982, Interim Award in *Dow Chemical v Isover-Saint-Gobain*, (1984) IX Ybk Commercial Arbitration 131.

[330] Pietro Ferrario, 'The Group of Companies Doctrine in International Commercial Arbitration: Is There any Reason for this Doctrine to Exist?' (2009) 26 Journal of International Arbitration 647, 663.

demonstrates that the theoretical foundation of the doctrine is based on the *lex mercatoria* and usages of international trade.[331] In addition, it appears that the operation of the doctrine is warranted in cases where: (a) the signatory and the non-signatory constitute one economic reality (*une realité économique unique*); are parts of the same group;[332] (b) the factual matrix of the case manifests an active role by the non-signatory third party in the negotiation, conclusion, performance, and/or termination of the contract;[333] and where (c) the common intention of the parties warrant the extension of the arbitration clause.[334]

The presumed parties' common intention, and the non-signatory's consent, in the context of the group of companies, is established where two essential elements are present: if: (a) the party dealing with the group genuinely believed that the non-signatory was a party to the agreement (the subjective element); and (b) that its belief was justified and reasonable. The latter pertains to the non-signatory's appearance as a genuine party (the objective element), evidenced through the corporate structure of the group, its relationship to the non-signatory, and the latter's active involvement in the negotiation, execution, and/or termination of the contract.[335] **4.205**

Thus, it seems peculiar to infer, from the above, the non-signatory's consent, or the parties' common intention. Particularly, it is blatant that all conditions relate, directly or indirectly, to the intention of the party requesting the extension and his/her expectations. Elements that seem, prima facie, pertaining to the group and the non-signatory entity, are actually used to determine, objectively, whether the party dealing with the group reasonably believed that the non-signatory member of the group was a party to the contract including the arbitration clause. **4.206**

This proposition is further confirmed by the fact that tribunals often extend the arbitration clause to the non-signatory, based on 'the common intention of the parties', where **4.207**

[331] ICC Case No 4131 of 1982, *Dow Chemical v Isover-Saint-Gobain*, (1984) IX Ybk Commercial Arbitration 131, 133–34.

[332] The more significant the degree of control, financially or managerially, the more inclined a tribunal will be to exercise jurisdiction. ICC Case No 5894 of 1991; ICC Case No 7155 of 1993; ICC Case No 8910 of 1998; ICC Case No 6000 of 1988, discussed in Brekoulakis (n 271) 154–55; *Kis France SA, Kis Photo Industrie SA v SA Société Générale, Sogelease Pacifique SA and others*, Cour d'Appel, Paris, 31 October 1989, in Albert Jan van den Berg (ed) (1991) XVI Ybk Commercial Arbitration 145.

[333] John Gaffney, 'The Group of Companies Doctrine and the Law Applicable To The Arbitration Agreement' (2004) 19 Mealey's Int'l Arb Rep 1, 2; Wilske, Shore, and Ahrens (n 326) 74; Gaillard and Savage (n 272) 284–85; Serge Gravel and Patricia Peterson, 'French Law and Arbitration Clauses – Distinguishing Scope from Validity: Comment on ICC Case No. 6519 Final Award' (1992) 37 McGill Law Journal 510, 531; *Kis France SA, Kis Photo Industrie SA v SA Société Générale, Sogelease Pacifique SA and others*, Cour d'Appel, Paris, 31 October 1989, in Albert Jan van den Berg (ed), (1991) XVI Ybk Commercial Arbitration 145, 147.

[334] ICC Case No. 4131 of 1982, *Dow Chemical v Isover-Saint-Gobain*, (1984) IX Ybk Commercial Arbitration 131, 136; Gaillard and Savage (n 272) 283–85, ('Clearly, however, it is not so much the existence of a group that results in the various companies of the group being bound by the agreement signed by only one of them, but rather the fact that such was the true intention of the parties [. . .] The existence of the parties' consent is thus clearly the key issue'); Born (n 1) 1447–48 ('it is those intentions, as reflected in the terms of the parties' agreements, that are the cornerstone of the group of companies doctrine').

[335] ICC Case No 4131 of 1982, *Dow Chemical v Isover-Saint-Gobain*, (1984) IX Ybk Commercial Arbitration 131, 134–35; Brekoulakis (n 271) paras 5.47–5.52; Youssef (n 276) 81; Philipp Habegger, 'Arbitration and Groups of Companies – The Swiss Practice' (2002) 3 European Business Organization Law Review 517, 535.

the conduct of the non-signatory has *confused* the counter party as to who is the genuine party to the agreement.[336]

4.208 Such confusion may be a result of the non-signatory's sheer negligence and their lack of awareness about the repercussions thereof. Confusion may even be deliberately induced in *mala fide*.[337] In both cases, justifying the extension of the arbitration clause based on the intention of the non-signatory or its consent seems specious.

4.209 Accordingly, it is submitted that the above indices constitute a sound basis for establishing an *expectation* of the party requesting the extension of the arbitration clause, and *assessing its reasonableness*.[338] The latter being objectively examined based on the structure of the group, its relation to the non-signatory member, and the latter's conduct throughout the contractual matrix of the case.[339]

4.210 In this regard, one asserts that the argument advocating that examining the related parties' conduct manifests their common intention is '*ignoratio elenchi*': it does not evince the parties' presumed common intention, but may determine if there is an abuse of rights.

4.211 The examination of the factual matrix of the case and the relevant parties' conduct, including that of the non-signatory, shall be undertaken to frustrate one's attempt to contradict its previous conduct to the detriment of another and to 'correct mistaken subjective assumptions or understandings at the time of contracting'.[340] Gary Born

[336] As stipulated by Professor Brekoulakis, 'the tribunal will examine the conduct and behaviour of the whole group that *led the other party to legitimately believe* that the non-signatory member of the group was a genuine party to the contract. Here, tribunals will focus on the conduct of the non-signatory member of the group to determine whether it adopted the behaviour of a "genuine party" that confused and misled the co-contractor' Brekoulakis (n 271) para 5.52; ICC Case No 5730 of 1988 (1990)117 Journal du Droit 1029 cited in Redfern and others (n 328) 101; Hanotiau (n 8) 44–45; ICC Case No 6000 of 1988 and ICC Case No 5103 of 1988, discussed in Brekoulakis (n 271) 155–56. The Egyptian Court of Cassation held that '[t]he fact that one of the parties to the arbitration is a company within a group of companies with one parent contributing in its capital is not proof that the latter is vested with the contractual obligations entered into by the former, which include an arbitration agreement *unless* it was proven that it had taken part in their execution or *created confusion regarding the party vested with the obligations* where its own will is mixed with the will of the other company'. Egyptian Court of Cassation, Hearing held on 22 June 2004, Challenges No 4729 and 4730, Judicial Year 72.

[337] Brekoulakis (n 271) paras 5.52–5.57.

[338] Youssef (n 276) 81, (providing that a *prudent* and *logical* analysis of the group of companies case law reveals that concepts such as '*legitimate expectations*' and '*protection of appearances*' are *relevant* to establish jurisdiction over non-signatories.

[339] Brekoulakis (n 271) para 5.47; Ferrario (n 330) 651; ICC Case No 11405 of 2001, (unpublished), cited in Hanotiau (n 8) 77–78. In ICC Case No 1160 of 2002, the Tribunal extended the arbitration clause by inferring consent from the corporate group structure and the active involvement of the non-signatory. It is worth noting that the non-signatory interfered in the contractual relationship *prior* to the conclusion of the contract, yet *decided not to sign it*, at the time of concluding the contract. This makes the rebuttable presumption that it did not consent to be a party or to be compelled to arbitrate even stronger, which further fortifies that extension may not be based on the non-signatory's consent. However, it is submitted that given the parent company's conduct, the counter party may have *reasonably* inferred that he was dealing with one contractual unit, and *believed* the non-signatory was indeed a party. Thus, it would be *abusive* to allow the non-signatory to hide behind the cloak of its separate legal personality and certainly *inequitable* to tolerate its inconsistent conduct that is contrary to the legitimate expectations of the counter party. ICC Case No 11160 of 2002, (2005) 16(2) ICC Bulletin 99, cited in Brekoulakis (n 271) paras 5.28–5.29.

[340] Born (n 1) 1455.

acknowledged the relevance of abuse of rights and provided that in such circumstances the doctrine of group of companies can be applied in a manner similar to 'abuse of right, relying on principles of good faith, equity and objective intent to supplement or correct subjective intentions of the parties to an arbitration agreement'.[341]

In conclusion, it appears that the principle of abuse of rights is vital in the context of extension of an arbitration clause to ensure the good administration of arbitral justice. The principle is explicitly endorsed in cases of piercing/lifting the corporate veil and in other cases to safeguard the parties' reasonable expectations and to maintain the fairness of the proceedings. Finally, while arbitral tribunals often extend an arbitration clause to a non-signatory on grounds of the group of companies doctrine by relying on the parties' common intention, arbitrators' decisions appear to reveal that the main enquiry is the existence of an expectation to one of the parties, and assessing the reasonableness of such an expectation, which greatly resembles the function of the principle of abuse of rights. **4.212**

IV. Conclusion

It would be a fallacy to claim that the principle of abuse of rights is alien or foreign to the law and practice of international arbitration. As evident from the above discussion, the principle is omnipresent. While the principle is not novel, its application in international arbitration is slowly gaining momentum given arbitrators' desire to search for genuine justice and to ensure the good administration of arbitral justice. As provided by one arbitral tribunal: **4.213**

> The principle [abuse of right] is old; one need only recall Cicero's *summum jus, summa injuria*. To say that the blind application of a rule may lead to iniquitous results is to recognise that the search for justice would fail if the law could do no more than validate relative positions of strength, or consolidate the status quo indefinitely. Thus, the exercise of a particular right may be inhibited if it would abase the law.[342]

Arbitral tribunals have effectively relied on abuse of rights to tackle different forms of abuse to ensure the good administration of justice. It provides arbitrators with a flexible tool to tackle various forms of procedural misconduct. A discussion of its application to different legal problems demonstrates its indispensability to international arbitration due to the interests that it advances. **4.214**

It is acknowledged that there are classic tools and existing legal rules at the disposal of arbitrators that can be utilized to administer arbitral justice. For example, treaties may include provisions regarding denial of benefits for entities that have no **4.215**

[341] ibid.

[342] *Himpurna California Energy Ltd v PT PLN (Persero)*, ad hoc arbitration under UNCITRAL rules, Final Award of 4 May 1999, (2000) XXV Ybk Commercial Arbitration 11, 92.

material economic activity.[343] Article 41(5) of ICSID and Article 39 of the new Rules of Stockholm Chamber of Commerce, which are manifestations of the abuse of rights principle,[344] may limit claims that lack legal merit and abusive claims/requests.[345] Provisions in arbitration statutes/rules may prevent inordinate delay and tactics in arbitration.[346] Arbitral tribunals may answer a party's abusive conduct by allocating the costs.[347] The doctrines of *lis pendens* and *res judicata* could apply to limit abusive parallel or subsequent proceedings.[348] In such cases, a stand-alone general principle of abuse of rights may appear superfluous. However, although these sanctions may comprise palliative tools, practice proves that they only tackle certain forms of abuse and remain largely inadequate to compensate/remedy the aggrieved party.

4.216 Whilst arbitrators often award and allocate costs against parties who engage in abusive conduct,[349] it is generally recognized that this practice fails to deter parties and their legal counsel from abusing their rights and engaging in procedural misconduct.[350]

4.217 It is true that the doctrine of *lis pendens* may be applied to preclude the risks associated with parallel arbitral proceedings.[351] For this doctrine to apply, the parties must be the same, the relief sought must be identical, and the facts and legal grounds must be the same.[352] The application of *lis pendens* in international arbitration is controversial.[353] Moreover, given the rigid requirements of the 'triple identity' test, it is submitted that it fails to remedy the enigmas associated with parallel proceedings, particularly in cases where the parties, causes of action and relief sought are not identical.[354] The inadequacy of *lis pendens* to tackle abuse of rights is reflected *exempli gratia* in the *CME*

[343] Lee (n 146) 366–67; *Pacific Rim Cayman LLC v The Republic of El Salvador*, ICSID Case No ARB/09/12, Decision on the Respondent's Jurisdictional Objections of 1 June 2012.

[344] Eric de Brabandere, 'The ICSID Rule on Early Dismissal of Unmeritorious Investment Treaty Claims: Preserving the Integrity of ICSID Arbitration', (2012) 9 Manchester Journal of International Economic Law 23, 24; Markert (n 73) 234–35.

[345] Yunus Emre Akbaba, 'Summary Procedure in the SCC Arbitration Rules of 2017: Shifting the Paradigm of Preliminary Objections in International Arbitration' (Kluwer Arbitration Blog, 1 February 2017) <http://kluwerarbitrationblog.com/2017/02/01/summary-procedure-in-the-scc-arbitration-rules-of-2017-shifting-the-paradigm-of-preliminary-objections-in-international-arbitration/> accessed 20 February 2019.

[346] Section 41 of the English Arbitration Act of 1996.

[347] Jenny Power and Christian Konrad, 'Costs in International Commercial Arbitration – A Comparative Overview of Civil and Common Law Doctrines' in Gerold Zeiler and others (eds), *Austrian Arbitration Yearbook 2007*, (Manz'sche Verlags- und Universitätsbuchhandlung 2007) 261 et seq; Welser (n 101) 165; Markert (n 73) 241; Park (n 127) 454.

[348] August Reinisch, 'The Use and Limits of Res Judicata and Lis Pendens as Procedural Tools to Avoid Conflicting Dispute Settlement Outcomes' (2004) 3 Law and Practice of International Courts and Tribunals 37.

[349] For example *Phoenix Action v The Czech Republic*, ICSID Case No ARB/06/5, Award of 15 April 2009, para 152; *Cementownia SA v Republic of Turkey*, ICSID Case No ARB(AF)/06/2, Award of 17 September 2009, para 171.

[350] Price and Wilske (n 112) 184; Gaillard (n 90) 27; Redfern and others (n 51) 244.

[351] Cremades and Madalena (n 203) 509; Pierre Mayer, 'Conflicting Decisions in International Commercial Arbitration' (2013) 4 Journal of International Dispute Settlement 407, 413.

[352] Miguel Temboury Redondo, 'Preliminary Judgments, Lis Pendens and Res Judicata in Arbitration Proceedings' in MA Fernandez-Ballesteros and David Arias (eds), *Liber Amicorum Bernardo Cremades* (La Ley 2010), 1138–39; Cremades and Madalena (n 203) 509–10.

[353] Born (n 1) 3793.

[354] August Reinisch, 'International Courts and Tribunals, Multiple Jurisdictions' in *Max Planck Encyclopedia of Public International Law* (Oxford University Press 2008) para 26; International Law Association, 'Final Report on Lis Pendens and Arbitration' (Toronto 2006) para 5.6, whereby a broader definition of the triple identity test was endorsed.

and *Lauder* cases discussed above.[355] One ventures that endorsing a general principle of abuse of rights comprises a more comprehensive and effective principle to deal with abusive conduct, including issues of parallel proceedings.[356]

Similarly, whilst the doctrine of *res judicata* operates to prevent the specific form of abuse associated with subsequent proceedings, the triple identity test mentioned above must be met.[357] It is thus acknowledged that the prevalent[358] strict application of the triple identity test fails to remedy manifest abuse of rights in this regard.[359] The application of the principle of abuse of rights is more effective as it may remedy any abuse pertaining to subsequent proceedings and its application does not rely on satisfying any rigid or formal requirements.[360] **4.218**

Given that a true abuse of rights does not breach any hard legal rule, 'it cannot be tackled by the application of classic legal tools'.[361] As the principle's operation presumes that the act is consistent with black letter law, it is an adequate remedy to tackle all forms of abuse that are not necessarily in breach of hard laws/rules. The importance of endorsing a general principle of abuse of rights to ensure the good administration of justice is not only appealing owing to its comprehensiveness and its ability to remedy forms of abuse that other rules fail to remedy. Its potency also stems from the fact that it is a general principle that can equally remedy any form of abuse that is not currently regulated by a specific rule:[362] **4.219**

> The principle also plays a role in the promotion of legal change. In an international society that itself continues to experience rapid and far-reaching change, longstanding general principles of law such as abuse of rights help to extend legal controls to previously unregulated areas, and to fill new gaps as they appear. As international lawyers rush forward to meet the challenges of the twenty-first century, they would be wise not to leave abuse of rights, one of their most basic tools, behind.[363]

[355] *Ronald S Lauder v The Czech Republic*, UNCITRAL Arbitration Proceedings, Award of 3 September 2001, para 177.

[356] Cremades and Madalena (n 203) 538; Campbell Mclachlan, *Lis Pendens in International Litigation* (Martinus Nijhoff Publishers 2009) 420–32 (providing that procedural formalities associated with the triple identity test may lead to an abuse of process).

[357] Wehland (n 226) para 6.113; *Wasteful Management Inc. v United Mexican States*, ICSID Case No ARB(AF)/00/3, Decision dated 26 June 2002, para 39; *Malicorp Limited v The Arab Republic of Egypt*, ICSID Case No ARB/08/18, Award dated 7 February 2011, para 103; ICC Case No 6363 of 1991, XVII Yearbook Commercial Arbitration 186, 198 (1992).

[358] Norah Gallagher, 'Parallel Proceedings, Res Judicata and Lis Pendens: Problems and Possible Solutions' in Julian DM Lew and Loukas A Mistelis (eds), *Pervasive Problems in International Arbitration* (Kluwer Law International 2006) 349; Wehland (n 226) para 6.117; Campbell McLachlan, Laurence Shore, and Matthew Weiniger, *International Investment Arbitration: Substantive Principles* (Oxford University Press 2010) 122–25.

[359] Dimsey (n 1161) 96; Bernardo M Cremades, 'Introduction' in Bernardo M Cremades and Julian DM Lew, *Parallel State and Arbitral Procedures in International Arbitration* (ICC Publications 2005) 10; Wehland (n 226) paras 6.114–6.115.

[360] Shany (n 210) 259; McLachlan (n 356) 420–32; Sheppard (n 215) 235.

[361] Gaillard (n 90) 18; Carmen Lopez and Lucy Martinez, 'Corruption, Fraud and Abuse of Process in Investment Treaty Arbitration' in Barton Legum (ed), *The Investment Treaty Arbitration Review* (3rd edn, Law Business Research 2018) 150.

[362] Ascensio (n 2) 765–67.

[363] Michael Byers, 'Abuse of Rights: An Old Principle, A New Age' (2002) 47 McGill Law Journal 389, 431.

4.220 Thus, a principle of abuse of rights is of paramount importance to ensure the good administration of arbitral justice. While it may crystallize its most potent manifestations in various principles and rules to tackle specific forms of abuse, endorsing it as a general principle remains indispensable to remedy all forms of abuse.

5
Conclusion

There is a dire need to prevent the transformation of international arbitration into a process profoundly tainted with procedural misconduct and abuse. The purpose of this book was to examine the recognition and development of abuse of rights as a general principle of law applicable in international arbitration to prevent the abuse of substantive and procedural rights. **5.01**

Further, the book examined the role and function of abuse of rights in international arbitration and reveals how its application ensures the good administration of arbitral justice. **5.02**

The results produced from this book comprise remarks on existing views and also a number of suggestions that mainly cover the following issues: (1) whether the principle of abuse of rights constitutes a general, or transnational, principle of law; (2) the core elements of abuse of rights and its scope of application; (3) concerns and limitations of the principle; (4) the importance of applying abuse of rights in international arbitration and its role in ensuring the good administration of arbitral justice; and (5) the nature of the principle and its operation as a general principle of substantive and procedural law in arbitration. **5.03**

I. Recapitulation

As discussed above, in order to examine whether abuse of rights can be considered a general principle of law, the principle's recognition in all systems of law is not required. The methodology employed intended to ascertain the prevailing trend within legal systems and establish the wide recognition of the principle. It is recognized that a principle that gains wide recognition can constitute a general principle of law, despite the fact that it is not recognized in a number of legal systems.[1] However, whilst the principle may not be readily recognized in some national laws, it remains important that its application does not defy the fundamental concepts of the main systems of law.[2] **5.04**

[1] Emmanuel Gaillard, *Legal Theory of International Arbitration* (Martinus Nijhoff 2010) 48–51.
[2] Harold C Gutteridge, *Comparative Law* (2nd edn, Cambridge University Press 1949) 6565.

5.05 A comparative examination of abuse of rights was undertaken in order to ascertain its wide recognition, identify its nature, analyse its application in national legal systems, and establish elements of commonality across different legal systems.

5.06 Based on a prudent synthesis of different legal systems, it was suggested that abuse of rights is an equitable principle in the *Aristotelian* sense, in that it clearly reflects equitable considerations, and primarily operates to ameliorate the harshness and rigidity of strict legal rules and contractual terms.

5.07 As a legal principle, its recognition and application naturally varies from one jurisdiction to another. Whilst its recognition is omnipresent, its legal basis and the manner in which it is applied is not the same. Thus, it was evident that the principle was formulated on statutory grounds in some jurisdictions, as in the case of Switzerland, Germany, and Egypt. A contrario, in France the courts arguably had a primary role in the principle's recognition, development, and application.

5.08 Similarly, the manner in which the principle is regulated and applied by courts may vary. Some jurisdictions sought to carefully define the principle and delineate its scope of application, such as the approach of Egyptian law and the law of Louisiana, where the principle is carefully defined and the criteria of abuse clearly set out. Other laws opted for a mere recognition of the principle and granted the courts the discretionary power to adopt the appropriate criteria of abuse.

5.09 The evolution of abuse of rights and its extension to limit the abuse of different rights is palpable. Although the principle originated in the arena of property law, it clearly extended to other areas of law, and is now considered by many jurisdictions as a general principle applicable in every department of law. This is equally evident with regards to the abuse of procedural rights, whereby some jurisdictions rely on the broad principle of abuse of rights to tackle any form of procedural abuse and other jurisdictions seek to include more defined statutory provisions to preclude procedural abuse.

5.10 The book also examined the recognition and application of abuse of rights in the common law systems. It was asserted that a general principle of abuse of rights is not acknowledged in the common law. However, it was argued that the common law has implemented other rules and principles, the operation of which may equally preclude different forms of abuse. Given the different rules/tools utilized to tackle substantive and procedural abuse, a distinction was made between substantive rights and procedural rights. It was argued that the operation of abuse of process in the common law parallels the principle of abuse of rights, and that the common law may limit other forms of substantive abuse if the conduct in question falls under the scope of a pre-existing tort.

5.11 Upon reviewing the principle's application in different legal systems, a delineation of the core elements of abuse of rights was embarked upon. As analysed, abuse of rights assumes the existence of an acknowledged legal right, presupposes that the act in question is made within the formal limits of the right, and that such right ceases legal protection given that it has been abused by the right holder.

The book discussed the concept of a right in the context of abuse of rights and endorsed the interest theory of rights, which advocates that a right denotes an interest recognized and protected by the law. It was argued that such an ideology of rights prohibited abusive exercise of rights and led to the formation of the abuse of rights principle. **5.12**

The book endeavoured to examine the different criteria adopted to find an abuse of right, and highlight the inherent limitation of each criterion. The study illustrated that the different criteria used by courts and tribunals are interrelated and overlap manifestly, which renders some of them superfluous. **5.13**

The study concluded that the criterion of reasonableness comprises an effective criterion of abuse, given that: (1) it covers certain applications of abuse of rights which may not necessarily be covered if other criteria are adopted; (2) it is widely used in civil law countries and international law; (3) it effectively encompasses other criteria; (4) it is not alien to the common law depiction of rights; and (5) it comprises an objective standard of abuse. **5.14**

On a different note, the role of other principles in precluding abusive practices was examined. In this regard, the interrelation between abuse of rights and the broader principle of good faith clearly demonstrated that abuse of rights is an application of the principle of good faith. The vertical interrelation between the principle of good faith and abuse of rights, and the perception that the former embodies the latter, suggested that jurisdictions that do not explicitly endorse the principle of abuse of rights, or adopt a restrictive application thereof, may still limit the exercise of rights on the basis of the principle of good faith. This was manifested by an examination of German law,[3] as well as US law.[4] Arbitral tribunals have also utilized the principle of good faith in order to preclude different forms of abuse.[5] **5.15**

Drawing on the analysis of the first two chapters, the study examined the application of abuse of rights in international arbitration and its role in tackling the rising phenomenon of abuse. The purpose of this chapter was to demonstrate that the application of abuse of rights is not foreign to the practice of international arbitration, and to suggest that a general principle of abuse of rights has emerged and developed owing to its paramount importance in ensuring the good administration of arbitral justice. **5.16**

The notion of administration of arbitral justice is largely ambiguous owing to the lack of any detailed study that delineates its meaning or its inherent elements. That said, prior **5.17**

[3] Judgment of 29 November 1956, 22 BGHZ 226, 230 (1957) translated in Vera Bolgar, 'Abuse of Rights in France, Germany, and Switzerland: A Survey of a Recent Chapter in Legal Doctrine' (1975) 35 Louisiana Law Review 1015, 1029–30.

[4] *Fortune v National Cash Register Co*, 364 NE 2d 1251 (Mass 1977) 1252–53.

[5] Decision rendered by the WTO Appellate Body in the case of *United States—Import Prohibition of Certain Shrimp and Shrimp Products* (12 October 1998) WT/DS58/AB/R, para 158; *Himpurna California Energy Ltd v PT PLN (Persero)*, ad hoc arbitration under UNCITRAL rules, Final award of 4 May 1999, (2000) XXV Ybk Commercial Arbitration 11.

to embarking on the interrelation between abuse of rights and the administration of arbitral justice, a clear demarcation of the latter was indispensable.

5.18 It was argued that the notion refers to the fairness of the proceedings, requirements of due process, and procedural efficiency. The study outlined how the application of abuse of rights balances the competing interests of due process, fairness, and procedural efficiency and then demonstrated how it ensures the good administration of arbitral justice.

5.19 It was submitted that abuse of rights strikes the balance needed between procedural efficiency, fairness, and due process. In recognizing abuse of rights as a general principle in arbitration, tribunals are equipped with a tool that can assist them in discerning the conduct of the parties and take into consideration the motives and purpose of any request that may affect the fairness of the proceedings or hinder the efficient conduct of proceedings. Upon a prudent balance of the competing interests, and based on the factual matrix of the case, arbitrators may determine whether such procedural request is reasonable.

5.20 The above submission was then tested and confirmed by an analysis of the application of abuse of rights to prevent common forms of procedural abuse, particularly in the context of: corporate and State manoeuvres to gain access to, or block, arbitral proceedings, parallel arbitral proceedings, and the extension of the arbitration clause to non-signatories.

5.21 This analysis demonstrated how the failure to apply the principle may seriously prejudice the opposing party and bring disrepute to the administration of justice. Thus, as the tribunals in the *CME/Lauder* cases failed to effectively apply abuse of rights, a material impediment to standards of fairness, requirements of due process, and the broader notion of administration of justice materialized, which was manifested by the conflicting awards rendered in the parallel proceedings.

5.22 The existence of other classic rules/principles that may tackle some forms of abuse in international arbitration was equally highlighted. An analysis of these rules and how arbitrators determine their scope of application evinced that they tend to be palliative rather than curative. Thus, whilst arbitral tribunals may answer a party's abusive conduct by allocating the costs, it is generally recognized that this practice fails to deter parties and their legal counsel from abusing their rights and engaging in procedural misconduct. Similarly, although the doctrines of *lis pendens* and *res judicata* may apply to limit abusive parallel or subsequent proceedings, the rigid requirements of the 'triple identity' test may fail to remedy the conundrums associated with such proceedings, particularly in cases where the parties, causes of action, and relief sought, are not identical.

5.23 Moreover, the various rules that attempt to tackle abusive conduct fragment and compartmentalize the approach to abusive practices, where different abusive behaviours will have to fit under different rules or doctrines.

In such cases, a stand-alone general principle of abuse of rights is far from being superfluous. The virtue and efficacy of a single theory with a wide scope of application and an overarching premise, is that it can be used to address different abusive behaviours, and equally enjoys the flexibility of general principles of law. It may remedy any abuse and its application does not rely on satisfying any rigid or formal requirements. 5.24

The book suggested that the importance of endorsing a general principle of abuse of rights was not only mandated by its role in ensuring the administration of justice, but also owing to its comprehensiveness and its ability to remedy forms of abuse that other rules fail to remedy. Its potency equally stems from the fact that it is a general principle that can equally remedy any form of abuse that is not currently regulated by a specific rule. While it may crystallize its potent manifestations in various specific principles and rules to tackle specific forms of abuse, endorsing it as a general principle remains indispensable to remedy all forms of abuse. 5.25

Drawing on the analysis of the abovementioned and based on the findings of the first three chapters, this study endeavoured to examine how abuse of rights is applied in international arbitration. Accordingly, Chapter 4 focused on discerning the legal basis of abuse of rights and examining its nature in international arbitration. Owing to the scope of the book, which focused on both substantive and procedural rights, a determination of the nature of abuse of rights in relation to substantive and procedural rights was warranted. 5.26

To that end, applying abuse of rights as a general principle of substantive law was demonstrated by an analysis of the views shared by scholars and its endorsement as a general principle by arbitrators. Tribunals recognize the application of the principle, not only as part of the applicable national law, but as a generally accepted legal principle. Moreover, the recognition of abuse of rights as a general principle of substantive law in international legal instruments was also discussed. 5.27

The discussion was not limited to the nature of abuse of rights from the perception of private law. Examining the principle's application in the domain of public international law was also achieved. Thus, it was highlighted that the principle is recognized as a general principle of law by prominent scholars; is endorsed as such by international courts and tribunals (including the ICJ, CJEU, WTO panels, and ICSID tribunals); and is applied in the context of a wide array of legal matters. 5.28

The book then provided a study on abuse of rights as a general principle of arbitral procedure. First, a general overview on the application of transnational principles of procedure in international arbitration was provided, and the non-comprehensive nature of the procedural framework of international arbitration was emphasized. Additionally, it was argued that an autonomous set of transnational principles have emerged in order to ensure the administration of arbitral justice. 5.29

Whilst the different representations of international arbitration were succinctly mentioned, the existence of an autonomous arbitral legal order was recognized and the 5.30

transnational depiction of international arbitration was endorsed. It was argued that international arbitration should be governed by transnational norms and procedural principles that emerge owing to their acceptance in different legal systems and as a result of their frequent application by international arbitrators.

5.31 Based on the above, it was submitted that abuse of rights constitutes a general principle of arbitral procedure given that: (1) its application to tackle different forms of procedural abuse is generally recognized in most legal systems, including the common law and international law; (2) it is recognized as such in international legal instruments and by distinguished scholars; and (3) it is constantly applied by arbitral tribunals as a general principle of law.

5.32 On a different note, an examination of how abuse of rights operates and applies as a general principle of arbitral procedure demonstrated that the element of reasonableness comprises the *raison d'être* and depicts the basis of abuse of rights.

5.33 A prima facie review of the principle's application may reveal that arbitral tribunals do not restrict themselves to a strict criterion of abuse but rather assess all the factual matrix of the case and endorse the same criteria used by national courts (intention,[6] reasonableness, and purpose of rights).[7] Some hailed the principle of abuse of rights as an effective remedy, but flagged that the lack of 'unifying criteria' of abuse is a disadvantage.[8]

5.34 One submits that the different conclusions reached by tribunals demonstrate the implementation of the balancing factor in applying abuse of rights as a general principle of law. As provided by one tribunal, the criterion of abuse should strike a fair balance between the need to safeguard one's rights and the need to deny protection to abusive conduct.[9]

5.35 In applying the balancing factor, a contextual analysis of the different competing interests at stake is conducted. Whilst it is true that there exists no abstract rule on how the balancing exercise is to be undertaken, or what the competing interests involved are, it is submitted that this conforms to the nature and function of abuse of rights: a principle that ameliorates the rigidity of the law and ensures the good administration of justice. Thus, the operation of this principle must be left as a flexible tool to be utilized by arbitrators given the specificities of the dispute in question. Accordingly, finding an abuse of right is a fact-based inquiry that demands arbitrators to balance all factors and interests involved in the case.

[6] *Pacific Rim Cayman LLC v The Republic of El Salvador*, ICSID Case No ARB/09/12, Decision on Jurisdiction of 1 June 2012, para 2.41; but see *Tidewater Inc, Tidewater Investment SRL, Tidewater Caribe, CA et al v The Bolivarian Republic of Venezuela*, ICSID Case No ARB/10/5, para 183.

[7] *Mobil Corp, v Republic of Venezuela*, ICSID Case No ARB/07/27, Decision on Jurisdiction dated 10 June 2010, paras 184–85; John Lee, 'Resolving Concerns of Treaty Shopping in International Investment Arbitration' (2015) 6 Journal of International Dispute Settlement 355, 356, and 360, 376.

[8] Lee (n 7) 376.

[9] *Renée Rose Levy and Gremcitel SA v Republic of Peru*, ICSID Case No ARB/11/17, Award of 9 January 2015, para 185.

It was clear that utilizing this criterion necessitated considering different interests depending on the nature of the dispute. Thus, evaluating the abusive nature of changing the corporate structure to gain access to ICSID arbitration raised different interests from those raised in the context of parallel proceedings, and the weight given to each interest differed based on the factual matrix of the case. **5.36**

However, it is important to note that examining various disputes that raise the same or similar questions provided sufficient evidence that the same legal and personal interests are examined to establish an abuse of right, which may assist in predictability and reliance on similar decisions. **5.37**

Exempli gratia, in the context of the initiation of parallel arbitral proceedings, the adoption of the balancing factor was apparent. In considering the existence of any abuse, tribunals balanced the competing interests involved which often include: the right to pursue different claims in different fora, against the risk of contradictory awards; preclusion of extra costs; the interest of procedural efficiency and ensuring the overall administration of justice; and also the conduct of the aggrieved party.[10] **5.38**

It was also highlighted that in balancing the competing interests, tribunals regularly considered the conduct of the aggrieved party and whether it was tainted with any abuse, in application of the principle of *he who comes to equity must come with clean hand*. Thus, in the case of *Ampal-American Israel Corp v Egypt* discussed above, the tribunal explicitly relied on the fact that the Respondent refused the consolidation of the arbitral proceedings, and also refused appointing the same arbitrator in the parallel proceedings to conclude that the initiation of the parallel proceedings were not abusive per se: 'it cannot be characterised as abusive especially when the Respondent has declined the Claimants' offers to consolidate the proceedings'.[11] **5.39**

II. Contribution and Recommendations

In an attempt to contribute to the legal debate on abuse of rights, and as a relatively novel study on its role in international arbitration, this book presents the following recommendations and considerations, the adherence to which may limit the rising phenomenon of abuse in international arbitration: **5.40**

First, the application of the general principle of abuse of rights presumes the existence of an acknowledged right and should operate to limit the exercise of *any* right conferred upon the parties by the applicable arbitration rules or laws. **5.41**

[10] *Ronald S Lauder v The Czech Republic*, UNCITRAL Arbitration Proceedings, Award of 3 September 2001, para 178; *Ampal-American Israel Corp et al v Arab Republic of Egypt*, ICSID Case No ARB/12/11, Decision on Jurisdiction of 1 February 2016, paras 321(iv) and 328–39.

[11] *Ampal-American Israel Corp, et al v Arab Republic of Egypt*, ICSID Case No ARB/12/11, Decision on Jurisdiction dated 1 February 2016, para 329.

5.42 *Second*, arbitrators' right/obligation to prevent procedural misconduct and abuse in international arbitration should emanate from their inherent duty to ensure the good administration of arbitral justice. Abuse of rights operates to enhance the efficiency of the proceedings, safeguard the fairness of the proceedings and the equality between the parties, preserve the integrity of the process, and uphold parties' reasonable expectations.

5.43 *Third*, abuse of rights should be treated and applied as a general principle of law in international arbitration. Whilst it is true that the principle exists and can be applied as a national legal construct, its wide recognition, significance to the arbitral process, and its frequent application by arbitrators testify to the effect that it should be considered and approached as a general principle of law.

5.44 More importantly, employing it as a general principle confers upon arbitrators a corrective tool of a clear equitable nature, and dispenses them with the restrictions and rigidity of parochial national rules, the application of which may defy the transnational perception of international arbitration.

5.45 *Fourth*, it is suggested that rights cannot be unreasonably exercised, and that such unreasonableness is not to be decided by any rigid rule or test, but by a flexible balancing exercise of the existing competing interests involved. Such balancing and compromise of competing interests creates a proper limit on each right and further advances the proper functioning of the legal system.

5.46 Accordingly, it is recommended that the balancing factor should be utilized by arbitrators as a criterion of abuse. The significance of the balancing factor emanates from its function, which seeks and maintains a fair balance between the competing interests of the parties involved, and from its wide recognition in the civil and common law legal systems, and in international law.

5.47 It is suggested that the balancing factor should contain sub-factors to guide decision makers, including, inter alia, the indices applied by courts as criteria of abuse (malice, the purpose of the right, the legitimate interest, and the comparative impairment test). The sub-factors shall also comprise all competing interests at stake, which will necessarily vary from one legal dispute to another.

5.48 *Fifth*, given the flexibility and extensiveness of its application, it is advocated that abuse of rights must be applied with utmost prudence and must be resorted to in exceptional circumstances where abuse is flagrant. Whilst it may introduce some uncertainties and may arguably impede legal certainty, it remains significant in order to reach an equitable and fair outcome.

5.49 Moreover, the study did not advocate an open-ended application of abuse of rights with no restraints, but rather suggested that by endorsing the element of reasonableness one should be able to ascertain his/her respective rights/obligations by examining the legal instrument in question (law/contract/treaty), and also recognize that rights are not absolute, but must be exercised reasonably.

Finally, while arbitrators may apply abuse of rights either as part of the applicable national law or as a general principle, where arbitrators are entitled to resort to general principles of law, it is propounded that abuse of rights should apply as an overriding principle of law, or a transnational public policy principle, in the context of procedural rights. This suggestion entails that whenever the conditions *sine qua non* for the principle's application are satisfied, arbitrators are to apply it notwithstanding the seat of arbitration, or the applicable law. **5.50**

Given the procedural framework of international arbitration, where existing laws and rules grant arbitrators the power to resort to generally accepted procedural principles, and due to the pivotal role of abuse of rights in ensuring the good administration of arbitral justice, it is submitted that it should operate as a principle of transnational public policy to prevent the abuse of arbitration related rights. Thus, it should apply in the context of procedural rights, notwithstanding the applicable rules and the *lex arbitri*. **5.51**

Based on the above findings and recommendations, it is truly hoped that this study could serve as a moderate contribution to this new and developing area of law, and fuel additional studies for further development.

Bibliography

Books and Chapters in Books

Abdelaziz MK, *The Civil Code in Light of the Jurisprudence and Doctrine* (Cairo 1985) vol 1

Abdelwahab MS, 'Extension of Arbitration Agreements to Third Parties: A Never Ending Legal Quest Through the Spatial-Temporal Continuum' in Franco Ferrari and Stefan Kröll (eds), *Conflict of Laws in International Arbitration* (Sellier 2010)

Abdelwahab MS, 'The Nuts and Bolts of Construction Arbitration in the MENA: Principles and Practice' in Stavros Brekoulakis and David Thomas (eds), *The Guide to Construction Arbitration* (Global Arbitration Review 2017)

Aboul-Enein MIM, 'Arbitration of Foreign Investment Disputes: Responses to the New Challenges and Changing Circumstances' in Albert Jan Van Den Berg (ed), *New Horizons in International Commercial Arbitration and Beyond* (Kluwer Law International 2010)

Alexy R, 'Individual Rights and Collective Goods' in Carlos Nino (ed), *Rights* (New York University Press 1992)

Alvarez H, 'Autonomy of International Arbitration Process' in Loukas Mistelis and Julian DM Lew (eds), *Pervasive Problems in International Arbitration* (Kluwer Law International 2006)

Amos M and Walton FP, *Introduction to French Law* (3rd edn, Oxford University Press 1967)

Andersen CB, '*General Principles of the CISG—Generally Impenetrable?*' in Camilla B Andersen and Ulrich G Schroeter (eds), *Sharing International Commercial Law across National Boundaries* (Wildy, Simmonds & Hill 2008)

Badia A, *Piercing the Veil of State Enterprises in International Arbitration* (Kluwer Law International 2014)

Barnett P, *Res Judicata, Estoppel, and Foreign Judgments* (Oxford University Press 2001)

Bauen M and Bernet R, *Swiss Company Limited by Shares* (Bruylant and Schulthess 2007)

Belobaba EP, 'Good Faith in Canadian Contract Law' in *Special Lectures of the Law Society of Upper Canada, Commercial Law: Recent Developments and Emerging Trends* (Toronto, De Boo 1985)

Bentham J, *An Introduction of the Principles of Morals and Legislation* (Athlone Press 1970)

Bentham, J, 'Of Laws in General' in HLA Hart (ed), *The Works of Jeremy Bentham* (Athlone Press 1970)

Berger B and Kellerhals F, *International and Domestic Arbitration in Switzerland* (3rd edn, Stämpfli Publishers 2015)

Berger KP, *The Creeping Codification of the Lex Mercatoria* (Kluwer Law International 1999)

Berger KP, '*The Creeping Codification of the New Lex Mercatoria*' (2nd edn, Kluwer Law International 2010)

Bernardini P, 'International Arbitration: How to Make it More Effective' in Laurent Levy and Yves Derains (eds), *Liber Amicorum En l'Honnour de Serge Lazareff* (ICC Publication 2011)

Besson S, 'Piercing the Corporate Veil: Back on the Right Track' in Bernard Hanotiau and Eric A Schwartz (eds), *Multiparty Arbitration* (ICC Publications 2010)

Besson S, 'Corruption and Arbitration' in Domitille Baizeau and Richard H Kreindler (eds), *Addressing Issues of Corruption in Commercial and Investment Arbitration* (Kluwer Law International 2015)

Biever R, 'Speech' in Council of Europe *Abuse of Rights and Equivalent Concepts: The Principle and its Present Day Application* (Proceedings of the 19th Colloquy on European Law, Luxembourg, 6–9 November 1989) (Strasbourg 1990)

Binder P, *An International Comparison of the UNCITRAL Model Law on International Commercial Arbitration* (1st edn, Sweet & Maxwell 2000)

Bingham T, 'The Problem of Delay in Arbitration' in Julian DM Lew and Loukas A Mistelis (eds), *Arbitration Insights: Twenty Years of the Annual Lecture of the School of International Arbitration, Sponsored by Freshfields Bruckhaus Deringer* (Kluwer Law International 2007)

Birnie P and Boyle A, *International Law and the Environment* (Oxford University Press 1992)

Bisaz C, *The Concept of Group Rights in International Law: Groups as Contested Right-Holders, Subjects and Legal Persons* (Nijhoff 2012)

Black's Law Dictionary (4th edn, West Publishing Co 1968)

Black's Law Dictionary (9th edn, West Publishing Co 2009)

Böckstiegel K-H, *Arbitration and State Enterprises: Survey on the National and International State of Law and Practice* (Kluwer 1984)

Böckstiegel K-H, 'Major Criteria for International Arbitrators in Shaping an Efficient Procedure', in ICC Bulletin Special Supplement, *Arbitration in the Next Decade* (1999)

Bonell MJ, *An International Restatement of Contract Law: The UNIDROIT Principles of International Commercial Contracts* (3rd edn, Transnational Publishers 2005)

Bonell MJ, *The UNIDROIT Principles in Practice* (2nd edn, Transnational Publishers 2006)

Born GB, *International Commercial Arbitration: Commentary and Materials* (2nd edn, Kluwer Law International 2001)

Born GB, *International Commercial Arbitration* (Wolters Kluwer 2009)

Born GB, *International Arbitration and Forum Selection Agreements: Drafting and Enforcing* (3rd edn, Kluwer Law International 2010)

Born GB, *International Commercial Arbitration* (2nd edn, Kluwer Law International 2014)

Boyd SC, 'The Role of National Law and the National Courts in England' in Julian DM Lew (ed), *Contemporary Problems in International Arbitration* (Springer 1987)

Brekoulakis S, *Third Parties in International Commercial Arbitration* (Oxford University Press 2010)

Brown C, *A Common Law of International Adjudication* (Oxford University Press 2007)

Brownsword R, 'Positive, Negative, Neutral: the Reception of Good Faith in English Contract Law' in Roger Brownsword, Norma Hird, and Geraint Howells (eds), *Good Faith in Contract* (Ashgate 1999)

Bücheler G, *Proportionality in Investor-State Arbitration* (Oxford University Press 2015)

Carbonneau TE, 'A Definition of and Perspective upon the Lex Mercatoria Debate' in Thomas E Carbonneau (ed), *Lex Mercatoria and Arbitration: A Discussion of the New Law Merchant* (Kluwer Law International 1998)

Cheng B, *General Principles of Law as Applied by International Courts and Tribunals* (Cambridge University Press 2006)

Collins L, *Dicey and Morris on the Conflict of Laws* (13th edn, Sweet & Maxwell 2000) vol 1

Cos K, 'Dépeçage or Consolidation of the Disputes Resulting from Connected Agreements: The Role of the Arbitrator' in Hanotiau B and Schwartz EA (eds), *Multiparty Arbitration* (ICC Publications 2010)

Council of Europe, *Abuse of Rights and Equivalent Concepts: The Principle and Its Present Day Application* (Proceedings of the 19th Colloquy on European Law, Luxembourg, 6–9 November 1989) (Strasbourg 1990)

Crawford J, *Public International Law* (Oxford University Press 2012)

Cremades BM, 'Introduction' in Bernardo M Cremades and Julian DM Lew (eds), *Parallel State and Arbitral Procedures in International Arbitration* (ICC Publications 2005)

Cremades BM and Caims DJA, 'Trans-national Public Policy in International Arbitral Decision-making: The Cases of Bribery, Money Laundering and Fraud' in Andrew Berkeley and Kristine Karsten (eds), *Arbitration: Money Laundering, Corruption and Fraud* (Kluwer Law International 2003)

Cromie S, *International Commercial Litigation* (2nd edn, Butterworths 1997)

D'Amato A, 'Good Faith' in Rudolf Bernhardt (ed), *Encyclopaedia of Public International Law* (Elsevier 2003) vol 2

D'Amato A, 'Good Faith' in Rudolf Bernhardt (ed), *Encyclopedia of Public International Law* (North-Holland 1995) vol 2

Daele K, *Challenge and Disqualification of Arbitrators in International Arbitration* (Kluwer Law International 2012)

David R, *The Legal Systems of the World: Their Comparison and Unification*', in '*International Encyclopaedia of Comparative Law* (Martinus Nijhoff 1975) vol 2

Davis BG, *Improving International Arbitration: The Need for Speed and Trust, Liber Amicorum Michel Gaudet* (ICC Publishing SA 1998)
de la Feria R and Vogenauer S (eds), *Prohibition of Abuse of Law: A New General Principle of EU Law?* (Hart Publishing 2011)
De Ly F, *International Business Law and Lex Mercatoria* (North Holland 1992)
De Ly F, 'Paradigmatic Changes—Uniformity, Diversity, Due Process and Good Administration of Justice: The Next Thirty Years' in Stavros Brekoulakis, Julian DM Lew, and others (eds), *The Evolution and Future of International Arbitration* (Kluwer Law International 2016)
Decock W, *Theologians and Contract Law: The Moral Transformation of the Ius Commune* (Martinus Nijhoff 1983)
Denning A, *Freedom Under the Law* (Stevens & Sons 1949)
Dimsey M, *The Resolution of International Investment Disputes: Challenges and Solutions* (Eleven International Publishing 2008)
Dworkin D, *Taking Rights Seriously* (Bloomsbury 2013)
Edmundson WE, *An Introduction to Rights* (2nd edn, Cambridge University Press 2012)
El-Ahdab AH, *Arbitration with the Arab Countries* (2nd edn, Kluwer Law International 1999)
Elkind JB, *Interim Protection: A Functional Approach* (Martinus Nijhoff Publishers 1981)
Emmanuel Gaillard, *Legal Theory of International Arbitration* (Martinus Nijhoff 2010)
Erk N, *Parallel Proceedings in International Arbitration: A Comparative European Perspective* (Kluwer Law International 2014)
Farnsworth EA, *Contracts* (2nd edn, Little, Brown and Company 1990)
Ferrari F, 'Forum Shopping in the International Commercial Arbitration Context: Setting the Stage' in Franco Ferrari (ed), *Forum Shopping in the International Commercial Arbitration Context* (Sellier European Law Publisher 2013)
Fiebinger R and Hauser C, 'An Arbitrator's View: Can Party Autonomy Hinder Procedural Efficiency' in Nathalie Voser (ed), *10 Years of Swiss Rules of International Arbitration* (JurisNet 2014)
Fleming J, *The Law of Torts* (8th edn, The Law Book Company 1992)
Fouchard P, 'Relationship Between the Arbitrator and the Parties and the Arbitral Institution' in *The Status of the Arbitrator*, ICC Bulletin-Special Supplement (ICC 1995)
Freeman AV, *The International Responsibility of States for Denial of Justice* (Longman 1938)
Friedmann W, *Legal Theory* (2nd edn, Stevens & Sons 1949)
Gaillard E, 'International Arbitration as a Transnational System of Justice' in Albert Jan van den Berg (ed), *Arbitration—The Next Fifty Years* (Kluwer Law International 2012)
Gaillard E and Savage J (eds), *Fouchard Gaillard Goldman on International Commercial Arbitration* (Kluwer Law International 1999)
Gaillard E and Pinsolle P, 'Advocacy in Practice: The Use of Parallel Proceedings' in Doak Bishop and Edward G. Kehoe (eds), *The Art of Advocacy in International Arbitration* (2nd edn, Juris 2010)
Gallagher N, 'Parallel Proceedings, Res Judicata and Lis Pendens: Problems and Possible Solutions' in Julian DM Lew and Loukas A Mistelis (eds), *Pervasive Problems in International Arbitration* (Kluwer Law International 2006)
Garnett RL, *A Practical Guide to International Commercial Arbitration* (Oceana Publications 2000)
Goodhart AL, *English Law and the Moral Law* (Stevens & Sons Ltd 1955)
Gordley J, 'The Abuse of Rights in the Civil Law Tradition' in Rita de la Feria and Stefan Vogenauer (eds) *Prohibition of Abuse of Law: A New General Principle of EU Law?* (Hart Publishing 2011)
Gordley J, *The Jurists: A Critical History* (Oxford University Press, 2013)
Greenberg S, Kee C, and Weeramantry JR, *International Commercial Arbitration: An Asia Pacific Perspective* (Cambridge University Press 2011)
Grossi P, 'Legal Absolutism and Private Law in the XIX Century' in Alessandro Pizzorusso (ed), *Italian Studies in Law* (Martinus Nijhoff, 1994)
Gutteridge HC, *Comparative Law* (2nd edn, Cambridge University Press 1949)
Hallowell JH, *The Decline of Liberalism as an* Ideology (Kegan Paul, Trench, Trubner & Co Ltd 1946)
Hanotiau B, *Complex Arbitrations, Multiparty, Multicontract, Multi-issue and Class Actions* (Kluwer Law International 2005)

Hanotiau B and Caprasse O, 'Public Policy in International Commercial Arbitration' in Emmanuel Gaillard and Domenico Di Petro (eds), *Enforcement of Arbitration Agreements and International Arbitral Awards: The New York Convention in Practice* (Cameron May 2008)

Hart HA, *Essays on Bentham* (Oxford University Press 1982)

Hofmann H, '*From Jhering to Radbruch: On the Logic of Traditional Legal Concepts to the Social Theories of Law to the Renewal of Legal Idealism*' in Damiano Canale, Paolo Grossi, and Hasso Hofmann (eds), *A History of the Philosophy of Law in the Civil Law World, 1600-1900* (Springer 2009)

Home H, *Principles of Equity* (Bell & Bradfute, Manners & Miller, A Constable & Co, and John Fairbairn 1825)

Honnold J, *Documentary History of the Uniform Law for International Sales: The Studies, Deliberations, and Decisions that Led to the 1980 United Nations Convention with Introductions and Explanations* (Kluwer Law 1989)

Hopt KJ, 'Legal Elements and Policy Decisions in Regulating Groups of Companies' in Clive M Schmitthoff and Frank Wooldridge (eds), *Groups of Companies* (Sweet & Maxwell 1991)

Horvath GJ and others, 'Categories of Guerrilla Tactics' in Stephan Wilske and Günther J Horvath (eds), *Guerrilla Tactics in International Arbitration* (Kluwer Law International 2013)

Hunter H and Sinclair AC, 'Aminoil Revisited: Reflections on a Story of Changing Circumstances' in Todd Weiler (ed), *International Investment Law and Arbitration: Leading Cases from the ICSID, Nafta, Bilateral Treaties and Customary International Law* (Cameron May 2005)

Hwang M, 'Why is There Still Resistance to Arbitration in Asia?' in Gerald Aksen and others (eds), *Global Reflections of International Law, Commerce and Dispute Resolution—Liber Amicorum in Honour of Robert Briner* (ICC 2005)

Inadomi MH, *Independent Power Projects in Developing Countries: Legal Investment Protection and Consequences for Development* (Kluwer Law International 2010)

Jaksic A, *Arbitration and Human Rights* (Peter Lang Publishing 2002)

Javier Trevino A, *Classic Writings in Law and Society* (2nd edn, Transaction Publishers 2011)

Jennings R and Watts A (eds) *Oppenheim's International Law* (9th edn, Oxford University Press 1992) vol I

Johnston D, 'Owners and Neighbours: From Rome to Scotland' in R. Evans-Jones (ed), *The Civil Law Tradition in Scotland* (Stair Society 1995)

José M and Tella F, *Equity and Law* (Martinus Nijhoff 2008)

Josserand L, *De I 'esprit des droits et de leur Relativité: Théorie dite dès l'Abus des Droits* (2nd edn, Dalloz 2006)

Kaufmann-Kohler G, 'Identifying and Applying the Law Governing the Arbitration Procedure—The Role of the Law of the Place of Arbitration' in Albert Jan van den Berg (ed), *Improving the Efficiency of Arbitration Agreements and Award: 40 Years of Application of the New York Convention*, ICCA Congress Series No 9, (Kluwer Law International 1999)

Kay M, *Blackstone's Civil Practice 2013* (13th edn, Oxford University Press 2012)

Kiss A, 'Abuse of Rights' in Rudolf Bernhardt (ed), *Encyclopedia of Public International Law* (North-Holland 1992) vol 1

Knapp V, *International Encyclopedia of Comparative Law* (Springer 1983) Part I, Chapter 2

Kolb R, 'General Principles of Procedural Law' in Andreas Zimmermann and others (eds), *The Statute of the International Court of Justice: A Commentary* (Oxford University Press 2006)

Kolb R, 'General Principles of Procedural Law' in Andreas Zimmermann and others (eds), *The Statute of the International Court of Justice: A Commentary* (2nd edn, Oxford University Press 2012)

Kolb R, *The International Court of Justice* (Hart Publishing 2013)

Korkunov NM, *General Theory of Law*, English Translation by WG Hastings, (2nd edn, The Macmillan Company 1922)

Kotuby CT and Sobota LA, *General Principles of Law and International Due Process* (Oxford University Press 2017)

Kreindler R, 'Arbitral Forum Shopping' in Bernardo M Cremades and Julian DM Lew (eds), *Parallel State and Arbitral Procedures in International Arbitration* (ICC Publishing 2005)

Kreindler R, 'Parallel Proceedings: A Practitioner's Perspective' in Michael Waibel and Asha Kaushal (eds), *The Backlash against Investment Arbitration* (Kluwer Law International 2010)

Kurkela MS and Turunen S, *Due Process in International Commercial Arbitration* (2nd edn, Oxford University Press 2010)

Lalive P, 'Transnational (or Truly International) Public Policy and International Arbitration' in Pieter Sanders (ed), *Comparative Arbitration Practice and Public Policy in Arbitration* (Kluwer Law International 1987)

LaLumiere C, 'Speech', in Council of Europe 'Abuse of Rights and Equivalent Concepts: The Principle and its Present Day Application' (Proceedings of the 19th Colloquy on European Law, Luxembourg, 6-9 November 1989) (Strasbourg 1990)

Lane PM, 'Dilatory Tactics: Arbitral Discretion' in Albert Jan van den Berg (ed) *Improving the Efficiency of Arbitration Agreements and Awards: 40 Years of Application of the New York Convention* (Kluwer Law International, 1999)

Lauterpacht H, *The Development of International Law by the International Court* (Cambridge University Press 1982)

Lauterpacht H, *The Function of Law in the International Community* (Oxford University Press 2011)

Levenstein M, *Maxims of Equity: A Juridical Critique of the Ethics of Chancery Law* (Algora 2014)

Levy L, 'Anti-Suit Injunctions Issued by Arbitrators' in Emmanuel Gaillard (ed), *Anti-Suit injunctions in International Arbitration*' (IAI Series on International Arbitration No 2, 2005)

Lew JDM, *Applicable Law in International Commercial Arbitration: A Study in Commercial Arbitration Awards* (Oceana Publications 1978)

Lew JDM, Mistelis LA, and Kröll S, *Comparative International Commercial Arbitration* (Kluwer Law International 2003)

Lieberman D, *The Province of Legislation Determined: Legal Theory in Eighteenth-Century Britain* (Cambridge University Press 1989)

Lopez C and Martinez L, 'Corruption, Fraud and Abuse of Process in Investment Treaty Arbitration' in Barton Legum (ed), *The Investment Treaty Arbitration Review* (3rd edn, Law Business Research 2018)

MacCormick N, 'Rights in Legislation' in PMS Hacker and J Raz (eds), *Law, Morality and Society, Essays in Honour of H. L. A. Hart* (Oxford University Press 1977)

Mahmassani, S, *The General Theory of the Law of Obligations and Contracts under Islamic Jurisprudence* (Beirut 1972)

Mann FA, *The Legal Aspects of Money* (5th edn, Oxford University Press 1992)

Mann FA, 'The UNCITRAL Model Law—Lex Facit Arbitrum' in Pieter Sanders (ed), *International Arbitration: Liber Amicorum for Martin Domke*, (Martinus Nijhoff 1967), reprinted in (2014) 2 Arbitration International 241

Mattei U, *Basic Principles of Property Law: A Comparative Legal and Economic Introduction* (Greenwood Press 2000)

McKendrick E, *Contract Law* (9th edn, Palgrave Macmillan 2011)

McLachlan C, *Lis Pendens in International Litigation* (Martinus Nijhoff Publishers 2009)

McLachlan C, Shore L, and Weiniger M, *International Investment Arbitration: Substantive Principles* (Oxford University Press 2010)

Meier A, 'Multi-party Arbitrations' in Manuel Arroyo (ed), *Arbitration in Switzerland* (Kluwer Law International 2013)

Meyer BF, '*The Swiss Rules of International Arbitration—Five Years of Experience*' in R. Füeg (ed) *The Swiss Rules of International Arbitration—Five Years of Experience* (Swiss Chambers' Court of Arbitration and Mediation 2009)

Michaels R, 'The Functional Method of Comparative Law' in Mathias Reimann and Reinhard Zimmermann (eds), *The Oxford Handbook of Comparative Law* (Oxford University Press 2008)

Morcos S, *Al Wafi Fi Sharh Al Qanun Al Madani (A Treatise on the Explanation of the Civil Code)* (Cairo 1988 edn) vol 2

Naimark R and Keer S, 'International Private Commercial Arbitration—Expectations and Perceptions of Attorneys and Business People' in Christopher Drahozal and Richard Naimark (eds), *Towards a Science of International Arbitration: Collected Empirical Research* (Kluwer Law International 2005)

Newcombe A, 'Investor Misconduct: Jurisdiction, Admissibility or Merits?' in Chester Brown and Kate Miles (eds), *Evolution in Investment Treaty Law and Arbitration* (Cambridge University Press 2011)

Newcombe A and Paradell L, *Law and Practice of Investment Treaties: Standards of Treatment* (Kluwer Law International 2009)

O'Connor J, *Good Faith in International Law* (Dartmouth Publishing Co 1991)

O'Malley N, *Rules of Evidence in International Arbitration: An Annotated Guide* (Informa 2012)

Onwuamaegbu U, 'International Dispute Settlement Mechanisms—Choosing Between Institutionally Supported and Ad Hoc; and Between Institutions' in Katia Yannaca-Small (ed), *Arbitration Under International Investment Agreements: A Guide to the Key Issues* (Oxford University Press 2010)

Oxford Advanced Learner's Dictionary (7th edn, Oxford University Press 2005)

Palombella G, 'The Abuse of Rights and the Rule of Law' in András Sajó (ed), *Abuse: The Dark Side of Fundamental Rights* (Eleven International 2006)

Paparinskis M, 'Inherent Powers of ICSID Tribunals: Broad and Rightly So' in Ian Laird and Todd Weiler (eds), *Investment Treaty Arbitration and International Law* (Juris 2011)

Park WW, 'Non-Signatories and International Disputes: An Arbitrator's Dilemma' in Permanent Court of Arbitration, *Multiple Party Actions in International Arbitration* (Oxford University Press 2009)

Park WW, *Arbitration of International Business Disputes: Studies in Law and Practice* (Oxford University Press 2006)

Park WW, 'The Procedural Soft Law of International Arbitration: Non-Governmental Instruments' in Loukas Mistelis and Julian DM Lew (eds), *Pervasive Problems in International Arbitration* (Kluwer Law International 2006)

Park WW, 'The Four Musketeers of Arbitral Duty: Neither One-For-All nor All-For-One' in Yves Derains and Laurent Lévy (eds), *Is Arbitration only As Good as the Arbitrator? Status, Powers and Role of the Arbitrator* (Kluwer Law International 2011)

Park WW, *Arbitration of International Business Disputes: Studies in Law and Practice* (2nd edn, Oxford University Press 2012)

Paulsson J, 'The Expectation Model' in Yves Derains and Richard H Kreindler, *Evaluation of Damages in International Arbitration* (Kluwer Law International 2006)

Paulsson J, *Denial of Justice in International Law* (Cambridge University Press 2005)

Paulsson J, *The Idea of Arbitration* (Oxford University Press 2013)

Peden E, *Good Faith in the Performance of Contracts* (LexisNexis Butterworths 2003)

Permanent Court of International Justice: Advisory Committee of Jurists, *Procès-verbaux of the Proceedings of the Committee, June 16th-July 24th 1920, with Annexes* (Van Langenhuysen Brothers 1920)

Petrochilos G, *Procedural Law in International Arbitration* (Oxford University Press 2004)

Petrochilos G, 'Three Pillars of International Public Policy' in Photini Pazartzis and others (eds), *Reconceptualising the Rule of Law in Global Governance, Resources, Investment and Trade* (Hart Publishing 2016)

Pfeiffer R and Wilske S, 'An Etymological and Historical Overview' in Stephan Wilske and Günther J Horvath (eds), *Guerrilla Tactics in International Arbitration* (Kluwer Law International 2013)

Planiol M, *Treatise on the Civil Law*, Translated by Louisiana State Law Institution, (1959)

Poudret J-F, Sébastien Besson, *Comparative Law of International Arbitration* (2nd edn, Sweet & Maxwell 2007)

Pound R, *The Spirit of the Common Law* (Marshall Jones Company 1921)

Pound R, *Jurisprudence* (West Publishing Co 1959) vol 1

Power J and Konrad C, 'Costs in International Commercial Arbitration—A Comparative Overview of Civil and Common Law Doctrines' in Gerold Zeiler and others (eds), *Austrian Arbitration Yearbook 2007* (Manz'sche Verlags- und Universitätsbuchhandlung 2007)

Prosser W, *Law of Torts* (3rd edn, West Publishing Co 1964)

Prosser W and others, *Prosser and Keeton on the Law of Torts* (5th edn, West Publishing Co 1984)

Rabban DM, *Law's History: American Legal Thought and the Transatlantic Turn to History* (Cambridge University Press 2013)

Raible M and Wilske S, 'The Arbitrator as Guardian of International Public Policy: Should Arbitrators go Beyond Solving Legal Issues' in Catherine A Rogers and Roger P Alford, *The Future of Investment Arbitration* (Oxford University Press 2009b)

Rainbolt GW, *The Concept of Rights* (Springer 2006)

Raz J, *The Morality of Freedom* (Oxford University Press 1986)

Redfern A and Hunter M, *Law and Practice of International Commercial Arbitration* (Sweet & Maxwell 1986)

Redfern A and Hunter M, *Law and Practice of International Commercial Arbitration* (2nd edn, Sweet & Maxwell 1991)

Redfern A and others, *Law and Practice of International Commercial Arbitration* (4th edn, Sweet & Maxwell 2004)

Redfern A and others, *Redfern and Hunter on International Arbitration* (5th edn, Oxford University Press 2009)

Redfern A and others, *Redfern and Hunter on International Arbitration*' (6th edn, Oxford University Press 2015)

Redondo MT, 'Preliminary Judgments, Lis Pendens and Res Judicata in Arbitration Proceedings' in MA Fernandez-Ballesteros and David Arias (eds), *Liber Amicorum Bernardo Cremades* (La Ley 2010)

Reinisch A, 'International Courts and Tribunals, Multiple Jurisdictions' in *Max Planck Encyclopedia of Public International Law* (Oxford University Press 2008)

Reinisch A, 'The Proliferation of International Dispute Settlement Mechanisms: The Threat of Fragmentation vs. the Promise of a More Effective System? Some Reflections From the Perspective of Investment Arbitration' in Isabelle Buffard and others (eds), *International Law between Universalism and Fragmentation* (Martinus Nijhoff 2008)

Reisman WM and Richardson B, 'Tribunals and Courts: An Interpretation of the Architecture of International Commercial Arbitration' in Albert Jan van den Berg (ed), *Arbitration—The Next Fifty Years* (Kluwer Law International 2012)

Sachs K, 'Time and Money: Cost Control and Effective Case Management' in Julian Lew and Loukas Mistelis (eds), *Pervasive Problems in International Arbitration* (Kluwer Law International 2006)

Sajó A (ed), *Abuse: The Dark Side of Fundamental Rights* (Eleven International 2006)

Salmond JW, *The Law of Torts* (Sweet & Maxwell 1936)

Sanhouri AEl-R, *Al Wasit Fi Sharh Al Qanun Al Madani (A Treatise on the Explanation of the Civil Code)* (Dar Al Shorouk 2010 edn) vol 1

Sayed A, *Corruption in International Trade and Commercial Arbitration* (Kluwer Law International 2004)

Schreuer C, 'Nationality Planning' in Arthur W Rovine (ed), *Contemporary Issues in International Arbitration and Mediation: The Fordham Papers* (Martinus Nijhoff, 2013)

Schwartz EA, 'The Rights and Duties of ICC Arbitrators' in *The Status of The Arbitrator*, ICC Bulletin-Special Supplement (ICC Publishing 1995)

Selden J, *Table-Talk: Being the Discourses of John Selden, Esq* (2nd edn, London J M Dent & Co 1819)

Shany Y, *The Competing Jurisdictions of International Courts and Tribunals* (Oxford University Press 2003)

Shany Y, 'Similarity in the Eye of the Beholder: Revisiting the Application of Rules Governing Jurisdictional Conflicts in the Lauder/CME Cases' in Arthur W Rovine (ed), *Contemporary Issues in International Arbitration and Mediation* (Martinus Nijhoff 2007)

Shaw MN, *International Law* (6th edn, Cambridge University Press 2008)

Sheppard A, 'Res Judicata and Estoppel' in Bernardo M Cremades and Julian DM Lew (eds), *Parallel State and Arbitral Procedures in International Arbitration* (ICC Institute of World Business Law 2005)

Silberman L and Ferrari F, 'Getting to the Law Applicable to the Merits in International Arbitration and the Consequences of Getting it Wrong' in Franco Ferrari and Stefan Kroll (eds), *Conflict of Laws in International Arbitration* (Sellier 2011)

Simpson AWB, *A History of the Common Law of Contract: The Rise of the Action of Assumpsit* (Oxford: Clarendon Press 1975)

Smit H, 'Proper Choice of Law and the Lex Mercatoria Arbitralis' in Thomas E. Carbonneau (ed), *Lex Mercatoria and Arbitration: A Discussion of the New Law Merchant* (Juris Publications 1990)

Smith HE, 'Property, Equity and the Rule of Law' in Lisa M Austin and Dennis Kilmchuk (eds), *Private Law and the Rule of Law* (Oxford University Press 2014)

Stavros Brekoulakis S, 'Parties in International Arbitration: Consent v. Commercial Reality' in Stavros Brekoulakis, Julian DM Lew, and Loukas Mistelis (eds), *The Evolution and Future of International Arbitration* (Kluwer Law International 2016)

Steingruber AM, *Consent in International Arbitration* (Oxford University Press 2012)

Storme ME, 'Case 22: Sitting on One's Rights—Belgium' in Reinhard Zimmermann and Simon Whittaker (eds), *Good Faith in European Contract Law* (Cambridge University Press 2000)

Taggart M, *Private Property and Abuse of Rights in Victorian England: The Story of Edward Pickles and The Bradford Water Supply* (Oxford University Press 2002)

Taruffo M, *Abuse of Procedural Rights: Comparative Standards of Procedural Fairness* (Kluwer Law International 1999)

The American Law Institute, *UNIDROIT Principles of Transnational Civil Procedure* (Cambridge University Press 2006)

Thompson J, 'Good Faith in Contracting: A Sceptical View' in Angelo Forte (ed), *Good Faith in Contract and Property Law* (Hart Publishing 1999)

Tony Weir W, 'The Common Law System' in René David and others (eds), *International Encyclopedia of Comparative Law* (vol II) *The Legal Systems of the World: Their Comparison and Unification* (JCB Mohr, Tubingen 1975)

van den Berg, AJ, 'Dissenting Opinions by Party-Appointed Arbitrators in Investment Arbitration' in Mahnoush Arsanjani and others (eds), *Looking to the Future: Essays on International Law in Honor of W. Michael Resiman* (Brill Academic 2011)

van den Berg, AJ, *Improving the Efficiency of Arbitration Agreements and Awards: 40 Years of Application of the New York Convention* (Kluwer Law International 1999)

Van Harten G, *Investment Treaty Arbitration and Public Law* (Oxford University Press 2008)

von Kann CE, *The College of Commercial Arbitrators, Guide to Best Practice in Commercial Arbitration* (Juris Publishing Inc. 2006)

Voser N, 'The Swiss Perspective on Parties in Arbitration: "Traditional Approach with a Twist Regarding Abuse of Rights" or "Consent Theory Plus"' in Stavros Brekoulakis, Julian DM Lew, and Loukas Mistelis (eds), *The Evolution and Future of International Arbitration* (Kluwer Law International 2016)

Voyame J, Cottier B, and Rocha B, 'Abuse of Right in Comparative Law' in *Abuse of Rights and Equivalent Concepts: The Principle and Its Present Day Application* (Proceedings of the 19th Colloquy on European Law, Luxembourg, 6-9 November 1989) (Strasbourg: Council of Europe, 1990)

Walde TW, '"Equality of Arms" in Investment Arbitration: Procedural Challenges' in Katia Yannaca-Small (ed), *Arbitration Under International Investment Agreements: A Guide to the Key Issues* (Oxford University Press 2010)

Wehland H, *The Coordination of Multiple Proceedings in Investment Treaty Arbitration* (Oxford University Press 2013)

Weiler T, *The Interpretation of International Investment Law: Equality, Discrimination and Minimum Standards of Treatment in Historical Context* (Martinus Nijhoff 2013)

Weinrib EJ, *Corrective Justice* (Oxford University Press 2012)

Welser I, 'Efficiency—Today's Challenge in Arbitration Proceedings' in Christian Klausegger and others (eds), *Austrian Yearbook on International Arbitration 2014* (Manz'sche Verlags- und Universitätsbuchhandlung 2014)

Welser I and Klausegger C, 'Fast Track Arbitration: Just Fast or Something Different?' in Gerold Zeiler and others (eds), *Austrian Arbitration Yearbook 2009* (Manz'sche Verlags- und Universitätsbuchhandlung 2009)

Welser I and Wurzer S, 'Formality in International Commercial Arbitration—For Better or for Worse?' in Gerold Zeiler and others (eds), *Austrian Arbitration Yearbook 2008* (Manz'sche Verlags- und Universitätsbuchhandlung 2008)

Wenger W, 'Art. 178 SPILA' in Stephen V Berti (ed), *International Arbitration in Switzerland: An Introduction to and a Commentary on Articles 176-194 of the Swiss Private International Law Statute* (Helbing & Lichtenhahn and Kluwer International 2000)

Willrich M, *City of Courts: Socializing Justice in Progressive Era Chicago* (Cambridge University Press, 2003)

Wilske S, '"Internationalisation of Law" in Arbitration: A Way to Escape Procedural Restrictions of National Law?' in Nedim Peter Vogt (ed), *Reflections on the International Practice of Law: Liber Amicorum for the 35th Anniversary of Bär & Karrer* (Helbing & Lichtenbahn 2004)

Wilske S and Horvath GJ (eds), *Guerrilla Tactics in International Arbitration* (Kluwer Law International 2013)

Youssef K, 'The Limits of Consent: The Right or Obligation to Arbitrate of Non-signatories in Group of Companies' in Bernard Hanotiau and Eric A Schwartz (eds), *Multiparty Arbitration* (ICC Publications 2010)

Yves Fortier L, 'The Minimum Requirements of Due Process in Taking Measures Against Dilatory Tactics: Arbitral Discretion in International Commercial Arbitration—"A few Plain Rules and a Few Strong Instincts"' in Albert Jan van den Berg (ed), *Improving the Efficiency of Arbitration Agreements and Awards: 40 Years of Application of the New York Convention* (Kluwer Law International 1999)

Zeiler G and others (eds), *Austrian Arbitration Yearbook 2008* (Manz'sche Verlags- und Universitätsbuchhandlung 2008)

Zeigler A and Baumgartner J, 'Good faith as a General Principle of (International) Law' in Andrew Mitchell and others (eds) *Good Faith and International Economic Law* (Oxford University Press 2015)

Zimmermann R and Verse DA, 'Case 22: Sitting on One's Rights—Germany' in Reinhard Zimmermann and Simon Whittaker (eds), *Good Faith in European Contract Law* (Cambridge University Press 2000)

Zimmermann R and Whittaker S, *Good Faith in European Contract Law* (Cambridge University Press 2000)

Zimmermann A and others, *The Statute of the International Court of Justice: A Commentary* (Oxford University Press 2006)

Zweigert K and Kötz H, *An Introduction to Comparative Law* (3rd edn, Oxford University Press 1998)

Articles

Alban JO, 'The General Principles of the United Nations Convention for the International Sale of Goods' (2012) 4 Cuadernos de Derecho Transnacional 165

Allan Farnsworth E, 'Good Faith Performance and Commercial Reasonableness Under the Uniform Commercial Code' (1963) 30 University of Chicago Law Review 666

Alting C, 'Piercing the Corporate Veil in American and German Law—Liability of Individuals and Entities: A Comparative View' (1995) 2 Tulsa Journal of Comparative and International Law 187

Ames JB, 'How Far An Act May be a Tort Because of the Wrongful Motive of the Actor' (1905) 18 Harvard Law Review 411

Ames JB, 'Law and Morals' (1910) 23 Harvard Law Review 97

Amos M, 'Abusive Exercise of Rights According to French Law' (1900) 2 Journal of the Society of Comparative Legislation 453

Anderson D, 'Abuse of Rights' (2006) 11 Judicial Review 348

Angus D, 'Abuse of Rights in Contractual Matters in the Province of Quebec' (1962) 8 McGill Law Journal 150

Anis Al-Qasem A, 'The Unlawful Exercise of Rights in the Civil Code of the Arab Countries of the Middle East' (1990) International & Comparative Law Quarterly 396

Anzorena CS, 'Multiplicity of Claims under BITs and the Argentine Case' (2005) 2(2) Transnational Dispute Management

Armstrong GM and LaMaster JC, 'Retaliatory Eviction as Abuse of Rights: A Civilian Approach to Landlord-Tenant Disputes' (1986) 47 Louisiana Law Review 1
Ascensio H, 'Abuse of Process in International Investment Arbitration' (2014) 13 Chinese Journal of International Law 763
Baldwin E, Kantor M, and Nolan M, 'Limits of Enforcement of ICSID Awards' (2006) 23 Journal of International Arbitration 1
Ballantine HW, 'Separate Entity of Parent and Subsidiary Corporations' (1925) 14 California Law Review 12
Berger KP, 'The Need for Speed in International Arbitration' (2008) 25 Journal of International Arbitration 595
Berger, KP, 'The International Arbitrator's Dilemma: Transnational Procedure versus Home Jurisdiction: A German Perspective' (2009) 25 Arbitration International 217
Blychak PM, 'Access and Advantages Expanded: Mobil Corporation v. Venezuela and Other Recent Arbitration Awards on Treaty Shopping' (2011) 4 Journal of World Energy Law and Business 32
Bolgar V, 'Abuse of Rights in France, Germany, and Switzerland: A Survey of a Recent Chapter in Legal Doctrine' (1975) 35 Louisiana Law Review 1015
Bonell MJ, 'A "Global" Arbitration Decided on the Basis of the UNIDROIT Principles: In re Andersen Consulting Business Unit Member Firms v. Arthur Andersen Business Unit Member Firms and Andersen Worldwide Societe Cooperative' (2001) 17 Arbitration International 249
Borman YR, 'Treaty Shopping Through Corporate Restructuring of Investments: Legitimate Corporate Planning or Abuse of Rights?' (2011) 24 Hague Ybk of International Law 359
Brazil-David R, 'Harmonization and Delocalization of International Commercial Arbitration' (2011) 28 Journal of International Arbitration 445
Brekoulakis S, 'Res Judicata and Third Parties' (2005) 16 The American Review of International Arbitration 1
Brekoulakis S, 'International Arbitration Scholarship and the Concept of Arbitration Law' (2013) 36 Fordham International Law Journal 745
Bridge M, 'Does Anglo-Canadian Contract Law Need a Doctrine of Good Faith?' (1984) 9 Canadian Business Law Journal 385
Bridge M, 'Doubting Good Faith' (2005) 11 New Zealand Business Law Quarterly 426
Brower CN, Brower II CH, and Sharpe JK, 'The Coming Crisis in the Global Adjudication System' (2003) 19 Arbitration International 415
Brower CN and Sharpe JK, 'Multiple and Conflicting International Arbitral Awards' (2003) 4 Journal of World Investment 211
Brower CN and Rosenberg CB, 'Why the Paulsson-van den Berg Presumption that Party-Appointed Arbitrators are Untrustworthy is Wrongheaded' (2013) 29 Arbitration International 7
Brown C, 'The Inherent Powers of International Courts and Tribunals' (2005) 76 British Ybk of International Law 195
Brown C, 'The Relevance of the Doctrine of Abuse of Process in International Adjudication' (2010) 7 Transnational Dispute Management 1
Brunner B, 'Abuse of Rights in Dutch Law' (1977) 37 Louisiana Law Review 729
Brunner C, 'Note—Federal Supreme Court, 28 April 2000' (2000) 18 ASA Bulletin 566
Burnett HG and Chrostin JB, 'Interim Measures in Response to the Criminal Prosecution of Corporations and Their Employees by Host States in Parallel with Investment Arbitration Proceedings' (2015) 30 Maryland Journal of International Law 31
Burton S, 'Breach of Contract and the Common Law Duty to Perform in Good Faith' (1980) 94 Harvard Law Review 369
Byers M, 'Abuse of Rights: An Old Principle, A New Age' (2002) 47 McGill Law Journal 389
Campbell D, 'Gathering the Water: Abuse of Rights After the Recognition of Government Failure' (2010) 7 Journal Jurisprudence 487
Catala P and Weir JA, 'Delict and Torts: A Study in Parallel, Part II' (1964) 38 Tulane Law Review 221
Cohen MR, 'On Absolutisms in Legal Thought' (1936) 84 University of Pennsylvania Law Review 681
Crabb JH, 'The French Concept of Abuse of Rights' (1964) 6 Inter-American Law Review 1

Cremades BM, 'Good Faith in International Arbitration' (2012) 27 American University International Law Review 761

Cremades BM and Madalena I, 'Parallel Proceedings in International Arbitration' (2008) 24 Arbitration International 507

Crosswhite M, 'Abuse of Process and Malicious Prosecution in Alabama' (1987) 38 Alabama Law Review 99

Cueto-Rua J, 'Abuse of Rights' (1975) 35 Louisiana Law Review 965

Cuniberti G, 'Parallel Litigation and Foreign Investment Dispute Settlement' (2006) 21 ICSID Review 381

Darwazeh N and Rigaudeau B, 'Clues to Construing the New French Arbitration Law' (2011) 28 Journal of International Arbitration 381

De Brabandere E, '"Good Faith", "Abuse of Process" and the Initiation of Investment Treaty Claims' (2012) 3 Journal of International Dispute Settlement 609

De Brabandere E, 'The ICSID Rule on Early Dismissal of Unmeritorious Investment Treaty Claims: Preserving the Integrity of ICSID Arbitration' (2012) 9 Manchester Journal of International Economic Law 23

De Ly F and Sheppard A, 'ILA Final Report on Lis Pendens and Arbitration' (2009) 25 Arbitration International 3

Dedek H, 'From Norms to Facts: The Realization of Rights in Common and Civil Private Law' (2010) 56 McGill Law Journal 77

Devine DJ, 'Some Comparative Aspects of the Doctrine of Abuse of Rights' (1964) 1964 Acta Juridica 148

Di Robilant A, 'Abuse of Rights: The Continental Drug and the Common Law' (2010) 61 Hastings Law Journal 687

DiMatteo LA and others, 'The Interpretive Turn in International Sales Law: An Analysis of Fifteen Years of CISG Jurisprudence' (2004) 34 Northwestern Journal of International Law and Business 299

Dockray MS, 'The Inherent Jurisdiction to Regulate Civil Proceedings' (1997) 113 Law Quarterly Review 120

Dubroff H, 'The Implied Covenant of Good Faith in Contract Interpretation and Gap-Filling: Reviling a Revered Relic' (2006) 80 St. John's Law Review 559

Duxbury D, 'Jhering's Philosophy of Authority' (2007) 27 Oxford Journal of Legal Studies 23

Eastwood G, 'A Real Danger of Confusion? The English Law Relating to Bias in Arbitrators' (2001) 17 Arbitration International 287

Edmeades B, 'Abuse of Rights' (1978) 24 McGill Law Journal 136

Eisenberg RA, 'Good Faith under the Uniform Commercial Code—A New Look at an Old Problem' (1971) 54 Marquette Law Review 1

Ellinghaus MP, 'In Defense of Unconscionability' (1969) 78 Yale Law Journal 757

Ellis J, 'General Principles and Comparative Law' (2011) 22 The European Journal of International Law 949

Elsing SH, 'Procedural Efficiency in International Arbitration: Choosing the Best of Both Legal Worlds' (2011) German Arbitration Journal (SchiedsVZ) 114

Exnicios JC, 'Abuse of Rights: An Overview of the Historical Evolution and the Current Application in Louisiana Contracts' (1987) 32 Law Review 946

Ferrari F, 'The CISG's Interpretative Goals, Its Interpretative Method and Its General Principles in Case Law (Part II)' (2013) 13 Internationales Handelsrecht 181

Ferrario P, 'The Group of Companies Doctrine in International Commercial Arbitration: Is There any Reason for this Doctrine to Exist?' (2009) 26 Journal of International Arbitration 647

Fletcher GP, 'The Right and the Reasonable' (1985) 98 Harvard Law Review 949

Fortese F and Hemmi L, 'Procedural Fairness and Efficiency in International Arbitration' (2015) 3 Groningen Journal of International Law 110

Foster H, 'Abuse of Rights—Civil Law—Legal Reasoning: Bradford v. Pickles Revisited' (1973) 8 University of British Columbia Law Review 343

Fridman GHL, 'Motive in the English Law of Nuisance' (1954) 40 Virginia Law Review 583

Fukunaga Y, 'Abuse of Process under International Law and Investment Arbitration' (2018) 33 ICSID Review 181
Gabriel H and Raymond AH, 'Ethics for Commercial Arbitrators: Basic Principles and Emerging Standards', (2005) 5 Wyoming Law Review 453
Gabrielle Kaufmann-Kohler G, 'When Arbitrators Facilitate Settlement: Towards a Transnational Standard' (2009) 25 Arbitration International 187
Gaffney J, 'The Group of Companies Doctrine and the Law Applicable To The Arbitration Agreement' (2004) 19 Mealey's Int'l Arb Rep 1
Gaffney JP, ''Abuse of Process' in Investment Treaty Arbitration' (2010)11 Journal of World Investment and Trade 515
Gaillard E, 'Thirty Years of Lex Mercatoria: Towards the Selective Application of Transnational Rules' (1995) 10 ICSID Review 208
Gaillard E, 'Transnational Law: A Legal System or a Method of Decision Making' (2001) 17 Arbitration International 59
Gaillard E, 'General Principles of Law in International Commercial Arbitration—Challenging the Myths' (2011) 5 World Arbitration & Mediation Review 161
Gaillard E, 'Abuse of Process in International Arbitration' (2017) 32 ICSID Review 17
Garnett R, 'National Court Intervention in Arbitration as an Investment Treaty Claim' (2011) 60 International and Comparative Law Quarterly 485
Goldoftas T, 'Abuse of Process' (1964) 13 Cleveland-Marshall Law Review 163
Goode R, 'International Restatements of Contract and English Contract Law', (1997) 2 Uniform Law Review 231
Gotanda JY, 'Recovering Lost Profits in International Disputes' (2004) 36 Georgetown Journal of International Law 61
Gradinaru N, 'Abuse of Rights' (2012) 4 Contemporary Readings in Law and Social Justice 1010
Graham P, 'The Will Theory of Rights: Defence' (1996) 15 Law and Philosophy 257
Gravel S and Peterson P, 'French Law and Arbitration Clauses—Distinguishing Scope from Validity: Comment on ICC Case No. 6519 Final Award' (1992) 37 McGill Law Journal 510
Greaves VE, 'The Social-Economic Purpose of Private Rights: Section 1 of the Soviet Civil Code. A Comparative Study of Soviet and Non-communist Law' (1935) 12 New York University Law Quarterly Review 439
Green LC, 'Comparative Law as a 'Source' of International Law' (1968) 42 Tulane Law Review 52
Gutteridge HC, 'Abuse of Rights' (1935) 5 Cambridge Law Journal 22
Gutteridge HC, 'Comparative Law and The Law of Nations' (1944) 21 British Year Book of International Law 1
Habegger P, 'Arbitration and Groups of Companies—The Swiss Practice' (2002) 3 European Business Organization Law Review 517
Hanotiau B, 'Complex Multicontract-Multiparty Arbitration' (1998) 14 Arbitration International 369
Hanotiau B 'Problems Raised by Complex Arbitrations Involving Multiple Contracts-Parties-Issues—An Analysis' (2001) 18 Journal of International Arbitration 253
Hanotiau B, 'Consent to Arbitration: Do We Share a Common Vision?' (2011) 27 Arbitration International 539
Hanotiau B, 'International Arbitration in a Global Economy: The Challenges of the Future' (2011) 28 Journal of International Arbitration 89
Hanotiau B and Caprasse C, 'Arbitrability, Due Process, and Public Policy Under Article V of the New York Convention' (2008) 25 Journal of International Arbitration 721
Hansen RF, 'Parallel Proceedings in Investor-State Treaty Arbitration: Responses for Treaty-Drafters, Arbitrators and Parties' (2010) 73 The Modern Law Review 523
Harrington Boyd JH, 'Socialization of the Law' (1917) 22 American Journal of Sociology 822
Harris C, 'Abuse of the Arbitration Process-Delaying Tactics and Disruptions: A Respondent's Guide' (1992) 9 Journal of International Arbitration 87
Hartkamp AS, 'Judicial Discretion Under the New Civil Code of the Netherlands' (1992) 40 The American Journal of Comparative Law 551

Hartkamp A, 'The Concept of Good Faith in the UNIDROIT Principles for International Commercial Contracts' (1995) 3 Tulane Journal of International & Comparative Law 65

Henriques DG, 'Pathological Arbitration Clauses, Good Faith and The Protection of Legitimate Expectations' (2015) 31 Arbitration International 349

Herman S, 'Classical Social Theories and the Doctrine of "Abuse of Right"' (1977) 37 Louisiana Law Review 747.

Higgins F, Brown W, and Roach P, 'Pitfalls in International Commercial Arbitration' (1980) 35 The Business Lawyer 1035

Hosking JM, 'Non-Signatories and International Arbitration in the United States: the Quest for Consent' (2004) 20 Arbitration International 289

Hunter M and Silva GCE, 'Transnational Public Policy and its Application in Investment Arbitrations' (2003) 4 The Journal of World Investment 367

Iluyomade BO, 'The Scope and Content of a Complaint of Abuse of Right in International Law' (1975) 16 Harvard International Law Journal 47

Jenkins I, 'Rudolf Von Jhering' (1961) 14 Vanderbilt Law Review 169

Joachim WE, 'The 'Reasonable Man' in United States and German Commercial Law' (1992) 15 Comparative Law Ybk of International Business 341

Jukier R, 'Banque Nationale du Canada v. Houle (S.C.C.): Implications of an Expanded Doctrine of Abuse of Rights in Civilian Contract Law' (1992) 37 McGill Law Journal 221

Kabra R, 'Has Abaclat v Argentina left the ICSID with a "mass"ive problem?' (2015) 31 Arbitration International 425

Karrer M, 'Arbitration Saves! Costs: Poker and Hide and Seek' (1986) 3 Journal of International Arbitration 35

Kaufmann-Kohler G, 'Globalization of Arbitral Procedure' (2003) 36 Vanderbilt Journal of Transnational Law 1313

Kerr M, 'International Arbitration v. Litigation', 1980 Journal of Business Law 164 (1980)

Kirby M, 'The Growing Impact of International Law on the Common Law' (2012) 33 Adelaide Law Review 7

Klemm U, 'Investment Through Third Countries: State Practice and Needs of Investors' (2009) 24 ICSID Review 528

Kolb R, 'Principles as Sources of International Law: With Special Reference to Good Faith' (2006) 53 Netherlands International Law Review 1

Kolo A, 'Witness Intimidation, Tampering and Other Related Abuse of Process in Investment Arbitration' (2010) 26 Arbitration International 43

Krauze M, 'English Law and the Doctrine of Abuse of Rights' (2012) 1 Oxford University Undergraduate Law Journal

Kryvoi Y, 'Piercing the Corporate Veil in International Arbitration' (2011) 1 Global Business Law Review 169

Lando O, 'The Lex Mercatoria in International Commercial Arbitration' (1985) 34 International and Comparative Law Quarterly 747

Lane BR, 'Kendall v. Ernest Pestana, Inc.: Landlords May Not Unreasonably Withhold Consent to Commercial Lease Assignments' (1986) 14 Pepperdine Law Review 81

Lawson JD, 'The Action for the Malicious Prosecution of a Civil Suit' (1882) 30 The American Law Register 353

Leahy ER and Pierce KJ, 'Sanctions To Control Party Misbehavior in International Arbitration', (1986) 26 Virginia Journal of International Law 291

Leboulanger P, 'Multi-Contract Arbitration' (1996) 13 Journal of International Arbitration 43

Lee J, 'Resolving Concerns of Treaty Shopping in International Investment Arbitration', (2015) 6 Journal of International Dispute Settlement 355

Lenaerts A, 'The General Principle of the Prohibition of Abuse of Rights: A Critical Position on Its Role in a Codified European Contract Law' (2010) 18 European Review of Private Law 1121

Lew JDM, 'Achieving the Dream: Autonomous Arbitration' (2006) 22 Arbitration International 179

Litvinoff S, 'Good Faith' (1997) 71 Tulane Law Review 1645

Lowe L, 'Overlapping Jurisdiction in International Tribunals' (1999) 20 Australian Ybk of International Law 191

Lyons D, 'Rights, Claimants, and Beneficiaries' (1969) 6 American Philosophical Quarterly 173

Majeed N, 'Good Faith and Due Process: Lessons from the Shari'a' (2004) 20 Arbitration International 97

Mantakou A, 'General Principles of Law and International Arbitration' (2005) 58 RHDI 419

Mantilla-Serrano F, 'Towards a Transnational Procedural Public Policy' (2004) 20 Arbitration International 333

Markert L, 'Improving Efficiency in Investment Arbitration' (2011) 4 Contemporary Asia Arbitration Journal 215

Mason A, 'Contract, Good Faith and Equitable Standards in Fair Dealing' (2000) 116 Law Quarterly Review 66

Mayer M, 'Conflicting Decisions in International Commercial Arbitration' (2013) 4 Journal of International Dispute Settlement 407

Mayer M and Sheppard A, 'Final ILA Report on Public Policy as a Bar to Enforcement of International Arbitral Awards' (2003) 19 Arbitration International 249

Mayrand A, 'Abuse of Rights in France and Quebec' (1974) 34 Louisiana Law Review 993

McIlwrath M and Schroeder R, 'The View from an International Arbitration Customer: In Dire Need of Early Resolution' (2008) 74 Arbitration 3

McLaughlin JT, 'Arbitration and Developing Countries' (1979) 13 The International Lawyer 211

Meyniel A, 'That Which Must Not be Named: Rationalizing the Denial of U.S. Courts with Respect to the Group of Companies Doctrine' (2013) 3 The Arbitration Brief 18

Miller AD and Perry R, 'Good Faith Performance' (2013) 98 Iowa Law Review 689

Mitchell AD, 'Good Faith in WTO Dispute Settlement' (2006) 7 Melbourne Journal of International Law 339

Mitchell M and Heaton D, 'The Inherent Jurisdiction of WTO Tribunals: The Select Application of Public International Law Required by Judicial Function', (2010) 31 Michigan Journal of International Law 561

Molineaux C, 'Applicable law in arbitration: The coming convergence of civil and Anglo-Saxon law via Unidroit and Lex Mercatoria' (2000) 1 Journal of World Investment and Trade 127

Mourre A, 'Arbitration and Criminal Law: Reflections on the Duties of the Arbitrator' (2006) 22 Arbitration International 95

Mrzayev R, 'International Investment Protection Regime and Criminal Investigations' (2012) 29 Journal of International Arbitration 71

Mustill M, 'The New Lex Mercatoria: The Next Twenty-five Years' (1988) 4 Arbitration International 86

Naimark RW and Keer SE, 'International Private Commercial Arbitration: Expectations & Perceptions of Attorneys & Business People' (2002) 30 International Business Lawyer 203

Nana Japaridze N, 'Fair Enough? Reconciling the Pursuit of Fairness and Justice with Preserving the Nature of International Commercial Arbitration' (2008) 36 Hofstra Law Review 1415

Nolan M, 'Issues of Proof of General Principles of Law in International Arbitration' (2009) 3 World Arbitration & Mediation Review 505

Note, 'General Principles of Law in International Commercial Arbitration', (1988) 101 Harvard Law Review 1816

Nygh PE, 'Foreign Status, Public Policy and Discretion' (1964) 12 International and Comparative Law Quarterly 39

O'Sullivan R, 'Abuse of Rights' (1955) 8 Current Legal Problems

Park WW, 'Private Disputes and the Public Good: Explaining Arbitration Law' (2005) 20 American University International Law Review 903

Park WW, 'Non-Signatories and the New York Convention' (2008) 2 Dispute Resolution International 84

Park WW, 'Arbitrators and Accuracy' (2010) 1 Journal of International Dispute Settlement 25

Parra AR, 'The 2006 Amendments of the ICSID Arbitration Rules', (2006) German Arbitration Journal (SchiedsVZ) 247

Paterson JM, 'Duty of Good Faith: Does it Have a Place in Contract Law?' (2000) 74 Law Institute Journal 47

Paulsson J, 'Arbitration Unbound: Award Detached from the Law of its Country of Origin' (1981) 30 International and Comparative Law Quarterly 358

Paulsson J, 'Delocalisation of International Commercial Arbitration: When and Why it Matters' (1983) 32 International & Comparative Law Quarterly 53

Paulsson J, 'May a State Invoke its Internal Law to Repudiate Consent to International Commercial Arbitration? Reflections on the Benteler v. Belgium Preliminary Award' (1986) 2 Arbitration International 90

Paulsson J, 'Unlawful Laws and the Authority of International Tribunals' (2008) 23 ICSID Review Foreign Investment Law Journal 215

Paulsson J, 'International Arbitration is Not Arbitration', (2008) 2 Stockholm International Arbitration Review 1

Paulsson J, 'Moral Hazards in International Arbitration' (2010) 25 ICSID Review 339

Perell PM, 'Res Judicata and Abuse of Process' (2001) 24 Advocates Quarterly 189

Perillo JM, 'Abuse of Rights: A Pervasive Legal Concept' (1996) 27 Pacific Law Journal 37

Petrova I, 'Stepping on the Shoulders of a Drowning Man' The Doctrine of Abuse of Right as a Tool for Reducing Damages for Lost Profits: Troubling Lessons from the Patuha and Himpurna Arbitrations' (2004) 35 Georgetown Journal of International Law 455

Pietrowski R, 'Evidence in International Arbitration' (2006) 22 Arbitration International 373

Pornbacher K and Dolgorukow A, 'Reconciling Due Process and Efficiency in International Arbitration—The Arbitrator's Task of Achieving The One Without Sacrificing the Other' (2013) 2013 Belgrade Law Review 50

Pound R, 'The Scope and Purpose of Sociological Jurisprudence' (1911) 25 Harvard Law Review 140

Pound R, 'The End of Law as Developed in Legal Rules and Doctrines' (1914) 27 Harvard Law Review 195

Pound R, 'Legal Rights' (1915) 26 International Journal of Ethics 92

Powers PJ, 'Defining the Undefinable: Good Faith and the United Nations Convention on the Contracts for the International Sale of Goods' (1999) 18 Journal of Law and Commerce 333.

Prebble Z and Prebble J, 'Comparing the General Anti-Avoidance Rule of Income Tax Law with the Civil Law Doctrine of Abuse of Law', (2008) 62 Bulletin for International Taxation 151

Price A and Wilske S, 'Costs and Efficiency in International Arbitration: The Arbitrators' Toolbox for Achieving the "Ideal"' 32 (2007) DAJV Newsletter 184

Pryles M, 'Lost Profit and Capital Investment' (2007) 1 World Arbitral & Mediation Review 1

Ramberg R, 'Piercing the Corporate Veil: Comparing the United States with Sweden' (2011) 17 New England Journal of International and Comparative Law 159

Rasmussen M, 'Overextending Immunity: Arbitral Institution Liability in the United States, England, and France' (2003) 26 Fordham International Law Journal 1824

Redmann G, 'Abuse of Rights: An Overview of the Historical Evolution and the Current Application in Louisiana Contracts' (1987) 32 Loyola Law Review 946

Reich-Graefe R, 'Changing Paradigms: The Liability of Corporate Groups in Germany', (2005) 37 Connecticut Law Review 785

Reid R, 'The Law and the Reasonable Man' (1968) 54 Proceedings of the British Academy 189

Reid E, 'Abuse of Rights in Scots Law', (1998) 2 Edinburgh Law Review 129

Reid E, 'The Doctrine of Abuse of Rights: Perspective from a Mixed Jurisdiction' (2004) 8 Electronic Journal of Comparative Law 1

Reinisch A, 'The Use and Limits of Res Judicata and Lis Pendens as Procedural Tools to Avoid Conflicting Dispute Settlement Outcomes' (2004) 3 Law and Practice of International Courts and Tribunals 37

Reiter BJ, 'Good Faith in Contracts' (1983) 17 Valparaiso University Law Review 705

Rhodes J and Sloan L, 'The Pitfalls of International Commercial Arbitration' (1984) 17 Vanderbilt Journal of Transnational Law 19

Risse J, 'Procedural Risk Analysis: An ADR-Tool in Arbitration Proceedings' (2009) 2009 Austrian Arbitration Ybk 461

Rivkin DW, 'Towards a New Paradigm in International Arbitration: The Town Elder Model Revisited' (2008) 23 Arbitration International 375
Rosenberg GA, 'The Notion of Good Faith in the Civil Law of Quebec' (1960) 7 McGill Law Journal 2
Saleh N, 'The Role of Intention (Niyya) Under Saudi Arabian Hanbali Law' (2009) 23 Arab Law Quarterly 347
Sanders PA, '"At Will" Franchise Terminations and the Abuse of Rights Doctrine' (1981) 42 Louisiana Law Review 210.
Sandrock O, 'Arbitration Agreements and Groups of Companies' (1993) 27 The International Lawyer 941
Santoro D, 'Forum Non Conveniens: A Valid Defense under the New York Convention' (2003) 21 ASA Bulletin 713
Sawyer DC, 'Revising the UNCITRAL Arbitration Rules: Seeking Procedural Due Process Under the 2010 UNCITRAL Rules for Arbitration' (2011) 1 International Commercial Arbitration Brief 24
Schauer F, 'Can Rights be Abused?' (1981) 31 The Philosophical Quarterly 225
Schlesinger RB, 'Research on the General Principles of Law Recognised by Civilized Nations' (1957) 51 The American Journal of International Law 734
Scholtens JE, 'Abuse of Rights' (1958) 75 South African Law Journal 39
Schwartz EA, 'Multi-Party Arbitration and the ICC' (1993) 10 Journal of International Arbitration 5
Schwarzenberger G, 'Uses and Abuses of the 'Abuse of Rights' in International Law' (1956) 42 Transactions of the Grotius Society, Problems of Public and Private International Law 147
Shookman J, 'Too Many Forums for Investment Disputes?' (2010) 27 Journal of International Arbitration 361
Silberman L, 'Report: International Arbitration: Comments from a Critic' (2002) 13 American Review of International Arbitration 9
Sinclair A, 'ICSID Arbitration: How Long Does it Take?' (2009) 4 Global Arbitration Review 18
Skinner M, Miles C, and Luttrell S, 'Access and Advantage in Investor-State Arbitration: The Law and Practice of Treaty Shopping' (2010) 3 Journal of World Energy Law and Business 260
Slate II WK, 'Cost and Time Effectiveness of Arbitration' (2010) 3 Contemporary Asia Arbitration Journal 185
Smith G, 'Dismissal of Arbitration Proceedings For Want of Prosecution' (2009) 5 Asian International Arbitration Journal 190
Sono K and Fujioka Y, 'The Role of the Abuse of Right Doctrine in Japan' (1975) 35 Louisiana Law Review 1037
Speidel RE, 'The 'Duty' of Good Faith in Contract Performance and Enforcement' (1996) 46 Journal of Legal Education 537
Stack D, 'The Two Standards of Good Faith in Canadian Contract Law' (1999) 62 Saskatchewan Law Review 201
Stapleton J, 'Good Faith in Private Law' (1999) 52 Current Legal Problems 1
Steyn J, 'Contract Law: Fulfilling the Reasonable Expectations of Honest Men' (1997) 113 Law Quarterly Review 433
Stipanowich T, 'Arbitration and Choice: Taking Charge of the "New Litigation"' (2009) 7 DePaul Business and Commercial Law Journal 383
Stipanowich TJ and Lamare R, 'Living with ADR: Evolving Perceptions and Use of Mediation, Arbitration, and Conflict Management in Fortune 1000 Corporations' (2014) 19 Harvard Negotiation Law Review 1
Strong SI, 'Limits of Procedural Choice of Law' (2014) 39 Brooklyn Journal of International Law 1027
Summers RS, '"Good Faith" in General Contract Law and The Sales Provisions of the Uniform Commercial Code' (1968) 54 Virginia Law Review 195
Summers RS, 'The General Duty of Good Faith—Its Recognition and Conceptualization' (1982) 67 Cornell Law Review 810
Sussman E, 'All's Fair in Love and War—Or is it? The Call for Ethical Standards for Counsel in International Arbitration' (2010) 7 Transnational Dispute Management 1
Sussman E, 'Why Arbitrate: The Benefits and Savings' (2010) 7 Transnational Dispute Management 2

Tamblyn N, 'Lawful Act Conspiracy: Malice and Abuse of Rights' (2013) Singapore Journal of Legal Studies 158

Taniguchi Y, 'Good Faith and Abuse of Procedural Rights in Japanese Civil Procedure', (2000) 8 Tulane Journal of International and Comparative Law 167

Tavender EDD, 'Considerations of Fairness in the Context of International Commercial Arbitrations' (1996) 34 Alberta Law Review 509

Taylor GDS, 'The Content of the Rule Against Abuse of Rights in International Law', (1973) 46 Ybk of International Law 323

Teitelbaum R, 'Case Report on Saipem v. Bangladesh' (2010) 26 Arbitration International 313

Terry A and Di Lernia C, 'Franchising and the Quest for the Holy Grail: Good Faith or Good Intentions' (2009) 33 Melbourne University Law Review 542

Tête WT, 'Tort Roots and Ramifications of the Obligations Revision' (1987) 32 Loyola Law Review 47

Tetley W, 'Good Faith in Contract Particularly in the Contracts of Arbitration and Chartering' (2004) 35 Journal of Maritime Law and Commerce 561

Thomas AL, 'Nonsignatories in Arbitration: A Good-Faith Analysis' (2010) 14 Lewis & Clark Law Review 953

Thomas E, 'Good Faith in Contract: A Non-Sceptical Commentary' (2005) 11 New Zealand Business Law Quarterly 391

Thompson RB, 'Piercing the Corporate Veil: An Empirical Study' (1991) 76 Cornell Law Review 1036

Tiryaki B, 'The Legal Results of the Abuse of Rights in Case of Contradiction to the Formal Rules of Contracts' (2008) 1 Ankara Bar Review 30

Topcan U, 'Abuse of the Right to Access ICSID Arbitration' (2014) 29 ICSID Review 627

Townsend JM, 'Non-Signatories and Arbitration' (1998) 3 ADR Currents 19

Uçaryılmaz T, 'Equitable Estoppel and CISG' (2013) 3(2) Hacettepe Hukuk Fak. Derg. 161

Veeder VV, 'The Lawyer's Duty to Arbitrate in Good Faith' (2002) 18 Arbitration International 431

Voon T, Mitchell A, and Munro J, 'Legal Responses to Corporate Manoeuvring in International Investment Arbitration' (2014) 5 Journal of International Dispute Settlement 41

Waincymer J, 'Promoting Fairness and Efficiency of Procedures in International Commercial Arbitration—Identifying Uniform Model Norms' (2010)3 Contemporary Asia Arbitration Journal 25

Walde TW, 'Procedural Challenges in Investment Arbitration under the Shadow of the Dual Role of the State' (2010) 26 Arbitration International 3

Wallwork A, 'A Requirement of Good Faith in Construction Contracts?' (2004) 20 Building and Construction Law 257

Walton FP, 'Motive as an Element in Torts in the Common and in the Civil Law' (1909) 22 Harvard Law Review 501

Walton FP, 'Delictual Responsibility in the Modern Civil Law (More Particularly in the French Law) as Compared with the English Law of Torts' (1933) 49 Law Quarterly Review 70

Williams GL, 'The Foundation of Tortious Liability' (1939) 7 Cambridge Law Journal 111

Wilske S, 'Cost Sanctions in the Event of Unreasonable Exercise or Abuse of Procedural Rights—A Way to Control Costs in International Arbitration' (2006) SchiedsVZ 188–191

Wilske S, 'Crisis? What Crisis? The Development of International Arbitration in Tougher Times' (2009a) 2 Contemporary Asia Arbitration Journal 187

Wilske S, Shore L, and Ahrens J-M, 'The 'Group of Companies Doctrine'—Where is it Heading?' (2006) 17 American Review of International Arbitration 1

Woolhouse SP, 'Group pf Companies Doctrine and English Arbitration Law' (2004) 20 Arbitration International 435

Yee WP, 'Protecting Parties' Reasonable Expectations: A General Principle of Good Faith' (2001) 1 Oxford University Commonwealth Law Journal 195

Yelpaala K, 'Restraining the Unruly Horse: The Use of Public Policy in Arbitration, Interstate and International Conflict of Laws in California' (1989) 2 The Transnational Lawyer 379

Yiannopoulos AN, 'Civil Liability for Abuse of Right: Something Old, Something New . . . ' (1994) 54 Louisiana Law Review 1173

Yiannopoulos AN, 'The Civil Codes of Louisiana' (2008) 1 Civil Law Commentaries 1

Yves Fortier L, 'Arbitrating in the Age of Investment Treaty Disputes' (2008) 31 The University of Southern Wales Law Journal 1

Zuberbühler T, 'Non-signatories and the Consensus to Arbitrate' (2008) 26 ASA Bulletin 18

Reports, Research Papers, and Web Notes

Akbaba YE, 'Summary Procedure in the SCC Arbitration Rules of 2017: Shifting the Paradigm of Preliminary Objections in International Arbitration' (Kluwer Arbitration Blog, 1 February 2017) <http://kluwerarbitrationblog.com/2017/02/01/summary-procedure-in-the-scc-arbitration-rules-of-2017-shifting-the-paradigm-of-preliminary-objections-in-international-arbitration/> accessed 18 February 2018

Arenas LC, 'Good Faith in the Lex Mercatoria: An Analysis of Arbitral Practice and Major Western Legal Systems' (PhD thesis, University of Portsmouth 2011)

Bayley JE, 'A Doctrine of Good Faith in New Zealand Contractual Relationships', (PhD thesis, University of Canterbury 2009)

Berger KP, 'The New Law Merchant and the Global Market Place: A 21st Century View of Transnational Commercial Law' <http://www.trans-lex.org/000002#Footnote-Inline-2e293518116d52d3f7fad10c233892fc > accessed 18 February 2018)

BIICL, 'Case Note: Karaha Bodas and Himpurna Arbitrations', 6 (2008) <http://www.biicl.org/files/3931_2000_himpurna_and_karaha_bodas_arbitrations.pdf> accessed 18 February 2018.

Brekoulakis SL, 'Arbitration and Third Parties', (PhD thesis, Queen Mary University of London 2008)

Cremades BM, 'The Use and Abuse of "Due Process" in International Arbitration', Alexander Lecture 2016, 6, <https://arbitrajeraci.files.wordpress.com/2018/07/the-use-and-abuse-of-e2809cdue-processe2809d-in-international-arbitration.pdf> accessed 18 February 2018

Desierto D, 'Arbitral Controls and Policing the Gates to Investment Treaty Claims against States in Transglobal Green Energy v, Panama and Philip Morris v. Australia', (Blog of the European Journal of International Law, 22 June 2016) <http://www.ejiltalk.org/arbitral-controls-and-policing-the-gates-to-investment-treaty-claims-against-states-in-transglobal-green-energy-v-panama-and-philip-morris-v-australia/> accessed 18 February 2018

Gerbay R, 'Due Process Paranoia' (Kluwer Arbitration Blog, 6 June 2016) <http://kluwerarbitrationblog.com/2016/06/06/due-process-paranoia/> accessed 18 February 2018

Explanatory Memorandum of the Egyptian Law No 131 of 1948 Promulgating the Civil Code

ICC Commission on Arbitration, 'Techniques for Controlling Time and Costs in Arbitration', ICC Publication No 843 (2007), 15 <http://gjpi.org/wp-content/uploads/icc-controlling-time-and-cost.pdf> accessed 18 February 2018

ICC Commission Report, ICC Dispute Resolution Bulletin, 'Decisions on Costs in International Arbitration' (Issue 2) (ICC 2015)

ICSID caseload statistics (Issue 2016-1)

International Bank for Reconstruction and Development, 'Report of the Executive Directors on the Convention on the Settlement of Investment Disputes Between States and Nationals of Other States', 18 March 1965, section 9

International Institute for the Unification of Private Law, Report by the Working Group for the Preparation of Principles of International Commercial Contracts, 6 June 2003

International Law Association, 'Final Report on Lis Pendens and Arbitration' (Toronto Conference 2006)

International Law Association, 'Interim Report on Public Policy as a Bar to Enforcement of International Arbitral Awards' (London Conference 2000)

International Law Association, 'Interim Report: 'Res Judicata' and Arbitration' (Berlin Conference 2004)

International Law Association, Resolution No 1/2006 (2006)

International Law Commission, 'Report of the International Law Commission Covering the Work of its Fifth Session', (UN Doc A/2456) in Ybk of the International Law Commission 1953 (United Nations 1959) vol 2

Lew JDM, 'Iura Novit Curia and Due Process', Queen Mary University of London, Legal Studies Research Paper No 72/2010

Paulsson J, 'Arbitration in Three Dimensions', LSE Legal Studies Working Paper No 2/2010

Peden E, 'When Common Law Trumps Equity: The Rise of Good Faith and Reasonableness and the Demise of Unconscionability', The University of Sydney, Legal Studies Research Paper No 06/57 (2006)

Perry S, 'Panel Forbids Duplicate Claims in Egyptian Gas Dispute' (2016) Global Arbitration Review, 2 <http://globalarbitrationreview.com/article/1036361/panel-forbids-duplicate-claims-in-egyptian-gas-dispute> accessed 18 February 2018

Pryles P and Waincymer J, 'Multiple Claims in Arbitration between the same Parties' (2008), 56 <http://www.arbitration-icca.org/media/4/63529655901040/media012223886747020multiple_claims_in_arbitrations_between_the_same_parties.pdf> accessed 18 February 2018

Queen Mary University of London and PricewaterhouseCoopers LLP, 'International Arbitration: Corporate Attitudes and Practices' (2006)

Queen Mary University of London and PricewaterhouseCoopers LLP, '2012 International Arbitration Survey: Current and Preferred Practices in the Arbitral Process' (2012)

Queen Mary University of London and PricewaterhouseCoopers LLP: 'Corporate Choices in International Arbitration: Industry Perspectives' (2013)

Queen Mary University of London and PricewaterhouseCoopers LLP: '2015 International Arbitration Survey: Improvements and Innovations in International Arbitration' (2015)

Reinhold S, 'Good Faith in International Law', Bonn Research Papers, Paper No 2/2013,

Resolution adopted by the International Law Institute, '*Arbitration between States, State Enterprises, or State Entities, and Foreign Enterprises*', Session of Santiago de Compostela, 1989 <http://www.idi-iil.org/app/uploads/2017/06/1989_comp_01_en.pdf> accessed 03 November 2019

Restatement (Second) of Contracts (1981)

Restatement (Second) of Torts (1965)

Restatement (Second) of Torts (1977)

Ripinsky S, 'Venezuela's Withdrawal from ICSID: What it Does and Does Not Achieve', International Institute for Sustainable Development, 13 April 2012 <https://www.iisd.org/itn/2012/04/13/venezuelas-withdrawal-from-icsid-what-it-does-and-does-not-achieve/> accessed 18 February 2018

Ryan M, 'Gaillard on Tackling Abuse of Process' (2015) Global Arbitration Review, 21 July <https://globalarbitrationreview.com/article/1034630/gaillard-on-tackling-abuse-of-process> accessed 18 February 2018

Shapiro SJ, 'The 'Hart-Dworkin' Debate: A Short Guide for the Perplexed', Public Law and Legal Theory Working Paper Series, Working Paper No 77/2007

Silva GC, 'Transnational Public Policy in International Arbitration' (PhD thesis, Queen Mary University of London, 2007)

Temmerman M, 'The Legal Notion of Abuse of Patent Rights', NCCR Trade Regulation, Working Paper No 2011/23

Thomson D, 'Israel Wins Gas Supply Claim Against Egypt', Global Arbitration Review, 7 December 2015, 1, <http://globalarbitrationreview.com/article/1034988/israel-wins-gas-supply-claim-against-egypt> accessed 18 February 2018

United Nations, 1075th Meeting (23 June 1970) in *Ybk of the International Law Commission 1970* (United Nations 1971) vol 1

Vicuña FO, 'Regulatory Authority and Legitimate Expectations: Balancing the Rights of the State and the Individual under International Law in a Global Society', ICCA, 15 April 2009 <http://www.arbitration-icca.org/media/0/12224293410150/regulatory_authority.pdf> accessed 18 February 2018

Ybk of the International Law Commission, 1075th Meeting (23 June 1970) (United Nations 1971) vol 1 <http://legal.un.org/ilc/publications/yearbooks/english/ilc_1970_v1.pdf> accessed 18 February 2018

Index